A MODERN ECONOMIC
HISTORY OF JAPAN

A MODERN ECONOMIC HISTORY OF JAPAN

Shō Ga Nai – It Is What It Is

Russell Jones

LONDON PUBLISHING PARTNERSHIP

Copyright © 2025 Russell Jones

Published by London Publishing Partnership
www.londonpublishingpartnership.co.uk

All Rights Reserved

ISBN: 978-1-916749-39-9 (hbk)
ISBN: 978-1-916749-40-5 (iPDF)
ISBN: 978-1-916749-41-2 (epub)

A catalogue record for this book is available from the British Library

This book has been composed in Adobe Garamond Pro

Copy-edited and typeset by
T&T Productions Ltd, London
www.tandtproductions.com

Printed and bound by
CPI Group (UK) Ltd,
Croydon, CR0 4YY

Contents

Preface		vii
Acknowledgements		xiii
Chapter 1	**Setting the Scene**	3
Chapter 2	**Reconstruction and Renaissance**	21
Chapter 3	**The Bubble Economy**	49
Chapter 4	**The Bubble Bursts**	73
Chapter 5	**The Crisis Deepens**	95
Chapter 6	**Leaving the Lost Decade Behind**	123
Chapter 7	**The Global Financial Crisis**	149
Chapter 8	**Out of the Frying Pan …**	159
Chapter 9	**Abenomics and After**	183
Chapter 10	**Conclusions and Prognoses**	209
Selected Charts		223
Bibliography and Sources		229
Notes		245
Index		259

Preface

'There is always light behind the clouds' — Japanese proverb

The modern economic history of Japan is an extraordinary tale and one that is known by surprisingly few. A modestly sized archipelago, prone to natural disasters, boasting relatively few raw material resources, situated at the edge of the East Asian landmass and long largely cut-off from the international community, Japan rose over the course of just 120-odd years from outright backwardness to the elite tier of the most advanced economies. This was a unique achievement and one that was realized despite the nation succumbing to a damaging interlude of ugly totalitarianism and subsequently suffering the most comprehensive and demoralizing of military defeats.

If Japan's progress before World War II was impressive, the decades following its subjugation and occupation by the United States saw it record sustained rates of economic growth that were hitherto unheard of: its pace of developmental catch-up exceeded all expectations as well as anything that had been witnessed before. Japan's record of unrelenting achievement up to the 1980s – especially where its trade performance was concerned – not only spawned a rising tide of envy and political resentment among its competitors but also encouraged them to adopt important aspects of the country's somewhat idiosyncratic economic model. In the meantime, the strength and direction of Japanese capital flows, together with the yen's gyrations on the foreign exchanges, were major considerations at international policymaking fora.

A common belief at this time, both in Japan and outside it, was that the country's success was set to continue, and that before long it would supersede the United States as the dominant global economic power. Such predictions, however, proved wide of the mark. Even as Japan was being feted as a prime example for others to follow, the powerful forces that had driven its post-war boom had already been waning for some time, and its model of economic development was becoming increasingly ill-suited to the requirements of high-income country status.

Encouraged by policy imbalances and efforts to assuage the ire of various trading partners, its rapid rate of expansion became more and more dependent on the unsustainable combination of asset price inflation and the rapid accumulation of private, and in particular corporate, debt. While this was bound to end in tears, and did, the extent of Japan's subsequent fall from grace in the 1990s and beyond – and in particular its struggles with financial sector dysfunction, deflation and demographic change – came as a surprise to most.

By the early 2020s Japan was once again, in the eyes of many international observers, a far away country about which relatively little was known – and the proportion who cared was smaller still. It had become something of an afterthought. The United States had re-established much of its historical economic superiority, not least where cutting-edge technology was concerned. European economic integration had advanced under the auspices of the European Union, albeit not without setbacks and the need to work through the painful process of successive crises. In Asia the focus was on China, which, freed from the shackles of communist economics, had taken over as the world's manufacturing superpower and was rediscovering much of the global pre-eminence it had enjoyed until the early nineteenth century. Only a small minority were aware, in anything beyond the vaguest of terms, of Japan's initial meteoric rise from impoverished backwater; the nature and extent of its wartime calamity; its remarkable mid-twentieth-century economic miracle; or the manner in which it came to be held up as an exemplar for other nations, both developed and developing, to follow. Instead, its relative underperformance, often exaggerated by the uninformed, was accepted as a given. Indeed, 'Japanification' had emerged as a derogatory byword for stagnation.

But this was to undersell a still vitally important, mature and sophisticated economy and to ignore the enduring lessons that Japan's unique, if often chastening, experience could offer on a number of levels. These extended beyond the process of successful and enduring economic development, to the management of asset price cycles and the currency markets; the complexities of combating deflation; the painful trade-offs implicit in successful structural reform; and, perhaps most pertinently of all at this juncture, how best to deal with the inexorable forces of demographic change.

Notwithstanding the powerful after-effects of the 1980s asset bubble, many of Japan's recent economic struggles and the associated policy conundra are bound up with its ageing and declining population. While few modern economies will experience these issues to quite the same extent as Japan, the trends are widespread. Policymakers across the advanced economies and beyond – not least those in China – are already being confronted by similar associated shifts in the underlying flows of savings and investment, intergenerational income inequalities, falling growth potential, structural pressures on the public finances, and a growing need to bolster productivity if they are to continue to expand at a rate remotely consistent with that achieved in the past. Furthermore, Japan has thus far dealt with these challenges and others without excessive social and political turbulence – something that seems highly unlikely elsewhere, especially now that populism has established such a hold on modern politics.

The Japanese experience has much to teach us all at a time of immense uncertainty, when the post-war Pax Americana is rapidly unravelling, and the rules-based international order is under so much duress.

*

I began to look at Japan and its economy in the late 1980s – not long after I had begun my career as an economist in the financial markets – when the country's influence was at its peak. I did my initial Japan watching from London but I went on to spend most of the 1990s in Tokyo, working as chief economist for two large international investment banks. I therefore observed the inflation of Japan's infamous asset price bubble from a distance, but then witnessed first hand the bubble's subsequent deflation and painful aftermath. The former was a period of burgeoning confidence, national pride and self-satisfaction that bled into arrogance and hubris. The latter was a period when, as suggested above, a plethora of supposed certainties about what had hitherto been the world's most successful economy were shown to be false. It was a fascinating, and frequently bewildering, time for a macroeconomist. I was privileged to have what amounted to a ringside seat for the tumultuous events that played out over those years.

I was also lucky in that during a brief academic career prior to joining the exodus to the world of finance that came in the wake of the City of London's 'Big Bang', my research had focused in part on the Great Depression of the 1930s. Unlike most of my contemporaries, I therefore had at least some understanding of what tended to happen during episodes of collapsing asset prices, financial trauma and rapidly falling confidence and output. I also had a sense of what, from a policymaking point of view, it was wise to do, and not do, about those issues. That said, I would be the first to admit that I, like most, initially underestimated both the extent and the duration of Japan's post-bubble blues, only really grasping their full depth and complexity with a significant lag. I too had ingested too much of the positive propaganda that swirled around the Japanese post-war economic miracle, and in particular the country's rambunctious late-1980s boom.

While I had moved away from Japan by the onset of the new millennium to plough an itinerant furrow that extended to a number of other major financial centres, I kept a close eye on the country. I found myself drawn to write about it whenever the opportunity arose, and my opinion on its progress was still on occasion sought out by investors and parts of the media. It was rarely far from my thoughts. It still held a fascination for me.

When, in 2023, I completed a macroeconomic history of the UK economy over the past half a century, I started looking for a new project to keep me occupied in semi-retirement. Attempting something similar on Japan, albeit with a slightly longer purview, appeared to be a logical next step. I was conscious, moreover, that relatively few high-level – or what might be termed panoramic – books on Japan's recent macroeconomic history existed in English. Fewer still had been written by Britons or, for that matter, by a Briton who actually had first-hand knowledge of the country, its economy, its financial markets and its policymaking community. There was a gap in the market, albeit a niche one.

In authoring the book, alongside my own recollections, previous writings and discussions with policymakers I have drawn overwhelmingly on sources available in English. My Japanese language skills, such as they are, have not permitted any alternative. This undoubtedly means that the richness of my research has been strictly bounded, but this is not to denigrate work on Japan undertaken in the English-speaking world of academia; at international institutions such as the International Monetary Fund, the Organisation for Economic Co-operation and Development or the Bank for International Settlements; or indeed by those economists who, like me, were employed by international banks and investment banks. I had no shortage of knowledge and expertise on which to fall back.

The approach I have adopted is that of a historical narrative with a strong bias towards the dynamics of economic, and especially macroeconomic, policymaking. That said, the book necessarily regularly explores the broader societal and political influences from which the process of economic development can never be divorced.

Although there is precious little original research in these pages – in essence the book represents a carefully assembled mosaic of circumstances, events and ideas drawn from existing literature – I recognize that this is a densely written tome, replete with facts, data and, on occasion, complex and unfamiliar concepts and arguments. Hence, where possible I have endeavoured to use well-chosen adjectives in place of rafts of statistics to establish a point, and I have also attempted to simplify for the lay reader, either in the main text or in an endnote, some of the more challenging notions explored. My hope is that the book will therefore appeal not just to economists but to a wider readership: anyone interested in Japan and its extraordinary journey or in the broader mechaics of economic development.

The book is made up of ten chapters, the first two of which are introductory. Chapter 1 traces Japan's erratic and often-torturous journey from an isolated and backward land in the middle of the nineteenth century to wartime defeat and US occupation in the late summer of 1945. Chapter 2 seeks to describe Japan's economic miracle of the 1950s and 1960s and the country's subsequent elevation to a position as the world's most admired, if not feared, competitor.

The detailed exploration of Japan's modern-day experience begins with a description of the bubble economy (chapter 3) and its immediate aftermath (chapter 4). The next two chapters cover first the financial crisis of 1997/1998 and then that crisis's subsequent reprise and the recovery of the early twenty-first century. Chapters 7 and 8 look at the global financial crisis and at how Japan coped with it, and at the devastating Fukushima earthquake. Chapter 9 focuses on the era of so-called Abenomics. Finally, the concluding chapter seeks to combine the various historical strands explored into some kind of coherent whole and to offer some lessons for the future. Towards the end of the book I have also provided a bibliography and some notes on sources. These are broken down on a chapter-by-chapter basis and presented together with a series of supporting charts that describe some of the more important trends alluded to in the narrative.

Author's note

Japanese names are presented in the text in the standard Japanese form by putting the family name first, followed by the given name.

Acknowledgements

There are a number of individuals without whose support and encouragement this book's publication would have been impossible.

First and foremost I would like to express my gratitude to my wife and family for their endless patience and understanding.

Second, I feel that I owe a longstanding – and hitherto outstanding – debt of gratitude to those individuals who worked alongside me during the years I spent in Tokyo at Union Bank of Switzerland and Lehman Brothers in the 1990s. They helped to make up for my many shortcomings as an economist and enabled me to revel in a fascinating voyage of discovery. Principal among these are Shima Chiharu, Stephen Church, Yamaura Fuyumi, Marshall Gittler, David Pike, Matthew Poggi and Robert Subbaraman.

Certain people were kind enough either to engage with me on the subject matter of the book or to provide detailed comments on the manuscript. These included Horii Akinarii, Dan Callahan, Saul Eslake, Jonathan Fried, John Llewellyn, Jim O'Neill and Bob Rayner. Silja Sepping kindly helped me assemble the charts. My sincere thanks to all of them.

Finally, I must thank my publishers, London Publishing Partnership, and in particular Sam Clark and Richard Baggaley. They were diligent, easy to work with and did a marvellous job of converting my initial efforts into something more fit for purpose.

Needless to say, the responsibility for any remaining errors in the text lies with the author.

A MODERN ECONOMIC HISTORY OF JAPAN

CHAPTER 1

Setting the Scene

'A journey of a thousand miles starts with one step' — Japanese proverb

PHOENIX FROM THE ASHES

When World War II ended, Japan was a physically devastated and emotionally traumatized pariah state. In mid August 1945 it would have seemed faintly absurd to suggest that this reviled, shattered, modestly sized country on the northwestern fringes of the Pacific Ocean would go on to experience the economic miracle that was to play out over the next 40-odd years. But during that extraordinary period Japan would consistently grow more quickly than other advanced economies, in both absolute and per capita terms; indeed, for a 20-year period, dramatically so.

The result of this was that despite accounting for only around 2.5% of the world's population and 0.1% of its inhabitable area, Japan attained one of the world's highest levels of national income. Its huge accumulation of external assets dwarfed those of other nations and became the mirror image of the United States's colossal burden of external liabilities. Its sophisticated products came to be renowned for their superior quality and state-of-the-art technological content, and Japanese commercial methods and industrial organization were widely touted as the best practice for others to follow. By the mid-to-late 1980s, the Japanese economy was commonly viewed as 'Number 1': the envy of the world.[1]

Japan's remarkable transformation had by this stage permeated to the very roots of its society. In the process, the lives of its people had been transformed out of all recognition. In 1945 almost half of Japan's working-age population was still engaged by the primary sector, particularly agriculture. Four decades later this figure had shrunk to around 5% of the total. Japan had become an overwhelmingly urbanized nation, dominated by its pathbreaking manufacturing industries and with an increasingly prosperous and diverse – if still highly protected and rather inefficient – service sector, renowned for the way it looked after its customer base. Its cities were clean and modern-looking, and they were well served by efficient transport networks. Its people were wealthy – and they looked it. It had developed a vibrant and cosmopolitan consumer culture. It could boast both the lowest infant mortality and highest life expectancy rates in the world, as well as an exceptionally high proportion of high school and university graduates. Even the historically lagging height and weight of Japanese citizens had begun to converge with the Western norm. Finally, despite the extent of its urbanization, the generally high population density and the dramatic changes to the nation's social fabric, Japan had largely avoided the criminality, violence and community decay that marked much of Western society, not least the United States. The country was prosperous, safe and largely content.

A NATION IN A HURRY

Japan's post-war economic miracle had a long gestation period. Crucial elements of it can be traced to the country's extended period of isolation prior to 1868. The Japan of the 200-year Tokugawa Shogunate period is often characterized as autarkic, quasi-feudal, technologically backward and militarily feeble.[2] No doubt there is truth in all this, but at the same time the country was already a significantly urbanized, ethnically and linguistically homogeneous nation, within which a protracted period of peace and political stability had fostered the development of a productive agricultural sector, unified markets, sophisticated transport and distribution systems, and complex commercial and financial arrangements.

Meanwhile, education was revered within the dominant native philosophy of Confucianism and was widely diffused, such that the nation enjoyed extraordinarily high levels of literacy for the time. The Samurai class[3] – which by this juncture were no longer required above all else to be warriors – had turned their attention towards administration, developing intricate bureaucratic and management processes that were still observable well into the twentieth century. Finally, the values of loyalty, rectitude and self-sacrifice were deeply imbued into Japanese culture. Not to put too fine a point on it, Tokugawa Japan embodied what are widely considered by development economists and economic historians to be some of the more important prerequisites for 'take-off'.

In 1853–54, the US navy essentially forced Japan to open its doors to the rest of the world. The Meiji Imperial Restoration that followed was the catalyst for a blizzard of (sometimes) chaotic experimentation and revolutionary change.[4] Initiated in large part by military men who saw international politics in social Darwinist terms, Japan's entire political, economic and social architecture was refashioned and modernized in an effort to insulate the nation from Western colonial intrusion and achieve greater equality in economic and political terms with the world's foremost powers. The implicit assumption was that this would not be possible without Japan itself emulating Britain and other European states and adopting an imperialist – supposedly civilizing – mission in Asia.

State Shintō – a chauvinistic variation on the theme of native ancestor worship – emerged to dominate Japan's polity, or *Kokutai*. Religion, respect for hierarchy, and the nation's ancient imperial lineage were forged into a distinctive cultural identity, the basic principles of which – the Japanese people's supposedly unique and sacred nature; a society that was innately harmonious and built on consensus; and, at its core, an emperor who enjoyed divine status – were in effect blended into an official ideology that was sustained by all the state institutions but especially by a powerful military, which answered directly to the emperor and retained an effective veto over major political decisions.[5] Over subsequent decades this creed would become increasingly dominant and influential, curdling into racist, nationalistic and autocratic dogma, with catastrophic results.

Integral to the rise of State Shintō was a constitution on the Bismarkian Prussian model introduced in 1889. In 1890 Japan became the first non-Western country to hold a general election for a national parliament: the Diet. The Diet was divided into two houses: the upper house, or House of Peers, which, like the cabinet and the judiciary, was appointed by the emperor; and the Lower House, or House of Representatives, which was elected on the basis of a very limited franchise. The latter's influence was initially largely confined to the government budget. A competent and respected civil service – which had learned much from the Samurai class and worked within a centralized system of government administration – and the cabinet (and particularly the representatives of the military within the latter) remained the dominant forces driving the governmental process in the emperor's name. Political parties in anything akin to the modern sense of the word only emerged – and began to take on broader responsibilities – as the parliamentary system matured in the twentieth century.

To underpin the system of government a modern system of public finance was put in place. In 1887 a progressive income tax was introduced to remodel a tax base that had previously been dependent on relatively inelastic sources of revenue, such as customs fees and levies on land and harvests.

Initially, in seeking to spark its modernization into life, Japan was content to hire highly qualified foreign experts and embrace en masse key elements of Western military, legal, educational, political, economic, financial and technological development, adapting them where necessary to the country's specific needs. In practical terms, this meant that many of the more egregious elements of free-market thinking were eschewed. From an early stage in the Meiji era, the interests of producers were prioritized over those of consumers, and significant government involvement in the sculpting of the economy's industrialization was embraced. This included the establishment of state-owned factories that, though they were commercially relatively unsuccessful, facilitated the training of Japanese engineers and had strong positive demonstration effects on emerging Japanese entrepreneurs. They were also subsequently sold on cheaply to private owners, under whom they were restored to profitability through restructuring and additional investment.

The wars fought in the 1890s and in the early twentieth century served to further entrench the role of government in the economy. However, unlike in the United States, for example, import tariffs were initially low as a result of the 'unequal commercial treaties' forcibly imposed on Japan by the Western nations at the outset of the Meiji era. They were only progressively applied to heavy industry from the beginning of the twentieth century, once Japan had been freed from these obligations.

Inward foreign direct investment and loans were also discouraged, except where they were deemed absolutely necessary (which in practice largely meant loans in a war context). Instead, the capital for Japan's development was provided in significant part from within the non-farm private sector itself in the form of retained earnings, the resources of rich merchants and business people, and personal and family savings. Fiscal transfers from agriculture to industry also played an important role, especially early in the Meiji era. Taxes raised on rural communities, many of which benefited from strong overseas sales of silk and tea, along with burgeoning domestic demand for rice, were used to finance public investment and industrial subsidies.

The first stock exchanges were established in Tokyo and Osaka in 1878, and from the late 1880s successive waves of joint stock company formation were observable. National savings to support capital accumulation were further encouraged through the promotion of post office based saving accounts and propaganda campaigns touting the doctrine of building national strength through popular sacrifice.

As every effort was made by the Meiji government to build a domestic industrial base, large, vertically integrated, family-run conglomerates with a bank at their core emerged. These *Zaibatsu*,[6] as they were called, were supported by a network of small and medium-sized subcontractors. In due course, the original *Zaibatsu* and their successors would come to exert enormous influence over economic and foreign policy and enjoy a symbiotic, if on occasion less than harmonious, relationship with the powerful military. The ascent of companies such as Mitsui, Mitsubishi, Yasuda and Sumitomo, which were to become household names around the world, can be traced back to this period. All that said, Japan's initial industrialization also owed a lot to the merchants, skilled engineers, craftsmen, rich farmers and village leaders who, across the country, helped to encourage the processes of technological diffusion and to foster business dynamism.

As far as the monetary system was concerned, the yen was created to replace various feudal monies in 1871. The US model of a national banking system in which certified private banks issued money against their specie reserves but where there was no central bank was initially applied, but this rapidly descended into inflation and disorder and was abandoned. After a period of austerity overseen by Matsukata Masayoshi, who served as finance minister for 15 of the 20 years between 1881 and 1901, the Bank of Japan (BOJ) was established in 1882, largely along the lines of the Belgian National Bank. The BOJ became the sole issuer of currency; it oversaw domestic financial activities; it provided the liquidity necessary to underpin economic growth; and, following a banking panic in Osaka and western Japan in 1890, it took on the role of lender of last resort. In this context, a commercial banking system more attuned to the needs of Japan's capitalist class emerged – although until the late 1920s the country was distinctly 'over-banked', and therefore inherently financially fragile. There remained too many small entities, lacking satisfactory information disclosure, risk management, portfolio diversification or project evaluation.

In 1897, at the urging of the still-influential Matsukata, Japan discarded the yen's erstwhile link to silver, which, although dominant as a means of international settlement in East Asia, had been persistently falling in value. Instead, in an effort to provide a more credible anchor of long-term macroeconomic stability and ease access to international capital markets – and despite considerable opposition from a business community worried about losing competitiveness – Japan followed the example of the major economies of the time and adopted the gold standard system of fixed exchange rates. They did so at a rate of ¥2 to the US dollar. Thereafter, Japanese inflation converged with world inflation, which over time tended towards zero.

COLONIAL EXPANSION

The Sino-Japanese War of 1894–95 saw an impressive Japanese military crush the forces of the corrupt and incompetent Qing dynasty of China. In so doing Japan assumed control of the island of Taiwan, established greater influence over Korea, and generally supplanted Chinese dominance in the region. Furthermore, the financial reparations Japan received from the vanquished

Chinese supported the initial adoption of the gold standard and offered some welcome, if temporary, relief from the balance of payments difficulties that had plagued the nation since the Meiji Restoration.

By the onset of the subsequent Russo-Japanese War of 1904–5, also fought over the issue of colonial influence in Korea and northern Asia, Japan's real gross domestic product (GDP) had more than doubled since 1870, and the country now had the ninth largest economy in the world.[7] From 1885 it had developed at a pace – just below 3.0% a year on average – that made Britain's early Industrial Revolution seem relatively pedestrian, and it already boasted many of the vestiges of a top-tier economy, including an impressive modern network of railway, telegraph and port infrastructure.

After its stunning victory over the Russian Empire – the first time an Asian nation had defeated a European power – and given its mounting colonial acquisitions, notwithstanding the overt racism of the time, the West had little choice but to take Japan seriously, both as a military force and as a trading partner and economic rival. It is noteworthy that the United States drafted its first plan for a war against Japan in this year.

Prejudice and discrimination were by no means unique to Europe and the United States, however. Japan's successful military adventures deepened the country's already palpable sense of uniqueness, destiny and ethnic and cultural superiority – setting the scene, as suggested above, for the brutal and self-destructive climax that ensued 40 years later.

The pace of Japan's real GDP growth slowed to less than 2% a year in the run-up to World War I. With the tacit support of the United Kingdom, Japan had largely financed its military operations by borrowing from Western investors in London and other international markets. The servicing of a substantial stock of war debt (the overall burden, more than half of which was held by foreign investors, peaked at around 65% of GDP and remained close to 60% of GDP in 1914) once again imposed a severe balance of payments constraint on the economy and necessitated an extended period of monetary and fiscal restraint.

THE FORTUNE OF WAR

The world's first truly global conflict was, however, to transform Japan's prospects, elevate its development to another level, and further enhance its geopolitical influence. Japan opportunistically allied with the Entente Powers,[8] although its military involvement was largely peripheral and limited to the occupation of Germany's various small colonies in East Asia, which it retained until World War II.

More pertinently, exclusion from the more destructive and financially demanding aspects of the hostilities enabled it successfully to fill the vacuum left by the major combatants, particularly the United Kingdom, in the supply of industrial and consumer goods to Asian and North American markets. Manufacturing output, exports and national income increased rapidly, with the benefits spreading to rural areas as well as cities. The annual average growth rate in real GDP exceeded 6% between 1914 and 1919. Industrial infrastructure – in the form of electricity generation capacity, communications systems and the railway and marine transportation networks – expanded in sympathy. Stock and land prices surged higher. The *Zaibatsu* made a killing. With overseas sales quadrupling, the current account moved back into healthy surplus, peaking at some 12% of GDP, while, in sharp contrast to the pattern observed in the economies of its allies, the public finances were greatly strengthened: the burden of public debt dropped to around 20% of GDP.

The only fly in the ointment was that, with so much demand for its productive capacity, goods and services inflation became increasingly elevated. After Japan had followed the United States in abandoning the gold standard in September 1917, domestic prices doubled in less than three years, triggering a rash of labour disputes. Japan, however, was by no means alone in experiencing high inflation at the time.

Overall, by any reasonable yardstick the nation enjoyed a 'good war'. By 1919 it was the second largest creditor country in the world after the United States, it would participate in the Paris Peace Conference as one of the so-called Big Five nations, and it was subsequently granted a seat on the council of the newly formed League of Nations.

TROUBLED TIMES

Unfortunately, however, once a hectic post-war boom had subsided, the nation was confronted by an altogether more challenging set of circumstances that was to have profound ramifications for its future. In many respects, the 1920s were, like the 1990s, something of a lost decade of financial distress and economic stagnation, although the ultimate political consequences were much more destructive than anything that was to occur 70 years later.

The asset price gains of the war and its immediate aftermath rapidly dissipated. International competition reintensified as the major Western economies reconstructed and returned to a peacetime footing, and Japan, as the marginal supplier, was often squeezed out of markets. Meanwhile, the global economy was beset by creeping protectionism (to which Japan contributed significantly) and a raft of financial fault lines and imbalances, together with a tendency towards deflation, as international primary product prices slumped.

Japan's economic problems were further deepened by the Great Kanto Earthquake of September 1923. This huge natural disaster resulted in 130,000 deaths, devastated much of Tokyo and Yokohama, left 2.5 million people homeless, and resulted in a short-term shock to GDP of some 29%.[9] To this day, the disaster is deeply etched into the nation's collective memory.

The 1920s also saw a series of bank runs and financial panics. These culminated in the *Shōwa* Financial Crisis of 1927, which played out just after Emperor Hirohito had inherited the chrysanthemum throne from his mentally ill father, Yoshihito, posthumously honoured as Emperor Taishō.

Although the population expanded at a rate of around 1.5% per annum, output growth across the decade was volatile, regionally uneven and modest overall, averaging only about 2% a year. Prices, meanwhile, in sharp contrast to during World War I, trended downwards, causing the real exchange rate to appreciate, especially in the first half of the decade, and encouraging the burden of public debt to rise steadily back up to more than 40% of GDP. This, despite the budget remaining close to balance throughout. Bankruptcies and bad loan problems multiplied, there were further violent labour disputes, market risk premia were elevated, and the external balance was again a perennial source of concern, as the massive external surpluses of World War I evaporated and with them much of Japan's cache of foreign reserves. Rural areas and the farming sector suffered disproportionately, not least because the government reorientated policy from seeking to support agricultural prices to instead providing cheap food for the increasingly urbanized population.

The 1920s were not without some silver linings, however. The *Shōwa* Financial Crisis belatedly led to a massive injection of public funds into the banks (facilitated in part by an extended reduction in military expenditure after the Washington Naval Treaty of 1922)[10], the disposal of bad debts via the creation of a 'bridge bank', improved financial oversight, and a much-needed streamlining of the banking sector. Prior to the crisis there were some 1,400 commercial banks in Japan. By 1932 the number had halved, and at the end of 1936 it stood at just over 400. This process of financial reconstruction and restructuring brought risk premia down and was to prove a crucial factor in weathering the storms of the Great Depression.

Notwithstanding the sluggishness of overall growth across the decade, technological catch-up with best overseas practice continued, and new industries such as chemicals, metals, electrical machinery and appliances, and aircraft manufacture emerged in the context of considerable industrial turnover and adjustment and rapid urbanization. This period also witnessed the initial emergence of some of the more distinctive and enduring elements of Japanese industrial organization and management. These included early iterations of the 'lifetime employment model', which was used to exert greater discipline and control over the workforce during World War II and subsequently became prevalent across Japan's larger firms in the context of the post-war labour shortage.

In the realm of politics, the 1920s initially saw the emergence of a number of progressive social movements and the development of the rudiments of a two-party political system based on the *Seiyūkai* and the *Kenseikai* (later *Minseitō*) parties.[11] Universal male suffrage was introduced in 1925, at a stroke quadrupling the size of the electorate, but hopes that all this would develop into an enduring liberal parliamentary democracy were frustrated. Prime ministers were still chosen by the *Genrō*, informal extraconstitutional advisors to the emperor. The political parties failed to establish an adequate popular base of support and remained detached from the average citizen, while successive administrations struggled to come to terms with the economy's difficulties. Governments were short lived. Parliamentary debate was raucous, even violent, and influence-peddling and corruption, often involving the powerful *Zaibatsu*, were endemic.[12] The weaknesses of the democratic process meant that the bureaucracy remained extremely powerful, but the military, frustrated by the increasingly liberal (or, to its mind, decadent, socialistic and anti-Japanese) urban culture of the time, and infuriated by the unwillingness of Western powers to treat Japan as a political, or for that matter racial, equal, increasingly hankered after greater influence and control.[13]

The anger and frustration in the military extended to poorly paid and mutinous mid-level officers, many of them from impoverished rural communities, who took the notion of *Kokutai* to extremes. To them the emperor was a direct descendent of *Amaterasu*, the Sun Goddess, whose predecessors had ruled the Yamato race, as the Japanese were wont to call themselves, for 2,600 years. They fantasized about restoring – through violence if necessary – a quasi-mythic Japan ruled by a warrior caste, where corrupt politicians and bureaucrats and greedy business entrepreneurs would play no part.

Against this volatile background, within mere days of the passage of the extension of the right to vote important freedoms began to be rolled back. The Diet gave new powers to the police to clamp down on political and social dissent. Groups with left-wing agendas were banned and their members rounded up. The media was subject to increasing control. After 1928, crimes against the *Kokutai*, both real and imagined, could result in the death penalty.

The Great Depression, and the deprivations and economic nationalism associated with it, only accelerated Japan's shift towards right-wing autocracy and its embrace of what was effectively a quasi-fascist imperial cult. Political assassinations multiplied extraordinarily. Between 1921 and 1936 the country experienced 64 major acts of political violence, including five attempted coups. Three sitting prime ministers, as well as numerous high-ranking cabinet ministers, officials, admirals and generals, were murdered, while the perpetrators were often seen across the country as heroes or popular avengers. In 1931 radical junior officers in the Kwantung Army, established in 1906 to protect

Japanese interests in Manchuria in northern China, staged a provocation by Chinese rebels in order to seize the region for Japan.[14] Though acting on their own initiative, their superiors, extending all the way up to the emperor himself, proved incapable of re-establishing the status quo ante and subsequently came to endorse their actions. The annexation of Manchuria marked the onset of a second phase of Japanese colonialism. It can be seen as the Japanese equivalent of Nazi Germany's quest for *Lebensraum*. By 1933 Japan had walked out of the League of Nations in protest against the international condemnation of its undeclared war in northern China.

FOOL'S GOLD

Japan's financial and broader economic frailties during the 1920s were such that, although the gold standard often dominated the policy debate and was viewed as a vital imprimatur of good housekeeping, and therefore crucial to raising foreign finance cheaply, successive governments baulked at returning to it after its abandonment towards the end of World War I.[15] In the end, however, in what proved to be a catastrophically badly timed decision, the Hamaguchi *Minseitō* Party administration – which assumed power just prior to the Wall Street Crash of October 1929, and within which the economically conservative Inoue Junnosuke was an influential finance minister – decided to take the plunge.[16]

Instrumental in the timing of this decision was the belief that the restoration of the gold standard would ease the imminent need to refinance Japan's sterling-denominated Russo-Japanese War debt and would facilitate the country's participation in the activities of the soon-to-be-established Bank for International Settlements (BIS). Against a background of severe fiscal and, to a lesser degree, monetary deflation, the formal link to gold was re-established in January 1930 at the old September 1917 rate of ¥2 to the US dollar. Despite some adjustment lower towards the end of the 1920s, the Japanese currency remained about 10% higher in real terms against both the dollar and sterling than it had been at the outset of World War I. For the link to gold to be sustainable, continued deflation would be unavoidable.

By this stage, however, the world was tipping into depression. Although returning to gold had the desired effect of allowing the government to refinance and extend the maturity of an important portion of its debt, the real economy flatlined, with rural communities again hit especially hard. The value of exports, dominated by raw silk and textile production, much of it for the US market, collapsed; private investment slumped; unemployment surged; the price level plunged along with the stock market; and social unrest fomented. In nominal terms, the economy contracted at a rate approaching

10% in both 1930 and 1931. The real value of debt and the cost of servicing it became increasingly onerous.

With capital fleeing the country, reserves ebbing away and the United Kingdom and other Western economies forced to devalue in September 1931, Japan's renewed attachment to gold lasted less than two years. In December 1931 a new government led by the *Seiyūkai* Party – under Inukai Tsuyoshi and in which the venerable elder statesman Takahashi Korekiyo returned as finance minister – bowed to the inevitable and immediately ordered an end to the formal link to gold.[17]

JAPAN'S KEYNES

Takahashi, however, went much further than abandoning gold in reorientating Japanese economic policy. Drawing on the ideas of John Maynard Keynes, Irving Fisher, Japanese theorists such as Amano Tameyuki and Fukuda Tokuzō, and the BOJ's deputy governor Fukai Eigo, the septuagenarian Takahashi cast aside conventional wisdom and introduced a revolutionary series of activist initiatives that predated the formalization of much macrostabilization theory and went some way beyond the response to the depression elsewhere, including Roosevelt's New Deal.[18] Takahashi instigated what was in effect a huge regime change: the world's first concerted programme of fiscal and monetary reflation.

First, the yen was allowed to depreciate in nominal terms by some 60% against the US dollar and by 44% against sterling over the next 12 months before being pegged. The fall in the real exchange rate amounted to some 20% over the period to 1935. Competitiveness was greatly enhanced, while Japan, like other countries at this time, also began to spin an ever-more-complex web of currency and capital controls and sought to further protect its major industries behind a steep wall of tariff barriers and quantitative import restrictions. As a result, a yen trading bloc, encompassing its colonial possessions in Taiwan, Korea and northern China, came into being.

Second, government expenditures were increased at a double-digit rate for two years and then maintained at a similar level for a further three. At the same time, income taxes were cut and transfers to sinking funds for the redemption of bonds were discontinued. As a result, for a period the budget deficit exceeded 8.0% of GDP, before correcting lower. The additional spending included large outlays for public works 'relief' programmes and infrastructure improvements, especially in rural areas, but also importantly for rearmament, and particularly for the burgeoning military intervention across Manchuria, which in due course resulted in the establishment of the Japanese puppet state of Manchukuo. Takahashi himself was no supporter of the militarists or of

Japanese colonial expansion – indeed rather the opposite – but such was the influence of the armed forces in cabinet, and according to the Meiji Constitution, that he had little choice but to acquiesce in many of their demands.

Third, the huge fiscal expansion and associated deficit financing were buttressed by aggressive domestic monetary policy action. This extended not just to a succession of official interest rate cuts (which brought the overnight call rate down from 5.5% to 2.6%) and an eightfold increase in the limit placed on the issuance of bank notes,[19] but also to the central bank, at Takahashi's request, committing for a temporary period to underwrite first newly issued Treasury bills and then, from November 1932, newly issued government bonds. By so doing, any risk of the 'crowding out' of private sector activity was avoided.

In this sense, Japan took macroeconomic policy to its limits, going beyond contemporary resort to quantitative easing and embracing what amounted to modern monetary theory and direct monetary finance.[20] It should be stressed, however, that what resulted, at least initially, was hardly an exercise in fiscal and monetary debauchery. To signal its longer-term commitment to fiscal discipline, the government promised that it would in due course seek to reduce gradually the outstanding stock of domestic public debt. While over the course of Takahashi's stewardship of the economy in the early to mid 1930s the Ministry of Finance (MOF) issued almost ¥2.8 billion of government bonds, all of which were sold to the BOJ, the Bank subsequently on-sold the vast majority of these in the open market, in the process absorbing the lion's share of the liquidity created.

Finally, Takahashi instigated a more active industrial policy: he made finance more readily available for importers; provided interest rate subsidies for industrialists, small businesses and farmers; and supported the activities of regional banks. This helped to make the most of the painful corporate and financial sector restructuring that had taken place in the 1920s and during the initial downturn in 1929 and 1930.

The new and unconventional policy mix was for a period a remarkable success. The narrowly defined money supply, which had been contracting sharply, began to rise. Falling price expectations were reversed, bringing down real interest rates, easing the burden of private sector debt, boosting confidence, and encouraging consumers and businesses to accelerate purchases. Aggregate demand, including exports, quickly recovered, with the macroeconomy growing at a real annual average rate of some 6% between 1932 and 1936.[21] The cyclical upswing began to bring the budget back towards balance and stabilized the burden of public sector debt at around 55% of GDP. Helped by the weaker exchange rate and import controls, the external account remained close to balance, even improving a little.

At a more micro level, the industrial policy bore fruit, while the large-scale government purchases related to military activities encouraged labour mobility and provided significant stimulus to the new heavy industries that had begun to emerge in the 1920s, and which were also benefiting from officially encouraged cartelization and laws limiting the market shares of foreign companies. Takahashi's reflationary strategy, it appears, helped to further restructure the economy.

Japan recovered earlier and faster from the Great Depression than did other economies, large or small. By the middle of the 1930s levels of resource utilization were again consistent with full employment – very much a rarity at the time. It was at this stage, however, that matters started to go awry.

Although the budget deficit had declined somewhat from its peak, Japan's government debt burden was significantly higher than the 40% of GDP it had been in 1929. Japan was also by this stage increasingly cut off from international financial markets, and the BOJ was finding it harder to on-sell its bond holdings. Whereas it had initially successfully sold 98%–99% of the bonds it had underwritten to commercial banks, by 1935 the proportion had dropped to under 80%. Market confidence in the policy mix was waning. The feeling was that in the absence of greater fiscal and monetary restraint, the inflation that had thus far remained largely quiescent would accelerate, the external balance would plunge into deficit, and the yen would come under renewed downward pressure. The by now physically ailing Takahashi therefore approached the 1936 budget process determined to restrain public spending and fiscally deflate in an effort to bring the budget back towards balance and lower the debt ratio. This meant not just the more efficient management of outlays on rural relief, but greater control over funding for the armed forces and associated ministries and, most importantly of all, the curtailment of the temporary expedient of the BOJ underwriting government debt.

DESCENT INTO THE DARK VALLEY

In late February of that year, however, after a series of acrimonious debates with the army and navy ministries, Takahashi and a number of other senior government figures became the latest in a long series of senior politicians to be assassinated by young right-wing militarists wedded to the burgeoning imperial cult, determined to purge Japan of Western liberal ideas. Officials sympathetic to him within the MOF were subsequently sidelined or expelled. Fiscal discipline first weakened than evaporated; the share of government spending, and in particular of military spending, in national income spiralled higher; the budget deficit increased dramatically; and with the precedent for direct monetary finance set, the BOJ became increasingly subservient to the politicians' – or, more specifically, the military's – whims. Its balance sheet exploded in size. The proportion of government bond issuance held by the central bank increased rapidly, ultimately peaking at more than 50% in 1944.[22] Unsurprisingly, inflation rapidly accelerated.

Takahashi's murder was symbolic of the fact that the parliamentary democracy that had been in headlong retreat in Japan since the mid 1920s was effectively over. Governments of national unity headed by military or sympathetic aristocratic figures superseded those of a single political party, and as the military leadership tightened its grip on the state machine, the latter part of the decade saw the country embark on a strategy of foreign conquest. In 1937 Japan expanded its military operations in China, capturing Peking, overrunning the cosmopolitan international enclave of Shanghai, and raping the city of Nanking. Diplomatic tensions with the United States and other Western nations progressively escalated thereafter, as Japan geared up for a broader conflict that would challenge the Asian colonial status quo.

Against this backdrop, the domestic economy – and, for that matter, the economies of its colonies – were increasingly mobilized to support the military and its expansionism. The proportion of a rapidly expanding national budget devoted to the armed forces approached 50%. Consumer price inflation, around 2% per annum under Takahashi, picked up to a double-digit rate. The exchange rate also began to weaken. To head off an increasingly acute balance of payments crisis, especially in the wake of the deep US recession of 1937–38, international trade and capital flows were subject to ever greater control. Domestic production, distribution, finance, energy supply, prices, wages and labour soon suffered the same fate. Conscription was introduced. The mobilization of national resources was consolidated under the Cabinet Planning Board, a bureaucratic superagency the dictates of which displaced much of the market mechanism. Japan increasingly became a command economy.

The *Kokutai* ideology also assumed greater influence at this time. Increasing efforts were made to restrict freedom of speech and encourage the 'spiritual mobilization' of the country. This extended to condemnation of 'selfish individualism', with its roots in European Enlightenment; blatant educational propaganda; and ever-more-insistent calls for greater personal sacrifice, devotion to the emperor and the sacred cause of Japanese exceptionalism.

WAR AND THE WAR ECONOMY

Economic growth in the later 1930s was domestically driven and robust, averaging around 5% per annum, with heavy manufacturing in metals, chemicals and engineering very much to the fore. Japan's economy dominated the region. Its total output at this time was around twice that of the rest of Asia (ex the Soviet Union) combined, while its merchant marine had become the third largest in the world.

A number of new *Zaibatsu* – without a bank at their core, more exclusively dependent on military contracting, and heavily invested in Korea and Japan's other colonies – emerged to challenge the 50-year dominance of the old industrial conglomerates. With mounting resort to cartelization and the rationalization of small businesses, the concentration of capital in the economy therefore burgeoned. In 1937 the ten largest *Zaibatsu* accounted for some 15% of the total capitalization of the corporate sector.[23] At the conclusion of the war in 1945 the figure had swollen to 35%.

By 1940, however, the macroeconomy had begun to falter. Activity was constrained by a shortage of foreign currency to pay for imports and by the slump in world trade that accompanied the outbreak of war in Europe. While stringent centralized planning and control could be used to 'hothouse' individual industries vital for the war effort, it was not conducive to a vigorous and broad-based expansion. Rationing became increasingly ubiquitous and luxury goods were hard to find.

In the autumn of the same year, as tensions deepened with the United States over the continuing war in China, Japan signed a tripartite 'Axis' pact with Hitler's Germany and Mussolini's Italy, although in truth Japan was to derive little military – or, for that matter, financial – profit from this unholy alliance. Things then came to a head in 1941. In July Japan's opportunistic occupation of French Indochina in the immediate wake of France's capitulation to Germany provoked the United States into freezing its holdings of Japanese assets and cutting off the nation's supply of oil, its primary source of energy. By the end of the year, viewing a 'Blitzkrieg strategy' as the only means to establish control over its supply of raw materials and achieve a favourable negotiated settlement in Asia, Japan had attacked the navy and airforce bases at Pearl Harbour in Hawaii, bringing it into direct conflict with the United States and its allies.[24]

Despite the rapid growth of the 1930s, the Japanese economy at this time was only about a fifth of the size of that of the United States; it was also smaller than those of the United Kingdom, Germany and Russia. The combined GDP of the Axis powers amounted to less than half of that of the Western Allies.[25] As World War II evolved into a full-scale global conflict, Japan was confronted by very challenging, if not impossible, economic odds. Nevertheless, under the leadership of militant right-wing Prime Minister Tōjō Hideki, the nation's armed forces initially achieved a remarkable sweep of victories, capturing a swathe of Western colonial territories in East and Southeast Asia, and across the South-West Pacific.

Japan's conquests at first saw them greeted by anti-colonial Asian nationalists as liberators who had dispelled the myth of white supremacy. However, the self-deterministic aspirations of indigenous Asian populations were of secondary importance in Japanese eyes to the natural resources these countries offered: resources that could ease domestic shortages and allow Japan to continue to wage total war. These extended to oil from the Dutch East Indies; copper, chromium and iron ore from the Philippines; and rubber and tin from French Indochina and Malaya.

The Japanese government continued to pay lip service to the notions of regional freedom from the yoke of Western colonial tyranny, shared development and the creation of an 'Asian Co-Prosperity Sphere' with a munificent Japan at its core. However, while in the pre-war period Japan's colonies had at least benefited in raw economic terms from its military developmentalism, the management of Japan's newly conquered territories proved unrelentingly autocratic and increasingly chaotic.[26] Military occupation descended into a vortex of exploitation, expropriation, enslavement, disease and starvation.

With the onset of full-scale war, the degree of central control over the domestic economy, and indeed over the population more generally, reached ever more extreme levels. Military-related output was paramount. Rationing became more and more austere. Power cuts were ubiquitous. Entertainment venues were shut down. Anything that smacked of extravagant living was denounced. There were no conduits for popular dissent.

In 1942, moreover, the Bank of Japan Act of 1882 was superseded by a new Bank of Japan Law, modelled on the Reichsbank Law of the Nazi regime, which narrowly focused the central bank on supporting the war effort and effectively left it unconditionally at the beck and call of the government, and in particular the MOF. Any restraint on the amount of credit that the BOJ could provide to the public sector was lost, while the Bank increasingly ensured that commercial lending was rationed via a limited number of authorized financial institutions in such a way that the major producers of war materiel – in effect the *Zaibatsu*, both old and new, and their suppliers – were prioritized.

In the following year the financial repression that had burgeoned through the 1930s was taken to its logical conclusion when the government established the National Savings Promotion Bureau to absorb any remaining private savings through neighbourhood associations – the funds could be withdrawn only for the purchase of government bonds. This both kept interest rates artificially low and enabled the government to place massive amounts of debt with impunity.

The increasingly intense mobilization of the economy for war was to prove a futile exercise, however. As early as 1942, the United States began to outproduce Japan in war materiel, and the gap was subsequently to widen dramatically. Not only did the United States go on to develop the most extraordinary war machine ever assembled, but as its forces progressively regained the territory that had been rapidly overrun at the start of the Pacific War, the economies of both the Japanese mainland and its occupied territories progressively broke down. This was especially the case once the United States began its strategic bombing campaign in late 1944. Japan was forced to shift more and more of its industrial capacity to Korea to escape its effects.

As the war proceeded towards its climax, Japan's public finances became increasingly disorderly and inflation on the black market ran rampant. Food production slumped by around a quarter. Absenteeism mushroomed, not least because workers had to spend much of their time sourcing enough to feed their families. The labour market became chaotic. Heavy industry – particularly the 'five key industries' of steel, aluminium, coal, shipbuilding and aviation – devoted almost its entire attention to the desperate needs of a military in headlong retreat. But despite some remarkable innovations (an important number of which would subsequently contribute to Japan's post-war renaissance), the quality and quantity of output inevitably fell far short of requirements as the country became increasingly starved of raw materials and intermediate inputs. Meanwhile, all non-strategic activities effectively ground to a halt, and in the face of the destruction of much of the Japanese merchant fleet, so too did the maritime trade linkages upon which the empire had depended so greatly.

ENDGAME

The final year of the conflict was characterized by an unrelenting series of disasters, both militarily and in economic and social terms. The Japanese armed forces were routed in a succession of brutal battles across the nation's hinterland, while US air raids flattened many urban areas and rendered living standards for much of the population deplorable. At the end of the war, around 2 million Japanese men had died in combat and some 8 million civilians – more than 10% of the population – had been killed or wounded. These figures include the 140,000 who died in Hiroshima and the 74,000 who died in Nagasaki, following the detonation of two atomic bombs, but they also extend to the 120,000 who succumbed in a single conventional fire bombing raid on Tokyo in March 1945. In total, the US bombing campaign reduced 60-odd Japanese cities and towns to rubble, with 40% of each city being destroyed on average. Around 2.5 million homes were damaged or destroyed. In Tokyo alone, a million buildings were demolished or severely impaired. The population of the capital fell from 6.75 million in 1940 to less than 3 million at the end of the war.

By mid 1945 two years of naval blockade had reduced key supplies of industrial raw materials to a trickle, and munitions output was in freefall. Japan's real GDP had shrunk by almost 50% from its 1941 peak and was only around a tenth of the size of that of the United States. Its public sector debt burden, though hard to estimate accurately, was the equivalent of more than 300% of its national income, and the BOJ's balance sheet was equivalent to more than 55%. Around a third of the nation's wealth was wiped out, including effectively all the assets put into military production and 25% of so-called peaceful physical assets.

Interestingly, however, while the destruction of urban housing was extensive, the damage to the railway network and the heavy industrial capital stock was more limited. The hydroelectric electricity generating stations were unscathed, and only about a third of the nation's steel, machinery, electrical and chemical manufacturing facilities were lost. The US bombing campaign was more indiscriminate than focused on industry per se. Less than half of the bombs dropped were specifically designated for industrial targets, and the accuracy of delivery was in any case limited. And unlike Germany, the Japanese mainland was of course spared a destructive invasion campaign.

It can in any event be argued that what matters most to future economic development is less the stock of physical assets destroyed during a war or natural disaster and more the quality of the human capital that is left, and the physical resources subsequently available to it. This contention was certainly to resonate in Japan's case over the following decades.

The colonial empire, meanwhile – which, at its August 1942 apogee, extended from Korea and Manchuria in the north to the borders of India in the west, Papua New Guinea in the south, and the Gilbert Islands in the east – was progressively overrun, and ultimately given up in its entirety. In the process, Japan lost access to many of the raw materials that had been vital to its previous development.

Even if it had not been invaded and the country overrun, Japan's defeat was absolute.

CHAPTER 2

Reconstruction and Renaissance

'There is victory in losing' — Japanese proverb

OCCUPATION — A GAME OF TWO HALVES

When Emperor Hirohito – previously remote, divine and infallible – spoke to the Japanese people for the first time to personally announce Japan's surrender in August 1945, he famously asked the nation to 'bear the unbearable'. The most obvious and immediate manifestation of this was for his subjects to acquiesce in the country's occupation by the US military, with the messianic General Douglas MacArthur, commander-in-chief of the United States Pacific Forces, installed as proconsul, or 'America's Shogun'. In so doing, the emperor signalled the demise of the *Kokutai* ideology, and left a proud people, unconquered for thousands of years, bewildered, its aspirations shattered and its spirit broken.

On a practical level, the immediate post-war situation was grim in the extreme. The government's finances were in disarray. Much of the economy was in a state of breakdown. Hard foreign currency reserves were non-existent. Inflation, bad enough in the later war years, soon degenerated into a complete collapse of the currency. The dollar/yen exchange rate, which was approximately 4.25 in 1939, was initially assigned a military conversion rate of 15, but this slipped to 50 in March 1947 and to 270 in July 1948. Looting, crime and corruption were rife. The black market, where many desperate people were forced to sell their few remaining assets, became ubiquitous. Unemployment was endemic; food was in chronically short supply and severely rationed, the situation not helped by a failure of the harvest in 1945; and malnutrition, tuberculosis and other communicable diseases were pervasive. To survive, millions faced little choice but to return to family farms from the burned-out cities. Those who remained were often reduced to living in shanties among the ruins or forced to seek shelter in subways.[1]

At the same time, some 7.2 million Japanese troops had to be demobilized, 4 million armament factory workers redeployed to peacetime activities, and 1.5 million civilians repatriated from colonies that had been overrun. Tens of thousands of Chinese and Korean workers that had been forcibly put to work in the coal industry were also returned home, resulting in major disruptions to power supplies.

Judged against this chaotic background, it can be argued that it was only the occupation that prevented Japan's complete collapse into an anarchic failed state.[2] But this was only the beginning of the story. Although the United States originally considered dismantling much of what was left of the capital stock and redistributing it among Japan's former enemies, the occupation, which stretched to April 1952, was ultimately also to lay a number of important foundations for the Japanese economy's – and the nation's – subsequent renaissance.

The arrival of the US forces in Japan saw two groups of officials vying for supremacy. One was liberal minded and included young 'New Dealers' intent on rooting out what they saw as Japan's feudal hierarchy, and putting into practice much of the Rooseveltian idealism of the 1930s. The other was more in tune with MacArthur's underlying philosophical beliefs: right wing, conservative and commercially minded. The former held sway initially, but circumstances, and MacArthur's powerful influence, dictated that the latter ultimately prevailed, in the process allowing important elements of the bureaucracy, fiscal system and economic structure in evidence since the Meiji era, and strengthened during the 1930s and the war, to endure – indeed, to flourish.

Consequently, the near-seven-year epoch of US oversight over Japan can be divided into two parts.

DEMILITARIZATION AND DEMOCRATIC REFORM

During the first phase, since the occupation was in effect an American monopoly, the nation's core geographical integrity was preserved. At the same time, the presence of the US military proved vital in keeping much of Japan's population alive and in encouraging Japan's ravaged industrial base to begin to reconstruct. The United States provided some $2 billion (around 0.5% of US GDP) in direct aid between 1945 and 1951, three-quarters of which went towards food, fuel and raw materials. This figure fell far short of the $13.3 billion (some 3% of US GDP) directed towards Europe under the Marshall Plan. However, US government programmes paid for over half of all Japan's import bill at this time, and Japan was also largely excused from having to pay reparations for its wartime misadventures.

Beyond providing basic sustenance and encouraging industrial reconstruction, the primary strategic focus between 1945 and 1947 was the dismantling of the Japanese war machine and the autocratic state that underpinned it. Political prisoners, most of whom were of the Left, were released; Japan's armed forces were rapidly disbanded; and a purge of wartime officials and war criminals was announced. However, the lack of Japanese speakers and the limited understanding among US officials of Japan's political, social and business institutions – together with the detached, 'rule from above' style of MacArthur and his cohorts – meant that there were always practical limits to the transformation of the system of governance. The occupation needed the bulk of the existing bureaucracy to function: it operated through the prevailing organs of the Japanese state. And ironically this meant the retention – even the strengthening – of many of the mechanisms of commercial oversight and control employed during the war. The economy initially remained rigidly planned, with limited interaction with the rest of the world.

That said, a new constitution that in essence remains operative today was hastily drawn up, and in November 1946 it was imposed on the subjugated nation and its government, then led by former diplomat and war critic Yoshida Shigeru, the dominant Japanese political figure of the time.[3] The new document formally repudiated war as an instrument of foreign policy and reduced the emperor to a mere 'symbol of the state'. His divinity was stripped away. Sovereignty was placed with the people. The state and the Shintō religion were separated. The peerage was abolished. The powers of the cabinet were increased. Women were given the vote, and allowed to stand for election.[4]

The Japanese people were guaranteed a broader range of inalienable rights than even their American overseers. These extended to free universal education, the protection of public health, the placing of women on an equal footing to men in matters such as inheritance and divorce, and free collective bargaining for wages and employment conditions. The latter resulted in the rapid establishment of trade unions, albeit within individual companies rather than across industries, which over time came to render them more sensitive to profitability when conducting wage negotiations. A remodelled, more liberal, more extensive and less elitist education system was also initiated, which proved to be a powerful conduit for improvements in the quality of the Japanese workforce.

At the same time, radical land reform sought to build on the erosion of the traditional power of large landowners seen during the war. This terminated decades of conflict between landlord and tenant and encouraged a class of small-scale landowners, which would provide important support for the successive conservative governments that came to dominate Japan's politics after 1945. Unlike during its previous flirtation with democracy, Japan would go on to enjoy a remarkable level of political stability.

The reanimation of competition in industry was also prioritized during this initial period. This extended to the dissolution of *Zaibatsu* holding companies, both old and new, together with the announcement of broader efforts to foster deconcentration. For example, a new Anti-Monopoly Act was introduced, based on US anti-trust law and overseen by a Fair Trade Commission (FTC).

REVERSE COURSE

The period of reform, though intense, was short lived. As the financial burden of the US presence in Japan mounted,[*] the appetite for staying on to further the process of Japanese democratization inevitably waned. More importantly, the Cold War began to grip the international community, and in this febrile atmosphere Japan was increasingly seen by the Truman administration as a potentially vital anti-communist bastion in East Asia, where both communist China and the Soviet Union appeared to harbour hegemonistic aspirations.

Rather than needing continued political reform and social restructuring, the US authorities came to the view that Japan instead required to be rapidly put back on its feet as an independent, economically stable and politically robust entity, albeit one that was now unambiguously sympathetic to the West rather than seeking to plough its own expansive furrow. In the process, the occupational authorities realigned themselves increasingly openly with the more conservative elements of Japanese society. MacArthur, at heart a reactionary, was happy to preside over this. Indeed, he saw the successful renaissance of Japan as a free-market capitalist economy, important trading partner and close US political ally as a means to further his own aspirations to be a Republican Party presidential candidate.

In this context, the emperor was dissuaded from abdicating and, through the often-flagrant manipulation of evidence at the Tokyo War Crimes Trial, excused direct responsibility for the conflict and allowed to escape any formal indictment as a war criminal. This despite the fact that he had at the time been commander-in-chief of the armed forces. Instead, the blame was put firmly at the feet of Tōjō, who was subsequently hanged in December 1948.

For his part, Hirohito was refashioned into an enduring otherworldly ceremonial symbol of continuity and the unity of the people – something that very much served the occupation's purposes of maintaining social stability. The purging of those individuals who had been at the core of the wartime regime and the military was also halted, and many were allowed to re-enter frontline politics and government, or, if not, act as behind-the-scenes

---

[*] In addition to the direct aid provided by the United States, around a million US troops were stationed there during the occupation at a cost of some $700 million per year.

powerbrokers, in the process further strengthening the old bureaucracy. Reform of the *Zaibatsu* and the broader governance of the Japanese corporate sector was similarly watered down. Anti-trust legislation was wound back. The Fair Trade Commission (FTC) soft-pedalled. The big banks were allowed to operate largely as they had before. The new labour unions, which had rapidly become militant, were reined in in uncompromising fashion, with government employees prohibited from striking. Finally, the defeat of inflation became an overwhelming priority.

TOEING THE LINE

Some effort had been made to stabilize prices in early 1946: new banknotes were issued, limits were placed on bank withdrawals, the wartime guarantees that had been used to encourage lending to arms suppliers were cancelled, and strict government controls were resumed. However, these initiatives foundered within six months in the face of continued supply shortages and the BOJ monetizing bonds issued by the Reconstruction Finance Bank (RFB), which had been established in January 1947 to provide financial support to key industries.[5] The consumer price index (CPI) increased almost fivefold between September 1946 and March 1949, and, as mentioned earlier, the yen's market value collapsed. As a result, the huge burden of government liabilities that had accumulated since the late 1930s was rapidly inflated away, as indeed was much of the real value of outstanding private sector debt and what remained of household savings.[6]

It took the so-called Dodge Line currency reform of spring 1949 to drive inflation out of the system.[7] This price stabilization programme embodied strict limits on public spending, tax reform, the elimination of the budget deficit, draconian credit controls, the abolition of many implicit subsidies to industry, a dose of broader deregulation in the domestic economy, and tighter foreign exchange and trade controls. The RFB was progressively wound down, allowing the large commercial banks to fill the vacuum, while the BOJ was afforded greater de facto control over official interest rate decisions and barred from directly financing government debt with a maturity of greater than one year.[8] Finally, the exchange rate was set at ¥360 to the dollar as a prelude to Japan in 1952 joining the International Monetary Fund/Bretton Woods system of fixed but adjustable exchange rates anchored by the dollar's enduring link to gold at $35 per ounce.[9]

The Dodge Line stabilized prices but proved to be unpalatable medicine. This was particularly the case as the world economy plunged into its first post-war recession in 1949. Recovery from the devastation of 1945 faltered. Bankruptcies and unemployment rose sharply and a number of bitter industrial disputes erupted. Yoshida's government came under acute duress. It was perhaps only the unchallengeable authority of the occupational forces that rendered the reform sustainable.

SALVATION

Miraculously, Japan's situation was then transformed by the onset of the Korean War in June 1950. Japan no longer had the autonomy to divert resources into its own defence: it had effectively become a US protectorate and would remain so after the signing of the US–Japan Security Treaty in September 1951, which took effect the following year. However, the United States saw Japan as a vital source of war materiel and a central logistical hub for the United Nations forces fighting the communists across the Korean peninsula. All told, some $2.3 billion of US procurement orders flowed to Japan between June 1950 and December 1953 – a sum exceeding the total aid received during the first five years of the occupation. Moreover, even after the hostilities in Korea had ceased, Japan remained a major source of supply for South Korea's reconstruction, receiving a further $1.75 billion from the United States between 1954 and 1956. And, of course, Japan knew how to make the most of the lifeline it had been thrown. Rapid development was, after all, in the country's post-Meiji Restoration DNA, and the war had provided ample experience of how to ramp up production in heavy manufacturing speedily for military purposes.

The early 1950s saw the basic industries boom and exports soar, encouraged by the fact that Japan was at this time one of the few industrialized economies with significant spare engineering and shipbuilding capacity. The foreign exchange earned (including from United Nations troops coming to Japan for rest and recreation) was channelled into the importation of the latest technologies developed in the United States and Europe, a factor that was to prove crucial to Japan's renaissance over the next two decades.

POLITICAL ECCENTRICITIES

One important consequence of the manner in which the occupation evolved, and particularly in the way the focus shifted towards Japan's rehabilitation as a Cold War ally after 1947, was that, despite the country being more outwardly politically stable than it had been before, the system of democracy remained idiosyncratic, even somewhat half-baked. Whatever the original intentions of Japan's US conquerors, the specifics of the 'Reverse Course' meant that the nation never entirely sloughed off its nationalist, authoritarian and corporatist past. For the next 50-odd years, it became in effect a conservative single-party state, albeit one led by a succession of sometimes aged, often nondescript, prime ministerial figureheads, who assumed the leadership largely because of their sensitivity to the demands of various interest groups and their acceptability to behind-the-scenes powerbrokers rather than because they were some all-powerful ideologue.

This was particularly the case following the 1955 merger of the Liberal Party and the Japan Democratic Party (with, it should be said, the tacit support of the US government) into a single entity: the Liberal Democratic Party (LDP).[10] Thereafter, as much as political philosophy, LDP factionalism (in effect parties within a party) – centred on the brazen patronage of individuals adept at fundraising, sustaining agricultural protection or delivering public works projects in Japan's limited number of disproportionately rural multicandidate constituencies – typically provided the most potent form of debate, if not opposition. Many Diet members inherited their constituencies from their fathers, or even their grandfathers (and it was always fathers and grandfathers rather than mothers or grandmothers), bringing a feudal element into politics. The level of national public discourse was often shallow and parochial; the electorate noteworthy in equal parts for its apathy and naivety. To maintain a veneer of active political multilateralism, the LDP even helped to finance the activities of the opposition parties, not least the Japan Socialist Party (JSP). By the early 1960s, party political opposition, much like labour militancy, had taken on an almost ritualistic quality.

While the Japanese political system ploughed its own eccentric but inexorably right-of-centre furrow, the bureaucratic elite – the best-educated and best-informed arm of Japan's institutional architecture – enjoyed considerable latitude. It was in effect left not only to preside over the detail of policy implementation, but to determine much of its basic thrust, focusing it in particular on the overarching goals of securing maximum economic advantage and catching up with Japan's most advanced competitors. As well as becoming a putative one-party state, Japan also developed into being a kind of bureaucratic developmental dictatorship.

Unfortunately, these arrangements were also to foment an enduring undercurrent of collusion, clientelism and corruption across big business, politicians, government officials and indeed organized crime. While this failed to stymie the subsequent economic miracle, it would consistently and undeniably taint Japanese life. Shocking political scandals would rear their heads with remarkable regularity in the decades to come, often being used to move a particular individual on who no longer quite fitted the bill of the LDP powers that be.

TAKE OFF

By the mid 1950s, Japanese production levels had exceeded those of the late 1930s. Not only was the economy's recovery from World War II complete, but the Korean War had kick-started a virtuous circle of sustained expansion.

The wartime destruction of much of the capital stock hastened the developmental process, in that it necessitated the construction of modern, state-of-the-art factories. It was further nurtured by an increasingly active industrial strategy that in important respects echoed wartime policy. This was conducted in significant part through the auspices of the MOF (particularly its Budget Bureau), which remained at the apex of the bureaucracy, and the Ministry of International Trade and Industry (MITI).

Established in 1949, the MITI was a descendant of the wartime Ministry of Munitions. The precise extent of its role in Japan's post-war renaissance is still debated, but there is little disputing that it became Japanese business's closest partner in government. With the support of the MOF, it oversaw accelerated depreciation for investment; provided low-interest-rate loans and tax deductions, especially for export earnings; sustained a web of tariffs and import controls; directed the allocation of initially scarce foreign exchange; deliberately truncated patent periods; and offered liberal doses of informal administrative guidance – all of which were aimed at boosting industrial and technological strength in specified sectors, assisting sunsetting in others and generally directing the economy's progress. In the meantime, foreign direct investment (FDI) was strictly limited because of the fear that it would stand in the way of the establishment of a sustainable indigenous industrial base.

An integral element of this strategy was the establishment of a group of highly competitive outward-looking companies that could act as the economy's developmental vanguard. Beyond the various micro measures mentioned above, the coalescence of these entities was supported by forced mergers, cartelization and the broader encouragement of the so-called *Keiretsu*. Linked through a web of large and stable cross-shareholdings that came to include as many as two-thirds of all corporate stocks (and which helped to keep foreign predators at bay), firms typically clustered around a single 'main bank' that provided financial oversight, acted as a sponsor or guarantor, and provided scarce capital. *In extremis*, the main bank could direct corporate reorganizations and downsizing programmes. *Keiretsu* members also tended to support each other's activities through repetitive trading with one another, bargaining collectively (including with foreign counterparties), exchanging personnel and pooling much of their technical research and market intelligence, not least on the progress of tastes and preferences overseas. The larger the firm, the more they depended on such arrangements. For some big enterprises, they amounted to more than half of their value added.

The structure of these groupings allowed them to indulge more in long-term business strategies rather than having to focus on short-term profit maximization to satisfy a plethora of diverse, often impatient, stockholders, as was usually the case in the West. In Japan, the overriding priorities became sales, the development of new products and increasing market share – the belief being that market dominance would ultimately bring larger and more sustainable financial rewards. And it often did.

The *Keiretsu* were to a significant extent reconfigurations of the *Zaibatsu*, albeit with some crucial differences. For example, hereditary family influence was much less in evidence, and they were less rigidly pyramidal and often more horizontal than vertical in nature. Stockholding was more diverse. *Keiretsu* banks also dealt with outsiders, and group insiders could deal with outside banks. A greater proportion of the economy remained outside these concentrations than during the heyday of the *Zaibatsu*, and they tended to be more dependent on state funding and direction than their pre-war predecessors.

Nevertheless, old *Zaibatsu* companies like Mitsubishi, Sumitomo and Mitsui once again came to exert a profound influence on the economy, just as newer groupings such as Furukawa, Asano, Ōkura and Nakajima also consolidated their presence at the forefront of Japan's renaissance.

As before, these entities were serviced by a network of small and medium-sized affiliates and suppliers that competed intensely with one another and were left to bear the brunt of the vicissitudes of the business cycle, acting in effect like shock absorbers for bigger business. Japanese industry therefore continued to exhibit a 'dual structure' of large islands of concentration surrounded by reefs of more atomized suppliers, some of which were to exhibit impressive entrepreneurial skills. As in the Meiji era, the dynamism of the lower strata of industry played an important role in driving the development process.

The workforce culture of the *Keiretsu* also warrants attention, in that it helped to improve the quality of labour and acted as an example for the rest of the corporate sector. Labour was in short supply in the 1950s and 1960s, and firms were keen to minimize employee turnover. *Keiretsu* employees – or, to be more precise, male *Keiretsu* employees – were expected to work hard and to exacting standards, observe a strict code of conduct and remain loyal to the firm, even in the face of the regular application of new technologies, product designs and production techniques. In return, they benefited from on-the-job training and, when necessary, reskilling; they were guaranteed long-term job security ('lifetime employment') and wage increases based in part on seniority; and, in many instances, they were provided with company housing. Staff were also consulted on major decisions. In this way, motivation and morale were sustained and changes in business strategy could be implemented with minimal resistance on the shop floor. Many large Japanese companies became social – almost religious – organizations. The legacies of wartime regimentation and the susceptibility of the workforce to soft indoctrination endured.

A HIGHER PLANE

The late 1950s and early 1960s saw Japan's expansion broaden out beyond the more traditional core heavy industries to electrical appliances, electronics, petrochemicals, synthetic fibres, machine tools, precision engineering and automobiles. At the same time, the economy shifted onto an unprecedentedly rapid growth trajectory and remained there until the onset of the first oil crisis in 1973. No economy had ever grown so consistently fast for so long.

In September 1960 the government of Ikeda Hayato announced, with some fanfare, its ten-year Income Doubling Plan. This helped Japan move on from a rare bout of social and political dyspepsia related to the extension of the 1952 US–Japan Security Treaty and it might also have had some effect in terms of boosting confidence in the future, both across industry and with the public. However, the reality is that the onset of the period of rambunctious expansion predated it.

Perhaps of greater symbolism and significance around this time were the Tokyo Olympic Games, the first to be held in Asia,[11] and Japan's admission to the Organisation for Economic Co-operation and Development (OECD). Both of these events occurred in 1964 and were widely considered to mark an end to Japan's pariah status and the country's return to the international community.

The total cost of the games, including their preparation, was around ¥720 billion, or some $2 billion (equivalent to just under a fifth of the core central government budget for the year). The prospect of Japan being the centre of international attention and welcoming a flood of overseas visitors also sparked major improvements in the nation's transport network. These included the first *Shinkansen,* or 'Bullet Trains'; upgrades to the nation's long-neglected highway system; and the rapid construction of a system of elevated expressways across the capital. In total, a further ¥994 billion, or $2.7 billion, was spent on infrastructure projects related to the games.

OECD membership signalled Japan's successful transformation into a fully industrialized economy, and indicated that the country had joined the 'club of the world's richest nations'. This provided greater opportunities to gain insights into policy best practice and to engage with the international community in resolving global issues. It also obligated Japan – as part of an associated commitment to the expansion of world trade on a multilateral and non-discriminatory basis – to step up the deregulation of imports and of the capital account of the balance of payments.

The latter was to prove challenging. Successive governments over subsequent decades ensured that the process was beset by considerable inertia. Formal barriers to trade for industrial products only converged with those prevailing in the other advanced economies in the late 1970s, while the agricultural sector remained heavily shielded, including by a plethora of non-tariff barriers, such as import quotas and licences. More importantly, the home market as a whole remained significantly protected by informal and social network obstacles that politicians and bureaucrats were reluctant to touch. The capital account was only fully liberalized in the 1990s.

The raw statistics of the high-growth period are worth dwelling on. During this remarkable epoch, the annual growth rate in real GDP was frequently well into double digits, peaking at some 13% in 1966! Even during the economy's brief – inventory-adjustment-driven – 'recessions', the overall expansion rate usually outstripped that of any other developed nation. And rather than doubling national income, as had been planned by Ikeda, it actually tripled between 1959 and 1971. The capital stock, meanwhile, grew at a rate of almost 8% a year, as against an average of 1.5% between 1913 and 1950. With the exception of Germany, this was a pace more than twice as fast as in the other major economies. Productivity growth averaged some 7.5% a year, against a 4.5% OECD average and the United States's 2.4%. Export volumes grew at an annual rate of more than 15%: almost twice the OECD average. What is more, on most measures of income inequality, such as the Gini coefficient, Japan was less unequal than any other top-tier economy.

By the early 1970s, Japan had made up huge ground with the Western economies in terms of per capita income and absolute levels of productivity, and it had overtaken France, the United Kingdom and Germany to become the second largest economy in the free world. It was a full-blown consumer society and had experienced a significant increase in middle class consciousness. Japan accounted for 15.7% of global crude steel production, 21% of global synthetic fibre production, 48.3% of global shipbuilding production, 14.2% of global passenger car production, and 30.5% of global commercial vehicle production. In the process, Japanese manufacturing companies had increasingly become household names across the world.

PARSING THE MIRACLE

The factors underlying Japan's remarkable transformation in the 1950s and 1960s were many and various, and it is difficult to be precise about the exact role of each. The driving forces often overlapped; they proved to be mutually reinforcing; and they extended beyond mere economics. Indeed, one of the most interesting aspects of Japan's economic miracle is that it did not really chime with any of the standard developmental models of the time. It was consistent neither with Marxist theory, Keynesian theory, free-market capitalist theory nor so-called dependency theory, with its emphasis on explicit import substitution.

What is clear, however, is that with the United States being sympathetic to Japan's economic cause for strategic Cold War reasons, the country enjoyed privileged access to an increasingly liberal system of global trade, which was itself expanding rapidly. The country faced limited constraints on its exports, while it could obtain the imported raw materials and other inputs on which it was heavily dependent with little difficulty.

The positive role of trade in Japan's development was further reinforced by what became an increasingly undervalued fixed exchange rate that, despite rising external criticism, the Japanese authorities baulked at adjusting upwards. Indeed, mention of revaluation was something of a taboo within government. The rate of ¥360 to the US dollar was considered sacrosanct throughout the high-growth era.

At the same time, Japan was able to purchase the latest technologies without having to bear the full costs of research and development, while high levels of domestic investment – gross fixed capital formation typically oscillated between the equivalent of 30% and 40% of GDP and peaked at 40.5% in 1961 – supported by high levels of domestic saving served to impel manufacturing industry towards the technological frontier and progressively boosted productivity. The emergence of the *Keiretsu*, and the economies of scale it fostered, also supported this process, as did a sustained shift of labour away from agriculture and forestry. Japan's industrialization went hand in hand with rapid urbanization and the remarkable growth of cities like Tokyo-Yokohama, Osaka and Nagoya.

The high level of domestic savings in part reflected what was at that stage a relatively meagre social security system and the fact that a significant part of household savings had to be allocated to mortgage payments, life insurance and large outlays such as weddings, school fees and downpayments on housing. Equally important, however, were cultural explanations. The values of loyalty, self-sacrifice and, in particular, thrift had become deeply instilled into the population's psyche. Borrowing was frowned upon as being indicative of desperation. Saving, on the other hand, was considered prudent and patriotic. Finally, Japan's system of postal savings – in effect a nationwide network of familiar consumer banks, with the capacity to accept deposits and provide a variety of other financial and social services – rendered the process of saving for individuals relatively straightforward, as it had done since its establishment towards the end of the nineteenth century.

For its part, the BOJ kept the structure of interest rates as low as possible, tightening policy only when the external balance deteriorated unduly and foreign currency reserves dropped below a minimum level. The inflation rate averaged around 5% on a GDP deflator basis through the 1950s and 1960s, while the official discount rate (ODR) fluctuated between 8.5% early in the period and 5.5%–6.5% towards its end. For this reason, real borrowing costs were generally subdued. However, the Japanese financial system was heavily regulated during this period, and the central bank, in concert with the MOF, actively used bank reserve ratio requirements and 'window guidance' on the growth and structure of loan provision as much as, if not more than, official interest rate adjustments in its management of the business cycle.

Turning to fiscal policy, while sectoral tax breaks and subsidies were used to manipulate the structure of output, the overall tax burden was kept low. In the 1960s it ran well below 20% of GDP; the OECD average was above 25% and the typical figure in Europe some seven percentage points higher. The budgetary stance was conservatively managed, following the so-called golden rule: that is to say, borrowing via so called construction bonds was used only to finance public investment. It was only in 1965 that the first 'deficit-financing bonds' were issued to address a temporary current revenue shortage. Consequently, the government typically ran a consistent primary surplus on its consolidated budget, and the public sector gross debt ratio was exceptionally low, bottoming out at only 4% of GDP in 1964. The burden of debt interest costs was similarly negligible. For all the financial carrots and sticks and associated administrative guidance used by the government to shape output, there was no discernible 'crowding out' of private sector activity by the public sector.

Once growth had been kick-started and had gathered momentum, demographic forces played a central role in expanding the domestic consumer market and maintaining labour input, especially as the education system – and the societal assumptions and expectations held about and of it – ensured that the workforce was of a high quality: literate, numerate and motivated. Between 1950 and 1973 a high birth rate meant that Japan's population expanded from 82.8 million to 109.5 million, i.e. it grew by almost a third. At the same time, the relative youth of the population – only 5%–8% of people were over 65 and the country enjoyed the industrialized world's most favourable balance of productive to non-productive population – meant that employees had to pay little by way of pension contributions or social security taxes to support the elderly. Furthermore, in a wage system in which pay was often in significant part determined by seniority, the young population helped to keep the overall wage bill competitive.

The high-growth period was further buttressed by stability or consistency on a number of levels. This extended beyond the dominance of right-of-centre political rule, to management methods; industrial relations; cooperation between state, private enterprise and various corporate bodies; and, in a broader sense, social attitudes and behaviour, and the widespread acceptance of the existing class structure. Japan also continued to allocate a relatively low proportion of national income to defence. A reinterpretation of the postwar constitution meant that the Japan Self-Defense Forces came into being in 1954 but were protected by the US defence and security umbrella; Japan generally spent less than 1% of GDP on the military – significantly less than most NATO members.

CHOPPIER WATERS

After Japan's remarkable run of success in the 1950s and 1960s, the 1970s brought new challenges.

Industrial pollution and associated health issues had become a growing problem as the economy rapidly expanded. Lead and mercury poisoning, smog in many major cities and the widespread contamination of rivers led to some tawdry scandals and a mounting public outcry. Successive rounds of legislation were belatedly introduced to address the threats posed by environmental damage, but opposition from the business community saw them persistently watered down. It was only in the early 1970s, with the establishment of the Environment Agency and the passage of a series of more robust parliamentary bills, that the legislative backdrop began to come to terms with the problem. At the same time, encouraged by the MITI, business began to recognize that pollution control and energy efficiency were in its own interest. By the mid 1980s Japan was for the most part no more polluted than most other major economies, and certainly less so than many developing economies.

The economy's trend expansion rate also began to shift down from the heady figures achieved in the 1960s, as technological catch-up progressed and the ability of high rates of investment to move the economy closer to the productivity frontier diminished. It was around this juncture that, in August 1971, the Nixon administration – no doubt in part because of Japan's intransigence in regard to a revaluation of the yen – unilaterally suspended the convertibility of the dollar into gold and imposed a 10% surcharge on imports in an effort to address the burgeoning tendency towards deficit in its external balance. By so doing, the US government threw the IMF/Bretton Woods system of fixed exchange rates into disarray. Efforts over the next 18 months to piece it back together around a devalued dollar and a greater degree of currency flexibility failed and the world toppled into a regime of floating exchange rates, within which the yen's longstanding undervaluation was progressively corrected. In the early 1970s the United States in essence decided to water down its paternal relationship somewhat with Japan in favour of greater economic self-interest.

The response of the Japanese authorities to the trauma of the long-overdue appreciation of the yen – it rose, in two stages, to ¥260 to the US dollar over the period to mid 1973 – and the fact that it was in future going to have to adjust to a less sympathetic United States in its trade and broader economic relations was to reflate aggressively. Public investment spending was ramped up sharply, pushing the consolidated budget into significant deficit for the first time since the immediate post-war era, and this was accompanied by a succession of official interest rate cuts and easier credit conditions. Broad monetary growth exploded higher, eventually peaking above 25% in annual terms.

This reflation coincided with the rise of Tanaka Kakuei, who became prime minister in July 1972. A relatively young (54), self-made and self-confident (even overbearing) figure – who was in many respects the personification of Japan's shady, money politics – he was different to his post-war predecessors and was set on delivering a bold new plan for the economy. Assuming that the country's high growth rate would be sustained – responding to his urgings, the government optimistically projected 9.5% per annum real growth for the five years to 1977 – Tanaka's aim was to redistribute the fruits of continued rapid expansion beyond the major urban centres to the rest of the country, in the process expanding the dominance of himself and his disciples across the LDP.[12]

The economy initially boomed in response to these initiatives. Real GDP growth reaccelerated to more than 8.0% in 1972 and 1973, while the unemployment rate dropped to barely 1% of the workforce. However, the current account balance, previously in consistent and growing surplus since 1968, swung into deficit, and both asset prices and goods and services prices surged higher. Speculative activity became rife in the stock and real estate markets. Annual CPI inflation moved into double digits. There was soon a sense that the expansion was unsustainable.

OPEC I: FROM BOOM TO BUST AND BEYOND

It was at this point that the first oil shock struck. Led by Saudi Arabia, members of the Organization of the Petroleum Exporting Countries (OPEC) introduced an oil embargo, targeting nations that supported Israel during the Yom Kippur War. Crude prices doubled in October 1973 and did so again in January 1974. Japan had built its rapid post-war expansion on a foundation of cheap energy. It was the world's largest oil importer, and it sourced around 90% of its oil from the Middle East. The country's terms of trade (the ratio of its export prices to its import prices) subsequently deteriorated by some 40%. Panic ensued across the population, with many seeking to hoard essentials of products considered to be prone to particularly sharp price rises.

Always sceptical of – even hostile to – Tanaka's plans, the BOJ had begun to tighten its stance in the spring of 1973, but the additional shocks to the price level left it a long way behind the curve. With the overall thrust of macroeconomic policy still expansionary and energy costs sharply higher, both actual and expected inflation continued to accelerate. Labour unions – their membership in high demand in a supercharged economy – initially prioritized the maintenance of living standards and demanded pay increases of more than 20% in 1973 and approaching 30% the following year. The annual rate of change in the CPI spiked to almost 25% in 1974 (then one of the highest rates in the OECD), while the external account plunged further into the red.

The BOJ was compelled to respond more forcefully. It pushed the ODR to a peak of 9% and sharply tightened window guidance on lending. Broad monetary growth – which, in keeping with the rise of monetarism, the central bank was paying more explicit attention to – fell back down towards single digits and dropped well into negative territory in real terms. Fiscal policy was also thrown into reverse in mid 1973 and early 1974, with public investment spending heavily curtailed. Tanaka's national remodelling plan was effectively abandoned almost as soon as it got underway.

The economy subsequently slumped into a bona fide recession. Indeed, in 1974 it suffered its first fall in real GDP since before the Korean War, with the peak-to-trough drop in industrial production amounting to some 18%. The unfamiliar inflationary uncertainties of this period encouraged the household saving ratio to jump, while corporate profitability, especially in manufacturing, was heavily squeezed, resulting in a long and deep adjustment in business investment. Over subsequent years, the unemployment rate was to more than double. Some outside commentators began to write Japan off.

The response to this 'sudden stop' in growth was dramatic, however. To guarantee future oil supplies Japan looked to suppliers beyond the Middle East, while cannily simultaneously providing generous aid for Arab governments and the Palestinians. At home, the government invested in nuclear power, imposed conservation measures, and offered energy-saving incentives to the corporate sector via discounted loans and special depreciation allowances. Capacity was quickly reduced or converted to new uses in the sectors that were hit hardest, while energy and raw material efficiency were generally encouraged. Automation burgeoned.

The crisis was a major factor in the shift of Japan's economy away from the oil-intensive, heavy industries – such as chemicals, steel, shipbuilding, cement and paper and pulp – that had led the way during the high-growth era and the country's journey up the value-added scale. Electronics, electrical machinery, precision engineering and other areas that demanded a high level of processing and more advanced technology, but that also had a high income elasticity, became its growth poles. The firms at its forefront, such as Sony, Toyota,

Matsushita, Honda, Sharp and Ricoh, established a major global footprint without being affiliated to any of the major established domestic *Keiretsu* groupings, although many set up vertically integrated industrial consortia of their own, often populated, as ever, by family-owned small and medium-sized parts manufacturers desperately competing to supply the dominant entity. It was in this context that Japanese firms perfected the 'just-in-time' system of inventory management.

Japanese auto makers were a particular beneficiary of the first oil crisis, frequently pioneering the employment of robotics and greater automation. In addition, the jump in gasoline prices helped Japan's smaller and more fuel-efficient models to gain market share in the United States at the expense of the 'gas-guzzling' Detroit competition. Furthermore, Japan's service industries, including those catering to other businesses, began to expand and mature, in the process accounting for a higher and higher share of overall employment. The 1970s also saw Japan begin to build a more comprehensive welfare state, expanding pension and medical insurance and putting more emphasis on the development of social overhead capital.

However, this rapid pace of structural change did not distract the authorities from sticking to their disinflationary guns. Indeed, inflation came to heel remarkably quickly. In this, policymakers were assisted by the particular nature of the Japanese system of wage determination. This was built around enterprise unions and the annual *Shunto*, or spring wage round, which determined basic pay for the next 12 months. The net result was greater commonality of interest and cooperation between management and workers, and a more centralized and synchronized process of wage bargaining – one less subject to coordination failure than in many other OECD economies. Equally, however, around a third of earnings was derived from semi-annual bonuses and overtime payments that were directly related to recent corporate performance. Workers proved less obsessed with real wage resistance and more malleable in the face of government exhortations for moderation than their Western equivalents, while overall pay levels were more responsive to labour demand and productivity considerations than elsewhere.

Basic wage demands fell sharply from 1975, while bonuses and overtime pay naturally adjusted lower in response to the squeeze on profits. Total annual wage inflation dropped from more than 27% in 1974, to just under 15% in 1975, and then to just over 9% by 1977. The annual rate of change in the CPI had dropped back into single digits by 1976 and was well below 5% in 1978. As wage and price inflation tumbled, the country's trade performance improved sharply, not least where its bilateral balances with the United States and the European Economic Community (EEC) were concerned. By 1979, Japan was running a current account surplus equivalent to some 1.7% of GDP.

The real economy began to move out of recession in early 1975, led not, as was typically the case, by exports and business investment but by residential construction and public investment. Fiscal retrenchment was short lived. A series of stimulus packages were instituted in late 1974 and 1975 that resulted in a positive fiscal policy impulse of more than 2% of GDP. Consumer spending also subsequently played a positive role, as the saving rate corrected lower, while net exports resumed their customary position as a key source of expansion. Overall business investment only began to recover from an extended period of adjustment in 1978.

Notwithstanding the weakness of corporate outlays on plant and equipment, the pace of the recovery was impressive relative to most of Japan's advanced economy competitors, and especially those in Europe, as was the speed with which price and wage inflation subsided. The flexibility of Japan's supply-side response to the oil crisis in the traded goods sector was remarkable. Indeed, it could be argued that given the size and nature of the first OPEC shock, the Japanese economy's rapid adjustment and revival in the mid 1970s was as impressive as the heady growth of the previous two decades. After all, external circumstances had been very much in Japan's favour during the previous epoch. The world economy had been enjoying a particularly long period of strong and stable growth, the ten was super-competitive, and lagging perceptions of Japan's strength and the studied prevarication of domestic policymakers had enabled it to maintain a trading regime that, in important respects, ran against the grain of international convention. None of this survived the first oil shock intact.

All this said, the heady growth of the 1950s and 1960s was consigned to the history books, as indeed, for that matter, was Tanaka's premiership. The 1974 recession saw his popularity ebb away, while revelations about his involvement in a succession of financial and vote-buying scandals left him with little choice but to resign. Behind the scenes, however, he remained the dominant figure in Japanese politics, earning the sobriquet 'Shadow Shogun'. This continued despite the notorious Lockheed scandal, which broke in December 1975 and rumbled on until 1983, forcing him out of the LDP to sit as an independent in the Diet.[13] Tanaka was incapacitated by a stroke in 1985 and eventually died in 1993, but his cohorts remained a powerful force in the LDP and Japanese politics, often exercising an effective power of veto over prime ministerial candidates into the early twenty-first century.

GLOBAL LOCOMOTIVE

By 1977, however, growth was slowing again. The recovery from the first oil shock had often remained tepid at best elsewhere, and this sparked pressure from the other advanced economies for Japan and Germany, whose external balances were back in healthy surplus, to encourage their currencies to appreciate and to expand domestic demand – in other words, to act as growth engines for the world economy.

The yen subsequently moved sharply higher, rising against the dollar from 290 to a mere 180. With inflation subdued, the BOJ cut the ODR in stages to a low of 3.5%, and window guidance on bank lending was relaxed. There also followed another bout of budgetary largesse, extending to successive rounds of public works investment and amounting in total to some 1.75% of GDP, even though the fiscal deficit was already at a post-occupation high of close to 5% of GDP.

These measures were in line with a 'Concerted Action Programme' formally adopted by OECD members in June 1978. This episode marked one among many occasions in which so-called *Gaiatsu,* or 'outside pressure', encouraged a notable change in Japanese economic policy.

Economic growth duly picked up in 1978 and 1979, led, as was intended, by domestic expenditures, although the new reality was that Japan's potential growth rate had by this stage slipped to around 4% a year, rather than being close to 7%, as the government had hoped. Moreover, the rejuvenated cyclical upswing came at the cost of an enduringly wide budgetary shortfall, which pushed the public sector debt burden up towards 50% of GDP – far above anything that had been seen since the end of the war – and added significantly to the debt service costs of the government.

OPEC II: RAPID ADJUSTMENT

In 1979 the world was hit by a second major oil shock. In January of that year Iran's Islamic Revolution saw diplomatic relations with the West deteriorate sharply, while OPEC once again adopted a stance of aggressively driving oil prices higher. The cost of a barrel of crude jumped from $12 at the end of 1978 to $34 in October 1981. Japanese import prices actually rose more during this period than they did during the first oil shock, and the deterioration in the terms of trade was also more dramatic, cumulating to almost 50%.

Fearing a repeat of the inflationary debacle of 1974, the BOJ sought to respond rapidly, and the ODR was ramped back up to 9% by March 1980. The prompt response paid dividends. Aided by the policy credibility it had earned through its disinflationary successes in the middle of the previous decade and, once again, by the particular mechanics of the Japanese labour market, the subsequent increase in consumer price pressures was much less dramatic than it had been six years earlier. CPI inflation peaked well under a double-digit annual rate in 1980 and had subsided to an average of only 2.7% by 1982.

The emphasis on disinflation, however, meant that the rapid expansion of the late 1970s was short lived. Real GDP growth slowed to around 3.5% in 1980 and 1981 from an unsustainable 5.5% in 1979, with domestic demand, and especially business investment, very sluggish. Unemployment increased but remained well under 3% of the workforce. Reflecting higher imported energy costs, the external balance moved back into the red in 1979 and 1980, but these deficits amounted to only around 1% of GDP and proved temporary. The current account was back in surplus in 1981 and has essentially remained in the black ever since.

Overall, Japan's relative performance during this period was again far superior to that of the other major economies, many of which suffered outright contractions (some of them serious), significant increases in joblessness, large external shortfalls, and extended periods of double-digit inflation and official interest rates. Also noteworthy is the fact that Japan had become the world's most efficient user of energy by the early 1980s.

NEW PRIORITIES

The second oil shock and the stagflation associated with it resulted in a significant reorientation of declared economic policy priorities across the developed world, exemplified most obviously by 'Reaganomics' in the United States and 'Thatcherism' in the United Kingdom. The new conventional wisdom was that the short-term fine-tuning of demand through fiscal policy and the prioritization of full employment should be set aside. Instead, the focus should be the re-establishment of relative price stability through tight monetary policy, and in particular high real interest rates and the restraint of monetary growth. At the same time, budgets should be brought back into balance, the state should be shrunk, direct taxes should be reduced, and deregulation and the freer operation of market forces should be pursued in order to enhance competition and bolster underlying growth.

The reality was that as events, politics and various technical complications intervened, the rhetoric associated with this policy revolution went considerably further than the substance. Nevertheless, by the early 1980s, Keynesianism had – at least in explicit terms – been consigned to the history books, and government intervention and the welfare states built over the course of the three previous decades or so had been sent into retreat.

In Japan, given its comparative success in addressing the vicissitudes of the 1970s, there was less clamour for a dramatic change of approach to policy. That said, the swing of the political pendulum in the West and the economic priorities that went with it did not go unnoticed or play out without effect. Furthermore, this period saw both growing international appreciation of

Japan's economic supremacy and the rise of Nakasone Yasuhiro: a brash and outspoken prime minister of some longevity who, in a break from the past, was recognized, even admired, abroad.

Nakasone, who enjoyed the sponsorship of Tanaka Kakuei, was an aristocratic right-wing nationalist. He was largely unrepentant about Japan's past, and he wanted to revise many of the institutional structures that had been imposed during the occupation and largely accepted thereafter, casting off the constraints on Japanese self-expression they had brought about. Leading the country from 1982 to 1987, he established close relations with Reagan and Thatcher and was happy to play up his sympathy for their worldview and approach to politics and present himself as the antithesis of his often gauche and unworldly predecessors. He professed a desire to 'internationalize' Japan, although the reality was that what internationalization meant to him, more than anything else, was being confident in advancing Japanese interests abroad. Consistent with this, he dared to suggest that Japan should ramp up its defence budget beyond 1% of GDP – something he achieved (just) in the final budget of his premiership.

Where economic policy was concerned, Nakasone's administrations prioritized two areas: the consolidation of the public finances and the reform of the financial sector, both of which dovetailed with the prevailing Western zeitgeist.

Japan's overall budget deficit remained around 4%–5% of GDP during the second oil shock, and the burden of government debt continued to mount, rising above the 50% of GDP mark in 1980. Debt interest payments accounted for more than a percentage point of GDP, crimping the scope for discretionary outlays.

These standard public finance metrics were by no means an outlier among the major economies at the time, and this was particularly the case relative to Japan's European competitors. Moreover, if the substantial assets accumulated in Japan's social security system were taken into consideration, then its indebtedness was well below the OECD average in net terms.[14] Nevertheless, with the MOF flexing its bureaucratic muscles, and increasingly concerned by the future liabilities that would accrue from a rapid ageing of the population structure – the nation's annual population growth rate had peaked at 1.35% in 1973, and by 1981 it was just 0.65% and set to continue to decline – the 1980s proved to be a period of sustained fiscal reconstruction.

Fiscal policy was tightened by between a half and one-and-a-half percentage points of GDP in every year from 1981 to 1987, and the overall budget balance moved back into surplus.[15]

The civil service was trimmed. Many of the subsidies and grants that characterized the high-growth era were withdrawn. Government spending increased by less than 1% per annum in real terms, and the share of government outlays in GDP was consistently reduced, while even if there were few explicit tax increases – an attempt to introduce a broad-based indirect tax failed to get parliamentary approval – the share of tax revenues also consistently rose. There was, in short, considerable 'fiscal drag' in the context of a progressive income tax scale and consistent economic growth.[16] As a result, the pace of the increase in the debt burden first slowed sharply and then came to a halt, allowing the weight of debt interest payments to stabilize at around 1.5% of GDP.

Reflecting the trend across many other advanced economies, this period also saw the at least partial privatization of, among others, the national telecommunications company the Nippon Telegraph and Telephone Corporation (NTT), Japan National Railways (JNR), Japan Airlines (JAL) and Japan Tobacco (JT).[17] In truth, however, although greater competition was encouraged, these reductions in public ownership were undertaken more for practical and financial reasons than for ideological ones, and there was little sense of them being part of a coherent plan. Inefficient and chronically overmanned, these public enterprises had all been a huge drain on the taxpayer for some time.

JNR in particular was as much a part of the social safety net as it was a national railway system. Despite large government subsidies it had run substantial losses since 1964 and the birth of the Shinkansen. At the time of its partial sell-off in 1987, JNR recorded a deficit of ¥37.1 trillion, equivalent to the national debt of several developing economies. The monolithic entity was split into seven slimmed-down groups, and its outstanding debt was transferred to a new company: the Japan National Railways Settlement Corporation (JNRSC), which was endowed with land and other assets disposed of at the time.[18] This particular privatization was arguably one of the most complex and bold attempted anywhere during the 1980s.

Turning to the financial sector, Japan's banks and other financial institutions had been rigidly regulated and siloed since 1945, with the paramount objective being to render them the servant of industry and economic rehabilitation. Innovation was stymied. Control was exerted by the quantity and allocation of credit available, rather than its price. A tentative process of regulatory relaxation got under way in the 1970s but it only really took off in the following decade as Japan built up increasingly large external surpluses; furthermore, it was widely recognized internally that an archaic, sclerotic and uncompetitive financial sector raised the cost of capital and threatened to become a serious constraint on growth. The Reagan administration's criticisms of Japan's protected financial markets – and, in particular, its suspicion that they had long helped to keep the yen artificially weak – also provided a degree of *Gaiatsu* to move the process along.

With the consistent resort to deficit finance, the 1980s saw the secondary market for government debt grow rapidly and it began to attract increasing international interest. Exchange controls were progressively removed. The strict segmentation of the sector was reduced, strengthening competition between banks and securities companies. Loan collateral requirements were relaxed. The number of short-term financial instruments multiplied, and the interest rates on them were increasingly market determined. Derivatives such as futures, swaps and options were introduced, and they quickly burgeoned. Foreign exchange market turnover in Tokyo exploded. A huge market for yen bonds sprung up in Europe (the Euroyen market). Foreign firms were allowed greater access, resulting in a flood of interest from overseas investors and commercial banks. Suddenly, almost from nowhere, Japan became one of the three major global financial centres, along with London and New York, and a rapidly increasing proportion of central bank reserves were held in yen, especially across Asia. It was becoming a reserve currency.

That said, there was one part of the financial sector that remained largely off limits to reform: the system of postal savings. It was one of Japan's largest employers, and through tax exemptions, generous terms and because of limited oversight it dominated domestic deposits, accounting for almost a third of the total by the mid 1980s.

The post office system had long enjoyed a cosy relationship with the ruling LDP's rural powerbase. The postmasters' association was one of the LDP's staunchest groups of supporters, and post offices often acted as a vote-gathering machine for the party. Furthermore, the Postal Ministry simply refused to give up being the system's overseer – a role it had played since 1874.

The postal savings system also lent almost all of the funds it collected from savers to the Ministry of Finance Trust Fund Bureau at interest rates below those on government debt. It was, therefore, a vital source of cheap finance for government-sponsored infrastructure projects and the priorities of industrial policy. It was not until the twenty-first century that thoroughgoing reform of postal savings was delivered – and, as we shall see, even then the process was politically fraught and the pace painfully slow.

LEADING THE 1980S RECOVERY

Despite the austere stance of fiscal policy in the first half of the 1980s, the economy accelerated markedly between 1983 and 1985, registering growth of some 5% per annum. A looser monetary stance in the context of financial liberalization acted to more than offset the fiscal squeeze – the ODR was progressively reduced to a low of 2.5% at the end of 1986, while window guidance on lending was very loose. Simultaneously, the reversal of oil prices to real levels last seen in the early 1970s meant that, by the middle of the decade, the world was recovering strongly, and nowhere more so than the increasingly dynamic Asian economies in Japan's immediate vicinity.

Subdued domestic cost pressures and a weak yen meant that Japan was extremely competitive during this period. Wage inflation dropped below 3% a year, while annual CPI inflation fell to 2.0% in 1985 and then a mere 0.6% in 1986. Along with business investment, net exports contributed strongly to the economy's expansion, and the country's share in total global exports rose to some 10% from a figure of 6.5% in 1979. Japan's already strong export orientation, if not mercantilist bias, was reinforced.

The yen's weakness was less the result of what was happening in Japan and more the flipside of a period of extraordinary, if increasingly unsustainable, US dollar strength. During the early 1980s the Reagan administration pursued a tax-cutting agenda and embarked on a rapid military buildup. Notwithstanding the Republican Party's professed attachment to fiscal probity, this swelled the US budgetary shortfall to an unprecedented peacetime proportion of GDP and left real interest rates at levels that attracted a flood of speculative capital into the US currency. In trade-weighted terms, the dollar reached all-time highs.

The combination of stronger growth, an expansive fiscal policy and a rapidly rising dollar pushed the US current account deeply into the red, with the deficit reaching some 3.5% of GDP at its peak. Meanwhile, Japan's external surplus, much of it with the United States, rose to more than 4% of its GDP, with the surplus on manufacturing trade peaking at more than 10% of GDP!

Net outflows of long-term capital from Japan burgeoned, reaching some $65 billion in 1985 and $137 billion in 1987 (a figure roughly matching the entire GDP of Switzerland). Around half of these outflows went to the United States, but by no means all of the money found its way into productive business assets. Japanese investment in overseas property and securities, especially foreign government bonds, jumped sharply, as for that matter did its foreign aid budget. In the process, Japan became the world's largest creditor nation and the US its biggest debtor.

Japan's huge external surpluses – driven in significant part by high-tech, high-valued-added products – together with its burgeoning net creditor status only added to the international resentment about its trade policies that had been building since the 1960s, much of it emanating from Washington and from US industry. Notwithstanding the effect of the egregious US policy mix on its own external balance and those of its major trading partners, the consensus was that Japan had not been playing by the global trading rules. Rather, Japan put undue emphasis on exports as a driver of growth, while the domestic market was rigged against foreign competition. Clearly, there are obvious parallels here with the way that the United States and others have tended to view China's development model over more recent decades.[19]

Initially at least, the standard Japanese response to these criticisms was that there was nothing intrinsically optimal about a zero external balance. Moreover, Japan had reduced its tariff barriers to negligible levels; beyond food and agriculture, its non-tariff barriers to trade were no higher than in the United States, and they were falling; and neither were its direct government subsidies egregious by international standards. Also, as a country geographically far removed from most other OECD nations, and with a still relatively young population and a natural resource endowment skewed to high-quality human capital, it was argued that there was bound to be a bias towards running an external surplus of some size. Finally, there was a feeling that the United States and others should look to their own economic shortcomings rather than jealously criticize and sanction Japan for its successes. If their own populations expressed a preference for Japanese goods, why should the Japanese themselves not do the same? Americans and Europeans should save more, cut their prices, improve the quality of their exports and work harder to break into the Japanese market.

In much of this, Japanese commentators had a point, but there was little doubt that navigating Japan's bloated and labyrinthine wholesale distribution system was a costly and complex process for foreign exporters. As much as it was a mechanism to put goods into the hands of consumers, like JNR it also served a secondary purpose as an unofficial domestic social security system – one built, in its case, on personal association and obligation. Furthermore, as noted earlier, a major characteristic of Japanese business practice was repetitive trading with suppliers through subcontracting. Such customs made it difficult for any newcomer, domestic or foreign, to enter a market. Meanwhile, the domestic retail market, especially for major household goods and cars, was traditionally controlled by local manufacturers. Again, newcomers could be discriminated against and excluded.

Finally, the Japanese bureaucracy had long seen it as its prerogative to encourage exporters, and to protect certain sensitive areas of the domestic economy through complex webs of regulation, including price controls and entry restrictions; licensing and certification procedures; and close connections between politicians, bureaucrats and businesspeople. The MITI had helped to nurture and sustain the large export-orientated companies within the *Keiretsu*. The Ministry of Health worked closely with pharmaceutical firms. The Postal Ministry worked closely with the communications industry. The Ministry of Agriculture worked closely with the farmers. And foreign firms were excluded from major public works projects because they had no experience in the Japanese market.

It was therefore hard to deny that exports held a special place in the Japanese governmental and business psyches, that existing players in Japan's domestic market remained protected by significant informal barriers to entry, or that Japan's volume of imports was lower than it might otherwise have been.

In the context of these considerations, policy began to shift on three distinct levels.

First, Japan agreed to extend the voluntary export restraints (VERs) it first introduced on textiles in the early 1960s, most conspicuously on cars, televisions and video tape recorders. Indeed, by the late 1980s some 20% of Japanese exports to the United States and the EEC were subject to some form of VER.

Second, Japan was content to work closely with the other major industrial nations to correct the dollar's dramatic rise, which the international policy-making community increasingly felt had overshot a value consistent with the US economy's underlying fundamentals. In September 1985 the so-called Plaza Accord, which combined coordinated rhetorical and more direct intervention in the foreign exchange market, added considerable momentum to a nascent correction in the US currency's value, as indeed did a decision of the BOJ to allow short-term market rates to increase temporarily.[20] The yen's rate against the dollar adjusted from a peak of 278 in November 1982 to 200 at the end of December 1985, en route to a level of around just 120 at the end of 1988.

Third, as we will see in the next chapter the Japanese authorities accepted that it was in the nation's own self-interest to respond more meaningfully in the years ahead to the increasingly strident diplomatic pressure it was under to move away from statism, open its markets and restructure its economy towards private, domestically led, growth. This was less an issue of the absolute size of the government's role in total output (which was well below the OECD average) and more about the nature of that role.

Of these three developments, it was the deliberate appreciation of the yen that had the biggest immediate resonance. The post-Plaza jump in the value of the Japanese currency was too rapid for Japanese industry to adjust to immediately. The economy slowed sharply, registering growth of only 2.5% in 1986, during what was known as the *Endaka fukyo*, or 'high-yen slump'. Export growth, particularly that of machinery, plummeted, and the contribution of net exports to growth swung into negative territory, while manufacturing sector profits also fell sharply. Many exporters looked to shift production offshore, not just into rapidly growing Southeast Asia but also into Europe and the United States too, often revolutionizing local work practices in the process.

REACHING THE PROMISED LAND

The first two chapters of this book have detailed how the Japanese economy went on a remarkable journey over the course of the 120-odd years following the 1868 Meiji Restoration, in the process overcoming numerous daunting challenges and repeatedly reinventing itself. It was the first economy to make the leap from underdeveloped status to fully developed, advanced status, avoiding, unlike so many other countries, the 'middle income trap'.[21] In so doing, it evolved from an alien, largely forgotten, deliberately isolated, vulnerable outpost on the edge of civilization to a huge, sophisticated, technologically advanced economy that had become both a role model for the rest of the world and, given its strong export orientation, a target for those envious of its success. Parvenus are invariably resented, and as John Maynard Keynes appositely put it: 'a debtor nation does not love its creditor'.[22] This was certainly the case with the United States in the mid 1980s.

By this time, Japan accounted for almost a tenth of global GDP, its stock of external assets was unparalleled, and the output of its major companies was ubiquitous. Furthermore, its influence on the world had by that stage begun to stretch beyond commerce and economic heft to culture, fashion, food, tourism and, despite its relative introversion, geopolitics.[23] By the same token, Japan, or at least its major cities, had become more cosmopolitan, at least superficially. Yet the residual unfamiliarity and opacity of Japanese society, together with the nation's chequered history, meant that the country was treated with considerable suspicion.

At the outset of its process of development, Japan possessed more of the prerequisites for success than others that would attempt to follow the same course. Culture – in the form of a solid work ethic, a reverence for education, the social status quo and a firm attachment to thrift – also played a positive role. And Japan managed, more successfully than most, to absorb and modify to its own purposes many institutional arrangements, ideas and technologies imported from elsewhere.

Demography – an often forgotten but inexorable force – also played an important part in Japan's advance. The country's population almost quadrupled between 1868 and 1986, growing particularly rapidly during the post-war high-growth era. And, as we will see, demography would continue to shape Japan's development, albeit in a much less constructive manner, in the late twentieth and early twenty-first centuries.

The nation's distinctive political system was a further recurrent factor at play. The influence and authority of an often less than impressive political class was throughout circumscribed not just by a strong and purposeful bureaucracy but also by big business; by financiers; on occasion by gangsters;

and, for one especially grim period, by a military that had run out of control. These peculiar arrangements undoubtedly had their downsides. They at times distorted and hindered development and sent Japan down unfortunate and costly blind alleys. But at other points, including after World War II, they provided a backdrop of stability and focus. They certainly acted to mould the particular form of progress that Japan enjoyed.

Japan's development was forged by its experiences in two world wars and their aftermaths. The first initially accelerated the country's progress dramatically before consigning it to a painful period of adjustment and consolidation. The second set its development back in even more spectacular and catastrophic fashion before yielding the circumstances that enabled an extraordinary 'second coming'. The post-war occupation and enduring US patronage played a seminal role, although it was perhaps as much because of the institutional and other consistencies it underpinned as it was due to the changes it brought about.

In many ways the economic system of the post World War II era had much in common with that established in the run-up to war (the so-called 1940 system). Beyond the enduring power and influence of a dedicated and determined bureaucracy, the workforce was kept quiescent; consumption was squeezed, and savings channelled into industry and government; the banks were encouraged to lend to affiliated companies; business and government planned ahead together, usually effectively; individual shareholder rights were heavily circumscribed; exports were prioritized; the domestic market was sheltered, and financial repression encouraged.

By the end of this period, few imagined that Japan's dramatic rise was likely to end abruptly. Indeed, most commentators both internally and externally expected it to continue unabated. Certainly, collective self-confidence within Japan itself was evolving into hubristic thoughts of unbounded Japanese supremacy and world leadership. But the late 1980s were to be the apogee of Japanese power and influence. The economic miracle subsequently ground to a juddering and painful halt. Over the next 40 years the country was spectacularly brought down to earth.

CHAPTER 3

The Bubble Economy

'Life has mountains and valleys' — Japanese proverb

WHAT COULD POSSIBLY GO WRONG?

Outwardly, the Japanese economy continued to outperform its major rivals substantially in the late 1980s. The cyclical upswing that followed the exchange-rate-driven slowdown of 1986 – subsequently entitled the *Heisei Boom* – was, as intended, domestically driven, robust and extended.[1] Employment became increasingly full. Investment spending and productivity growth were extremely impressive. Goods and services price inflation picked up from uncomfortably low levels but remained largely quiescent, and well below the G7 average. The consolidated budget balance continued to improve, moving well into the black, and the burden of government debt and debt interest payments began to subside. Significant – if imperfect and patchy – efforts were made to deregulate domestic markets, enhance competition and encourage import penetration, and the external surplus declined consistently as a proportion of national output, just as the international community desired. Nevertheless, Japan added significantly to its already impressive stock of external assets.

In this context, the Japanese people came to enjoy a level of prosperity that would have been beyond the wildest dreams of previous generations. For most, post-war frugality was well and truly left behind. City centres, particular Tokyo's, where many large companies had their increasingly lavish headquarters, were modern, vibrant and clean, appearing to outsiders to exude wealth. Japanese industry was renowned for its embrace of cutting-edge technologies, and its international hegemony continued apace. Overseas tourism was burgeoning in the United States, Europe and beyond. Rich Japanese individuals were buying up the world.

Perhaps unsurprisingly, all this success bred arrogance and exceptionalism and a belief that Japan's supremacy was destined to endure. To many at home, and for that matter abroad, the country had taken on an aura of invincibility. If, as was widely believed at this time, there was to be a 'Pacific Century', Japan was seemingly bound to be its trailblazer – the model for others to follow. It was feared. It was the future.

The real economy's continued ebullience and perceived success was only part of the story, however. This period also witnessed one of recent economic history's most remarkable bouts of asset price inflation. Impelled by historically low interest rates and rapid credit expansion, and amplified by the innovative opportunities offered by financial deregulation and the particular institutional architecture of Japanese commerce and society, soaring stock and land prices were integral – even defining – elements of the riotous late-1980s boom.

As ever with such episodes of unbridled excess, however, the boom was built on sand. It became increasingly dependent on temporary stimuli, misconceptions and wishful thinking, and it inevitably proved unsustainable. In the meantime, it fostered huge wealth inequalities, market distortions and resource misallocation, and it incentivized widespread, and at times brazen, financial malfeasance. An inescapable, debilitating and chastening hangover ensued, although few could have predicted its magnitude or duration. In its aftermath, the presumption of Japan's enduring economic superiority was utterly crushed.

CHANGE OF TACK

As suggested towards the end of the previous chapter, there was by the mid 1980s a growing acknowledgement within the Japanese bureaucracy that the economy needed to be reorientated away from its long-standing dependency on exports and towards the expansion of domestic demand and personal consumption. This fundamental conclusion was central to a number of official documents published by various arms of the government at the time, of which the 'Mayekawa Report' – produced under the direction of former BOJ Governor Mayekawa Haruo at the instigation of Prime Minister Nakasone – is the most widely quoted and was the most influential.[2]

The rationale for abandoning what was in effect a neo-mercantilist development strategy had two elements. First, the desire to assuage international criticism of Japan's huge external surplus and growing share of global export markets, and so prevent the application of more draconian protectionist measures against it.[3] Second, a recognition within Japan that a highly regulated, high-cost and inefficient non-traded-goods sector was imposing an increasing burden both on the economy's praetorian guard of export manufacturers and, more pertinently, on the Japanese people as a whole. The latter were confronted by high prices, diminished choice, overcrowding, poor-quality living accommodation, long working hours and shortcomings in infrastructure. Notwithstanding the huge improvements in income, wealth and other developmental metrics since World War II, the domestic population was being denied the full benefits of their country's economic success. Finally, the old model was likely to prove increasingly ill-suited to a mature economy with a rapidly ageing population, where innovation and entrepreneurship would assume greater importance in driving growth.

The consensus was, therefore, that Japan needed to implement a programme of structural reforms across areas as diverse as housing, construction, finance, retailing and distribution, agriculture, employment conditions, and the tax system if the economy's enviable record of achievement was to be continued and social stability maintained. However, there were considerable differences of opinion over the pace, priorities and precise nature of the changes that would have to be forthcoming. After all, they would involve countless painful trade-offs and impinge upon many powerful vested interests that had long been able to extract significant rents from the status quo. The inertia in sensitive areas of policy that had been such a constant over the previous 40 years was therefore unlikely to dissipate immediately.

The external adjustment that was at the core of many of the international community's calls for a new approach to development in Japan was, however, in an overwhelming sense a macroeconomic, rather than microeconomic, policy issue. At the same time, structural reform was likely to prove politically and socially more palatable when the economy was expanding at a decent clip, and when people felt financially secure and confident about the future. The levers of monetary and fiscal policy would therefore have to do much of the heavy lifting, especially during the preliminary stages of the process of change.

The matters of greatest urgency were achieving a more sympathetic constellation of exchange rates and impelling the domestic economy out of the relative torpor into which it had descended in 1986.

MONETARY LAXITY

In the wake of the Plaza Accord signed by the finance ministers of the G5 nations in September 1985, Japanese monetary policy was strongly influenced by developments on the foreign exchanges. The international desire to correct the dollar's chronic overvaluation against the yen and other currencies led the BOJ initially to encourage short-term market interest rates to rise somewhat, even if it left the ODR at the 5% level it had been set at since late 1983. But the rapidity of the subsequent fall in the dollar/yen rate, together with its deflationary implications for the Japanese economy, was such that by the end of the year the central bank felt it necessary to reverse course dramatically. The ODR was cut four times over the next twelve months or so, bringing it down to what was at the time an all-time low of 2.5%. Furthermore, any meaningful restraint on bank lending was temporarily removed. The yen nevertheless continued to trend upwards against the dollar until Q1 1988, eventually reaching a high against the US currency of approaching 120. In overall nominal effective terms, the yen's appreciation between late 1985 and mid 1988 amounted to some 60%.

The annual rate of broad monetary growth, meanwhile, accelerated from around 8% a year to well into double digits, eventually peaking first at around 12% in early 1988 and then at some 15% in Q2 1990.[4] This was far in excess of the growth rate of nominal GDP, which averaged 5.7% per annum between 1985 and 1989. The process of financial deregulation that was then in train meant that the Bank had a less precise understanding of how monetary considerations affected the economy than it had had hitherto. But that said, the extended superfluity of monetary growth clearly pointed to a sizeable build-up of excess money balances. Moreover, the results of surveys of opinion by both the BOJ and others were abundantly clear that lending conditions were considered to be easy, especially by larger firms, and that corporate liquidity remained plentiful until the end of the decade.

The growth in bank advances traced a similar pattern to the broad money supply. Bank credit extended to the corporate sector – which had been rising steadily since 1981 – registered a particularly rapid expansion rate. There was at the same time a shift away from more traditional business loans and towards those related in one way or another to real estate investment. Real estate developers, construction and finance companies borrowed an estimated ¥41.0 trillion, or the equivalent of some 12% of GDP, from Japan's banks during this period.

The late 1980s also saw financing from the capital markets in the form of share offerings, corporate bonds, convertible bonds and bonds with warrants increase rapidly, especially in 1989 when some ¥28 trillion of additional cash was raised in this way. Indeed, the combination of low interest rates and rapidly rising share and land collateral prices enabled Japanese companies essentially to borrow for free, in the process giving them a huge cost-of-capital advantage over their US and European counterparties and an overwhelming incentive to invest – in almost anything that potentially offered a positive return. This was particularly the case when companies raised cash in dollars on the Euromarkets and swapped the proceeds back into yen. The disparity in effective borrowing costs in Japan's favour over the United States was for a time in the region of 400 basis points.

In this context, the ratio of total private credit to GDP rose from around 0.8 in 1980, to 1.0 in 1985, and to more than 1.2 in 1990. The total financial deficit of the non-financial corporate sector (its excess of investment over savings) peaked at around 9% of GDP at the end of 1989. By this stage the financial sector had also fallen into significant deficit, when it was usually close to balance or even enjoying a small surplus.

In summary, over the course of 1986, and for the next three years or more, monetary policy in Japan was unambiguously easy, and it sparked a raucous expansion of credit and a hectic investment boom. With the risk of excessive goods and services price inflation perceived to be low in an environment of subdued international commodity prices, residual yen strength, gradual domestic deregulation and a significant increase in manufacturing import penetration, it was only in May 1989 – by which time the impetus behind the economy's expansion was colossal – that the BOJ began to unwind the succession of official interest rate cuts that had taken the ODR to a record low. By this time, however, with inflation trending upwards, real borrowing costs were significantly below their levels of two years earlier. The nominal policy rate would have to rise considerably to rein in the cyclical upswing.

MORE FISCAL RESTRAINT

A further reason the thrust of monetary policy was kept so accommodative for such an extended interlude in the late 1980s was because the bias of fiscal policy remained towards consolidation and restraint. Growth in both government consumption and, especially, government investment was heavily constrained. There was a major stimulus package in May 1987 extending, inter alia, to some ¥5 trillion of public investment. However, even though this appears to have boosted private sector confidence, such was the subsequent rise in tax revenues – a function in part of the very high level of transactions in the share and real estate markets – that the fiscal stance was tightened by around two percentage points of GDP between 1986 and 1989 and the consolidated budget swung into the black for the first time since the early 1970s. The elasticity of tax revenue growth with respect to nominal GDP growth jumped well above its long-term average in the mid to late 1980s.

By the end of the decade, Japan boasted a budget surplus of 1.8% of GDP, which was comfortably the largest in the G7. As a consequence, the gross government debt ratio had fallen some five percentage points from its 1987 peak of 75.5% of GDP.

With one eye on the country's ageing population structure, this period also saw the biggest tax reform since the occupation, albeit only after the initial plans had been watered down and with a significant delay before its completion. Prime Minister Nakasone had wanted to introduce a major reorientation of the tax system in 1987 or 1988, including a general sales tax of 5%, but widespread public opposition to the rise in indirect taxes and a series of associated electoral setbacks for the LDP were such that Nakasone resigned and was replaced by Takeshita Noboru in October 1987.

The vexed issue of tax reform therefore had to be referred to a Diet Commission to find an acceptable compromise. In the end, following a series of income tax giveaways for households and companies, including adjustments to Japan's relatively high marginal rates, tax-exempt saving was abolished; a capital gains tax was applied to individuals' security transactions; and, most importantly of all, a consumption tax (a form of VAT) was introduced in May 1989 at a rate of 3%. The tax base was therefore broadened and the tax take to some extent shifted away from direct levies. There was also a clear suggestion that the consumption tax rate would subsequently have to be increased progressively as the population aged.

BOOM, BOOM, BOOM

Notwithstanding the continuation of fiscal restraint, forceful monetary stimulus in the context of financial deregulation, weak commodity prices (Japan's terms of trade improved by some 57% between January 1985 and August 1986), and the general ebullience of global economic activity in the second half of the 1980s meant that the Japanese economy, and in particular domestic expenditure, was soon once again expanding at a rate some way in excess of trend – and, for that matter, at a higher rate than the economies of its major competitors. Real GDP growth averaged 5% per annum over the years 1987–1989, while real domestic demand growth averaged more than 6.5% per year. Activity also held up particularly well in Japan after the October 1987 global stock market crash. By 1989 the economy was beyond full capacity. It exhibited a positive 'output gap' of more than 1.0% of real potential GDP, and this was set to increase further over the subsequent three years.[5] The contribution of net exports to growth during this period was consistently, and significantly, negative, and the external surplus fell from its 1986 peak of some 4.5% of GDP to 2% of GDP in 1989. The politically sensitive bilateral trade imbalance with the United States declined by some 30%.

As hinted earlier, the cyclical upswing was an investment boom more than anything else. The housing sector rebounded strongly, particularly in 1986 and 1987, after six years of decline – a consideration that was encouraged by

Japanese baby boomers being at the peak of their spending capacity, especially where mortgages were concerned. However, the dominant driving force of the expansion was private business investment, which increased its share of nominal GDP from around 15% in 1986 to more than 20% at the peak of the cycle – a level comparable to that seen during the high-growth period of the 1950s and 1960s. Remarkably, at its zenith, Japanese business investment exceeded total plant and equipment spending in gross terms in the far larger US economy.

The investment upswing began in the credit-condition-sensitive non-manufacturing sector, as was typical in the post-war Japanese economy. However, it subsequently became broad based, especially once the pace of the yen's rise eased in late 1988; as resource utilization rates surged; as asset price inflation amplified profits growth; as labour came to be in increasingly short supply; and as new technological advances in areas such as ICT, retailing, finance and transport were adopted.

The expansion of personal consumption was less dramatic and was marked by significant volatility around the time of Emperor Hirohito's severe illness and subsequent death early in 1989 and the introduction of the 3% consumption tax a few months later. Indeed, despite support from strong real disposable income and employment growth, the sharp rises in stock and land prices, and a buoyant housing sector, personal consumption's share of nominal GDP fell throughout the late 1980s.

Only about 14% of Japanese household assets were held directly in stocks, while turnover in housing was low. The household wealth effect was therefore limited to around 4% of any capital gain, with a lag of about a year. Consistent with this, the household saving ratio fell only modestly during the boom, from some 16% of disposable income in 1986 to 14% in 1990. For all the strength of the overall cyclical upswing, and in particular of domestic demand, the shift to a consumer-led economic model proved to be more easily said than done. Overturning a commercial and, for that matter, political system – constructed around the priorities of big business rather than the average person in the street – would take time.

Despite the strength of the cyclical upswing and the erosion of excess capacity, inflation was slow to pick up. Indeed, the headline CPI inflation rate fell close to zero in 1987 (the lowest rate in the G7) and was only around 1% when, in the spring of 1989, the introduction of the consumption tax temporarily added just over a percentage point to the annual rate. Even at the peak of the business cycle in the first half of 1990, underlying CPI inflation remained a mere 2.0% a year: a reflection of moderate wage growth, increased import penetration in manufactures, and falls in the cost of machinery in the context of technological advances.

EXTERNAL ADJUSTMENT

The sharp fall in Japan's current account surplus outlined above represented a remarkably rapid degree of external adjustment. This was particularly the case given the extent of the improvement in the country's terms of trade in 1985 and 1986, the fact that at the outset of the adjustment the absolute level of Japan's exports was more than 50% higher than its imports, and that the income elasticity of Japan's exports (mainly high-value-added manufactures) was around twice that of imports (mainly raw materials and oil). Furthermore, there was limited scope to direct Japan's specialized suite of high-productivity exports to the domestic market, and the accumulation of net external assets implied a structural increase in Japan's net investment income.

Beyond the sustained strength of domestic demand, the rise of the yen after 1985 played a central role in overcoming these constraints on adjustment. The real effective appreciation of the currency was not far short of the jump in the nominal rate, amounting to some 46% between the Plaza Accord and December 1987. This dramatically crimped the profitability of the export sector while making imports cheap enough that longstanding business arrangements that restricted the sale of foreign goods in Japan were increasingly watered down or cast aside.

At the same time, the exports of the Asian newly industrialized economies (NIEs) – many of which were benefiting from copying elements of Japan's development model and whose currencies depreciated in sympathy with the dollar – had become more sophisticated and of higher quality, and thereby more attractive to Japanese consumers. The rapidly expanding NIEs were also a favoured destination for Japanese FDI – which in total increased almost sixfold in dollar terms between 1985 and 1989, and at its peak amounted to more than 2% of GDP – as companies sought to circumvent the high yen by developing lower-cost production bases offshore, avoid VERs and escape the rapidly rising cost of domestic land. This initially actually boosted Japanese exports of capital goods, but over the longer term it reduced domestic export capacity, facilitating lasting external adjustment.

Export volume growth was stagnant in 1986 and 1987 and recovered only slowly thereafter. Japan's global export market share, which had been rising since the late 1960s, therefore retreated from its peak of 10.3% in 1986 to 8.5% in 1990. Import volume growth, meanwhile, surged, averaging more than 10% per annum between 1986 and 1989, such that the real trade balance moved into sustained deficit and the share of imports in GDP rose to 3.75%. This was still much lower than in other OECD economies, especially the closely integrated European ones, but represented a significant increase from a low of around 2.5%. Even more impressively, the end of the decade saw the share of manufacturing imports in the total approach 50%, as against a mere 20% in 1980. Japan's manufacturing trade surplus declined from a peak of more than 10% of GDP to some 6%.

STRUCTURAL REFORM

Deregulation and supply-side reform represented a means not only to augment the impact of the high pressure of domestic demand and currency-driven shifts of relative prices on the external account, but also to enhance domestic competition, improve the allocation of resources, raise productivity and advance the lot of Japanese consumers.

In 1980 more than half of Japan's total value added was produced by regulated industries and around a quarter originated in sectors that could be characterized as heavily regulated and in which bureaucratic interventions played a central role in corporate strategies. Vast swaths of the Japanese economy were characterized by complicated standards, certification, licensing and tendering processes, and distortionary taxes, all overseen by government officials often working opaquely behind the scenes via a nudge here and a wink there.

There was limited enforcement of anti-monopoly law, and the free formation of prices was severely constrained. Differences in legal frameworks put limits on the sales promotions that overseas producers relied heavily on in other external markets. Intellectual property rights were heavily protected. The retail sector was comprehensively controlled to shield smallholders, while sales networks in general were often controlled via exclusive dealer arrangements by manufacturers, not least in the area of autos and household appliances. The dominance of cross-shareholdings restricted foreign mergers and acquisitions (M&A) activity to minimal levels.

With *Gaiatsu* acting as an important catalyst for change, however, the decade saw programmes of deregulation implemented in areas ranging from building and land use to agriculture and finance, and from distribution and travel to road haulage and government procurement. There were some notable areas of progress. Along with yen strength, the partial deregulation of air travel, for example, helped to spark a travel boom. The number of Japanese overseas tourists doubled between 1985 and 1989, contributing to a widening external travel deficit that went a long way towards offsetting the positive impact of increased net investment income on the current account balance.

Nevertheless, despite the publicly expressed aspirations of the authorities in this regard, the overall process of deregulation was partial and uneven. For example, the implicit subsidies to agriculture, including through the price support schemes that covered 80% of production, remained among the highest in the OECD and were close to double the OECD average. Japanese agriculture therefore had far too many small plots where the scope for economies of scale was limited. Agricultural productivity suffered heavily as a consequence, amounting to only around one-third of the US level.

Furthermore, the *Keiretsu*, as well as tried and tested customs such as the widespread habit of repetitive trading with trusted suppliers through subcontracting, endured. The stability and long-term planning and development such arrangements facilitated remained powerful catalysts for their retention.

These business practices acted more like import tariffs than fixed quotas, however, and as the yen's sharp rise in the middle of the decade dramatically cheapened the costs of imports – import prices fell continuously from mid 1985 to mid 1987, with the annual rate of deflation peaking at close to 20% in 1986 – business practices began to change. The incentive provided by movements in the exchange rate was simply too much for many Japanese companies to ignore.

The problem was that a reversal of the yen's strength could encourage the changes in business practices to unwind. There therefore remained at the end of the decade a requirement for more far-reaching measures to make the service sector more responsive to the demands of the market. It was in this context that the US and Japanese governments launched the Structural Impediments Initiative (SII) in July 1989 to identify obstructions in both countries that conspired to impede trade and balance of payments adjustment. In the SII's final report, published in June of 1990, among other measures Japan agreed to implement an expansive long-term programme of public works spending on social overhead capital; to encourage leisure activities; to increase land supply for houses in urban areas through more rational taxation of land and a review of regulation; to further liberalize the retail sector; to strengthen the application of the anti-monopoly law, which, despite being based on its US counterpart, was very loosely enforced; to promote sorely lacking inward FDI (Japan did not figure in the top 25 nations with respect to FDI inflows); and to make the *Keiretsu* system more transparent. The future direction of policy was therefore clear. The key question, however, would be the pace and sequencing of change.

ASSET PRICE EXCESS

Asset price inflation was nothing new to Japan. As noted in chapter 1, there had been a huge asset bubble during and after World War I, while there were further bursts of rapid stock and land price inflation during previous post-war periods of credit expansion and boom conditions in the late 1950s and early 1970s. Indeed, land prices rose enormously during the high-growth era. For plots used for housing, prices were seven times higher in 1974 than they had been in 1960.

The rise in asset prices in the 1980s – and in particular from 1986, after which they became progressively more divorced from the trend in nominal GDP – was particularly egregious, however. It pervaded almost every corner of society, in the process supercharging the boom in the real economy and, in particular, in business investment. The word 'bubble' is the only term that can adequately capture the nature and the atmospherics of what occurred during this period.

The Nikkei 225 stock price index was ultimately to peak at 38,915 at the end of 1989, or some 3.1 times its level when the Plaza Accord was signed in September 1985. In just over four years the market capitalization of the Tokyo Stock Exchange (TSE) rose from the equivalent of 60% of GDP to about 1.5 times GDP, and the TSE came to account for more than 41% of the total value of world equities. The Nikkei would subsequently not exceed its December 1989 peak until February 2024.

The cumulative rise in stock prices played out despite the sharp worldwide adjustment in equity markets in October and November 1987. As suggested earlier, Japan was affected much less by this event than most other countries: prices fell by some 23% from their peak as against typical falls of 35%–40% in the United States and Europe. By April 1988 the losses had been recouped, and the equity market was once again surging higher. With the authorities doing their best to sustain confidence and encouraging the major securities houses not to unload their huge stock holdings, Black Monday failed to shatter the conviction that the Japanese economy would continue to grow rapidly and outperform, not least because it put off the date when monetary policy would have to be tightened. The bull market remained intact for another two years or so.

The speculative frenzy of the late 1980s was such that companies increasingly sought to boost their profits by playing the stock market. This so-called *Zaitech*, or 'financial engineering', was often undertaken with borrowed money siphoned into special *Eigyo Tokkin* accounts held with brokerage houses that were deliberately skewed towards investment in speculative, high-risk assets. What is more, in many cases the brokerage houses were confident, or foolish, enough to guarantee the corporate owner of the account against losses. Some 15% of the total earnings reported in 1989 by companies listed on the TSE were accounted for by *Zaitech*. For many of Japan's largest companies, the proportion was 40% or 50%. For some, it was greater still.

The rise in land prices lagged stock prices a little. It spread outwards from Tokyo to other major cities, such as Osaka and Nagoya, and then to much of the rest of the country, albeit much less dramatically. However, there were significant differences in land price increases with respect to location and land use. Commercial land increased in value faster than residential land, and the appreciation of industrial land lagged behind both.

The Urban Land Price Index eventually peaked in September 1990 at a level almost four times higher than it was at the time of the Plaza Accord of September 1985. As the decade progressed, the price of the average dwelling in Tokyo reached 7.5 times the income of the average wage earner. An equivalent plot of land came to cost some 30 times more in Japan's capital city than it did in London, 50 times more than in San Francisco, and 100 times more than in Los Angeles. Two-generation mortgages, and sometimes even three-generation ones, flourished. The size of housing units decreased, such that the average area per person fell to less than half the equivalent in the United States. Japanese housing also had fewer amenities and was increasingly inconveniently located. Many Japanese simply gave up trying to get on the property ladder. At the end of 1989 the government estimated that Japan's property market was worth more than ¥2,000 trillion, or four times the estimated ¥500 trillion value of US property. In early 1990 Japan could in theory have bought all property in the United States by selling metropolitan Tokyo.

Real aggregate asset prices – a weighted average of equity, residential and commercial real estate prices deflated by the GDP deflator – rose more in Japan during the late 1980s than it did in any other OECD economy with the exception of Finland, and it rose between two and three times more than was the case in the other larger advanced nations. The combined capital gains registered on shares and real estate from 1986 to 1989 were staggering, amounting to more than 450% of GDP.

The bubble also caught the attention of gangsters and criminals, who saw the manipulation of land and share prices as a means to make quick and easy money, and it brought out the worst in Japan's often cosily conspiratorial governing classes. For example, in 1986 the recruitment company Recruit Cosmos sought to bribe dozens of leading bureaucrats and politicians by offering them shares in a subsidiary company prior to its flotation. When the scandal subsequently came to a head in late 1988 and early 1989 it not only greatly complicated the passage through the Diet of the government's consumption tax plans but also resulted in the resignations of Prime Minister Takeshita Noboru, Finance Minister Miyazawa Kiichi and the leaders of two opposition parties.

DECONSTRUCTING THE BUBBLE

Japan's extraordinary asset price bubble was promoted by the interaction of a series of powerful, overlapping and mutually reinforcing considerations, many of which are depressingly familiar to economic and market historians. The most important of these factors were extended monetary policy accommodation; the structure of taxation and regulation; the aggressive behaviour of financial institutions; weak disciplinary mechanisms, whether operative on the financial sector, companies or individuals; and overconfidence and euphoria.

Monetary Missteps

There was a strong correlation between credit expansion and asset prices across all the major economies in the 1980s but this was particularly the case in Japan. Low interest rates and easy financial conditions acted to change perceptions of the economic outlook for the better in 1986 and then sustained a high level of optimism about the potential pace of economic growth in subsequent years. At the same time, however, monetary laxity improved bank balance sheets and boosted collateral values through its effects on land and share prices and helped speculators to fund their activities. The transmission mechanism of loose monetary policy in the late 1980s extended far and wide and involved a number of positive feedback loops that augmented its effects, but more than anything else it transformed the activities of Japan's corporate sector.

In hindsight, the BOJ, under the guidance of Governor Sumita Satoshi (a former MOF official), kept policy too loose for too long. For example, Taylor rule analysis* suggests that short-term rates were progressively too low between mid 1987 and mid 1989, with the maximum extent of the policy error amounting to around 2.5 percentage points before correcting.[6] This was in significant part down to the strong influence exerted by the framework of international policy coordination that followed the Plaza Accord, particularly in regard to the dynamics of the foreign exchange market. In responding to this agreement, it is noticeable that the BOJ, no doubt encouraged by the MOF, proved much more compliant and expansive than did the more independently minded Deutsche Bundesbank, the central bank of the other major current account surplus nation of the time.[7]

Of the five ODR reductions after January 1986, only the first was purely at the instigation of the Japanese central bank. The other four were profoundly shaped by broader considerations. The second and third were policy adjustments made simultaneously with the Federal Reserve, and the fourth and fifth came in the context of joint governmental statements on the international environment released with the United States and then with the G7.

Behind the scenes, however, the BOJ was increasingly concerned about becoming constrained in its actions, and it worried that the thrust of policy – and in particular its effects on domestic monetary growth and asset

---

* Under the Taylor rule, the appropriate policy interest rate is deemed to be a function of the estimated real equilibrium rate, the deviation of inflation from its targeted level, and the output gap.

prices – would ultimately prove destabilizing. From as early as the summer of 1986 it was fretting about a build-up of future inflationary potential. By the time the final cut in the ODR to 2.5% was implemented in February 1987 as part of coordinated efforts to put an end to the dollar's post-Plaza plunge (the so-called Louvre Accord), the Bank was keen to see it quickly reversed.[8] But with the US currency subsequently proving reluctant to recover and the US authorities still pushing Japan to take further action, the BOJ encouraged domestic money market rates to edge lower in May, even if it did leave the ODR unchanged.

Tighter window guidance on bank lending was instituted in Q2 1987. But this departure was swimming against the riptide of historically low interest rates, and in any case by this stage financial liberalization and the expansion of various financial intermediary channels beyond the Bank's influence had undermined the effectiveness of this hitherto tried and trusted policy tool. As noted earlier, corporate financing via the capital markets was skyrocketing. What is more, the banks increasingly booked loans overseas – so-called impact loans – to bypass the mandated limits. The total of the latter grew from around $50 billion in 1986 to $400 billion in 1990.

Short-term rates were finally edged back up a little in August 1987, but the events of Black Monday, which sparked fears of another October 1929, forced the BOJ into a volte-face, as all the major central banks acted to sustain market confidence and prevent the slide in stock prices gathering momentum. The dollar, moreover, was still proving reluctant to bottom out. It continued to fall against the yen into year end and remained fragile in the early months of 1988.

By the middle of 1988, however, as the recessionary fears of late 1987 dissipated, the United States and West Germany had begun to push their own official interest rates upwards and the BOJ was determined to follow suit. The economy was growing well beyond its potential rate, and there was mounting evidence of financial excess. Short-term market rates were guided consistently higher from the middle of the year. By November 1988 interbank rates had also been more or less completely liberalized, which meant that the overnight (or call money) rate thereafter assumed much greater importance in policy, in a manner akin to the US federal funds rate. Any direct link between lending rates and the ODR had also been effectively severed, but it nevertheless retained a considerable symbolic role, and the Bank was keen to reinforce the message of what it was doing to market rates with a change in what still remained at that stage the most closely watched indicator of its monetary stance. The problem was that industry and much of the domestic commentariat were less than convinced of the wisdom of such action.

One widely held concern was that should the BOJ step up the pace of interest rate normalization, the dollar's fall could resume and international cooperation would be set back, if not collapse altogether – and all on Japan's watch. At the same time, notwithstanding the strength of domestic economic activity, money and credit growth, and asset prices, annual CPI inflation remained close to zero in the middle of 1988 and only rose above 1% towards the end of the year. There was, in addition, the uncertain effect on economic activity of the prospective introduction of the consumption tax in April of 1989 to consider.

In the end the ODR was raised by 0.75 percentage points at the end of May 1989, while the call for lenders to be more disciplined in terms of both the quantity and the quality of their loans was strengthened, with lending for activities related to real estate a particular focus. Bank lending to the real estate industry and to non-bank financial companies that provided an additional conduit of finance to real estate related activities rose from 10% to 26% of total loans outstanding over the course of the 1980s.

There then followed two further ODR hikes of 0.5 percentage points in mid October and on Christmas Day 1989, taking the BOJ's benchmark rate to 4.25%, its highest level since late 1985. While real long-term interest rates remained exceptionally low at a little above 2%, the yield curve inverted in late 1989 and perceptions of the availability of loans began to deteriorate. There was therefore little doubt that the thrust of monetary policy had become more restrictive, and that the structure of interest rates had shifted upwards into a new, and higher, range.

Indeed, with Sumita Satoshi replaced as BOJ governor in November 1989 by Mieno Yasushi, Japan was embracing a very different monetary regime. Mieno was a conservative career central banker. He was held in high regard by his colleagues and had long been groomed for the top job at the Bank, where he was often referred to as 'the prince'. He had spent most of his 30-odd-year career focused on domestic issues. He had limited international experience, spoke little English, and during his time as deputy governor he had been a stern, if less than public, critic of the policies pursued between 1986 and 1989. He was seen internally as someone who could retrieve a degree of de facto independence from an MOF that had long dominated the Japanese bureaucracy and to which the BOJ was still legally beholden. For a time, at least, it would not be an exaggeration to say that Mieno was viewed by many as a Japanese Paul Volcker: a man who would rebuild the central bank's credibility after a period when it had largely ebbed away.

Sadly, it never quite worked out that way. The problem he was confronted with was that the change of stance came too late. Both the domestic economy and asset price inflation had by this stage run out of control, and the likelihood of anything approaching a soft landing was slim in the extreme.

Looking back, the persistently low-interest-rate structure in both nominal and real terms in the late 1980s encouraged the belief that monetary policy would remain loose indefinitely. There was, for example, no major change in implied forward rates out to three years until late 1989, after the first two ODR hikes. This was a primary consideration both in the inflation of the asset bubble and in the economy's unsustainable rate of expansion.

Many have concluded, therefore, that the BOJ should have begun to adjust policy to moderate rate expectations and suppress credit growth as early as the beginning of 1987. This makes sense, but the problem with such arguments is that focusing conventional monetary policy predominantly on asset markets itself ran the risk of unacceptable broader macroeconomic instability.[9] It is a relatively blunt tool, operating with significant, but unreliable lags, and its ultimate effects are uncertain and spread far beyond the financial sector. A small official interest rate premium put in place to encourage financial stability could lead to the worst of both worlds: uncomfortably low inflation and continued asset price excess. But taking aggressive official interest rate action to counteract an asset boom could easily encourage the opposite problem and plunge the real economy into deep recession and encourage outright deflation, especially where private indebtedness was high, as was the case in Japan, particularly for the corporate sector. Total private sector debt increased from 165% of GDP in 1985 to 210% of GDP in 1990.

There were also the politics of the situation to consider. Deliberately instituting a policy that either pricked an asset bubble that was swelling the wealth of a sizeable portion of the electorate (including many politicians) or that risked recession and unemployment was bound to be unpopular. Similarly, if Japan had unilaterally disengaged from the foreign exchange market cooperation of that era, the Reagan administration – and for that matter the EEC – would probably have responded with more punitive trade sanctions. Just as the Bank had feared as early as 1986, Japan's commitment to international policy cooperation became a powerful constraint on its actions and on its ability to manage the domestic economy.

With BOJ official interest rate policy so constrained, others have suggested that the Japanese authorities should have lent more heavily against the financial wind through the greater employment of what is today known as macroprudential policy. In other words, window guidance should have been tightened earlier, and more aggressively, especially where real estate related loans were concerned. At the same time, limits could have been imposed on loan-to-value and loan-to-income ratios, and dynamic or countercyclical capital and liquidity buffers could have been introduced. In the stock market, margin requirements could have been adjusted more forcefully.

Again, this makes sense, but many of these tools were not part of the international policy mainstream at that time. Indeed, the 1980s had seen a distinct trend away from the direct interventions and quantitative controls that were common in earlier decades. It was only towards the end of the decade that the BIS sought to implement minimum common capital adequacy standards, while macroprudential policy was only formalized in the wake of the Global Financial Crisis (GFC) of 2007–2009. Finally, it remains questionable how effective such policy initiatives would have been when confronted by historically low interest rates, financial liberalization and the extraordinarily positive momentum of stock and land prices.

Given the political and practical constraints on monetary policy, it has further been argued that fiscal interventions should have shouldered more of the burden of macro stabilization: budgetary policy should have been more restrictive and provided more of an offset to the laxity of monetary policy. Again, however, it is hard to escape the fact that the politics of additional fiscal restraint would have been complex both at home and abroad. Tax reform, including a reduction in the burden of income tax, was a government priority; fiscal policy had already been tight for some years; and tightening even more aggressively, potentially further boosting an increasingly substantial budget surplus, would have been bound to incur the wrath of the international community.

Overall, the trade-offs and constraints that Japanese policymakers, and in particular those at the BOJ, faced in the late 1980s were unenviable to say the least. Once Japan committed to the exchange rate and external imbalance priorities of the international community, its room for manoeuvre was hugely curtailed. Indeed, it could be argued that its central role in the inflation of the bubble was almost preordained.

Geography, Psychology, Taxation and Regulation

Land is Japan's most scarce resource and has long occupied a central position in the nation's psyche as the most enduring and dependable store of value. In the 1980s most Japanese had only ever known a world in which land prices usually went up and, indeed, where the price of real estate typically increased faster than that of other real assets. A major and extended fall in land prices was to all intents and purposes beyond their ken.

Much of the mountainous archipelago that makes up Japan is unsuited to human habitation or development, and as a result its population (the second largest in the OECD) and industry are clustered into a relatively small number of urban areas, many of which, including Greater Tokyo, are located on the central Kanto Plain of the island of Honshu. The capital – which makes up just 4% of the land mass – had experienced large-scale inward migration during the high-growth era and was home to around a quarter of the country's population in the late 1980s. It accounted for 40% of total sales and

55% of all bank lending, and it was also where many government activities were concentrated.

The structure of regulation and taxation acted to limit the effective supply of land further while also stimulating its demand, not least that of a speculative nature.

Housing and construction were tightly controlled. In urban areas there were limitations on where development could take place, on the number of floors a building could have, and on the proportion of a lot's land that could be utilized. Even then, only around 40% of Tokyo's authorized height to building ratio was used because leasing laws dating back to 1941, originally designed to protect tenants from eviction, discouraged high-rise multifamily rental housing. The average building height in Tokyo was just 2.8 storeys. For a city of its scale, Tokyo had very few skyscrapers, and the same was true of other Japanese cities.

At the same time, land benefited from preferential tax treatment relative to other financial assets.

Three landholding taxes were levied at a municipal level, the most important of which was a fixed assets tax set at 1.4% of the assessed value of land, buildings and depreciable assets. However, because of special provisions for residential land – and as the official assessed values of land failed to keep pace with market values – the effective landholding tax rate was much lower: only a mere 0.2% or 0.3% in the late 1980s.

For its part, inheritance tax was highly progressive, with 13 marginal rates rising from 10% to 70%. However, its provisions favoured land over all other types of wealth. The assessment values used by the National Tax Agency for inheritance tax were typically about 70% of the already understated official valuation of land prices. Hence, in the year 1990, in imposing inheritance tax, the tax authorities worked on the basis of land prices that were only about half the full market value. And this estimate does not take into account the fact that assessment values for small residential plots were further reduced. In contrast, inherited financial assets were taxed at their full market price. This discriminatory treatment in favour of land provided a strong incentive for landowners who intended to make bequests to hang on to their holdings. Indeed, it encouraged landowners to convert financial assets into land, and even for people to borrow money to buy land for inheritance purposes as the full amount of the associated debt was tax deductible.

The system for capital gains tax (CGT) was complex, but CGT on land essentially depended on the length of tenure: the longer the tenure, the lower the liability. Owner occupiers were also exempt from CGT for small gains, and until 1988 CGT could be avoided on an owner-occupied property altogether if it were rolled into another property. As for corporations, with the capital gains from land price inflation only subject to tax when realized, once a company had acquired land, its incentive to use it was limited and its incentive to sell it less still.

The structure of corporate income tax provided a further encouragement for firms to purchase land. The debts incurred in the process, including interest costs, together with the taxes paid on landholding could be entirely deducted from profits.

All this resulted in the accumulation of huge latent capital gains for the corporate sector. Indeed, they were estimated at more than ¥500 trillion, or the equivalent of more than 130% of GDP, at the end of 1988, a year in which almost 80% of unutilized land owned by the corporate sector was not earmarked for any particular use in the near or intermediate future.

The nature of land transactions taxation provided yet another constraint on the liquidity of the property market. Land transaction taxes were levied at the prefectural, municipal and national level, with the total tax rate working out at about 5.5% in effective terms. With as much as 80% of the cost of a new home in many areas taken up by the value of the land, this implied that transactions taxes could account for as much as a quarter of housing construction costs! Landholders therefore had a strong incentive to demolish and rebuild their existing home rather than upscale on new land. The secondary market for homes suffered hugely as a result.

Finally, elements of both landholding and inheritance tax, extending to deferment and the waiving of taxes altogether, favoured farmland over residential land even in urban areas. This encouraged the existence of a large number of small city farms that prevented more rational use of scarce real estate. In 1989 agricultural land occupied 12% of all urban areas, and there were 30,000 hectares of farmland in Tokyo alone.

The nature of land regulation and taxation effectively left the supply of land semi-fixed at an inadequate level, at a time when demand was fuelled by excessively lax monetary conditions and a supercharged economy. In such an environment, rapid real estate price inflation was inevitable.

Land price inflation also cross-fertilized with the stock market. As corporate land holdings were valued at purchase price under Japan's accounting system, the asset base of many firms was chronically understated at a time when the extensive cross-shareholdings within the corporate sector reduced the number of marketable stocks by as much as 60%. The price to earnings (PE) ratio on the Nikkei 225 index, which surged upwards from 1985, remained extremely high throughout the late 1980s, often in excess of 50 and never dipping below 40. For comparison, the PE ratio on the S&P 500 in the United States peaked at around 20 in mid 1987 and averaged around 12 during the decade as a whole.

Aggressive Financial Institutions

Financial institutions in Japan became increasingly forceful in their business strategies from 1983, but especially from 1987. This widespread inclination reflected in large part the financial deregulation of the time. Deregulation shrank the banks' customer base and threatened to exert a lasting squeeze on their profitability, incentivizing them to develop new products and take on additional risk, and pushing them to the limits of legality and beyond. The lifting of restrictions on non-financial firms' fundraising in the securities markets, the fact that banks themselves were only permitted phased entry into the securities business, and the progressive liberalization of interest rates on deposits all conspired to encourage the banks to lend more aggressively, and, as suggested earlier, particularly to small firms backed by property holdings and to those in real-estate-related sectors or in search of a mortgage.

The major banks increased their share of the mortgage market from 13% to 22% in the second half of the 1980s, and the share would have been much larger were it not for the government-sponsored Housing Loan Corporation (HLC), which lent money to home borrowers at subsidized (significantly below market) rates.

The capital base of the banks also increased considerably during this period through several channels. First, the strong cyclical expansion swelled banks' gross profits, boosting retained earnings and Tier I capital. Second, Tier II capital was greatly enhanced by unrealized gains on securities holdings. Controversially – and in contrast to the conventions in the United States and the United Kingdom, for example – under the BIS's capital adequacy regulations first introduced in the 1988/1989 financial year, Japanese banks were allowed to count 45% of their unrealized capital gains on securities holdings towards their capital. This had to be equal in total to at least 8% of their assets once those assets had been weighted according to their riskiness.[10] In the financial year ending in March 1989, an average of more than 40% of the reported profits of Japan's major banks can be traced to this source. And third, banks increased their equity financing in the context of favourable market conditions. Between 1987 and 1989 the main banks issued some ¥6 trillion of cheap equity and equity-related finance.

Many other loans backed by property were provided by Japan's non-bank financial institutions – including leasing companies, consumer finance companies and mortgage companies – and they too were almost entirely dependent on bank credit for their funding. These often-private entities tended to focus their activities on the more speculative property players, prepared to pay high rates of interest for financing. The banks' advances to the non-banks were frequently used to channel funds to risky or shady borrowers they preferred not to be seen to lend to directly and, as time went by, to circumvent the official restrictions on loans to property companies.

The ebullience of asset prices was central to the banks' immediate profitability and to their meeting their capital requirements – and, thereby, to their ability to lend. The dynamics of Japanese bank capital at this time had the perverse effect of incentivizing them to procyclically increase the risk of their loan portfolio. Their underlying profitability and capital adequacy was a fraction of what they reported during the bubble years. Any precipitous decline in asset prices would decimate the balance sheets of much of the financial sector.

Corporate Indiscipline

Historically, the main bank system that underpinned much of the *Keiretsu* during the high-growth period had acted as the primary mechanism to impose financial and broader discipline on firms' corporate governance. However, as the grip of the system inevitably began to loosen in the face of structural change, and deregulation encouraged firms to begin to raise increasing amounts on the capital markets, this mechanism was weakened. Neither shareholders nor creditors, meanwhile, provided an adequate substitute. Considerations such as large enduring cross-shareholdings, the application of the cost method of accounting, cosy relationships between corporate leaders and bureaucrats, and poor levels of transparency and disclosure did not help.

With financial innovation burgeoning and risk-taking activities moving beyond traditional channels, Japan needed an alternative – stronger – framework of corporate oversight and hazard control, especially across the financial sector. Administrative guidance and the paucity of written rules associated with it were found wanting. But, unduly influenced by the fact that there had not been a major threat to the soundness of the financial system in the post-war era, the authorities failed to fill the gap. The MOF and the BOJ were found wanting. They lacked specialized resources, their efforts in this regard hindered by the prevalence of frequent job rotation. Supervisors and regulators simply could not accumulate the necessary experience required.

Not for the first time in history, a period of asset price excess was exacerbated by inadequate governmental oversight.

Overconfidence and Euphoria

As suggested earlier, even before the inflation of the late 1980s bubble, Japan's remarkable economic renaissance and extended period of outperformance had kindled a sense of self-confidence that encouraged the belief that the country's post-war miracle could be extended indefinitely. The *Endaka Fukyo* slowdown of the middle of the decade might have sparked doubts about this in some quarters, but these were soon dispelled once the domestically led recovery got underway and Japan's economic superiority over the other advanced economies seemed to have been re-established. The common mantra – one that was also peddled by many outside commentators – was that 'Japan was different'. It made its own rules.

The stock market's resilience to Black Wednesday in October 1987 and the rapid accumulation of external assets in the context of the economy's cumulative current account surpluses were key elements of this hubris. Together they fed the belief that high investment returns could be sustained with limited risk.

At the height of the domestic property boom, Japanese investors stampeded into the US property market, purchasing iconic assets such as the Exxon Building and the Rockefeller Center in New York and a selection of high-end golf courses and hotels. Total Japanese investment in US property rose from $1.9 billion in 1985 to $16.5 billion in 1988, and it was still running at $14.8 billion in 1989. The art world was also dominated by cash-rich Japanese bidding for masterpieces of all shapes and sizes.

The overseas activities of Japanese financial institutions, meanwhile, expanded out of all recognition. By the end of 1989 more than 40% of total international bank lending was conducted by Japanese entities. Large-scale takeovers of foreign banks and securities companies by Japanese firms were common. At the same time, notwithstanding the extortionate cost, those foreign financial institutions that remained independent from Japanese ownership were desperate to demonstrate their global reach by expanding their operations in Tokyo, the world's most rapidly growing and seemingly successful financial hub.

JAPAN'S MINSKY MOMENT

Driven by a powerful cocktail of well-meaning but ultimately distortionary international cooperation, related macroeconomic policy missteps, regulatory shortcomings, biases in the tax system, institutional idiosyncrasies and the enduring weaknesses of human nature, Japan's bubble economy of the late 1980s was an extraordinary – at times almost surreal – affair during which much of a nation hitherto widely respected for its stoicism, self-discipline and business acumen lost touch with reality. Notwithstanding the impressive record of orthodox economic performance that went with it, the bubble represented one of the more extreme episodes of financial and asset price excess of the twentieth century.

Japan gorged on credit, and land and share prices were bid up to levels appreciably divorced from underlying fundamental considerations. Many of the basic laws of economics were downplayed, if not ignored altogether. The banks collectively took leave of their senses. A corporate sector that had been the foundation on which the nation's post-war economic renaissance was built was drawn into a vortex of overconfidence, reckless expansion and speculation. But the intoxication spread much further than this. Towards the end of the 1980s everyone from householders to bureaucrats and from politicians to gangsters was consumed by the tumult. Almost all rationality was lost.

In hindsight, the bubble period provides a stunning endorsement of the behavioural analytical framework of asset markets developed by the American economist Hyman Minsky.[11]

Minsky believed that the financial system and the way it behaved were central to the manner in which economies evolved across the business cycle. The financial system should not be dismissed, as many economists were wont to do, as merely a conduit that dutifully channelled funds from savers to borrowers. Its comportment could and would change, and as it did so it would exert a powerful impact on the rest of the economy.

Minsky's central idea was that relative stability will tend to encourage complacency, and that complacency can encourage a system to become unstable. The assumption that the good times will continue to roll will encourage the taking of ever greater risks in the pursuit of profit. The seeds of instability and ultimate adjustment are inevitably sown during periods of success and abundance.

Building on this, Minsky further suggested that the provision of credit goes through three stages. In the initial stage, normally following a previous period of instability or crisis, lenders and borrowers are cautious. Modest sums are advanced and borrowers are keen to ensure that they can comfortably repay both the principal and the interest on a loan. In the second stage, as the business cycle picks up steam and confidence increases, lenders make loans for which the borrower can only afford to pay the interest. The assumption is that the asset that provides the collateral for the loan will continue to rise in value and allow the principal of the loan to be paid off later. In the final stage, when the previous downturn or crisis is a distant memory, loans will be made to entities that can pay neither the interest nor the principal. The expectation of continued increases in the value of collateral is all that underpins the loan.

Finally, Minsky's analytical framework suggested that at some stage there will be an event or series of events that causes asset prices to correct and triggers a collapse in the whole credit-based house of cards. At this point there is a recognition that there is debt in the system that can never be paid back and a fire sale of assets follows, with catastrophic consequences. Economists sympathetic to this schema subsequently came to call it a 'Minsky moment'.

Japan was on the cusp of a Minsky moment at the end of 1989. The BOJ had reached the conclusion that the situation was unsustainable. The dizzying cycle of spending and speculation was increasingly disorderly, even chaotic. The abandonment of moral scruples and the levels of financial malfeasance and abuse were unacceptable. The huge wealth disparities the bubble had encouraged between 'asset haves' and 'asset have nots' threatened the very fabric of Japanese society. Asset price inflation was a harbinger of goods and service price inflation. The longer that adjustment was delayed, the greater the ultimate adjustment would be.

UP ON THE ESCALATOR, DOWN IN THE ELEVATOR

The hope, if not the expectation, was that Japan's policymakers – who had done such an impressive job and dealt with so many other challenges over the previous 40 years – could engineer a soft landing. Few, however, realized quite how difficult a task this would be or how traumatic the consequences the pricking of the bubble, and its malign interaction with numerous underlying structural fault lines, would prove. Japan's circumstances were to change out of all recognition over the following years. Its economic miracle was over. The country was about to enter its 'lost decade'. The notion of its economic supremacy would be shattered beyond repair.

CHAPTER 4

The Bubble Bursts

'After victory, tighten your helmet strap' — Japanese proverb

REALITY BITES

When, after a five-day streak of new all-time highs, the Nikkei 225 closed at 38,916 at the end of the final trading session of 1989, hopes for another stellar year for Japan, its economy and its markets were elevated. Many domestic stockbrokers confidently predicted that the country's most widely quoted and internationally familiar index of stock prices could reach the 50,000 level before long, and that the by-now-well-established combination of robust economic growth, relative price stability and international outperformance would be sustained. Neither did many foreign commentators demur. There were, of course, some Cassandras, including the perennial sceptics who had long questioned the foundations of Japan's economic miracle, but they were very much a minority. Most were happy to believe that Japan's predominance – in so many senses of the word – would continue. This was despite the by-now-obvious shift in priorities at the BOJ, and among the authorities more generally, and the fact that the global business cycle had begun to lose momentum, en route to recession in 1991.

The new year, however, saw Japanese long-term interest rates climbing steadily – first to 6% and then towards 7% – as the yen continued the slide that had begun in late 1988. Meanwhile, rather than continuing its remorseless ascent, as widely predicted, the equity market trod water in a way it had rarely done since the autumn of 1987. Initially, most observers viewed this as merely a temporary pause in the longstanding rally, but by the second half of February the Nikkei was under much more severe duress. Although the ever-business-friendly LDP had won a slightly larger than expected majority in Lower House elections held that month, Japanese stocks became subject to wave after wave of often frantic selling.[1] Sentiment had turned dramatically for the worse. The back of the bull market was broken.

While politicians began to fret – and complain about the short-sighted habits of speculators and the destructive activities of foreign investors – true to its new mission, the BOJ and its austere governor kept up the pressure to drive the excesses out of asset markets; bring the rampaging economy to heel; and forestall, or at least moderate, a broader rise in inflation. The ODR was raised by a further percentage point to 5.25% in early March. By early April the Nikkei was trading back under 28,000: a fall of some 28% from its peak.

To universal sighs of relief, there followed a brief rally, but Governor Mieno and his colleagues had not finished applying their sobering disinflationary medicine. After all, the yen had continued to fall against the dollar, 10-year bond yields showed little sign of reversing course, the annual rates of broad money and bank lending growth were still running well into double digits, companies were flush with cash and sanguine about financial conditions, and there was scant evidence that land prices had begun to adjust downwards.

Furthermore, despite the more restrictive monetary policy stance, the real economy retained considerable positive momentum. Business confidence was still elevated. Profits growth, although off its highs, remained robust. After a brief inventory adjustment around the turn of the year, industrial production and manufacturing capacity utilization surged to new highs. The broad-based boom in business investment continued, its share in overall GDP exceeding 20% in nominal terms. Private consumption was underpinned by ever-fuller employment and accelerating wage growth, which approached a cyclical high of 5% a year. Consequently, driven by domestic demand Japan was set to achieve an annual growth rate in excess of 5% in 1990, resulting in a positive output gap of some four percentage points of GDP; a further contraction in the external surplus to just 1.5% of GDP; and, as tax revenues continued to exceed expectations, a consolidated budget surplus of some 2% of GDP.

The situation confronting a central bank still troubled by asset market immoderation, robust growth and the potential for a wage–price spiral was further complicated in early August 1990 when Iraqi armed forces invaded Kuwait, pushing up oil prices and elevating Japan's headline annual CPI inflation rate to more than 3.5% – a clip not seen for a decade.[2] As the international community considered its response, yields on Japanese government bonds (JGBs) surged towards 8% and the Nikkei swooned once again. Despite objections from the MOF, which favoured a cautious line because of the uncertainties thrown up by the geopolitical situation, the BOJ remained uncompromising in its approach, hiking the ODR again to 6% at the end of August. Nor were Mieno and his colleagues finished. The Bank publicly questioned the importance of the stock market to the real economy and then pushed the overnight call money rate, by then its primary policy tool, up to more than 8% in the period to early 1991. At the same time, increasingly severe restraints were imposed on bank lending for anything related to the real estate market.

In the end, the Nikkei slumped to just above 20,000 in early October before staging another limited rebound. At its nadir, it had lost almost half its value in nine months, and three years of bull market had been wiped out – the bloated equity portfolios held by banks and businesses slashed in value. This in itself was enough to leave the country in a state of shock. But even more pertinently, by the end of the year land prices – especially those in the major urban centres – finally started to retreat from their stratospheric highs, beginning a persistent downtrend that, although few would have been able to believe it at the time, would ultimately extend into the next century. Meanwhile, corporate bankruptcies multiplied, and in early 1991 broad monetary growth and bank lending growth began to collapse, losing altitude in a manner not seen since the war.

The bubble had well and truly burst, the long expansion that began in 1986 was in its death throes, and a downturn of uncertain proportions beckoned.

THE CYCLE TURNS

The first half of 1991 saw inventories once again mounting, and much more dramatically relative to industrial shipments than had been the case in late 1989 and early 1990. Business sector confidence and spending softened significantly. The capital–output ratio had by this stage moved far above its long-term trend, with the efficiency of investment spending heading remorselessly in the opposite direction. Too many projects had become high risk and low return. Residential investment also slumped in the face of the significantly higher structure of interest rates and softening land prices.

Personal consumption, however, as was customary, proved to be the most stable component of domestic demand across the business cycle. It was sustained at this juncture by the limited direct exposure of households to the stock market and bank loans, the low level of homeownership, and persistently limited unemployment; personal consumption even began to reverse the decline in its share of GDP that had been in evidence since 1983.[3]

A rebound in exports – encouraged by the delayed effects of the yen's decline in 1989 and the first half of 1990 – together with solid public investment outlays also moderated the initial slowdown and sustained the upswing for a while longer, albeit at a reduced pace. In the end, not least because of significant statistical carryover from 1990, real GDP growth averaged a more than respectable 3% for 1991 as a whole, some way above the OECD average.

Bond yields were by now well past their peak, however, and firmly established on a firm downtrend, and the extended expansion was clearly on borrowed time. Nevertheless, given residual concerns about the high outstanding balance of liquidity in the economy (and especially that held by large corporates); the enduring tightness of the labour market; and the fact that, boosted by energy prices, headline CPI inflation was still above 3%, the BOJ continued to take a hard monetary policy line.

It was not until mid 1991 that there was a tentative reversal of course. The call money rate was initially edged down from its 8.0%-plus highs in May. Then, together with the ODR, it was reduced by a further half percentage point in July. Window guidance on bank lending was also abolished at this juncture, the feeling being that in the context of financial liberalization, interest rate changes had become a more effective tool with which to regulate commercial bank advances.

While the BOJ bided its time, however, corporate insolvencies further escalated, especially in the non-manufacturing sector and particularly among real estate firms; evidence of bank distress accumulated; and there were early signs of a slump in domestic wholesale prices that was to endure for the rest of the decade and beyond. The BOJ was one of a lengthy line of central banks that kept fighting the last battle well after it had been won – something that was to haunt them for many years to come. It was only in the final quarter of 1991, when the Bank engineered a more rapid reduction in the call money rate and twice cut the ODR by half a percentage point, that it began to grasp the degree to which circumstances had changed and the extent of the trouble the real economy and the financial sector were in. It should be stressed, though, that the notion that the economy's malaise was bad enough that the call rate would ultimately be cut to zero and then remain there, or lower, for the better part of a generation was little short of inconceivable.

INTO RECESSION

The downturn intensified in 1992. Broad monetary growth continued to slump, turning negative in annual terms in the second half of the year. In the real economy, industrial production, business confidence and business investment were the most obvious casualties, with the latter falling more than 7% in real terms and its share in GDP beginning to return to more normal levels (at least for Japan). Employment growth slowed, especially for those on part-time contracts, and wage inflation moderated as bonuses and overtime hours were cut to reduce labour costs. The unemployment rate started to edge up, towards 3% of the workforce, and the positive output gap declined. To compensate for the weakness of domestic demand, Japanese companies also increasingly looked overseas for sales. This export drive provided some support to GDP growth, which averaged around 1% for the year, but at the price of further international resentment.

Property prices, meanwhile, continued to retreat from their previously sky-high levels, but the most immediate and conspicuous demonstration of Japan's developing crisis in the eyes of the international media and investment community remained the stock market's dramatic reversal of fortune. In March the Nikkei dropped through the 20,000 level for the first time since February 1987, pushing the market's PE ratio down to around 40, which when adjusted for cross-shareholdings left it below the US level of 25. This was not the end of the bear market, however. By August the Nikkei had dropped to a six-and-a-half-year low of 14,309, which represented the better part of a two-thirds decline from its highs. The equity bull market of the late 1980s had completely evaporated. The combined losses caused by falling stock and land prices at this juncture amounted to a remarkable ¥700 trillion.

All this left the banking sector facing an acute profits squeeze. The major banks' unrealized capital gains on their stock portfolios had similarly fallen by some two-thirds from their peak by March 1992, and they continued to fall thereafter. Since they had little ability to issue new equity in such unforgiving market conditions, they could only meet their capital requirements at the end of the 1991/1992 financial year by issuing subordinated debt to insurance companies and slashing their overseas lending.

At the same time, the fall in land prices, which amounted to some 25% by this stage, meant that many of the loans made directly to the real estate industry or indirectly to it via non-bank financial companies (which had, in the late 1980s, accounted for more than a quarter of all loans outstanding) soured. The MOF estimated the total of non-performing loans (NPLs) at 2% of overall advances at this stage, but this was only a snapshot of an ever-rising total – and in any case it was a gross understatement of the real situation. The figure was flattered by the way the statistics were calculated. For example, they included loans where no interest had been paid for six months but excluded loans on which interest payments had been reduced; they also omitted the loans of bank affiliates and those made to non-banks that had been relieved of interest payments during government-encouraged rescue operations. The official NPL numbers also benefited from the opacity of Japanese accounting – which the MOF was content to tolerate, or even encourage – and from the subterfuge and mendacity of many banking executives, who were reluctant to admit publicly to the true condition of their balance sheets. Such issues were to continue to blight the process of dealing with the aftereffects of the bubble economy into the next century.

The BOJ cut rates again in April and July 1992, such that the cumulative decline of 3.75 percentage points over the 13 months or so from the previous peak was the most rapid since the war. By this stage, however, official interest rate reductions were exerting only a limited effect beyond providing some stimulus to the housing market. With corporate debt at record levels and industrial capacity increasingly excessive, few businesses wanted to borrow more unless they were in distress and even fewer banks wanted to lend to anyone but a shrinking population of the most creditworthy borrowers – a group that largely excluded the small and medium-sized enterprises (SMEs) that had traditionally been at the leading edge of Japanese cyclical upswings. The highly leveraged corporate sector's financial balance had begun a decade-long swing back from the unprecedented deficit equivalent to some 9% of GDP recorded in 1990 to an unprecedented surplus of a similar magnitude. The process of credit intermediation – the lifeblood of a capitalist economy – had dropped into exceptionally low gear. Japan was falling into a Keynesian 'liquidity trap', whereby the strength of balance sheet adjustments in the private sector were such that orthodox monetary policy was largely neutered.

Nevertheless, the failure of the BOJ to ease policy further in the latter part of 1992 is difficult to fathom. While additional rate cuts might not have provided much by way of stimulus, they were surely a better option than doing nothing, not least because, with disinflationary pressures building (CPI inflation was falling towards 1%), they would have encouraged real interest rates to fall faster at a time when the equilibrium real rate – that consistent with output at potential and stable inflation – was negative, and probably increasingly so.[4]

KEYNESIAN KEIZAI[5]

If the BOJ was still intent on playing monetary policy hardball, the government and the MOF were less sanguine about the situation. Although the fall in asset prices and the profit squeeze had hit government revenues hard – there was a large drop in the elasticity of tax revenues with respect to GDP in the early 1990s[6] – March saw the public investment budget for the 1992/1993 financial year front-loaded to give the economy a temporary fillip. Then, at the end of August, a ¥10.7 trillion (1.8% of GDP) fiscal package was announced. Together with financial assistance for SMEs and the government-sponsored HLC, some ¥8.6 trillion of this was earmarked for public works.

After more than a decade of restraint, and with Japan having some of the weakest automatic stabilizers among the major economies – that is to say, the level and cyclical variation of unemployment and other social welfare benefits was limited – fiscal policy had entered an extended phase of intermittent discretionary expansion.[7] Especially given the adjustments going on across corporate sector balance sheets, this was the logical step to take, although the sporadic manner in which it was subsequently enacted left much to be desired.

Around this time, the MOF, shocked by the continued weakness of asset prices, also introduced measures designed to dissuade the banks from unwinding their cross holdings of shares and to temper the immediate burden of ever-increasing bad loans. With tacit official approval, many banks continued to extend credit to essentially insolvent borrowers. Finally, not only were the government's further privatization plans for NTT, JR and JT postponed, but a scheme was announced to help with the disposal of bad loans.

Banks were encouraged to sell the collateral (repossessed properties) on failed advances to the Cooperative Credit Purchasing Company (CCPC), a new agency established by the banks themselves, which would then try to liquidate these assets. This announcement stabilized stock prices temporarily, but the problem was that the scheme only accelerated property sales and thereby created even more sour loans, not least because the collapse in real estate values was accelerating and was now spreading beyond the major urban areas. There remained at this stage no direct provision of public funds to address asset price deflation or the knock-on effect on the financial sector.

By early 1993 the ODR was back at the 2.5% level that prevailed from late 1986 until mid 1989 – a level that was widely believed to have been a primary catalyst for the final, and dramatic, phase of the bubble economy. But the country was now fully in recession rather than suffering a temporary slowdown driven by the exchange rate, which had been the case six years earlier. For 1993 as a whole, the annual real growth rate amounted to a mere 0.3%: the worst outturn since the outright decline in 1974 in the wake of the first oil shock. The adjustments in corporate profitability, business spending, hiring, working hours and pay accelerated. Indeed, plant and equipment investment fell at a double-digit real rate over the course of the year, and its share in nominal GDP receded to around 15% – some five percentage points off its peak. The steepest declines in investment were observable in real estate, finance, manufacturing and construction: the sectors that had expanded the most in tandem with the escalation in asset prices in the late 1980s. The output gap turned negative for the first time since 1987. Import volumes continued to fall, and despite the extended strength of the yen, VERs that impacted almost 8% of merchandise exports, and a renewed loss of export market share, the current account surplus was once again stable, at around 3% of GDP, or twice its 1990 low. Only public investment and housing investment, both directly supported by government policy, kept the economy's head above water.

Notwithstanding the temporary pick-up in residential construction spending, there was no sign of an end to the slide in land prices, the escalation in bankruptcies or the accumulation of bad debts on the balance sheets of the banks. The credit crunch therefore continued even though – in sharp contrast to the three previous years – the MOF began actively to encourage the banks to increase lending. What is more, trade tensions with the United States had escalated once again, the net result of which was a renewed surge in the value of the Japanese currency. By mid August 1993 it had risen against the dollar by more than a third from its April 1990 low and was approaching the psychologically important 100 level.

Monetary conditions remained onerous. The historically low level of nominal short rates was not low enough, and nor were matters being helped by the fact that however much the MOF wanted the banks to lend more, it was simultaneously encouraging them to boost their operating margins to help address the impact of the burgeoning bad-loan problem on their profits. They were therefore failing to pass lower policy rates on in their entirety. The net result of these contradictory urgings was that total loan growth almost ground to a halt, while subordinated debt sales continued to be essential to the banks achieving their capital adequacy targets.

Unsurprisingly, therefore, the BOJ guided short-term interest rates down further in the second half of the year, and in September 1993 the ODR was reduced to a new low of 1.75% – far below the policy rate in any other OECD economy.

POLITICAL UPHEAVAL

The economy's extraordinary change in fortune since the late 1980s boom was mirrored by a collapse in the popularity of the hitherto unassailable LDP. The two phenomena were undoubtedly related to some degree, but the first half of the 1990s also saw a surge of disquiet about the longstanding traits of influence peddling, corruption and sleaze in Japanese politics, and the related focus on individuals rather than issues. Calls for political reform became more voluble, and the LDP suffered a series of high-profile defections, ostensibly related to these demands but also down to certain individuals seeking to develop their personal powerbases. The party then lost its majority at a general election in July 1993 and subsequently failed to form a government for the first time since 1955.

What followed was an administration led initially by Hosokawa Morihiro of the recently formed Japan New Party. Hosokawa was himself a former LDP Diet member, a grandson of a wartime prime minister and a distant cousin of the emperor. He oversaw a hastily cobbled together eight-party rainbow coalition of left, right and centre, made up of people who had scant experience of running much at all, let alone the world's second largest economy. It lasted only eleven months, and Hosokawa himself survived only nine of those before being superseded, briefly, by Hata Tsutomu of the *Shinseitō* party.

While it lasted, the coalition ostensibly championed two things: structural and political reform.

Where the first of these priorities was concerned, it is hard to conclude that it accelerated the process of supply-side enhancement to any significant extent. Indeed, the government's major economic policy achievement was less in the area of structural policy and more the further application of fiscal stimulus, albeit extended to tax relief.

As for the second priority, after an extended legislative tussle, the coalition did make some progress in advancing electoral reform before it inevitably fell apart amid widening ideological disagreements and, ironically, following a campaign finance scandal. As a result of its efforts, the old system of 130 multimember seats delivering 511 representatives to the Lower House was replaced at the 1996 general election by a new system of 300 single-member seats elected through plurality and 200 proportional representation seats elected from regional blocks.[8]

However, the reform failed to result in the emergence of a stable two-party system in which there were regular alternations in power. Nor for that matter did it end Japan's money politics. The focus on individuals and the prevalence of pork barrel spending might have been tempered a little, but they endured, not least because there was still a significant power imbalance between the rural and urban electorates.

The LDP quickly resumed its dominance of Japanese politics. The Hosokawa/Hata government was followed in June 1994 by another coalition that, despite being nominally fronted by Morayama Tomiichi of the JSP, was in reality controlled by the LDP. This administration lasted until the autumn of 1996, by which time the LDP's president, Hashimoto Ryūtarō, had taken over as prime minister. Hashimoto failed to win an overall majority at the subsequent Lower House elections but won enough support at the expense of the Socialist Party to consolidate the LDP's position further.

MORE FISCAL LARGESSE

In the meantime, land prices fell faster in 1993, despite continued easing of official interest rates, than they had in 1992; more than 14,500 companies went to the wall. This brought the total number of bankruptcies since the bubble burst to almost 46,000 and left the sum of bad debts at ¥24.6 trillion. Against this background, there were two further fiscal packages in 1993. The first, in April, sought to extend the stimulus provided by the previous two and amounted to some ¥13.3 trillion in total (2.8% of GDP), including another ¥10.6 trillion of public works spending, together with further help for SMEs and additional funding for the HLC. It also embodied the front-loading of 75% of the public works earmarked for the budget of the 1993/1994 financial year into the first half of the fiscal year. The second package, in September, was broader in scope, extending beyond public works outlays and funding for SMEs and the HLC to the promotion of deregulation; it totalled around ¥6.2 trillion, or 1.3% of GDP.

February 1994 saw yet another round of fiscal expansion. The package added up to just over ¥15.0 trillion, or 3.1% of GDP, this time and was the largest yet. It centred on a substantial temporary personal income tax cut (amounting to ¥5.5 trillion or 1.25% of GDP) as much as on public works spending.

It brought the total headline amount of fiscal support provided over a period of just under two years to more than ¥45 trillion, or almost 10% of GDP. Even allowing for the fact that the impact on the economy of additional spending on goods and services in national accounts terms fell far short of this figure, the cumulative positive impulse of fiscal policy between 1991 and 1995 was some five percentage points of GDP.

As noted in the previous chapter, with the population set to decline and age rapidly it had been clear for some time both that the Japanese tax system was ripe for further reform and that the adjustments in structure made in the mid-to-late 1980s had to be taken further. In the first place, the government needed to rely less on direct taxes, which accounted for some two-thirds of all revenues – a figure almost twice the OECD average. At the same time, the income tax system was steeply progressive in the middle-income ranges, where neither tax brackets nor allowances had been adjusted since the previous decade. Finally, taxation of the self-employed was inefficient, and the taxation of interest and retirement income was unduly light. The country, in short, required a more extensive income tax base, less progression and higher indirect taxation.

As a result, a bill proposing a set of new tax reforms was presented to the Diet in October 1994. It did not directly lower income tax rates but it did substantially raise the thresholds at which those tax rates applied and increased work-related tax allowances by some 8.5%. Furthermore, even if this permanent tax relief was to be offset by an increase in the consumption tax to 5% in the 1997/1998 financial year, the temporary 1994 income tax cuts were extended into the 1995/1996 financial year, albeit at a reduced level of ¥2.0 trillion.

By this stage the consolidated budget deficit was approaching 5% of GDP and the gross debt burden some 87% of GDP, both well above the OECD averages. Moreover, despite the dramatic falls in interest rates across the maturity spectrum, net debt interest payments were edging higher.

DEFLATION BECKONS

Helped by the strength of global activity, sustained fiscal largesse stirred the economy back into some sort of life in 1994, with private consumption and residential investment the primary sources of expansion. But the reprieve proved short-lived, not least because the BOJ continued to drag its feet on monetary policy, and the yen appreciated further, breaking through to a new high against the dollar of ¥96.00 in November. Overall growth for the year amounted to just 1%: a little better than it had been in 1993 but hardly indicative of a meaningful recovery. Business investment continued to slide, declining by another 6% in real terms. This period was also noteworthy because it witnessed the first signs of outright goods and service price deflation: the annual rate of change in the GDP deflator turned negative in the second half of the year. The CPI would soon follow.[9]

The end of 1994 saw Mieno Yasushi stand down as BOJ governor, having completed his five-year term of office. Maintaining the tradition that the head of the central bank should be drawn alternatively from the Bank and the MOF, he was replaced by the lifetime MOF official Matsushita Yasuo, who was considered to be more moderate and pragmatic. Mieno had certainly done what was initially asked, and indeed expected, of him: he brought the curtain down on the bubble economy. The problem was that he did not know when to stop applying his deflationary medicine: official interest rates remained on hold throughout his last year in the job despite a persistently strong yen and evidence that Japanese inflation was dropping to dangerously low levels. The Nikkei ended the year back below 20,000. Mieno had begun as a hero, especially at the BOJ itself, but he ended up as something of a villain. Certainly, few tears were shed on his departure, either at the MOF or in the prime minister's residence. In the eyes of some, he proved to be less a Japanese Paul Volcker and more a 1990s version of Clément Moret, the Bank of France governor who in the first half of the 1930s almost deflated the French economy to death.

OTHER TREMORS

On 17 January 1995 the Great Hanshin Earthquake, which registered 7.2 on the Richter scale, devastated the city of Kōbe, its port (the sixth largest container port in the world) and its environs. Almost 6,500 people died, one in five buildings in the area were destroyed, and much of the local infrastructure was severely damaged. Just as in the 1920s, a period of financial crisis and profound economic adjustment was compounded by a major natural disaster, although the short-term hit to GDP this time was, at 2%, a fraction of what it had been in 1923.[10]

Then, just over two months later, on 20 March 1995 five members of the Aum Shinrikyo cult launched a chemical attack on the Tokyo subway, one of the world's busiest commuter transport systems, at the peak of the morning rush hour. Thirteen people were killed and many more injured, some seriously.

Furthermore, in the background trade tensions with the United States flared up once again, pushing the yen to more new highs. The Japanese currency peaked at just below 80 against the US dollar in May: a level that represented an 18% appreciation relative to the 1994 average.

Unsurprisingly, these three events exerted a significant negative impact on business and consumer confidence, and for a period the shallow cyclical upswing was stopped in its tracks. In these circumstances the process of deflation also received new impetus. Wholesale and consumer prices and the GDP deflator all fell in 1995 in year-over-year terms.

It might have been expected that such was the extent, the varied nature and the close proximity of the shocks that they would afford the Japanese authorities an opportunity to launch a more forceful and comprehensive attack on the economy's problems by instituting a sustained and coordinated burst of fiscal and monetary reflation. But what followed was something altogether more modest. The government merely introduced a limited supplementary budget designed to finance reconstruction and relief work in the areas affected by the disaster, and after more than a year of stasis the BOJ finally saw fit to cut the ODR by a further 75 basis points, to 1.0%. Similar timidity characterized the approach both to the core underlying problem of a collapsing real estate market and to the process of structural reform.

FINANCIAL MICAWBERISM

At the end of March 1995 the MOF estimated that the total burden of NPLs across the financial system amounted to ¥40 trillion: some 5.8% of all outstanding advances, or the equivalent of around 8.5% of GDP. The dead weight of these compromised assets varied enormously across the sector, however. The main banks, which accounted for some 40% of total loans made by private sector entities, had made considerable progress in addressing the NPL issue through write-offs, restructurings, sales to the CCPC and increased loan loss provisions. In March 1995 they stated that their share of the NPL total was ¥12.5 trillion, which was a significant fall from the peak of ¥13.8 trillion reported in September 1993; the decline had, though, come at the cost of their declaring losses in the course of the 1994/1995 financial year, and those losses had only been contained by their revaluing the unrealized capital gains on their securities portfolios by more than 50%. As a result, their risk-adjusted capital-adequacy ratio fell by almost a percentage point to 8.9%. Their core capital – that excluding unrealized capital gains and loans – was much lower. Indeed, it was one of the lowest among the major economies' banking sectors.

Notwithstanding the frantic balance sheet gymnastics of the major banks, the financial system's problems – and thereby its underlying fragilities – did not end there. They were spread much wider.

For example, the life insurance industry had begun to come under growing duress. Like the banks, insurance companies saw a growing proportion of their loans, which accounted for more than a third of their assets, sour. More pertinently still, in an environment of historically low interest rates and weak stock prices, the returns on their assets began consistently to fall below the guarantees offered to their clients.

The greatest difficulties, however, were to be found among the second-tier regional banks, the credit and agricultural cooperatives and various non-bank financial institutions, where exposure to bankrupt and near-bankrupt entities was acute. This was particularly the case where the *Jusen,* or housing loan companies, were concerned. And it was here that the next stage of Japan's financial crisis played out.

The *Jusen* were initially founded by banks and other financial entities in the early 1970s with the encouragement of the MOF to augment the existing supply of housing loans. Driven by increased competition in the late 1980s to skew their loan portfolios away from mortgagees and towards risky real estate developers, they had little expertise in commercial lending and rapidly found themselves under mounting balance sheet pressure once real estate prices began to fall. By 1993 they had already been the beneficiaries of two MOF-organized rounds of loan forgiveness and interest rate concessions by their founder banks, under the so-called convoy approach. However, these interventions were merely designed to tide them over until land prices recovered. That recovery never materialized. Indeed, by the end of 1994 the country-wide decline in land prices from the peak was about a third on average. In the six major cities, land prices had approximately halved. The *Jusen* were doomed. It was only a matter of time before they collapsed.

When they were finally wound up in the summer of 1995, around three-quarters of the *Jusen*'s loan books were non-performing and their aggregate losses amounted to ¥6.4 trillion – a figure far beyond the amount that their founder banks could possibly cover. The government had no choice but to step in to liquidate the failed entities and create a public asset management company (the Resolution and Collection Bank) to manage their bad assets.[11] The *Jusen*'s losses were allocated to the founder banks (¥3.5 trillion), lender banks (¥1.7 trillion) and agricultural financial institutions (¥0.53 trillion). The residual ¥680 billion ($6.7 billion) was covered by the taxpayer, albeit only after a fierce debate in the Diet.

The *Jusen* problem was the first case in which public money was used to deal with the fallout from the bubble directly, and despite the relatively small sum involved it provoked strong resentment well beyond the political class. Indeed, the public bitterness was sufficiently intense that the further application of public funds was thereafter considered to be acceptable only as a last resort. Although the Japanese authorities could no longer credibly avoid recognizing that the financial sector's problems ran deep and wide, and that this risked a run on the broader banking system, the *Jusen* issue reinforced the centrality of forbearance to financial policy. In the absence of a comprehensive legal framework for the resolution of major banking sector issues, financial institutions would continue to be granted considerable latitude in the way that their balance sheets were presented. More specifically, this meant in regard to the veracity of their assessments of loan quality and the value of the collateral associated with those loans. In the meantime, the hope was that the economy and the asset markets would ride to the rescue before too long.

Sticking to this approach of 'buying time' was at the very least bound to be something of a white-knuckle ride, however. There were further runs on a number of other small financial institutions over the summer of 1995, and the MOF felt it necessary to reassure depositors that their savings would be safe should the overall situation deteriorate dramatically by announcing that the Deposit Insurance Corporation (DIC) would protect all deposits for five years, while also committing to addressing the NPL problem over a similar horizon.[12] This was a momentous decision that only served further to embed the strategy of toleration and indulgence of financial institutions. The recognition of losses and the process of balance sheet adjustment would inevitably be impeded.

In the meantime, the DIC would need more funds if it was to become a credible comprehensive safety net in the eyes of the public. Up to this point its financial resources were extremely limited. In June 1996 a five-year programme of progressively higher bank contributions was announced to this end. The DIC was also granted greater latitude to borrow, supported by a government guarantee.

Confidence in the Japanese financial system was dealt a further blow around this time by the revelation that a single bond trader working for Daiwa Bank in the United States had concealed trading losses of more than $1 billion and that Daiwa had itself deliberately deceived the US authorities about what had taken place. This episode suggested that the slack internal risk controls and irregular practices that multiplied during the rapid overseas expansion of Japan's banks in the bubble years endured. It also bred a feeling in the international investment community that neither the MOF nor the BOJ had an adequate grasp of what was going on in the Japanese financial sector. The sense abroad was that the Daiwa incident was only the tip of the iceberg.

Unsurprisingly, the continued fall in land prices, the heavy burden of NPLs, the growing difficulties being experienced by smaller financial institutions, the question marks that were being raised over the banking sector's operating procedures, and the nature of the regulatory environment in Japan began to be reflected in higher borrowing costs in the interbank market: a phenomenon that became known as the 'Japan premium'. This in turn made it harder for the stronger institutions to take over the weak. The 'convoy' system that had long been the default response in Japan to periods of financial duress, and which sat alongside forbearance in dealing with the fallout from the bursting of the asset bubble, was no longer viable.

TEMPORARY RESPITE

Thankfully, some relief from these financial fragilities was forthcoming in the second half of 1995. The yen's sudden surge at the beginning of the year unwound in the face of extensive intervention in the foreign exchange market by the Japanese authorities and as US Treasury Secretary Robert Rubin's efforts to establish a strong dollar policy gained credibility. Official reserve assets rose by an amount equal to half of the current account surplus in 1995.

The Japanese government also saw fit to respond to the economy and the financial sector's continued difficulties with yet another large bout of fiscal expansion, this time amounting to ¥14.2 trillion (3% of GDP) and containing the largest allocation yet towards public investment (¥8 trillion), although as usual the headline figure significantly exaggerated the impact on final demand. In July the BOJ acted to push the call money rate below the 1% ODR and then in September it set the latter at a mere 0.5%, all of which helped to bring real short-term market interest rates down to a level last seen in the 1970s.

Growth picked up again towards the end of the year, and there were hopes that the more sympathetic exchange rate environment and this latest round of fiscal and monetary support might finally be enough to stabilize matters and draw a line under the crisis. This was especially the case as the global environment seemed to be set fair. Indeed, as we shall see, 1996 proved to be the best year for the Japanese economy and for Japanese share prices since the bubble burst. It was, however, to prove a false dawn.

PONDEROUS SUPPLY-SIDE REFORM

As outlined in the previous chapter, there had been a growing focus on structural reform in the guise of deregulation and the enhancement of competitive forces in Japan during the 1980s, and especially after 1985. It was recognized in numerous official reports that macroeconomic policy could not by itself deliver the overlapping objectives of narrowing price differentials with other advanced economies, sustained improvements in the standard of living of the population, the enduring requirement for business to adapt to changing demands and new technologies, improved access for foreigners to the domestic market, and the moderation of the external surplus and thereby trade frictions. Hence, often responding to criticism from, and sometimes working with, the United States, numerous areas of the economy were singled out for change, including distribution, telecommunications, finance, transport, energy and agriculture. It was further recognised that the *Keiretsu* and certain other longstanding business practices and cultural preferences, not least those that served to reduce foreign influence in the economy, would have to evolve if the process of reform were to reach a successful conclusion.

Some progress was made in all these areas over the course of the previous decade, and overall government intervention in the economy was reduced, but the process was hesitant and uneven, and far from complete. It was estimated by the Economic Planning Agency (EPA) that regulated industries still accounted for some 42% of total value added in 1994 – a drop of only eight percentage points since 1980 – while 23.6% was highly regulated, which actually represented a small increase on the 1980 figure! Prices in many sectors, and especially those that were most heavily regulated, remained high, and disincentives to spend were material. Administrative procedures often remained overly complex and opaque. Significant parts of the service sector were sheltered to a greater or lesser degree from external entities. The system of taxation was prone to distortions and was inefficient. New business opportunities were stymied. Investment was stifled and saving encouraged.

Consequently, the pressure for further reforms, including from the United States and the international community more broadly, remained strong in the early 1990s, often touching on regulatory and industrial practices dating back to the 1940s. This was particularly the case given the rebound in the external surplus after 1990, mounting evidence that Japan's underlying productivity and growth performance had deteriorated, and as the country's ageing population increasingly impinged on its future prospects.

The mid 1990s saw the working-age population peak, and the overall population reached the same milestone in the second half of the following decade. Labour productivity growth across the business sector slumped from an average of close to 4% a year in the late 1980s to less than 1% in the first half of the 1990s, and it varied greatly from sector to sector, with manufacturing exporters outperforming, domestic services generally lagging, and the beleaguered financial, construction and real estate industries particular stragglers. Nor did the tendency for the banking sector to keep some troubled companies in business through debt forgiveness and by lowering contracted interest rates help the overall situation. The economy's potential growth rate, which had run as high as 4.5% for a time during the bubble period, subsequently slipped to well below 2%.

There therefore followed a further slew of reform packages, some of which were bound up with successive fiscal packages (including the 1994 and 1995 income tax cuts) and which embodied more than a thousand individual proposals. There was also recognition by the authorities that interventions in markets should be the exception rather than the rule. 'Freedom in principle and regulation as the exception' was the stated mantra, while timetables for policy implementation were adopted and regular commitments to review progress were made.

Some of the more important additional reforms came in finance, energy, transport and communications, where relative prices fell significantly, and these sectors saw their rates of investment hold up relatively well during this period. Perhaps most important of all, however, were reforms related to the distribution system, which accounted for some 14% of total value added in the early 1990s. A series of changes to the laws relating to large-scale retail stores streamlined the process of establishing such entities and reduced the impediments on the operation, resulting in their rapid growth and a sharp decline in the multitude of inefficient small shops. Together with the impact of the prolonged economic downturn and currency strength, the relaxation of warehousing fees and the acceptance of more foreign certification inspection data, this reduced the monopolistic influence of domestic manufacturers; encouraged competition among firms and price sensitivity among consumers; and accelerated import penetration, reductions in standardization of pricing and resort to discounting.

Unsurprisingly, given the events of late 1980s, a further area of change was in respect to the real estate market. A number of changes in taxation were forthcoming, including the introduction of a national land tax at a rate of 0.3% from 1993, albeit with broad exceptions; increases in assessment values for inheritance tax that brought them closer to market prices; and a reduction in the various tax incentives to maintain farmland in urban areas. These all acted at the margin to discourage the hoarding of real estate holdings somewhat and increase the efficiency of land use. The supply of land was also improved by the relaxation of zoning laws and an easing of the outdated tenant protection laws, which had acted as a form of rent control, via changes in residential and commercial leases for new contracts. On the other hand, an increase in capital gains tax on the sale of landholdings worked in the opposite direction to these changes.

Most Japanese individuals were still subject to higher real estate prices relative to their income, and had less living space per person than elsewhere, while high land prices remained an important impediment to new business development. More clearly needed to be done. Too many government interventions still encouraged the inefficient use of land.

Other reform initiatives came in the form of a strengthening of the FTC's ability to enforce competition policy; less complex regulations on inward FDI; the further liberalization of the financial sector, in particular the money and debt markets; and in regard to the hitherto often rigid siloing of different subsectors. At the same time, the number of agricultural products that were subject to quotas was reduced and tariffs were substituted for those that remained; some government corporations were merged or privatized; and the door was opened to new carriers in the telecoms sector and NTT's monopolistic position was further eroded, not least through the separation of mobile communications from its purview.

Finally, an Administrative Procedures Law was passed in 1994 that sought to increase the transparency and limit the sweep and arbitrary nature of much bureaucratic decision-making, although it still excluded many critical areas such as taxes, patents and immigration matters. Allied to this, an independent Administrative Reform Committee was established in December 1994 to oversee the deregulation process from the beginning of the 1995/1996 financial year to the end of the 1997/1998 financial year.

Reviewing all this, the overall burden of government regulation and intervention was further reduced across the Japanese economy over the first half of the 1990s. The system became less opaque, and importantly this extended at least to some degree to the informal administrative guidance that had been such a feature of the post-war period.

The EPA estimated that the various deregulatory measures implemented between 1990 and 1995 resulted in a 1.7 percentage point boost to nominal GDP and created more than a million jobs. However, the EPA's calculation was on a gross basis and neglected to include the negative side-effects of policy change, such as the closure of small-scale retailers or employment rationalization. The net impact of deregulation was doubtless still positive, just not to the degree suggested. Overall, the deregulatory process remained gradual and piecemeal, and it was often reliant on small, incremental, changes. There were very few industries in which entry barriers were comprehensively swept away or the underlying forces of demand and supply were left to their own devices.

For all the constant background noise in this area of policy, the packages exhibited notable similarities, repeatedly going over old ground. Too many suggestions made by domestic businesses or by Japan's foreign interlocutors were ignored. Too many initiatives were vague and imprecise or merely amounted to a commitment to review an issue. There was no real overarching plan and no powerful independent body with robust funding and statutory powers to oversee the process and to publicize the benefits. Nor was there much of a sense at the end of the period that the process of deregulation would speed up, or indeed that there was sufficient adaptability in public administration to make that happen. To many external observers, the conclusion remained that the various domestic vested interests retained undue influence and that Japan continued to do as little as it could get away with. Domestically, pessimism among businesses about the future rate of output growth showed no sign of moderating.

STRUCTURAL BREAK

The first half of the 1990s saw an enormous change in Japan's economic circumstances. Once the grossly inflated asset prices of the previous decade commenced what was an inevitable fall back to earth, the economy lost impetus and sank into a protracted and obdurate recession, the like of which had not been witnessed in the post-war period. In the process, numerous excesses and unsustainable imbalances accumulated during boom years began to unwind in malign fashion. It was a period of pronounced cyclical and structural adjustment followed by what was to prove a modest expansion – one that was heavily dependent on policy support and in which business investment spending was particularly slow to pick up and was narrowly focused on IT-related outlays when it did.

Perhaps most importantly, the financial sector – recently subject to liberalization, and much of which had lost all sense of moderation, even reality – was consumed by a rising tide of NPLs. It was forced to restructure or write off many of these troubled assets, increase its loan loss provisions and pull in its horns, not least to meet its capital requirements. The spigot of loans hitherto advanced to real estate related activities and on the basis of supposedly ever-appreciating land collateral values was turned off. Credit conditions became more austere, not least for the SME sector.

There remained, however, persistent suspicion of a lack of disclosure and transparency across the sector, and there was therefore huge uncertainty as to the full extent of its underlying balance sheet issues, especially where the smaller regional banks and the non-banks were concerned. Financial statements had too often been found to have concealed important transactions and obligations that rendered an entity much less sound than previously believed.

Lacking a comprehensive legal framework for the resolution of a major financial crisis, wary of voter anger about the corporate extravagancies and malfeasance of the previous decade, and concerned about the loss of face implied by more complete disclosure of the truth, successive governments were reluctant either to admit the extent of the problem with which they were confronted or to apply large-scale public funds by way of a solution. Rather than lance the boil, they preferred instead to fall back on the convoy system, blanket deposit insurance and a strategy of forbearance in the hope that economic conditions and the markets would turn around, facilitate a process of gradual provisioning and write-offs, and resolve matters over time, thereby saving their blushes. Lessons could and should have been drawn from the transparent and forceful way the Nordic financial crises, which initially overlapped with that of Japan, was resolved. Alas, they were not.[13]

The corporate sector, which had also been increasingly drawn into stock and land price speculation, saw its profitability slump and cost of capital surge, and it was similarly confronted by the urgent necessity to focus on balance sheet repair. A brutal inventory adjustment ensued and investment spending on plant and equipment – which had become grotesquely bloated and increasingly inefficient during the latter stages of the upswing but which had been the domestic lifeblood of Japan's post-war economic miracle – was repeatedly slashed. With the population set to age rapidly, and the workforce set to shrink, there remained a reluctance to lay staff off. However, little was done to offset the natural wastage of labour, overtime and bonus payments were sharply reduced, and basic wage increases were curbed. With a persistently strong yen adding to their woes, manufacturing companies continued to seek to cut production costs by shifting their operations overseas, most obviously to Asia, and particularly where machinery and transport goods were concerned. In this environment the household sector increased its propensity to save and was happy to hold a rising proportion of its financial assets in cash.

The goods and service price inflation that at the beginning of the decade had been such a concern for the BOJ all too rapidly morphed into the opposite problem of deflation. CPI inflation was already uncomfortably low by 1993, and by 1995 it had dropped into negative territory, in the process adding to the real burden of debt across the economy.

Meanwhile, despite the strength of the yen and a renewed decline in Japan's export market share after 1993, the weakness of domestic demand kept the external balance in significant surplus; trade tensions with its competitors, particularly the United States, were therefore prone to intermittent escalation. Japan remained under international pressure to open its domestic markets and reorientate its economy away from exports.

As the financial sector and the economy reeled, bank lending and monetary growth collapsed, inflation dissipated and the external surplus became more entrenched, macroeconomic policy was dramatically reoriented.

After some regrettable initial hesitation, and notwithstanding a difficult-to-understand extended pause in 1994, policy rates were progressively reduced towards the zero bound, albeit to limited effect beyond the residential construction sector. In terms of standard macroeconomic theory, Japan was operating on the flat part of the LM curve, where monetary policy was apt to 'push on a string.'*

---

* The IS-LM model – which stands for 'investment–saving' (IS) and 'liquidity preference–money supply' (LM) – is a Keynesian macroeconomic model that shows how the market for economic goods interacts with the loanable funds market, or money market. It is represented as a graph in which the downward-sloping IS and upward-sloping LM curves intersect to show the short-run equilibrium between interest rates and output. The relative slopes of the two curves equate to the relative strength of monetary and fiscal policy. When the LM curve is flat, monetary policy will be weak.

In such circumstances, the suggestion is that fiscal policy, as represented in theoretical terms by a relatively steep IS curve, should pick up the slack, and fiscal policy did indeed become more expansionary in the 1990s. The consolidated budget swung into substantial deficit and the stock of outstanding government debt rose sharply. Indeed, the entire improvement in the budget position over the 1980s was reversed.

This was to a significant extent the result of non-discretionary factors, and in particular a sharp drop in tax revenues and an increase in outlays on unemployment relief and other social benefits. However, public sector demand also became the prime source of discretionary support for the economy after 1991, increasing its share in GDP, helping to fill the cavernous hole that had opened up in corporate demand, and preventing a more catastrophic fall in real GDP.[14]

That said, there was little effort to coordinate fiscal policy with monetary policy, as there had been in Japan in the early 1930s, and the nature of the fiscal stimulus employed was flawed on a number of other levels. Reflecting presentational creative accounting, the announced size of the various fiscal packages consistently exceeded the underlying effect on final demand by anything between a half and two-thirds. The packages also typically followed conservative, even contractionary, initial budgets. Significant sums (as much as 30% of the cost of some projects) were expended on the acquisition of land, which, while it might have moderated the rate of real estate price deflation and to some degree sustained confidence, was merely a transfer of assets. As financial liberalization reduced market interest rates, the government-subsidized loans that fleshed the packages out became less attractive and suffered from limited take-up. Even when they were accessed, they largely merely substituted for private sector equivalents.

There was, moreover, a sense that the various fiscal interjections were hastily cobbled together, with limited thought given to consistency, sustainability or the maximization of their medium-term impact. They were never incorporated into an extended plan with specified targets. Their positive effects were episodic rather than continual, which did little to reduce underlying private sector uncertainty. The associated public investment ran into significant implementation issues, especially at the local government level. The project selection process was politically skewed and left much to be desired, and rates of return were frequently disappointing.[15] The bulk of the income tax cuts when they came in 1994 and 1995 were temporary rather than permanent, which reduced their effect.

It is little surprise, therefore, that subsequent estimates of the multipliers associated with these fiscal packages are modest, their weakness compounded by the tendency of the banking sector's problems to limit private sector follow-through and by the corporate sector's focus on deleveraging. The multiplier estimates for public spending typically fall between 0.4 and 1.1, with a declining trend over time. Those associated with tax measures range from 0.2 to 0.5.

The continued belief that the economic trials and tribulations of the period would prove temporary, and that attention would soon have to turn once again to public sector debt consolidation, played a role in these shortcomings. One is left with the conclusion that the efficiency of fiscal policy as a counter-cyclical device would have been improved by Japan having more expansive automatic stabilizers, including in the form of a more comprehensive social security system.

For its part, micro reform continued in the early 1990s much as it had in the 1980s. There were unquestionably some areas of progress, which expanded markets, reduced prices, raised real incomes and created new business opportunities. But given the significant flattening of the trajectory of economic output and a greater vulnerability to future shocks, the reform process fell well short of what was required. Powerful vested interests continued to exert a malign influence, the evolution of reform in general remained gradual and piecemeal and was beset by inertia that bled into policy rigidity, and the political upheavals of the period did little to help. It is interesting to note that the former *Zaibatsu* (Mitsui, Mitsubishi, Sumitomo, plus the three bank groups of Fuji, Sanwa and Daiichi-Kangyo) retained a share in the economy in terms of capital, assets, sales and current profits of around 18% in 1994.

A more urgent and expansive approach to reform had to become an increasing priority if growth potential were not to continue to slide and if the economy was to avoid more regular setbacks.

Overall, Japan's asset price bust of the early 1990s had much in common with both previous such episodes and those that followed it. What was to mark it out as exceptional was the length of time it took the authorities truly to come to terms with its extent and its broader implications. The contrast with the remarkable way Japan adapted to, and moved on from, the two oil shocks is stark.

CHAPTER 5

The Crisis Deepens

'Good medicine tastes bitter' — Japanese proverb

FLATTERING TO DECEIVE

There is no question that 1995 was a difficult year for Japan. The shock and horror of the Great Hanshin Earthquake, the belated arrival in the country of urban terrorism, and the continuing financial fallout from the bursting of the late 1980s asset bubble, including its enervating influence on real activity, together conspired to leave both the macroeconomy and national confidence at a low ebb. The next 15 months, however, were to see the overall tenor of things temporarily improve. Growth picked up somewhat, as for a while did share prices. Bank lending, especially for house purchases, rebounded modestly, and this helped to buoy broad monetary growth. While a succession of smaller banks and finance companies continued to fail, important parts of the financial sector appeared – to the extent that it was possible to judge – to be on the mend. Corporate indebtedness began to subside, and the financial position of firms improved. The slide towards deflation was halted. Official interest rates stopped falling. There was, in short, something of a sense of a return to normality.

Unfortunately, this was to prove all too ephemeral. The worst of Japan's remarkable economic fall from grace was still to come, as a series of overlapping negative shocks malignly interacted with one another in the context of its significant enduring underlying fragilities. The period from the middle of 1997 until the end of 1998 was to prove little short of catastrophic – it was at that time, arguably, the worst financial crisis suffered by an advanced nation since World War II. It is no exaggeration to say that for some months the fear was of a total meltdown in the world's second largest economy.

FALSE DAWN

After four years of scant growth, an acceleration in the pace of real activity gradually became observable during the second half of 1995. Another sharp burst of public investment spending following the implementation of the ¥14.2 trillion September fiscal package pushed its share in GDP to a peak of 8.6% and elicited a particularly rapid expansion rate in the first quarter of 1996.[1] Thereafter, following a brief hiatus in the following quarter, the cyclical upswing appeared to gather momentum and broaden out, with all the major components of private sector demand contributing positively. Japan's real GDP growth rate of some 3.5% in 1996 was its fastest since 1990, and the most impressive recorded that year among all the major economies.

A pick-up in personal consumption was encouraged not just by consistent, if modest, growth in real disposable incomes and by faster employment growth, but also by a turn in the durable goods replacement cycle and a dip in the household saving rate. Residential construction was boosted by lower borrowing costs, including – importantly – the favourable rates offered by the HLC.[2] Business investment emerged from several years in the doldrums – responding to improved corporate profitability, the super low interest rate environment, and the desire on the part of larger manufacturing firms to improve competitiveness – such that this vital component of demand's share in GDP recovered to close to the average of the previous two decades. And finally – and albeit with something of a lag – net exports were buoyed by the effect of domestic destocking on import volume growth, a pick-up in global activity and a significant depreciation of the yen. The Japanese currency was relatively stable in the first half of 1996 at a level some 25% off its April 1995 high against the dollar. Exports of capital goods and cars were particularly strong while, supported by continued outflows of FDI, trade became further focused on Asia.

The recovery progressively excised the surplus capacity that had accumulated since 1992, although the unemployment rate dropped only marginally from the then post-war high of 3.5% recorded in the spring of 1996 and wage inflation, particularly where basic pay settlements were concerned, remained subdued. The weakness of wage growth and unit labour costs left consumer prices more or less stable. CPI inflation averaged just 0.1% for the year, comfortably the lowest rate in the OECD, but hardly a help in reducing the economy's huge nominal burden of debt.[3] In the meantime, back down to a mere 1.5% of GDP, the current account surplus for once was a less than burning issue.

TEMPORARY FINANCIAL RESPITE

The combination of easy monetary conditions and cyclical recovery acted to swell the banks' operating profits, in part because they neglected to pass on the full benefits of lower interest rates to their customers. This allowed them to reduce the publicly declared burden of NPLs and, more pertinently, their unprovisioned NPLs, including by sales to the CCPC, albeit at prices that were a declining proportion of their face value. At the same time, as outlined in the previous chapter, the DIC's resources were strengthened through higher insurance premia and greater latitude to borrow with a government guarantee, while a new Financial Supervisory Agency (FSA), notionally independent from the MOF, was established to pursue a more transparent and rules-based (rather than case-by-case) system of banking oversight. Against this background, the hope flourished that the systemic NPL problem could be consigned to the history books by April 1998, and that regulators would thereafter be able to apply a new framework of Prompt Corrective Action (PCA) smoothly in the event that any bank's capital ratio deteriorated unduly in an altogether less fraught environment.

Encouraged by the rising optimism about the health of the banks and the financial system more generally, the government decided in November 1996 to proceed with a five-year strategy to complete the process of reform begun in earnest in the 1980s, the intention being to render the sector 'free, fair, and global'. Christened the 'Big Bang', after the moniker applied to the sweeping changes introduced by the Thatcher government in the UK financial services sector a decade earlier, it encompassed a wide range of initiatives. These extended to the relaxation of residual controls on foreign exchange and cross-border capital transactions; the removal of the post-war ban on holding companies; the liberalization of brokerage commissions on stocks; the dismantling of market segmentation; reduced restrictions on bank financing options; longer opening hours for retail banks and cash dispensers; greater freedom in the management of pension funds; fewer restraints on derivative trading; and a movement to mark-to-market accounting practices.

The idea was to increase competition, lower costs, expand choice and raise efficiency, in the process encouraging the Japanese financial system to catch up with best practice elsewhere. As with the City of London in the 1980s, however, reform would inevitably bring with it significant disruption and rationalization. Outdated business practices would be challenged and replaced. Mergers and acquisitions would multiply. The least efficient enterprises would shrink or be put out of business entirely. There would be new players and greater foreign involvement. Jobs would be lost.

The assumption, if not the expectation, within government was that the process of financial sector change and modernization could be carefully controlled and that the inevitable side-effects could be kept to manageable proportions. The problem was that the sanguinity of late 1996 would prove to be a mirage. Beneath the veneer of a modestly improved macro environment, the reality was that few, if any, of Japan's underlying financial problems had been comprehensively addressed. Notwithstanding the evidence of a gradual upturn in the balance sheet health of the financial sector as a whole, the situation varied enormously from institution to institution. Some banks remained in a very fragile, even unsustainable, condition. Land prices, and thereby the value of underlying loan collateral, continued to slide. Bankruptcies and the liabilities associated with them were still escalating. The banks' Tier 1 capital continued to fall towards the BIS limit of 4%. There also remained a strong suspicion – encouraged not just by the long history of obfuscation, deceit and corruption across the corporate sector and public institutions in Japan, but by what had been unearthed at those entities that had already been liquidated – that important transactions and obligations had regularly been concealed and that the real stock of bad loans and loans at risk of becoming so was considerably higher than was being officially disclosed.

Furthermore, 1996 saw some important hints that a full-blown banking crisis could be just around the corner. The share prices of banks with larger portfolios of bad debts continued to trend downwards, while Nippon Credit Bank, Hokkaidō Takushoku Bank and the Long-Term Credit Bank – all sizeable institutions – announced either big losses or drastic, often panic-stricken, restructurings, including the closure of their overseas operations. In addition, there were the continuing struggles of the life insurance companies, whose projected yields for policyholders greatly exceeded the returns that were being generated in an environment of such low interest rates.

HITTING THE WALL

Notwithstanding these issues, however, the pace of economic growth quickened markedly in the first quarter of 1997 as householders accelerated spending, including on house purchases, in anticipation of the planned hike in the consumption tax to 5% in April of that year. This was only to be expected, and the confident belief within government at this time was that, after a brief correction in domestic demand in the following quarter, the recovery that had begun in late 1995 would resume. The economy might not be able to sustain the sort of growth rates achieved in the 1980s, but the stagnation of the first half of the decade could be confined to the history books.

Instead, what followed was a vastly different, and much more challenging, set of circumstances for the Japanese economy and the country's policymakers. Unduly zealous fiscal consolidation, a catastrophic financial crisis that spread across much of the rest of Asia, and the enduring and unfortunately underappreciated legacies of the bubble economy cross-fertilized with one another in devastating fashion. This combination of forces soured into a poisonous cocktail of further asset price deflation, surging insolvencies, collapsed confidence, financial sector breakdown, a renewed slump in credit supply and demand, and an extended drop in private expenditures, especially business sector outlays.

Rather than rebound in the second half of 1997, real GDP remained below its Q1 1997 level across the balance of the year. In total, the economy contracted in six quarters out of seven (and throughout calendar year 1998), with a peak-to-trough decline in output of more than 5%. Unemployment surged towards an unheard of 5% of the workforce, for a period exceeding the jobless rate in the United States for the first time since World War II.[4] The output gap once again widened dramatically. Deflationary pressures re-intensified, with the annual rate of change in domestic wholesale prices, the CPI, the GDP deflator and overall wages all turning negative. The only consolation was that a portion of these declines reflected the impact of deregulation rather than excess supply. Stock prices fell by around a quarter in the second half of 1997, to plumb new post-1990 lows, and then fell further still in 1998. Land prices continued to fall for the rest of the decade and some way into the next. Led by a sharp decline in import volumes, net exports provided the only positive contribution from private demand to real GDP growth in 1998 and, helped by better terms of trade, the external surplus swelled again to some 3% of GDP. For a while, the situation threatened to spin completely out of control before it was salvaged by another dramatic, if belated, reorientation of policy.

COUNTING THE COST

Prior to exploring the dynamics of this downturn further and outlining the specifics of when and how policy was recalibrated, it is worth outlining in some detail the size, nature and ramifications of the total losses already incurred as a result of asset price deflation by this juncture. Notwithstanding the other shocks that struck in 1997 and 1998, it was these, more than anything else, that lay behind the economy buckling once again in such spectacular fashion.

By 1997 Japan had been confronted by total capital losses cumulating to around a quadrillion yen (some $7 trillion). This represented approximately two full years of GDP, or 14% of the value of the nation's total assets when the bubble burst at the end of 1989. About two-thirds of the total loss came in the form of the value of real estate holdings (a fall of some 27% from the peak). The remainder can be ascribed to stock price declines.

Households were hit hardest, followed by non-financial corporations, then financial entities. Little of the fall in asset values was matched by corresponding falls in liabilities, which declined by a mere ¥100 trillion or so. Total national net worth was therefore reduced in a manner largely corresponding to the drop in asset values.

As we have seen, much of the correction in asset prices came early in the decade, but asset price deflation was still a fact of life in the mid 1990s. Land prices peaked in 1991 at around six times 1970 levels but subsequently fell on average by around 4.5% a year, with the deepest declines in the commercial sector. Equity prices were more volatile than land prices, with particularly sharp falls seen in 1990 and 1992. Thereafter, there was rather less of a trend but no sustained recovery.

Household net worth fell by about a sixth over this period, mostly in the form of land holdings. This was the equivalent of some 20% of annual disposable income. Negative equity and mortgage arrears surged. Efforts were made to rebuild savings. There was a reluctance to invest in housing further. Risk aversion dominated investment portfolio selection, with the share of assets held in equities dropping to less than 5%, or about a quarter of the level then prevailing in the United States.[5]

The losses of non-financial corporates were more or less evenly split between land and equities. The overall fall in their net worth was equivalent to some 16% of their total balance sheets, or nearly twice the level of current profits earned by all companies with capital of more than ¥10 million over the intervening period. This was at the core of the surge in bankruptcies. The corporate sector's financial behaviour matched the timidity of households, with a particular reluctance to borrow, especially from the banks, and invest.[6]

The biggest effects on the real economy can be traced to the financial sector, even though the direct effect on their balance sheets only accounted for about 20% of the total, largely through holdings of equities. Nevertheless, as already pointed out, the sector's capital base was squeezed hard, as the capital gains on securities held since the 1970s and 1980s were largely wiped out. For example, the banks suffered a decline in the market value of their listed equities of some ¥43 trillion over the eight years to March 1997. They were also hurt to the extent that the value of the collateral that they held against their loans – land, for the most part – collapsed, generating a bad-loan problem of huge (but uncertain) size.

The banks' health was further undermined by increased competition following an extended period of gradual liberalization. The Big Bang might have been designed to accelerate this process, but it had already been in train for some two decades.

Finally, there was the matter of regulatory forbearance to consider. The sustenance of severely damaged, often insolvent, financial firms via incomplete disclosure or by being forcibly merged with a healthier rival reduced the incentive to develop expertise in risk analysis and management.

The net result of all these issues for the financial sector was chronically low returns (the average return on investment for the banking sector was a mere

0.5% in the 1994/1995 financial year), a continuation of excessive risk taking and what amounts to the cardiovascular system of a modern market economy having precious little ability to absorb any major new setbacks.

BUDGETARY BELT TIGHTENING

As suggested above, a tighter budgetary stance was the initial catalyst for the economy hitting the buffers in 1997. Following the expansionary September 1996 package, the impetus of fiscal policy was thrown into reverse as policymakers sought to rein in the persistent widening of the central and local government budget deficits and moderate the upsurge in overall public indebtedness. By 1996 the consolidated budget shortfall had swollen to some 5% of GDP, far in excess of the G7 and OECD averages; the burden of gross government liabilities was rapidly converging on 100% of GDP; and, despite historically low interest rates, the burden of debt service costs was rising in sympathy.

There was also, however, the increasingly pressing need to prepare for the impact on the public finances of the rapid ageing of the population structure.

It was estimated around this time that the progressive collapse in the nation's birth rate from 4.5 children per family in 1947 to 1.4 children per family in 1995 together with the longest life expectancy in the OECD meant that, by 2025, the Japanese population would be the oldest of all the advanced economies and that only two other OECD members would have a higher ratio of elderly to working-age people. What is more, even though the number of elderly would begin to stabilize after 2025, the low birth rate would ensure that both the active population and the total population continued to fall rapidly. By 2050 the latter was expected to have dropped by more than 20% from its projected peak in the 2010s. This was unheard of for a modern peace-time economy and would clearly have huge implications on a number of levels.

As the labour force declined, trend growth would slow and become increasingly dependent on the pace of productivity improvements – which, latterly, had decelerated significantly of course. Saving and investment would fall – the latter by more than the former – as, unlike in many societies, there was little evidence that the Japanese elderly dissaved significantly. There would be reduced demand for housing and lower house prices. And, most pertinently for fiscal policy, government spending would remain under persistent upward pressure from rising public pension obligations, increasing medical costs for the elderly and the need for widespread long-term care, while tax revenue growth would be constrained.

Despite a number of policy changes extending to increases in the retirement age and higher contribution rates, state pension benefits were projected to rise from 10% of GDP in 1998 to 16% by 2025, while spending on health care was expected to jump from 2% of GDP to 5% over the same period.[7] Consequently, assuming other public spending shares were held constant, government spending in GDP would spiral upwards to more than half of national income by 2025, some 10 percentage points higher than the average of the previous decade. This was widely believed to represent a powerful constraint on future private sector dynamism.

Japan clearly needed to go further with its reforms to public pension and social security systems, look to increase the birth rate and female and elderly participation, and explore greater inward migration. At the same time, the application of broader structural policy initiatives aimed at raising productivity was a greater priority than ever. But these were medium-to-long-term solutions. In the short term the feeling was that the priority was to reverse the expansionary fiscal policy bias of the prior five years or so and to bear down on the budget deficit. This was even though it had been central to the economy registering any growth at all over this period.

Hence, in addition to the expiration of the ¥2 trillion temporary income tax cut in December 1996 and the consumption tax hike scheduled for April 1997, social security contribution rates were further increased and public investment outlays cut back sharply in the 1997/1998 financial year budget. In overall terms, fiscal policy was tightened by well over a percentage point of GDP in calendar year 1997. Furthermore, in November of that year a Fiscal Structural Reform Act (FSRA) was passed to impose caps on major government spending categories sufficient to halve the combined central and local government deficit to 3% of GDP by FY 2003 and to ensure that the sum of taxes, payroll contributions and the fiscal shortfall would not exceed 50% of GDP. The intention was to put in place an extended fiscal squeeze akin to that of the 1980s, even though the underlying health of the economy was much less robust.

The impact of this fiscal policy volte-face, and particularly the consumption tax hike, proved much greater than expected, however. For example, retail sales fell 16% immediately after the indirect tax change, to a level some 5% below the level a year earlier, and subsequently struggled to recover. Housing starts also traced a similar pattern. In this environment, inventories rapidly escalated, production was cut back, profits and business sentiment subsided, and plant and equipment investment once more retreated. The upswing ground to a juddering halt.

THE ASIAN CRISIS

The unexpected weakness of domestic spending in Q2 1997 was then compounded by the eruption early in the following quarter of a devastating financial crisis across much of the rest of Asia. The region had been experiencing an extended period of rapid, credit-fuelled growth and asset price inflation similar in some respects to Japan's bubble era. Matters were further complicated by a series of fixed and quasi-fixed currency pegs that came to be viewed as implicit guarantees of exchange value, that encouraged a flood of short-term external borrowing and that prevented appropriate central bank responses to growing evidence of overheating. The situation became increasingly unsustainable as external deficits burgeoned, and the exchange rate regimes were swept away by powerful speculative forces. Asset markets and currencies collapsed as capital flows into the region dramatically reversed.

Further echoing Japan's experience, the situation was exacerbated by poor data transparency, weak corporate management and risk control, the lax enforcement of prudential rules, inadequate supervision, excessive government involvement in lending, and poor overall governance and political uncertainty. A number of banking sectors imploded, necessitating a series of large-scale IMF-funded rescue packages, the quid pro quos for which were severe deflation and the implementation of structural reform programmes. Real activity in the economies affected fell on average by more than 5% in 1998, and only around two-thirds of the loss was recovered in 1999.

As a consequence, the yen rapidly appreciated both regionally and in effective terms. The volume of Japanese export sales to its most important market[*] first slowed, then slumped. What is more, the already acutely fragile Japanese banks, which had remained heavily invested in the region after the bubble years, were seriously exposed. More than 4% of the major banks' outstanding loans were in the countries most affected. The Asian Crisis thereby added significantly to the Japanese banks' profitability, NPL and capital adequacy issues.

Macroeconomically, the only saving grace was that the negative effects were mitigated somewhat by terms-of-trade gains from weaker global commodity prices. The total adverse impact of the Asian Crisis on Japan's real GDP was in the region of 0.5% in 1997 and about 1.25% in 1998.

FINANCIAL DISINTEGRATION

As already suggested above, however, the Japanese financial sector's problems in 1997 and 1998 ran far deeper than its exposure to the rest of Asia – and they were much more grave than was generally realized. In the autumn of 1997 – against a background of sharply deteriorating business conditions, overcapacity, low underlying profitability, further asset price falls and the prospect

---

[*] Asia as a whole accounted for more than 40% of total overseas sales.

of more intense competition – a series of large-scale financial firms collapsed. Key among these failures were Hokkaidō Takushoku Bank, Japan's tenth largest lender and the dominant bank on the northern island of Hokkaido; Sanyo Securities, the country's seventh largest stockbroker; and Yamaichi Securities, one of the so-called Big Four brokerage houses.

The impact on private sector confidence, trust and risk appetite was devastating. Credit intermediation, already seriously impaired, slumped further. The interbank markets froze. Lenders were reluctant to lend, especially to small companies. Where they could, borrowers looked to pay back loans and baulked at taking out further advances. In a classic 'flight to quality', depositors shifted funds away from financial institutions considered to be weak, often preferring the security of foreign banks. That said, there was at least no widespread run on deposits.

International perceptions of the Japanese financial sector, already poor, soured further, adding to pressures on profitability. By the end of the year, the 'Japan premium' had jumped from an average of around 10 basis points over the previous year to almost 100 basis points, and it subsequently oscillated between 20 and 80 basis points. The amount that Japanese banks had to pay over and above the government for longer-term borrowings also rose progressively, from 0.2 to 0.8 percentage points by the third quarter of 1998.

U-TURN

As the gravity of the situation deepened, the authorities belatedly came to realize that they had to change course and that this meant resorting to all the available levers of policy. However, as was seen across the world both in the Great Depression and, more recently, in the GFC of the early twenty-first century, major policy recalibrations take time both to reach critical mass and to exert the desired impact. They involve significant information, decision-making and implementation lags. They also tend to go through several iterations, the initial variants of which prove inadequate before they are sufficiently honed to be effective. In Japan this process was further complicated and extended by the societal imperative to build consensus for a course of action. In the meantime, there was extended uncertainty and debate, even panic; considerable market volatility; and the potential for social and political turmoil.

RETURNING TO THE FISCAL ACCELERATOR

The draft budget compiled for the 1998/1999 financial year was initially designed to comply with the austere medium-term approach to fiscal policy laid out in the unfortunately timed FSRA, and it prioritized the restraint of public investment spending that had driven much of the growth that Japan had achieved after the collapse of the bubble. However, it was clear to most observers well before the end of calendar year 1997 that the FSRA had been overtaken by events and would have to be fundamentally revised. As Keynes and, for that matter, Takahashi had suggested in the 1930s, fiscal deflation in the midst of a burgeoning economic downturn was self-defeating. It would both exacerbate the recession and leave the public finances in a worse condition than they were initially.

In May of 1998 a cyclical flexibility clause was added to the Act, and the designated year for the achievement of the Act's targets was pushed out to the 2005/2006 financial year. In the meantime, emergency stimulus measures were prepared, extending to renewed direct tax relief, crucial help for the financial sector, additional loans from public sector financial institutions to ease credit conditions, and the reanimation of public works outlays. These initiatives were formally presented in a ¥16.6 billion package – the largest yet – delivered in April 1998 and financed by two supplementary budgets, one brought down in February 1998, the other in June.

Unfortunately, this amounted to a cumbersome and protracted policy U-turn – one that was greeted negatively both by the financial markets and by the business community. Indeed, remarkably, the initial response of the government to the sharp deterioration of the economy in mid 1997 was merely to promote further deregulation (of which more later), which, while laudable in and of itself, was hardly the most appropriate response to what rapidly developed into a precipitous downturn. It was not until well into 1998 that the fiscal stance became expansionary, by which time the recession was more than a year old and had metastasized alarmingly. In addition, many of the measures taken to support the economy at this time again gave the impression of being rushed and were of limited potency. The income tax cuts were explicitly temporary, which reduced their effectiveness on spending behaviour. The additional public spending programmes were insufficiently thought through, focused on the politically powerful construction sector, and continued to offer low and declining rates of return, while a sizeable portion depended on the compliance of cash-strapped local authorities and were subsequently delivered neither in short order nor in full.

Following the LDP-controlled government's loss of a considerable number of seats in the upper house of the Diet in July 1998, Hashimoto Ryūtarō resigned as prime minister and head of the coalition government and was replaced by Obuchi Keizō, previously the foreign minister. In framing fiscal policy for 1999 it was recognized that the economy remained weak and fragile, and therefore acutely vulnerable to another premature tightening of fiscal policy. What followed was effectively a 15-month budget that combined a second supplementary budget for the 1998/1999 financial year and the regular budget for the 1999/2000 financial year. What is more, the application of the FSRA was suspended.

The expansionary elements of these departures were presented in yet another fiscal package – at ¥23.9 trillion in total, once again the largest yet – in November 1998. It encompassed a permanent reduction in the top marginal rate of income tax from 65% to 50%, costing ¥4.0 trillion, and a reduction in the corporate tax rate from 46.4% to 40%, costing more than ¥2.0 trillion. There was also another ¥8.1 trillion of public investment commitments together with a further series of measures to ease the credit crunch and reduce the rate of corporate failures. These included expanded public lending at subsidized interest rates, not least via the HLC, and, most importantly, a large extension of the credit guarantee programme available to SMEs through to March 2001, which provided the banks with 100% coverage against losses and ultimately swelled to nearly ¥30 trillion (6% of GDP) by 2001.[8] Finally, and perhaps most extraordinarily, the government distributed ¥700 billion of shopping vouchers (¥20,000 per eligible person) with a sixth-month expiry date to families with children and to the elderly to be used for purchases at local retail outlets.[9]

This brought the total headline figure for the eight fiscal packages announced to that date during the 1990s to a staggering ¥103.4 trillion. In overall terms, fiscal policy remained expansionary through the turn of the millennium. The total extent of budgetary largesse cumulated to three percentage points of GDP over a three-year window.

There were by this stage, however, growing concerns that with the consolidated budget deficit exceeding 7% of GDP and the gross burden of debt spiralling to 125% of GDP and beyond, the scope for further fiscal stimulus was now limited given the nation's future demographic challenges. Neither the bond market nor the credit rating agencies had been impressed with the rise in government debt issuance in late 1998 and 1999. Long-term interest rates had risen sharply, threatening to crowd out much of the latest fiscal package's reflationary effect.

In this context, even if fiscal policy remained expansionary, public sector reform took on a higher level of priority. In June 1999 legislation was passed to reorganize 22 existing ministries and government agencies into just 12 entities and to create a new Cabinet Office, all within five years. There was, in addition, a further sale of NTT shares in late 1998, as well as an announcement about greater efforts to improve the prioritization of medium-term public spending programmes, to enhance public project evaluation and procurement, to encourage government decentralization, and to restructure the financing of the Fiscal Investment and Loan Programme (FILP) such that it became subject to more market discipline. Pensions, health care and local government were also highlighted for further surgery, and there was a recognition that the overall tax burden (including social security contributions), which was exceptionally low relative to that in other advanced economies, would have to rise considerably in future.

All this implied that, over the longer term, the consumption tax would have to rise much further; various allowances and tax credits in the personal tax system, not least those for the self-employed, would have to be reduced; and the entire system of tax administration would have to be made more efficient. There was also the increasingly vexed issue of environmental taxation to consider. The fiscal policy agenda for the early years of the twenty-first century stood to be a full one, although whether the economy's performance would be conducive to its completion remained moot.

PUSHING THE LIMITS OF MONETARY ORTHODOXY

As the financial crisis developed, the BOJ was forced aggressively to fulfil its role as lender of last resort.

It injected substantial amounts of liquidity into the interbank market while also providing large loans (albeit sometimes reluctantly) to troubled institutions to allow them to continue to function while they were wound down. What the Bank did in regard to Yamaichi Securities was particularly pertinent. Towards the end of 1997 it became clear that Yamaichi, which had assets of ¥3.7 trillion (or $30 billion), had suffered massive off-balance-sheet losses. The securities house was not just a major player in the domestic financial markets: it also had a sizeable international presence, especially in Europe. As such, it was in many ways akin to Lehman Brothers in 2008. Yet, as noted in the previous chapter, Japan was without a bankruptcy law consistent with an orderly resolution of such a company. Without knowing whether Yamaichi was solvent or insolvent, the BOJ decided to provide unlimited liquidity to the firm, such that all the exposures of domestic and foreign market participants against it were transferred to the central bank. The threat of a systemic meltdown was avoided,[10] but the central bank's balance sheet ballooned in size, expanding at an annualized rate of almost 200% between October 1997 and March 1998.

Reflecting collapsing inflation expectations, widespread risk aversion, the reduced private sector demand for capital and the belief that short-term rates would remain exceptionally low for an extended period, long-term interest rates also fell sharply during this time, ultimately dropping below 0.75% in

October 1998 – then the lowest rate ever recorded – before rebounding into 1999 in the face of the concerns about fiscal sustainability mentioned earlier.

These considerations encouraged the yen to weaken initially against the other major currencies, although the high (40%) weighting of Japan's trade towards the crisis-hit Asian economies meant that there was little adjustment lower for the Japanese currency in effective terms, either nominal or real. Furthermore, the sudden unwinding of the so-called carry trade in mid 1998 ushered in a period of yen strength in the run-up to the millennium.[11] All this in turn acted to keep overall monetary conditions unduly tight for an extended period.[12] They were, for example, consistently more restrictive than during the previous recession of 1991 and 1992. Taylor rule analysis on the basis of various alternative inflation objectives indicates that the call money rate should have been increasingly negative in the late 1990s.[13]

Despite the tightness of monetary conditions, which was exacerbated by weakness in both the supply of and demand for credit, and the initial inertia in fiscal policy described above, there was once again a difficult-to-fathom reluctance on the part of the BOJ to reduce its call money target rate further. It was held at the then record low of just under 0.5% for a total of three years, and throughout the first 15 months of the crisis.

It was only in September 1998, after a third successive quarterly contraction in real GDP had been announced and a sovereign default by Russia had added to global uncertainty and risk aversion, that the central bank took the plunge and cut by a further 0.25 percentage points, adding that it would also provide whatever degree of liquidity was required to encourage market stability. It then followed this departure with a series of measures designed to enhance the effectiveness of the policy. These included a blanket guarantee on all deposits and interbank transactions; the beginning of a progressive expansion of the range and duration of the securities accepted, and the counterparties permitted to take part in, its open-market operations; and the extension of a temporary lending facility to refinance 50% of the increase in loans provided by financial institutions and so help firms with their year-end funding.[14]

The sudden jump in bond yields around the turn of 1998 in the wake of the November fiscal package, together with the persistent strength of the yen, then sparked pressure for another easing of monetary policy. This went hand in hand with a wider debate about the overall approach the BOJ should take in the exceptional circumstances of the time. Discussions extended to whether or not it should now shift its focus to more quantitative intermediate goals, such as monetary base or commercial bank reserve growth, or the expansion rate of its balance sheet; whether it should adopt an explicit inflation target to anchor inflation expectations; whether, as one senior official and a number of outside commentators suggested, it should *raise* policy rates to boost the income of a household sector that was a net creditor; and even whether it should be deliberately irresponsible in its approach to policy in an effort to boost inflation and reduce real interest rates.[15] There was also some discussion about resort to a repeat of the Takahashi strategy of the early 1930s.

In the end, in February 1999 the call rate was cut further to 0.15% and subsequently encouraged, through generous liquidity injections, to fall as close to zero as possible. This marked the first time that the lower bound on interest rates had been approached in a major advanced economy in the postwar era. Then, in April, the Bank stated that this near-zero-rate stance would be maintained until a steady growth path emerged and deflationary concerns were over. This was another path-breaking measure: the first application of explicit 'forward policy guidance'.

Market rates at longer terms subsequently dropped to similar record lows to the call rate, and long-term rates reversed much of their previous rise. In the autumn of 1999 the Bank announced that it would supplement its efforts to ensure the permeation of the zero-rate policy with the acceptance of US Treasury bonds as collateral to help address potential problems emerging from the Y2K issue.[16]

Notwithstanding the BOJ's pioneering initiatives, resort to more radical monetary policy options was at that stage eschewed for a wide range of reasons, some of which appear contradictory. They included, for example, the legal and organizational complexities involved; scepticism about their potency; fears that inflation, not least in asset markets, would be rekindled; and the potentially damaging real economy, financial and political side-effects that might ensue. Where the latter were concerned, there were worries, for example, that the explicit adoption of quantitative easing might slow down restructuring, raise risk premia, depress confidence, increase savings, expose the Bank to large balance sheet losses, and, as in the late 1930s, offer additional degrees of spending freedom to potentially irresponsible politicians, thereby stoking excessive inflation. Besides, the Bank was by this stage already buying outright some ¥400 billion a month of government bonds. Ostensibly, this was consistent with the long-term trend increase in the demand for cash within the economy, but it could be argued – and indeed was argued, by the Bank – that it in itself already represented a significant degree of debt monetization.

CHANGES TO THE BANK OF JAPAN LAW

Beyond the caution surrounding the monetary policy regime, significant and long-overdue changes were made to the institutional framework within which the BOJ operated as the crisis mounted. In particular, April 1998 saw a new legal structure for the Bank come into effect. Encouraged by institutional developments in other economies, and by the widespread belief that a more independent BOJ would have responded more effectively to the excesses of the late 1980s, this embodied the repeal and replacement of various laws dating back to February 1942 and World War II that had left it subject to the control of the MOF and the government.[17] Consequently, both the BOJ's freedom of action and the transparency of its decision-making processes were enhanced, and Japan followed the example of greater central bank autonomy and openness set since the late 1980s by New Zealand, Canada, Chile, the Czech Republic, the United Kingdom and others.

Under the new legal framework, the primary objectives of the central bank were twofold. First, there was the pursuit of price stability and thereby the sound development of the economy. However, as suggested above, price stability was not at this stage formally defined, which complicated the response to the crisis of the late 1990s.[18] Second, there was the smooth settlement of payments across the financial system, and thereby the encouragement of overall financial stability.

Notwithstanding the extraordinary and rapidly evolving circumstances in which the new law came into force, the basic rationale was to improve the credibility of the Bank's commitment to low inflation, to reduce uncertainty, and in the process to lower associated risk premia in financial market prices.

To achieve these goals, the administrative architecture of the Bank was remodelled. There would be a single decision-making body: the Policy Board, which comprised the Bank's governor, two deputy governors and six other members drawn from beyond the Bank. Two representatives of the government (in practice one from MOF and one from the EPA) could attend the meetings of the board, as necessary. However, while they could make propositions, including the demand that the implementation of a policy decision was delayed until the following meeting, they were barred from voting.

Governors and board members were appointed by the government for a period of five years, and their appointments had to be confirmed by both houses of the Diet. Up to six executive directors and a number of policy advisors were appointed by the MOF on the recommendation of the Policy Board. Members of the board other than the governor and his deputies would be chosen on the basis of academic experience or proven expertise in economics or finance. The board would also have to publish an immediate summary of its discussions, together with a full record of meetings at a later date. Every six months the Bank would in addition have to report on its activities to the Diet.

Because of retirements and resignations on the part of a number of senior Bank officials – including the governor, Matsushita Yasuo, and his deputy, Fukui Toshihiko, both of whom accepted responsibility for a series of all-too-familiar bribery and information scandals during the mid 1990s – only one of the top officials from the previous regime at the Bank remained in place in April 1998. To restore the Bank's reputation, and give the impression of wiping the slate clean, the new governor, Hayami Masaru, was recruited from beyond the ranks of either the Bank or the MOF.

Although he had worked at the BOJ for 34 years from 1947 until 1981, and during that time come to occupy a number of senior positions including that of executive director, Hayami had latterly been the president of the trading company Nissho Iwai.[19] He was to prove a controversial appointment. Indeed, on occasion the criticism of his record from domestic politicians and the international press was to turn decidedly personal and ugly. This was not so much because of his previous history at the Bank or anything untoward he had done during his business career, although his record at Nissho Iwai was, to say the least, chequered. Rather, it was because he was already 73 years old when he returned to the Bank (and he sometimes acted his age in public) and, more substantively, he was not afraid to express his scepticism about unorthodox policy initiatives and his belief that deflation could only be defeated once politicians had adequately confronted the underlying structural problems of the Japanese economy. Hayami's commitment to the need for aggressive monetary reflation therefore came across as less than complete, and in this context he was an important catalyst for the Bank's sluggish and largely conventional response to the intensification of the crisis in 1998.

Hayami's policy conservatism, and in particular his lack of enthusiasm for policies that might have involved closer cooperation with the government, may also have been encouraged by the BOJ's newly enjoyed autonomy. That is to say, he became something of a prisoner of its greater independence and the need to establish its credibility under the new regime. In this, he may have been influenced by the fact that there was, in contrast to the old 1942 legislation, limited guidance in the new Bank of Japan Law as to how the impact of unconventional monetary policy on the bank's balance sheet and matters of its longer-term solvency were to be dealt with.

But whatever the thinking behind his views, their importance should not be underestimated. Monetary policy is always something of a confidence trick. It works in part through the management of expectations and partly because people thereby believe it will work. If the governor of the central bank were casting aspersions on monetary policy's potency, why would others refrain from doing so? And if the markets and the general population were sceptical about its effects, then, in the sort of situation Japan found itself in during the late 1990s, there was a risk that deflation expectations would become embedded.

BELATED RESORT TO PUBLIC FUNDS

With the dramatic intensification of the financial sector's problems in the autumn of 1997, whatever the thrust of monetary and fiscal policy, it became clear that the large-scale provision of public funds that had so far been eschewed by successive governments was unavoidable if the situation was to be stabilized. In late December it was announced that PCA powers would be applied in a 'flexible manner' until April 1999 for banks not operating internationally. More pertinently, up to ¥30 trillion ($240 billion, or 5.75% of GDP) would be made available before the end of the 1997/1998 financial year to bolster the resources of the DIC further (¥17 trillion), thereby protecting the depositors of failed institutions; and to recapitalize the balance sheets of weak but solvent banks (¥13 trillion), and so accelerate bad loan write-offs. The magnitude of the funding proffered was influenced by the NPL totals detailed in financial entities' half-year statements; that is to say, ¥28.1 trillion (4% of total loans, and 5.6% of GDP), slightly higher than end-of-March figure of ¥27.9 trillion.

However, the government also asked the banks to classify their loans on the basis of the probability that they be repaid, and this indicated that even at what was to prove a relatively early stage in the downturn, only about 88% of all bank loans were viewed as being reasonably certain to be reimbursed in full. Furthermore, the lion's share of the remainder was considered to be at considerable risk. The suggestion once again was that the NPL problem ran much deeper than hitherto presented, and that the public funds made available at this stage would in due course prove inadequate.

Notwithstanding this, rather than forcing the banks to use the public funds made available to write off their bad loans, the authorities left it up to the banks to request assistance. The banks, however, were sufficiently fearful of the stigma of the restructuring conditions attached to the money on offer – even though they were less than stringent[20] – that in the end only ¥1.8 trillion (0.4% of GDP), a small fraction of the sum available and about 4.7% of total Tier 1 and Tier 2 bank capital, was utilized – and even then in a rather indiscriminate fashion. Nearly all the banks requested a mere ¥100 billion in the form of subordinated debentures or loans with a call option at their discretion, and the government was reluctant to separate out the weakest banks. The average cost of the funds was below the level that would have been demanded in the market.

This is not to deny that this effort at recapitalization had some positive effect. The banks' accounts for the end of the 1997/1998 financial year revealed that the capital adequacy ratios (CARs) of applicants had risen slightly and that most of the major banks were comfortably able to meet their requirements.

However, in achieving this they were helped by the fact that, although they were mandated to begin to adopt the more stringent US standards for the reporting of problem loans,[21] a number of other accounting adjustments – including freedom to write up the value of land assets from acquisition cost to market price, and the deduction of clients' time deposits holdings from loan balances – were announced to boost their capital position and in an effort to encourage them to lend.

Meanwhile, there was no let-up in the recession. Business confidence remained at a low ebb, credit intermediation was still dysfunctional, the inefficiency and overcapacity in the financial sector had not gone away, and the concerns about the banks' attitude to transparency and disclosure around NPLs only burgeoned. Financial market pressures – including renewed stock price weakness, credit rating downgrades, a rewidening of the Japan premium and a similar jump in the margin the banks paid over the risk-free rate for longer-term funding – therefore intensified as 1998 progressed. What is more, the Clinton administration in the United States – already deeply involved in the IMF bailouts of Japan's Asian neighbours, and increasingly concerned about the potential for financial contagion from Japan to other major economies – called on the Japanese government to adopt a forceful approach to the crisis. Given all this, the authorities had little choice but to respond with a more comprehensive strategy for dealing with the banking sector's problems. Not for the first time, the government of the day could point to *Gaiatsu* as the reason it had to take a difficult decision at home.

The upshot was what was termed the 'Total Plan'. This was initially thrashed out in July of 1998 and was finally passed into law in October, while in the meantime the new FSA and the BOJ conducted their own audits of all the major banks. The Total Plan framework, and the associated Financial Revitalization Law and Bank Recapitalization Act, allowed the temporary nationalization, public administration or sale or liquidation of failed banks, and it included greatly increased funds for recapitalization. A Financial Revitalization Committee (FRC) was established to oversee the FSA until 2001 and to assume responsibility for crisis management.

A second supplementary budget for the 1998/1999 financial year earmarked ¥60 trillion (12% of GDP) for the financial crisis. This included the ¥17 trillion from the initial plan allocated to the DIC plus ¥43 trillion in additional funds that could be applied at the regulator's disposal. Of the latter sum, ¥25 trillion was assigned to the recapitalization of weak but viable banks and ¥18 trillion put towards the establishment of 'bridge banks' to manage, collect and dispose of failed institutions' bad assets and allocated for temporary nationalizations of failing banks. The latter would be undertaken by the Resolution and Collection Corporation (RCC), a wholly owned subsidiary of the DIC, which grew out of the RCB established to resolve the *Jusen* crisis. Importantly, the RCC was also allowed to buy compromised assets from solvent banks.

The latter part of 1998 and early 1999 saw a wave of bank failures that extended beyond smaller regional entities to the systemically important Long Term Credit Bank (October 1998) and Nippon Credit Bank (December 1998), both of which were found to be undercapitalized and were subsequently nationalized. In each case, the condition of the bank's balance sheet was discovered to be much worse than had hitherto been reported. In the case of Long Term Credit Bank, for example, its capital deficit was initially estimated at ¥340 billion, but by August 1999 the shortfall was put at ¥3.5 trillion! The 'window dressing' of accounts – or sometimes outright fraud – was shown to be rife, illustrating once again the historical shortcomings of Japanese auditing practices and underlining the huge uncertainties surrounding the issue of NPLs.

In March 1999 the remaining large banks received further, much larger, injections of public capital – ranging from ¥150 billion to ¥1 trillion and totalling ¥7.4 trillion (1.5% of GDP, or some four times as much as was provided in the first round of recapitalization a year earlier) – to resolve their NPL problems in return for various commitments to the FRC to rationalize their business models, the progress of which would be regularly reviewed.

Most of these injections took the form of preferred equity, which qualified for Tier 1 status in CAR minima. The rest took the form of subordinated debt, which counted towards Tier 2 capital. The price charged varied considerably from bank to bank, although it was lower on average than with the previous round of injections. Recipient banks also planned to raise an additional ¥2.2 trillion in capital from private sources, most of which was from *Keiretsu* affiliates. With the government providing a quarter of these banks' total capital and a third of their Tier 1 capital, BIS CAR requirements were subsequently comfortably met.

The banks' and other financial institutions' NPL estimates and provisioning standards subsequently improved somewhat, and it became harder to hide financial losses with impunity. In March 1999 the NPL total for all deposit-taking institutions was put at ¥38.7 trillion, or 5.6% of credit exposure and 7.9% of GDP, as against ¥38.0 trillion in March 1998. For the major banks, the equivalent figures were ¥20.3 trillion, 5.7% and 4.1%. The provisioning requirements for the recipient banks became 100% for loans to those in bankruptcy, around 70% for loans to those considered to be in danger of bankruptcy and without coverage of collateral or guarantees, and 15% for loans considered to require close monitoring. The major banks had previously only provisioned 52.1% for those in danger of bankruptcy and 1.6% for those in need of attention: 10.4% and 1.2% of their loan books, respectively.

In this environment, the FSA quickly gained credibility, and a semblance of financial stability was re-established. The Japan premium retreated to 1997 levels and bank stocks rallied. Additionally, late 1999 and early 2000 saw the announcement of mergers that would in due course result in the establishment of two new megabanks that could compete with Bank of Tokyo Mitsubishi, the one major Japanese bank to have come through the 1990s with a portion of its integrity intact. First, Fuji Bank, Dai-ichi Kango and the Industrial Bank of Japan came together to form the Mizuho Financial Group, and then Sanwa and Tokai combined to form UFJ (the United Financial of Japan).

The risk of a systemic collapse under the huge weight of NPLs was fended off. There remained a sense, however, that the conditions demanded for the public funds were unduly soft. While foreign operations were wound down, the number of directors reduced and operating expenses cut, remuneration incentives for bank executives remained absent; the efforts to reduce capacity through mergers only went so far; investment in new technology was under-emphasized; and, most importantly of all, credit risks were still neither adequately assessed nor priced. At the same time, the disposal of real estate capital was limited, in part because of its legal complexity. With a limited focus on ROE, bank profitability stayed low. The risk therefore remained that when the next cyclical downturn arrived, and further problem loans built up, the banks' balance sheets would again be unable to sustain the necessary write offs, more entities would have to be closed, and the process of recapitalization would need to be repeated.[22]

RECOVERY (OF A SORT)

In response to the broad-based reorientation of policy, and the re-establishment of a degree of stability in the financial sector, the dramatic downturn which began in April 1997 – and which was at its worst towards the end of 1998 – drew to a close in 1999 and a modest and fragile upswing ensued. Initially encouraged by another strong surge in public sector investment in Q1, average real GDP growth for the year edged into positive territory, while the pick-up in business confidence, industrial production, manufacturing profits and exports, not least to a rebounding Asia, was more impressive and consistent across the year. The stock market also recovered somewhat, with the Nikkei 225 rising from below 13,000 in October 1988 to almost 19,000 by the end of 1999.

However, the rise in public works spending rapidly subsided through the year as local government outlays fell short of expectations, and a further ¥18 trillion (3.4% of GDP) stimulus package (the ninth since August 1992, bringing the cumulative headline total to ¥132.4 trillion), including some

¥6.8 trillion of additional government investment projects, was announced in November 1999. In the meantime, the labour market remained extremely weak, with an increasing proportion of those who were unemployed out of work for an extended period and with the participation rate in decline; the real estate market retreated further; bank lending was still falling; and prices and wages continued to drop in year-over-year terms, although thankfully there was no sign of a downward spiral developing. There were also the vexed issues of how the economy would perform when the substantial degree of macro policy support was withdrawn and how the financial sector would cope with any further shocks. Japan was clearly not yet out of the woods, and its structural shortcomings were far from fully addressed.

ADAPTING TO GLOBALIZATION

Persistent and well-designed structural reform, as we have already noted, is a vital component of economic policy. It helps an economy to adjust constructively in the face of the never-ending progression of perturbations that inevitably confront it and to achieve a brisk and sustainable growth of productive capacity by ensuring that resources flow readily from low-productivity to high-productivity activities and from declining sectors into growing sectors. In the process, it delivers lower prices and a stimulus to domestic demand and improves living standards. Some improvements had been made in the 1980s and early 1990s but, as illustrated in the previous chapter, market forces across much of the service sector remained compromised by government interventions of one form or another, inflating Japan's cost structure, constraining the development of new technologies and firms, and imposing a dead weight on productivity. Much work remained to be done.

The traumatic events of 1997 and 1998 no doubt added to the pressure for reform. But there were a range of other fundamental considerations that made it essential that Japan made significant mutually reinforcing advances in this key area of policy. Globalization was intensifying, with the increasing integration into the world economy of China and the countries of the former Soviet Union, ushering in an age of more intense international competition and increased pressure for companies to produce innovative goods at attractive prices. The influence of new information technologies was burgeoning, further expanding markets and their contestability. The initial eclipse of the bubble economy had left in its wake significant imbalances in corporate sector personnel, fixed capital and financing that needed to be unwound, especially in small and medium-sized non-manufacturing companies. There were many resources that needed to be reallocated and utilized more efficiently. The rapid ageing of the population, meanwhile, put a particular premium on productivity enhancement if the economy were to continue to expand at anything like an acceptable rate. The nature of corporate governance was beginning to diversify, with the gradual erosion of the influence of the *Keiretsu* and the main bank model, and its high dependence on debt. Corporate pension funds were chronically underfunded, having consistently failed to generate the returns necessary to meet their obligations. Finally, notwithstanding the demonstrable flexibility of the Japanese labour market over several decades, the systems of lifetime employment and seniority-based wages were looking increasingly inconsistent with slower underlying growth and demographic change.

Japan's supply-side to do list was long and challenging.

Despite the risk that tougher economic times, and the immediate social and political imperatives that went with them, would encourage policymakers to call a temporary – or, for that matter, lasting – halt to the process and protect the status quo, successive Japanese governments continued the process of structural reform during the late 1990s, Moreover, the measures went beyond those that were touched on above – that is, changes to financial sector regulation, the new legal framework for the BOJ, the tax system, the manner in which the public sector operated and the modifications to the social security system – and embodied the strategic decision to move from a system of regulation-based prior intervention to one based on retroactive supervision, with a greater role for the judicial system.

The years 1996 through 1999 saw a succession of revised three-year action plans for reform that successively embodied thousands of initiatives for different parts of the economy. As these plans were put into operation, to varying degrees, entry barriers were further reduced, red tape cut, cartels weakened and competition enhanced in the distribution, telecoms, air and land transport, electricity supply, petroleum products, construction and agricultural sectors. At the same time, the lifting of the 50-year-old ban on holding companies was designed to encourage restructuring and synergistic M&A activity, and it was made easier for job-placement firms, including for temporary workers, to operate.

Despite these continued efforts to reduce government intervention and control, however, the rhetoric of reform still went some way beyond its substance. Perhaps unsurprisingly, the process remained haphazard and pedestrian, for the most part embodying a plethora of minor technical recommendations and proposals (many of which were restatements of existing announcements) rather than immediate sweeping changes. Urgency was lacking. It was the low-hanging fruit that was harvested. There were once again a lot of earnest progress reports and analyses of the potential positives of reform for the economy, but a sharp break with previous regulatory practices was for the most part eschewed. Another issue was that there was no overarching independent body driving the process.

At the end of the 1990s, therefore, the influence of the small and medium-sized business lobbies and their LDP sympathizers, which had the most to lose from reform, remained palpable. Japan was an economy still only in gradual transition from heavy regulation and bureaucratic paternalism to a more market-based system. There was much to be done, not least in agriculture, where producer support levels remained very high; in telecoms, where NTT retained important monopoly powers; in the area of land-use taxation and regulation, which continued to encourage resource inefficiency and high real estate prices; and where the ability of companies to confront over-staffing and engage in larger-scale redundancies were concerned. And Japan could ill-afford further foot-dragging.

A LOST DECADE

Rather than gradually emerging from the post-bubble asset price deflation quagmire of the first half of the 1990s as most domestic policymakers and many external commentators expected, Japan instead saw its economic crisis deepen alarmingly as the millennium drew to a close. A nation previously feted as the world's most successful economy and a role model for others had in effect suffered a lost decade, the details of which make for sobering reading.

Japan had one of the worst growth performance records in the OECD, especially after 1992. It suffered not one but two catastrophic recessions, the second of which was one of the sharpest seen in a developed nation since the Great Depression. The recessions bookended what was a brief, and for the most part hesitant and uneven, phase of recovery. There was consistent downward pressure on the price level, including a two-thirds decline in real estate values and an extended financial crisis that in 1998 verged on complete systematic meltdown. Interest rates plumbed depths that were hitherto unknown in any economy at any time, while government indebtedness exploded to levels normally associated with major wars.

At the macro level, the country continued to run up large external surpluses and accumulate a huge stock of foreign assets, but even these can be interpreted as symbols of weakness – the result of shattered confidence and a chronic excess of private sector savings – rather than strength. At the micro level, many Japanese companies remained household names but they had become increasingly multinational in terms of production and outlook, while the domestic landscape remained notable for service sector inefficiency, high prices and a swelling corporate underclass.

Japan's demise in the 1990s reflects a toxic mixture of the cyclical and the structural: exogenous shocks and internally propagated problems; and numerous policy errors. As detailed in the two previous chapters, the initial trigger was the deliberate monetary-policy-induced deflation of an increasingly frenzied and socially divisive asset price bubble at a time when the world economy was slowing down. But what is also clear is that monetary policy was then left too tight for too long. It took the BOJ some nine years to bring the policy rate to the zero bound, and because of the descent into deflation, real short-term borrowing costs remained positive more or less throughout, which was clearly less than appropriate for such a compromised financial system and macroeconomy. The searing experience of undue monetary policy laxity in the late 1980s prompted the opposite mistake in the 1990s, underlining how policymakers all too often become prisoners of their own history, or at least of their most recent mishap. There was then the matter of a BOJ governor who appeared to question whether monetary policy, or at least unorthodox monetary policy, had any potency at all.

The high interest rates of the early 1990s raised the cost of capital, slashed private sector net worth and provoked swingeing cuts in investment spending. But by the time that policy rates were being reduced, business and consumer confidence were weak and fragile, and borrower balance sheet adjustments restricted the demand for credit at any given level of interest. What is more, with banking sector profitability crushed between the hammer of collapsing collateral values and the anvil of the evaporation of hidden profits on equity holdings, the willingness to lend was similarly constrained.

Yet, while non-performing loans escalated to enormous, if uncertain, levels and the process of financial intermediation was severely compromised, the problems of the banks were allowed to fester, until, following the broader Asian Crisis, the system threatened to collapse altogether. Only then was recapitalization resorted to and a supervisory and prudential framework remotely consistent with the reorganization of the sector forthcoming. At a minimum, earlier action to recognize problem loans and raise adequate provisioning would have helped identify the capital shortage and jump-start the process of restructuring.

Fiscal policy was equally flawed. In contrast to the early 1930s under Finance Minister Takahashi, it was largely uncoordinated with monetary policy. Rather, it was applied in a rushed, episodic and inconsistent manner, with scant regard given to cost control or economic efficiency. The reversion to restraint in 1997 was a particularly egregious error. The private sector response to expansionary budgetary initiatives remained disappointing. Exigency and at-times-crass political manipulation of spending priorities led to the channelling of resources into low-return public works projects, often in out-of-the-way places, and into loans that added to microeconomic distortions and the contingent liabilities of government.[23] The cost of land purchase continued to take up a large proportion of the money allocated. Planned investments regularly exceeded actual implementation.

Tax cuts were assigned a secondary role, their effectiveness stunted by their frequently temporary nature, and despite some changes the overall tax system was allowed to remain replete with iniquities and at odds with the necessities of the nation's rapidly aging population. Notwithstanding their regularity and headline size, Japanese fiscal packages failed to exert a lasting influence on growth expectations, no doubt in part because weaknesses in the banking sector curtailed their multiplier effects. Overall, they typically temporarily filled holes in aggregate demand rather than establishing a launching pad for a sustained expansion.

What also became clear over the course of the 1990s, and especially in the second half of the decade, was that the feverish speculation of the bubble economy had glossed over a multitude of deepening structural problems. By the onset of the Asian Crisis, Japan was beset by a chronic misallocation of resources, with its traditional engines of growth – demographics and capital accumulation – exhausted and both the private and public sectors weighed down by excessive leverage. For its part, corporate Japan had too many people, too much plant and equipment and too much debt in places where they produced too little and at too high a cost. There was an urgent need to construct a new growth model based on domestic demand, the more efficient use of labour and capital, and consumer rather than producer sovereignty.

However, with the buffer of a large structural external surplus buying it the sort of time denied its Asian neighbours in 1997 and 1998, Japan found it hard to cast off the statism that had been at the core of its development since the Meiji Restoration and that remained a notable feature of its post-war high-growth era. Corporate restructuring was slow in coming and remained largely confined to the larger firms, especially those in manufacturing. Successive governments were happy to pay lip service to structural reform and deregulation but – in the absence of a coherent concept of the state's role during a period of market-led growth and suitable independent oversight – progress was disappointing: hesitant, fragmented, disjointed. The public sector's influence in the economy remained too pervasive, along with the socialization of risk and moral hazard. Transparency and accountability were still lacking, and too many markets were distorted, uncompetitive and vulnerable to special interests. Whole islands of the economy – agriculture, construction, smaller companies, even telecoms – remained to a significant degree sheltered from the chill winds of competition. Insolvent 'zombie' firms were allowed to linger and constrain investment by sound firms.

It is difficult to escape the conclusion that Japan's lost decade had many roots, in social, cultural and political factors. Failure to come to terms adequately with the economy's deep-seated malaise and the reluctance of business managers to revise customs such as lifetime employment and seniority-based wages can be traced in part to the hubris that accompanied the catalogue of previous successes. The opacity of Japanese accounting and supervisory procedures and the predominance of shame as a motivating force in a consensus-based society added to the inertia in the process of understanding and adjustment. Equally, the intensity of 1990s global capitalism – with its unforgiving competition, its wide income inequalities and its requirement for rapid decision-making – sat rather uncomfortably in a society that has also entertained a distrust of free markets, looked for guidance from the centre and prided itself on its inclusiveness and homogeneity. Last, the democratic process remained idiosyncratic and immature. Japan was in effect a one-party gerontocracy where gerrymandering was rife, where prevarication and procrastination were a way of life, and where patronage was often dispensed with brazen vulgarity.

The question was, where would Japan go as it entered a new century? Could its politicians and broader policy-making community cast off old habits? How would the country address the fact that, in the eyes of many, macroeconomic policy had effectively been exhausted? Could it finally embrace a more aggressive and time-constrained strategy of deregulation and reform? How would it cope should another large external shock strike it? Would such a shock finally be the catalyst for fundamental change, or would Japan timidly fall back on a dangerous strategy of 'economic Micawberism'? Would the population remain so stoic if the economic woes of the previous decade continued?

CHAPTER 6

Leaving the Lost Decade Behind

'Continuance is strength' — Japanese proverb

GETTING REAL

Some four years after the previous bout of optimism, the dawn of the new century brought fresh hope that the economic outlook had finally changed for the better, and that a decade of stagnation, deflation and dysfunction in the banking sector could be consigned to the past. Unfortunately, the year 2000 was to prove another false dawn. The economy was soon to become mired in a third downturn since the collapse of the bubble and yet another episode of acute financial crisis that threatened to descend into complete meltdown.

This latest bout of trauma, however, served finally to concentrate policy-makers' minds sufficiently for them to put in place a thoroughgoing and lasting response to the financial sector's problems, while the corporate sector subsequently embarked on an impressive period of much-needed balance sheet restructuring. Underpinned by a sympathetic international environment, a sustained expansion would follow that endured until the GFC plunged the entire world into its deepest downturn since the 1930s.

That said, the Japan of the early years of the twenty-first century was a rather different animal to that of its extended post-war boom and epoch of unrelenting outperformance. Even if its export industries continued to impress, it was a more mature and less vibrant economy. Full employment did not return. Deflation stubbornly refused to disappear. Asset markets struggled to recover. Interest rates remained exceptionally low. And the burden of public sector debt continued to escalate to extraordinary peacetime levels. The challenges therefore remained many and various.

FLATTERING TO DECEIVE ONCE MORE

The recovery that had commenced in 1999 briefly strengthened in the first half of 2000, broadening out beyond exports and manufacturing production to services, at least to a limited extent. Business confidence and investment picked up, and the labour market stabilized. While the continued tendency of prices to fall was hardly welcomed, it at least helped to sustain real incomes and personal consumption.

At around 1.5%–2.0% a year, underlying growth potential remained less than half what it had been prior to the bursting of the bubble, and the cyclical upturn remained fragile. The dominant driving force for the expansion was the global IT boom rather than internal considerations. Beyond that, Japan's structural vulnerabilities were very much in evidence. The profitability of many domestic sectors remained modest, and the investment 'accelerator' – enfeebled by excesses of debt, capacity and labour, especially in non-manufacturing – was a pale shadow of its old self. Unemployment proved reluctant to decline and the share of long-term joblessness remained on a rising trend. Wage growth was barely positive, and to the extent that wages did grow, it was largely because of overtime and bonus payments, such as they were. The household saving rate was stubbornly elevated.

In the background, NPL disposal was laborious and bank balance sheets remained weak, despite the recapitalization of 1999. A return to profitability at the banks in large part reflected further sales of cross-shareholdings at a time when the stock market was temporarily buoyant. Indeed, the Japanese stock market peaked in 2000 at a price-to-earnings (P/E) ratio higher than during the bubble! Excluding stock and real estate holding disposals, the major banks continued to record losses, as they had done on this basis since the early 1990s. Lending continued to fall, as both the demand for and the supply of credit stayed at a low ebb.

Three considerations conspired to bring the recovery to an end.

First, and most importantly, the global IT boom of the late 1990s turned to bust after the spring of 2000, tipping the world into recession in the following year. Global equity prices began an extended retreat from their highs, which unsurprisingly engulfed Japan's stock indices. The Nikkei index fell by more than half over the next two years, to plumb yet-deeper post-bubble lows. The heady days of 1989 seemed a world away.

Second, once the impact of the ¥18.0 trillion November 1999 fiscal package faded, and in particular once public investment outlays fell away, the private sector of the economy lost a vital crutch and, as had been the case since the bursting of the bubble, struggled to stand on its own two feet. Fiscal policy was tightened by more than a percentage point of GDP in 2001.

Third, under the guidance of Hayami Masaru, the BOJ, which had seemed impatient to end its policy of zero interest rates plus generous liquidity provision (ZIRP) almost since its inception, edged the call money target up to 0.25% in August 2000. It did so despite rising bankruptcies, continued deflation, the weakness of lending activity and broad money growth, and the fact that monetary conditions had tightened sharply over the previous three years as real interest rates and the real effective exchange rate moved higher. The Bank's rationale for this change of stance was that the ZIRP had always been a temporary response to a specific set of difficult circumstances that had now elapsed. Moreover, there was in its eyes a mounting risk of renewed asset price excess, unmoored inflation expectations and other unwelcome ramifications from the policy, including reduced pressure for restructuring at the banks and in the broader corporate sector, and delays in fiscal adjustment. Not for the first time since 1990, the Bank's judgement and timing were to prove maladroit; it was to run into considerable criticism as a result, not least from the government.[1]

In hindsight, it is clear that the Japanese economy had begun to lose momentum just as the BOJ abandoned the ZIRP, and it was, from that point onwards, heading inexorably towards another recession. Inventories rapidly accumulated. Exports, industrial production, corporate profits and business and consumer confidence all slumped. Real GDP growth slowed, then turned negative for three successive quarters in 2001, and, even allowing for reduced growth potential, a large output gap once again opened up, deepening deflationary pressure. The unemployment rate rose to yet another post-war high of almost 5.5% of the workforce, and there was a growing shift towards the employment of cheaper temporary and part-time workers as firms struggled to curtail labour costs. Household income growth, already feeble, softened once again as overall wages fell in absolute terms.

Most importantly of all, however, the financial sector's problems rapidly re-intensified. The NPL total rebounded. The scope for the banks to fall back on unrealized stock gains to sustain their profitability and meet their capital requirements was curtailed by the Nikkei's renewed slide. The value of loan collateral continued to decline as the extended slump in land prices was given renewed impetus.

ACTION STATIONS AGAIN

This series of events necessitated yet another major policy response. A fiscal package, this time amounting to ¥11 trillion (2% of GDP) in headline terms, was launched in October 2000, although on this occasion less than half of the total was devoted to public infrastructure outlays and none of that amount was allocated to the cash-strapped local governments. The stimulative impact was concentrated into the first quarter of 2001 and rapidly dissipated thereafter. Indeed, the primary effect of the package was to slow the rate of decline in public investment spending temporarily rather than reverse its course.

As we shall see, this marked the onset of a period when fiscal policy, and in particular public works investment, was to be much less to the fore in the process of sustaining the economy than had been the case in the 1990s. The priority instead switched to fiscal consolidation and tax and public sector reform, although it should be stressed that progress in all these areas was to prove halting and – in the case of the budget deficit and the debt burden – short lived.

In the absence of a sustained and powerful dose of fiscal largesse, greater onus fell on monetary policy to address the new downturn. The Hayami BOJ had to unwind its dreadfully timed tightening of August 2000 within a mere seven months. Furthermore, with many politicians and much of the wider commentariat questioning the value of its independence as the need for such a humiliating volte-face became clear, the Bank was impelled to adopt a new and, for that time, radical modus operandi in the search for a means to reinvigorate the process of monetary policy transmission and turn the economy around.

QUANTITY SUPERSEDES PRICE

Encouraged by MOF officials and members of the government, rather than focusing on the overnight rate as an intermediate target, the BOJ took the decision to concentrate instead on maintaining ample liquidity in the form of the outstanding current account balances (effectively the sum of required and excess reserves) held with it by the commercial banks. The overnight rate duly fell back to zero, but, more pertinently, by highlighting the role of bank reserves in policy, the BOJ became the first central bank in the modern era to embark on a strategy of quantitative easing, or QE.[2]

The March 2001 announcement by the Bank proved to be the thin end of an increasingly unorthodox wedge of monetary policy – one that endured until March 2006 and was then applied with even greater force during the GFC and its aftermath. The BOJ's direction of travel in the post-bubble period was to provide a template that other central banks would in due course choose to follow once their own official interest rates had converged on the zero bound.

In this context, the full extent of the BOJ's 2001 regime shift – which continued once Hayami Masaru had been replaced as governor in March 2003 by the resurrected Fukui Toshihiko – is worth dwelling on in some detail.[3] The new strategy came to embody six evolving elements.

First, as deflation remained a stubborn problem, and financial fragility continued to be a source of concern, the current account balance (reserve) target was raised progressively from ¥5 trillion at the policy's outset to a peak of some ¥30–35 trillion from April 2004. There were also several episodes – including after the September 11, 2001 terrorist attacks on the United States and at the end of successive accounting years – when the Bank decided that it should temporarily be more generous in its provision of funds to the banking system than was suggested by its official objective.

Second, the BOJ at the outset committed to continuing to use its ¥400 billion per month of outright purchases of long-term JGBs as part of its liquidity provisions, in the process exerting downward pressure on bond yields and potentially moderating any 'crowding out' of private sector activity. However, these regular bond-buying operations were eventually ramped up to ¥1.2 trillion a month from May 2004 as well as being extended to a wider range of maturities. Consequently, in an echo of the Takahashi approach of the 1930s, the Bank found itself indirectly monetizing more than a third of the general government net borrowing requirement. Bond yields remained below 2% throughout the early 2000s, often traded below 1% and bottomed out at around 0.35% in April 2003.

Third, in addition the Bank progressively expanded the breadth and maturity of its short-term money market operations – in due course extending them to corporate bonds, commercial paper (CP), asset-backed commercial paper (ABCP) and other asset-backed securities (ABSs) – as it sought to address specific weak points in financial intermediation.

Fourth, beyond expanding and finessing its management of market liquidity, to better manage expectations, the BOJ committed to maintaining its quantitative approach to policy until the core CPI inflation rate became positive on a sustained basis, thereby strengthening the initial forward guidance that had been issued in 1999 but which the Bank seemingly ignored in August 2000. In October 2003 the guidance was further refined. Thereafter, the Bank undertook to maintain its super-abundant liquidity provision around the zero bound until actual inflation had been positive for some months and a majority on the Policy Board believed inflation would remain in positive territory.

Fifth, towards the end of 2002 the BOJ established a standby facility that allowed banks to divest themselves of their equity holdings at a time when liquidity and confidence in the stock market were at a particularly low ebb. This initiative was designed to reduce the banks' vulnerability to stock price declines. Prior to its introduction, the major 15 commercial banks held some ¥19.8 trillion of stocks against Tier 1 capital of ¥15.9 trillion. The facility was meant to be wound up in September 2003 but was eventually extended by a year. All told, the Bank bought some ¥2.1 trillion of stocks rated BBB or higher at market prices – the equivalent of some 6% of the banks' total equity.[4]

Finally, at the behest of the MOF, the BOJ conducted intermittent bouts of large-scale foreign exchange intervention in order to cap what was viewed as excessive yen strength. However, the immediate effects of these operations were limited, both in terms of the yen's performance and, for that matter, on the monetary base. Any immediate tendency for the intervention to inflate the latter was subsequently sterilized, albeit sometimes with a delay.

NOVELTIES, UNCERTAINTIES, PROS AND CONS

In choosing to embark on this quantitative approach – and set aside the misgivings it had previously expressed at the end of the 1990s about the associated potential for losses on its asset holdings, moral hazard, impaired confidence, higher risk premia and slower corporate restructuring – the BOJ entered what was largely uncharted territory. In the process, it saw both the size and the composition of its balance sheet change out of all recognition. Its assets increased from the equivalent of some 10% of GDP in mid 2000 to more than 30% of GDP when the policy began to be wound down in 2006; what is more, a portion of those assets (albeit a relatively small portion) was, contrary to standard central banking practice, anything but risk-free.

The key question is therefore whether these unconventional departures, and the risks to which they exposed the BOJ, were worth it? Unfortunately, reaching a definitive judgement in this regard is difficult. The counterfactual is unknowable, it can only be surmised, while it is always challenging fully to grasp the dynamics of opaque concepts such as sentiment and the ever-mercurial financial markets. Nor is our understanding helped by the fact that the Bank, for its part, often appeared confused and less than consensual about precisely how QE was meant to work; in its aftermath, the BOJ was at least circumspect, if not downright sceptical, in its own assessment of the policy's impact.

What we know for sure is that, although monetary conditions eased for a while after the policy's inception, there was no rapid end to the downturn in 2001. The enduring weakness of bank and corporate sector balance sheets would have been active constraints on any monetary initiative, however conventional or unconventional: both the demand for and the supply of loans remained weak. For this reason, although the monetary base exploded higher after April 2001, the annual rate of broad monetary growth remained in a very low range, and actually declined over the period in which the strategy was in place. Deflation, meanwhile, proved stubbornly persistent. The CPI inflation rate did not return to positive territory until 2006, and even then fleetingly.

At the same time, the exchange rate remained subject to bouts of strength; the stock market, even if it did eventually rally, remained acutely depressed; inter-bank market activity declined dramatically; credit spreads became a less reliable measure of risk; bank profits were diminished by the associated flatness of the yield curve; and the incentive for corporate restructuring was reduced. In particular, QE delayed the recognition of problem loans and made it easier for borrowers to remain 'current' on their repayments.

On the other hand, the generous liquidity provided by the Bank moderated inter-bank and other risk premia where they had become unduly exaggerated. It is noticeable, for example, that the so-called TIBOR–LIBOR spread – an indicator of the degree of financial stress on Japanese banks relative to other banks – was broadly flat after the introduction of QE until the GFC.[5] There were, in addition, discernible policy duration effects from the Bank's forward guidance: interest rate expectations were lowered, especially at shorter maturities, and well into the process of recovery. The entire yield curve was therefore lower, for a substantial period, than it would otherwise have been, as indeed was the term structure of real interest rates.[6] That said, the latter tendency might have been further enhanced had the BOJ announced a formal inflation target akin to the 2% objectives set by other major central banks.

Overall, it is hard to draw the conclusion that the BOJ's QE policy of the early 2000s represented a transformative breakthrough. It delivered net positive results, but they should not be unduly exaggerated. Perhaps the wisest judgement to make is that it was certainly a better option than merely managing liquidity to keep the policy rate back at zero and suggesting that thereafter the central bank was largely powerless. This was particularly the case in 2001 and 2002, when Japan's rolling financial crisis was again severe and there was the risk of meltdown. It is to this vexed period that we now turn.

ANOTHER FINANCIAL CRISIS

As suggested earlier, the onset of the latest economic downturn saw the banks' NPLs once again on the increase. The official total for the end of the 2000/2001 financial year, based on the individual banks' own estimates, increased to some ¥34.0 trillion for all banks (equivalent to some 6% of GDP), up from ¥31.8 trillion in the 1999/2000 financial year. There remained a keen sense, however, that, despite some improvements in accounting practices, loan classifications were still frequently based on wishful thinking and an unwillingness on the part of bank managements to push client firms in trouble towards bankruptcy. Remarkably, the bank mergers that followed the recapitalizations of the late 1990s had revealed that very dissimilar loan classifications could be applied by different banks to the same borrower. Banks regularly failed fully to acknowledge the credit risk of borrowers, and their ability to service their debt, often preferring instead to lower contracted interest rates to keep firms going. The authorities were complicit in this, pushing the banks to continue to lend to SMEs, for example, irrespective of their financial condition. Unsurprisingly, therefore, the alternative estimates of the NPL total produced by many in the private sector (including the major international investment banks operating in Japan) – estimates that embodied broader definitions of the problem – were as much as three times higher than the official figure, or the equivalent of approaching 20% of GDP.

The recapitalizations of the late 1990s had only provided temporary respite and, notwithstanding the emergence of a small number of mega banks, had not provided enough of a catalyst for the restructuring of the banking sector, and especially its balance sheet. This was particularly the case among the regional banks. Capacity remained excessive, cost structures were too high and profitability and capital were too low. All the while, NPL disposal continued to be slowed not just by the timidity of bank management but also by the illiquidity of the real estate market, uncertainty over the residual value of collateral and difficulties in enforcing claims. Loan loss provisions and write-offs, although they had in some instances picked up, were inadequate. In the meantime, the problems of the insurance sector were also burgeoning. Engulfed by the wide gap between promised returns on existing policies and the rock-bottom rate of return on assets, as well as their own NPL issues, a succession of life insurance companies failed in the 2000/2001 and 2001/2002 financial years.

Once again, the overall financial situation threatened to spin out of control. The nettle of dealing with the fall-out from the bursting of the bubble had to be grasped once and for all.

A NEW POLITICAL BROOM

This was the situation when, in late April 2001, Japan welcomed a new prime minister. Mori Yoshirō had taken over from Obuchi Keizō a year earlier when the latter suffered a stroke, but he was gaffe prone, and increasingly unpopular as the economy and stock market once again slumped; his term of office was a disaster and he was forced to resign. He was replaced by Koizumi Junichiro, who in comfortably defeating the consistency candidate Hashimoto Ryūtarō benefited from rule changes that gave the LDP party rank and file greater influence in choosing a leader.

With his bouffant hair, youthful looks and professed love of Elvis Presley, Koizumi cut a very different figure to the staid image of his predecessors. He had charisma. Remarkably, he was even something of a sex symbol. Nor, in contrast to those who went before him, was he associated with Tanaka

Kakuei and his acolytes. Indeed, he was strongly influenced in his open and relatively unpolluted approach to politics by Fukuda Takeo, Tanaka's arch enemy within the LDP.[7] Koizumi was also possessed of an impressive intellect. He was a trained economist, having completed his university education in the United Kingdom. He used the media well too, eschewing the often-vacuous ambiguities of previous Japanese prime ministers and putting his ideas across to the electorate in pithy soundbites.

Ideologically, Koizumi presented himself as a free-market liberal reformer in the Thatcherite mould – one who wanted to shift the LDP's focus further away from its traditional rural heartland, and the corruption and nepotism that went with it, and more towards Japan's underrepresented younger urban population. He appointed a cabinet based more on merit than on factional power, and he talked of new supply-side initiatives and of implementing substantial changes in the way the public sector operated, including at the previously sacrosanct postal savings system, which he characterized as a quasi-government-run slush fund, ripe for privatization.

As time went on, however, it became clear that his agenda was more traditionally LDP in tone. He would portray Japan's problems as a spiritual crisis. He proved to be an unrepentant nationalist, akin to Nakasone. He was a staunch supporter of the US–Japan security relationship. Beyond finance, his record on reform was patchy at best. He was also content to defer to the fiscal conservatives at the MOF. Rather than driving significant and broad-based structural change, his enduring popularity was grounded in the fact that his time in office coincided with the resolution of the banking crisis and a long-awaited lasting recovery.

DOING THE RIGHT THING

Koizumi initially developed his policy agenda under the guidance of a new Cabinet Office and Council on Economic and Fiscal Policy (CEFP), both originally established by the Mori administration; the prime minister chaired the latter himself. His programme, launched in June 2001, was clearly coloured by his professed policy predilections, although it also drew on much work undertaken by the previous government, and in important respects had a familiar feel about it. The lip service paid to privatization, deregulation, competition-enhancement and entrepreneurship was hardly new, but the rhetoric was clearer and more direct.

More importantly, it was around this time that Koizumi and the broader policymaking community at last took on board the notion that little could be achieved in the absence of a definitive resolution of the NPL problem. There could be no renaissance of the Japanese economy without a profitable financial sector that allocated credit confidently and efficiently. With Keio University free-market academic and respected media pundit Takenaka Heizō installed as minister of economic and fiscal policy, and subsequently also as minister for financial services, the next two years, and particularly the period from the autumn of 2002, finally saw the implementation of a comprehensive financial sector strategy based on the provision of public funds. The strategy, which sought to address the shortcomings of previous interventions,[8] encompassed ten crucial elements, which can be summarized as follows.

First, there were much greater efforts to ensure realistic valuations of compromised assets. These began towards the end of 2001 with a series of special inspections of 149 large borrowers at the major banks by a reconstituted FSA.[9] The FSA's investigations were complemented by similar inspections of 97 banks undertaken by the BOJ. The results of the two surveys confirmed that the banks' self-assessments of asset quality had been consistently, and often significantly, over-optimistic. According to the FSA, for example, the extent of NPLs had been understated by at least a quarter and the provisioning and write-off requirements by at least a third.[10] The official NPL statistics were updated commensurately to a figure of more than ¥43 trillion for the banks (8% of GDP) and more than ¥54 trillion (10% of GDP) for all financial institutions.

Second, as a consequence, loan classification and provisioning were strengthened from the 2003/2004 financial year. Prudential norms were subsequently further strengthened by the broader introduction of mark-to-market accounting and the use of discounted cash flow methodology to value loans and harmonize loan classification across major creditors. An Accounting Standards Board of Japan was established to oversee the task of bringing accounting standards up to best practice.

Third, under a Programme for Financial Revival introduced in October 2002, the major banks were required to accelerate the disposal of compromised assets from their balance sheets, halving the headline NPL ratio by the end of the 2004/2005 financial year. This was to be achieved by selling them directly to the market, by pursuing bankruptcy procedures or by rehabilitating borrowers through out-of-court workouts. Any remaining bad loans could be sold to the RCC, which was given a trust bank license, allowing it to repackage the assets it bought for sale. The RCC would play an important, if indirect, role in assisting heavily indebted companies.

Fourth, additional public funds were made available for recapitalization beyond the injections of ¥1.8 trillion and ¥7.4 trillion made in 1998 and 1999. In exchange for this government support, compromised banks were required not just to dispose of bad assets but also to write down the capital of existing shareholders, to replace senior management and to submit a reorganization plan that would be regularly reviewed by the FSA. This is what happened in May 2003 with the country's fifth largest lender, Resona Bank, which was created from a merger of Daiwa and Asahi banks. Resona's reconstitution is now widely viewed as a critical turning point in the crisis.

Fifth, the sum of equities held by banks was to be reduced to a level equivalent to 100% of their Tier 1 capital by September 2006. In addition to the BOJ's stock purchasing facility, the government set up its own Bank Shareholdings Purchase Corporation (BSPC) in January 2002 to assist in these efforts. The BSPC had purchased some ¥1.6 trillion of stocks by 2006, bringing total purchases by the public sector to some ¥3.7 trillion.

Sixth, limits were also placed on the amount of deferred tax assets (tax credits based on expected future profits) that banks could count towards their Tier 1 capital ratio. In 2003, for example, such assets accounted for nearly half of Tier 1 capital across the major banks, adding to concerns about the ability of these entities to absorb further losses.

Seventh, banks were required to undertake governance reforms consistent with Basel Committee guidelines, such as the appointment of outside directors and the establishment of a board auditing committee.[11]

Eighth, in April 2002, consistent with the notion of restoring market discipline and reducing moral hazard, the authorities proceeded with the planned restrictions on the protection of time deposits. However, this saw the migration of deposits to the bigger banks, from time accounts to current accounts, and into cash, suggesting that private sector confidence in the banks remained low. For this reason, in October 2002 the government decided to postpone further restrictions until the 2005/2006 financial year.

Ninth, to complement the changes imposed on the banks, the government took steps to facilitate the restructuring of heavily indebted borrowers. In 2003 the Industrial Revitalization Corporation of Japan (IRCJ) was established to purchase distressed loans from banks and to work directly with any creditors who were still believed to be viable. This initiative built on previous efforts to speed up and broaden out the insolvency system via the Civil Rehabilitation Law of April 2000.[12] More specifically, in addition to the updated accounting and auditing framework, there were new guidelines for out-of-court corporate settlements, and government support for debt/equity swaps and corporate reconstruction funds. Over the ICRJ's four-and-a-half-year existence, it provided 41 instances of support, mainly for entities in non-manufacturing. The total debt of these companies amounted to around ¥4.0 trillion.

Finally, the purchases and sales of NPLs via the IRCJ and the RCC acted to build a market for restructuring by enhancing price discovery, resolving credit disputes and providing legal clarity and accountability. As asset prices staged a recovery from their early 2000s lows, the costs of the interventions by the ICRJ and the RCC declined. The IRCJ actually made a small profit over the course of its existence.

FINALLY, A LASTING RECOVERY

Japan's recovery from its third post-bubble recession actually began to establish itself before the Koizumi government's financial strategy had gained traction. Its initial complexion was redolent of the 1999–2000 upswing, in that it was very much export led, albeit on this occasion with demand from Asia (China, especially) to the fore. Indeed, by 2008 Asia accounted for around half of Japan's exports. A requirement for an inventory rebuild after the steep stock adjustment of late 2000 and early 2001 helped, as did a weaker yen. Notwithstanding the limited effects of the BOJ's direct interventions, the Japanese currency's real effective value would start to fall in late 2000, and ultimately decline by some 40% over the period to the fourth quarter of 2007. Business confidence, profits and industrial production then all responded. Electronics and auto exports were particularly strong at the outset of the upturn, and the current account surplus, which had diminished somewhat at the turn of the millennium, jumped back above 3% of GDP.

The domestic economy remained sluggish, however, and for a time the fear was of a repeat of the aborted take-offs of 1996 and 2000. The business investment accelerator was again constrained by corporate balance sheet adjustment and a high capital–output ratio, and private consumption was suppressed by soft income growth, the high level of joblessness and a lack of household risk appetite. And, of course, asset prices remained under duress and the process of financial intermediation was still compromised. Deflation, meanwhile, was deeply embedded, such that nominal GDP continued to fall until 2003; indeed, it failed to re-attain its 1997 peak until 2016! That said, there was little evidence that the persistently falling price level encouraged businesses and consumers to delay purchases significantly. Rather, it just cast a depressing pall of perception over the economy and made the process of balance sheet adjustment across both the private and the public sectors harder.

By the middle years of the decade, however, with the global economy – and the rest of Asia in particular – buoyant, the recovery process had gathered momentum and broadened out, as a virtuous circle between private income and employment, spending and output growth developed, and as the long-overdue shift in strategy towards the financial sector in 2001 and 2002 bore fruit. With business investment belatedly gaining traction and coming increasingly to the fore, private domestic demand was stronger than in the two previous short-lived recoveries, although the expansion was still heavily export dependent. Export volumes grew strongly throughout, and Japan ran up a succession of larger and larger external surpluses, which peaked at close to a record 5% of GDP in 2007. On the other hand, public demand – in contrast to much of the 1990s – tended to subtract from growth.

The strength of exports meant that there remained an imbalance between the manufacturing sector, where profitability rebounded impressively, and the more domestically focused non-manufacturing sector, where smaller companies dependent on bank finance dominated. Moreover, this was reflected in significant regional disparities in economic performance.

Nevertheless, despite the shortcomings of the cyclical upswing, real GDP growth averaged 1.7% a year between 2003 and 2007, with a peak of 2.2% in 2004. By September 2005 the upswing had developed into the longest of the post-war era. More impressively, GDP per head, arguably the best macro measure of national living standards, expanded at a rate of 2.1% per annum, matching the OECD average from 2002 to 2007. Reflecting a rebound in productivity, and particularly in manufacturing, this was a far better performance than in the 1990s, and it began to reverse Japan's rapid slide down the major economies' per capita income rankings.[13]

Bank stock prices bottomed out in March 2003, as asset valuations became more realistic; non-viable institutions were wound up; and the consolidation of the sector, not least at the regional level, accelerated. The banks' total bad loans fell to ¥35 trillion in 2002 (6.7% of GDP), ¥26 trillion in 2003 (4.9% of GDP), ¥17.5 trillion in 2004 (3.3% of GDP) and just ¥13.0 trillion in 2005 (2.4% of GDP), by which point the government announced that the NPL problem was over.[14] For its part, Tier 1 bank capital bottomed out at 4.9% of assets in 2002 and had risen to almost 8% by 2007. Bank lending growth finally turned positive in annual terms in August 2005, having fallen more or less consistently since the mid 1990s. The cumulative contraction in bank credit amounted to more than 25%.

All told, the authorities deployed some ¥47 trillion of public funds (around 9% of 2002 GDP) to address the banking crisis. In addition to ¥12.5 trillion of capital injections, this included grants of loss coverage of ¥18.6 trillion and asset purchases of ¥9.8 trillion. Impressively, though, almost three-quarters of this sum was recouped.

CORPORATE RESTRUCTURING

The accelerated process of bank balance sheet adjustment and the economy's extended recovery together combined to promote an improvement in the financial situation of the broader corporate sector. In particular, the 'three excesses' that had weighed on firms since the bursting of the bubble – those of corporate debt, productive capacity and labour – were addressed by a wave of cost cutting, rationalization and increased focus on core areas of business, in the process helping further to normalize the business cycle and render the expansion more sustainable. The diminished need to pay off debt in particular freed up funds for investment and labour income as the upswing matured. After its initial hesitancy, business fixed investment spending was especially strong in 2005, while the headline unemployment rate, which peaked at around 5.5% in 2002, had by 2007 dropped back below 4%.

Looking at the detail of this tripartite process of adjustment, the ratio of non-financial corporate debt to GDP declined from its peak of 130% in 1989 to just 80% by 2005 – that is to say, to its 1986 level. The overall corporate sector's financial balance, deep in the red at the end of the late 1980s boom, moved far into surplus, registering a peak of 11% of GDP in 2004 before falling back towards zero as the expansion matured.

For its part, the ratio of corporate fixed assets to sales, which had risen throughout the 1990s, peaked at around 220% in the early 2000s before declining to 190% in 2007, as the rate of retirement of the capital stock accelerated. By the mid 2000s the BOJ's quarterly *Tankan* business survey indicated that firms believed the capacity overhang had largely been eliminated and that they felt more comfortable in expanding the stock of plant and equipment to meet demand growth.

The *Tankan* survey also suggested that the excess of employment, built up during the bubble era when fears of an enduring labour shortage encouraged overzealous hiring, had finally dissipated by 2005. Consistent with this, labour's overall share in national income traced a similar declining path, dropping to some 55% of GDP from a peak of more than 60% in 1994, with the process extending to firms of all sizes after 2002. The corporate sector's profit-to-sales ratio, meanwhile, moved inexorably in the opposite direction, also returning to its pre-bubble level. Wage costs were in part restrained by a gradual shift away from full-time to part-time and temporary employment. The evolution of the wage structure also played a role. Base salaries were kept low, as seniority-based pay was scaled back somewhat, while performance-based remuneration in the form of overtime and bonuses claimed a larger share of total compensation.

FISCAL REVERSAL

As suggested previously, the role of fiscal policy was different in the early 2000s to what it had been in the 1990s. Koizumi viewed Japan's long-standing reliance on fiscal stimulus and especially public works spending as a default option in the face of tough economic times as at best having run its course and at worst as being a source of political sleaze and resource misallocation. He was determined it should be set aside, or at least relied upon to much less of an extent.

With the MOF happy to support the prime minister with warnings about the growing unsustainability of Japan's public finances, and because of its fear that the country was confronted by 'Ricardian equivalence' – the tendency of a forward-looking private sector to offset the impact of fiscal expansion by saving more because it fears that taxes will have to be raised later – there were only two small supplementary budgets in the 2001/2002 financial year.[15] Fiscal policy was therefore actually tightened substantially around the bottom of the cycle. Thereafter, it was broadly neutral. Positive budgetary impulses were short lived and subsequently unwound. The sustained strength of net exports and the rehabilitation of the financial sector from 2002 meant that the economy absorbed both the 2001 tightening and the subsequent absence of sustained fiscal support much better than it had dealt with its intermittent withdrawal in the 1990s. However, whatever Koizumi's preferences, there was no repetition of the sustained decade-long fiscal squeeze of the 1980s and, importantly, there was no increase in the consumption tax during his tenure.

Looking at the detailed fiscal accounts in the early 2000s, relying on a roughly equal split of spending restraint and revenue increases, the headline broadly defined government deficit – which of course said little about the underlying thrust of policy on a period-to-period basis – fell from a peak of around 7.5% of GDP in 2002 and 2003 to some 3.0% of GDP in 2007. The gross debt ratio stabilized around 157% of GDP in 2004 and 2005 before edging down slightly over the next two years.

On the spending side, as the prime minister desired, public investment's share in GDP fell further from its 1996 peak, dropping from 6% of GDP in 2002 to just 4% of GDP in 2007. However, the allocation of public investment lacked the necessary transparent cost and benefit analysis for it to be efficient. Too much spending remained focused on the wrong projects and in the wrong places, and rates of return were disappointing.

Public sector wages were also constrained, although they rose faster than those in the private sector, and the impact on the budget was counterbalanced by higher social security outlays in the context of consistently high unemployment and the ageing population structure. Real public consumption spending averaged around 2.0% a year during the upswing. Additional spending restraint flowed from the fact that net debt service payments fell from around 1.0% of GDP a year at the start of the decade to close to zero, as the effective interest rate of Japanese government debt collapsed in the context of persistent deflation and QE.

On the revenue side, social security contributions were increased. In particular, the public pension system underwent a major reform in 2004, designed to limit pension spending to 9.25% of GDP over the following decade and to ensure sustainability over the long term. At the core of this were progressive increases in contribution rates from 13.6% in the 2004/2005 financial year to 18.3% in the 2017/2018 financial year, with the further proviso that they indexed to any significant changes in the number of contributors to the system or to average life expectancy. Finally, in 2007 the government phased out the temporary income tax cut of 1999.

There was throughout a sense that public sector reform was too vague and lacked ambition, both in terms of the medium-term targets for key budget metrics such as the central and local government primary balance, which tended to rely on over-optimistic assumptions, and more generally in the way that the Japanese government operated. The role of public sector financial institutions in the allocation of capital, while reduced, was still significant and distortionary, while other public sector agencies and special budget accounts – even if they had been scaled back by a combination of abolition, privatization and transformation into independent agencies – continued to exert undue influence. Market mechanisms in the provision of healthcare and other services were limited. The system of public employment was inefficient, lacking in flexibility.

The restructuring of the tax system was limited, such that it continued to distort the allocation of labour and capital, weighed on output and constrained revenue growth. The politically toxic consumption tax remained at 5% – the lowest major indirect tax rate in the OECD – while the corporation tax rate of 40% was the highest in the world. The income and corporation tax bases remained too narrow. There were too many deductions, loopholes and inconsistencies. The self-employed enjoyed generous relief, while female labour participation was held back. The system of local taxation was overly complex. There was no taxpayer ID system to ensure compliance.

Overall, persistent deflation and the paucity of nominal GDP growth made fiscal adjustment harder. But notwithstanding Koizumi's declared predisposition towards budgetary reform, the complexity of the issues and the political obstacles to constructive change also remained onerous. Progress was underwhelming.

SUPPLY-SIDE POLICY AND THE PRODUCTIVITY PROBLEM

All this raises the question of the role of broader supply-side policy in the economy's structural adjustment. As we have already seen, it had long been recognized that, given the nation's challenging demographics, it was vital to improve productivity if the underlying rate of economic growth were not to continue to slow, or even peter out altogether.

Aggregate labour productivity per hour worked was still some 30% below the US level at the start of the century, so there was plenty of scope for catch-up. The problem was not the highly competitive manufacturing sector, which continued to enjoy a high and sustained rate of productivity growth. Rather, it was the need to reverse a sharp fall in service sector productivity growth, which had dipped from 3.5% a year between 1976 and 1989 to only 0.9% a year between 1999 and 2004.

The reforms of the insolvency system, improvements in the accounting and governance frameworks, the emergence of out-of-court corporate workouts, and the development of a market for the restructuring of distressed assets were all encouraging developments in this regard, not least as they potentially served to draw in private capital and expertise from overseas, as indeed did a generally healthier banking system and more efficient allocation of capital. However, these developments went only so far. Even if they were less than half what they were in the bubble era, networks of stable shareholdings were still widespread, at around 20% of the total. Outsiders on boards were in short supply. Japanese institutional investors remained reluctant to remove underperforming management, and the corporate bond market was underdeveloped, never coming close to making up for the extended decline in bank credit.

According to the government, more than 6,000 regulatory reform measures were undertaken over the decade to 2005, and its own index of regulation fell from 100 at the outset of this period to 35 at the end. The decline was initially more pronounced in manufacturing, but it subsequently became more distinct in non-manufacturing industries such as electricity supply, trucking and telecoms, where there had been large price falls and increases in demand.

The government's structural reform agenda in the 2000s was laid out in a series of detailed annual three-year programmes based on reports provided by the Cabinet Office Council for Regulatory Reform (later the Council for the Promotion of Regulatory Reform). The 2007 programme, for example, identified 15 priority areas including education, information technology, distribution and energy.

Among the obvious achievements made in this period was the progress made in the enforcement of competition law by the FTC through the 2005 revision of the Anti-Monopoly Act. Equally heartening were special low-regulation zones established as testing grounds for national reforms. There was also, from 2004, a much-needed shift in focus towards the social welfare system, including medical services, nursing and education.

Criticism of the reform process remained widespread, however. Policy rhetoric continued to go beyond substance. The drafting of many associated laws was often vague and careless. Ex ante permits and licences were still ubiquitous in many areas. There remained a lack of transparency and excessive scope for administrative arbitrariness. The power of vested interests, including in various ministries, remained strong. The pace of change was inconsistent. Reform remained a piecemeal and unduly pedestrian process.

Consequently, market entry was constrained, FDI extremely limited and the service sector in general rather sclerotic. Import penetration increased only slowly. Venture capital was in short supply. M&A activity was still lacking, with few hostile deals. Little effort was made to increase the role of foreign workers, and the labour market exhibited growing dualism. The share of non-regular workers who had temporary contracts was skewed to young, female, part-time employees, who were less expensive for employers to hire and who increasingly took on the mantle of second-class citizens.

As the cyclical upswing matured, the outstanding reform agenda in services therefore remained a substantial one. The competition laws and powers of the FTC could be further strengthened and the processes of application, screening, assessment and evaluation for the special regulation zone programme rendered less complex and slow. There remained a requirement further to reduce the obstacles to the establishment and expansion of large-scale retail stores. The electricity and gas industries needed independent regulators to guarantee fairer competition, to expand consumer choice over suppliers and to engineer the formal separation of vertically integrated incumbents. There were high barriers to entry in the port system. There was inadequate airport capacity, undue regulation of landing slots and undue restrictions on the selling of airline tickets directly to consumers at competitive prices. Business services were dominated by powerful and defensive professional associations and closed off to international competition by an unwillingness to recognize foreign certification. The agricultural sector remained one of the most heavily protected in the major economies.

Product market reform needed to be combined with labour market reform. Dualism and the inequality of income and opportunity associated with it needed to be tackled by lower employment protection for regular workers, the expansion of social insurance schemes to more non-regular workers, and more training to enhance non-regular workers' human capital and employability. Spending on Active Labour Market Policies (ALMPs) was far below that in Europe.

Finally, women accounted for more than two-thirds of non-regular workers, and more than 40% were employed part time. However, more needed to be done to raise female participation and to bring them into the full-time workforce if the effects of population ageing were to be addressed. This meant that aspects of the social security system that reduced work incentives for women had to be wound back, and there needed to be greater availability of childcare at a reasonable cost. Furthermore, lingering misogynistic attitudes and the notion that only extended working hours were proof of career commitment had to be tackled.

POSTAL SAVINGS REFORM

As far as Prime Minister Koizumi's strongly expressed desire to privatize the postal savings system was concerned, progress was limited there too.

In the early 2000s the postal savings system employed more than 250,000 staff, boasted 25,000 post offices and 26,500 ATMs; it was the world's second largest mail delivery service and still accounted for 23% of all the cash deposits in Japan. Its total assets cumulated to some ¥227 trillion or, if the postal insurance system is factored in, ¥350 trillion: a quarter of total personal financial assets. Furthermore, despite some reforms, it was still a main source of funding for the government's second budget, the FILP. It was a mammoth and – in the eyes of many in the LDP and beyond – highly treasured national asset.

Nevertheless, as suggested above, Koizumi had for decades identified the postal savings system as a source of patronage and corruption and the beneficiary of unfair and distortionary government support. It restricted competition, weighed on banking sector profitability and functioned as an active constraint on societal change. In seeking to privatize it, he was both laying down a powerful political marker and taking on some of Japan's most powerful vested interests, not least in his own party.

As a first step, Japan Post, a government-owned corporation, was established in April 2003 to replace the old Postal Services Agency. The initial idea was to split it into four companies: a bank, an insurance company, a postal service company and a fourth entity to run the post offices as retail outlets for the other three. Each would then be privatized in April 2007.

In August 2005 the Lower House of the Diet passed a bill to complete the reform but only by a handful of votes, with many LDP members voting against. The bill was then defeated in the Upper House because of defections from the ruling coalition. Remarkably, Koizumi's response was to dissolve the Lower House, expel the LDP rebels and call an immediate general election, which he presented as a referendum on the postal privatization process. To the surprise of many, the prime minister won a resounding victory – the LDP's best result since 1986 – and a final version of the bill was approved in October of that year. Japan Post was abolished and a state-controlled holding company established to oversee the four separate entities mentioned above. There was then to be a ten-year transition period during which the savings and insurance companies would be fully privatized, with the government remaining involved with the other parts of the system to ensure that it met its full-service mandate.

It was at this stage, however, that Koizumi surprisingly lost interest, not just in reform but in being prime minister altogether. Rather than using the increased authority afforded him by his resounding electoral victory and his success with postal privatization to force through a more radical programme of policy change, he declined to seek re-election as party leader and stepped down in September 2006. He was replaced as prime minister by his protégé, Abe Shinzo.

Abe was the grandson of Kishi Nobusuke, who was prime minister between 1957 and 1960 and had been a member of the wartime junta; he was even arrested in the immediate post-war period as a war criminal. Abe was at this stage a more traditionally minded LDP leader, less wedded to the idea of reform than Koizumi, either of the postal system or more generally. With a long record of historical denialism – a trait he shared with many on the right of the LDP – what was most important to Abe was the loosening of the US-enforced post-war settlement, including the constraints imposed on the Japanese military.

This failed to resonate with the electorate, however, and his political light and health rapidly faded, such that he resigned a year later. The feeling at the time was that his rapid departure would mark the end of his frontline political career but, as we shall see, he was in due course to make a remarkable comeback.

Away from the machinations of the LDP's leadership, the truth was, however, that there was little real understanding or consensus about precisely how the detail of postal privatization should unfold. The process became mired in a huge political quagmire. There was fierce opposition from those who feared job losses and the closure of post office branches that effectively served as community centres and LDP vote-gathering bases in many rural areas. There followed endless legislative delays, detours and volte-faces. In the end, a majority privatization process, which still saw the government maintain a one-third share, was only completed in October 2021.

RUSHING FOR THE EXIT ONCE MORE

In early 2006, some five years into the cyclical upswing, the Fukui-led BOJ persuaded itself that the two conditions it had set for it to end its QE policy were met. It therefore announced that it would abandon its ¥30–35 trillion target for the banks' current account balances, curtail its ABS and ABCP purchases, and gradually drain liquidity from the money markets – all while aiming to keep overnight interest rates at zero. However, in a concession to a government concerned about its ability to finance a still-substantial budget deficit and an onerous debt burden, the Bank's monthly JGB purchases were sustained at ¥1.2 trillion.

Although the Bank also stressed that the pace of any further monetary tightening would be gradual and that a historically low level of official rates would prevail, the adjustment of policy was not without controversy. While the output gap had been largely eliminated by this stage, CPI inflation was barely back in positive territory, having essentially been negative (sometimes significantly so) for more than a decade, excluding the transitory impact of indirect tax hikes. As a result, the actual consumer price index was some five percentage points off its highs. Meanwhile, other important measures of goods and service price inflation remained negative in annual terms. Some 15 years on from the bursting of the bubble economy, both land prices and the Nikkei stock index – while by this stage demonstrating signs of greater stability – remained at mere fractions of their highs and had seemingly decoupled even from a depressed level of nominal GDP.[16]

In seeking to flesh out its new strategy, based on the views of Policy Board members, the BOJ outlined an operational definition of relative price stability of 0%–2% a year for the CPI, with a central tendency of 1%.[17] This was, of course, below the formal and informal inflation targets set by other central banks, which tended to coalesce around 2%. In the eyes of most commentators at home and abroad, it was too low, especially as the Japanese CPI, like most such indices, had at least some upward bias. That is to say, it exaggerated the actual pace of inflation.[18]

The Bank's rationale for this aberrantly low definition of price stability was that Japan had historically experienced more subdued inflation than elsewhere. This was no doubt true. But by stressing that 'Japan was different' in this regard, it seems to have been keen to deflect from its responsibility for previous policy errors and the development of deflation. More pertinently, a 1% target raised the risk that following negative demand shocks, the central bank would more regularly hit the zero bound constraint than its contemporaries, real interest rates would rise to inappropriate levels, and QE would have to be resurrected.

In addition, the Bank suggested that policy would in future be assessed not just by reference to the most likely scenario for output and prices over the next 1–2 years, but also by whether significant risks were developing where long-term growth and price stability were concerned. Its judgements on these matters would then be presented in detail in its regular 'Outlook Reports' and 'Economic Assessments'.

There appear to have been two important undercurrents to the shift in policy and the proposed adjustments to the Bank's modus operandi. First, once the financial crisis of 2001–2002 had passed, there was scepticism about the effects of QE beyond its signalling role around the zero-rate stance. Hence, moving away from a quantitative approach would have little negative effect on the economy. Second, there was a desire for continued discretion and a rejection of hard and fast policy rules around inflation. The latter in turn reflected an enduring obsession with the threat of asset market excess and resource misallocation as well as a fear that the BOJ had neither the tools nor sufficient understanding of the monetary policy transmission mechanism to achieve a formal inflation target consistently.

Notwithstanding these considerations and their veracity, by July of 2006 the Bank had smoothly transitioned to a more orthodox monetary framework, with the banks' current account balances normalized, while also raising the policy rate to 0.25%. Reflecting the scaling back of its open market operations and the natural unwinding of its holdings of shorter-term government securities, the BOJ's balance sheet shrank by around 20%, to ¥116 trillion. However, the complementary lending facility for banks introduced in early 2001 remained in place, and it had been unable to unwind its bank stock holdings.

Unlike in 2000, the BOJ's exit strategy was not associated with an immediate collapse in the recovery. Nor did it encourage a jump in long-term interest rates. Ten-year JGB yields remained in the 1.5%–2.0% range. A second 25 basis points rate hike followed in February 2007 as the Bank remained concerned by the effects of the historically low level of rates in both nominal and real terms. By this time there were also signs that land prices had finally begun to rebound after 15 years of persistent decline. Again, therefore, it seems that it was concerns over the longer-term risk factors – asset price excess and resource misallocation – rather than the immediate outlook for CPI inflation that were dominating the Bank's decision-making process. Indeed, its short-term inflation forecasts for 2006 and 2007 had proven too high and had to be revised down.

Not everyone at the Bank bought fully into this view, however. One of the deputy governors, Iwata Kazumasa, voted against the second rate hike. To his mind, the contemporary inflation rate, which remained around zero, simply did not justify it. Nor for that matter did market-based inflation expectations, which remained under 1% and were falling from mid 2006. Taylor rule analysis suggests that the Bank's policy rate should have been negative from 1998 to the end of 2006.

STORM CLOUDS GATHER

Although the expansion survived the BOJ's policy recalibration, it began to lose momentum in 2007. Personal consumption, which had been subdued throughout the upswing, was constrained by the phasing out of the temporary income tax breaks of 1999 and by the continued weakness of wage growth, even as the unemployment rate fell back below 4% for the first time since 1998. Business and residential construction investment growth slackened, the latter after revisions to building standards laws.[19] Bank lending also began to slow once more, particularly where advances to non-manufacturers and SMEs – which accounted for almost half of all bank loans and had benefited the least from the upswing – were concerned.

The slowdown then turned into a full-blown recession through the course of 2008 as the GFC dealt the Japanese economy a huge blow. By this stage, the reins of the central bank had been passed to Shirakawa Masaaki, another BOJ lifer.[20] As we shall see, his term as governor was to prove both extraordinarily challenging and extremely controversial.[21]

BETTER LATE THAN NEVER?

The new millennium had begun with Japan facing another recession and an existential financial crisis. Seven years later, however, in the run-up to the GFC, it finally appeared to have shrugged off its lost decade. It had enjoyed a sustained cyclical upswing and its underlying performance, as measured by real per capita income growth, was akin to that of its major competitors, albeit a pale shadow of what it had been before 1990.

This apparent process of normalization reflected the enduring strength of its highly competitive export industries in the context of an extended low-inflation global boom – the 'Great Moderation'[22] – and, importantly, the fact that its policymaking community had at last abandoned a strategy of forbearance, if not wishful thinking and Micawberism, and actively sought to come to grips with the post-bubble problems of its financial sector. Asset valuations became more realistic. The disposal of NPLs was accelerated. Bank capital was improved. Financial supervision was strengthened. The various negative feedback loops between the banks and the real economy that had previously weighed heavily on the economy's progress could be gradually unwound, and the corporate sector was able to escape from the onerous burdens of excessive debt, capacity and labour.

The extended delay in addressing the financial fallout from the bursting of the bubble – Japan's financial crisis was far longer than most historical examples of such episodes – came at a huge price, however. A vast amount of wealth was destroyed and much output permanently lost. Many lives were turned upside down. Some longstanding illusions about Japan's position in the global economy were shattered. But perhaps most pertinently of all, Japan's public finances were set on an unsustainable and politically challenging path that in 2007 policymakers had barely begun to address.

There also remained a sense that Japan's economy was fragile and still vulnerable to shocks. The process of population ageing – with all its unfamiliarities, uncertainties and need for societal adjustment – had barely begun. Growth was overreliant on external demand. The non-manufacturing sector was still held back by overburdensome regulation and government interference. It lacked flexibility and dynamism. A number of domestic service industries remained effectively isolated from international competition. The profitability of the banks, while improved, remained below that seen in Japan's competitors.

The tendency towards deflation proved hard to overcome and to purge from the mindsets of households and corporates alike. The lack of room for manoeuvre when it came to policy was not just confined to fiscal policy. Official interest rates may have been edged up from the zero bound, but the entire term structure remained historically extraordinarily low. Furthermore, while the BOJ had journeyed further down the unconventional path than any central bank since the Great Depression, it had done so under sufferance, often indicating that it had a higher tolerance for deflation than was wise, and it made a number of crass errors in its haste to return policy to normality. The bank therefore remained something of an enigma to many observers. Could it be relied on to do the right thing should things sour once again?

Politically, the Koizumi era of the early 2000s had been refreshing on some levels, and the prime minister certainly 'got' the overwhelming importance of dealing with the financial sector's difficulties in a way that his predecessors had not. But in many respects, in 2001 and 2002 he had little choice but to grasp this nettle. The country was on the edge of a precipice. Neither does the common characterization of Koizumi as a successful reformer really hold water. He had much in common with his predecessors, and in many ways he reverted to type. His record was inconsistent to say the least. He also left the political stage just when it could be argued that his ability to really deliver change was at its apogee.

The reform of Japan's economy continued to be stymied by the enduring power of political conservatism and various vested interests. Many of the longstanding attitudes and cultural values that served to get the country into such a mess in the first place endured. Transparency and accountability were often lacking.

PUTTING THE LOST DECADE INTO CONTEXT

Finally, it is worth examining how Japan's experience in the wake of the bursting of the bubble compares with the typical pattern observed after major financial crises in the modern era.

The historical record since the late nineteenth century demonstrates that after sizeable financial traumas the path of output tends to be depressed substantially and persistently, with no rebound to the pre-crisis trend over the medium term. Japan certainly fits this bill. However, growth usually eventually returns to its pre-crisis rate, which was not the outcome in Japan, and in this it appears that demography played an important role.

The depressed output path observable in post-financial-crisis economies usually results from three considerations. First, there is a long-lasting reduction in the employment rate due to lower participation and higher structural unemployment. Second, there is a lower capital-to-labour ratio because of constrained credit supply, lower collateral values, weaker corporate balance sheets and heightened general uncertainty. And third, there is lower total factor productivity (TFP) because of a shortage of capital (especially for higher-risk projects) and less innovation because of reduced R&D spending. Again, Japan fits this template quite well.

Following most financial crises, the initial output loss is mainly accounted for by TFP, but unlike the employment rate and the capital-to-labour ratio, the level of TFP tends to recover to its pre-crisis trend over the medium term, while capital and employment suffer more enduring losses to trend. These patterns appear to have applied in significant measure in Japan.

Past episodes also indicate that a crisis will be more obdurate if it extends to a currency collapse. Despite some initial weakness in the yen, this did not happen after the bubble. Indeed, within a few years currency strength was the bigger concern.

In searching for alternative explanations for the stubbornness of Japan's difficulties, one is inevitably drawn both to the particularly dramatic extent of the initial correction in domestic asset prices and corporate indebtedness and to the economy's especially high pre-crisis investment share.

In the past, extended post-crisis adjustment phases were also associated with limited policy space. In this regard, Japan was lucky, initially at least, to have had considerable room for policy manoeuvre. That it still suffered a particularly long hangover after the bubble again perhaps also reflects the various shortcomings of the post-crisis monetary and fiscal response.

Lastly, both a favourable external environment and improved structural policies in the wake of a financial crisis can help to moderate the time it takes to recover. Japan clearly benefited from the former for much of the mid-to-late 1990s, and especially after 2002. In the absence of the Great Moderation, its export-dependent economy would have suffered much more. As for the latter, as we have seen, Japan's record was mixed. Although no doubt a positive influence, it is hard to conclude that it had a huge effect on the recovery process.

Japan's experiences in the 1990s and early 2000s no doubt have much in common with previous financial crises elsewhere. But what marks the Japanese narrative out as exceptional are the degree of initial asset price and credit excess, the economy's extraordinarily high pre-crisis capital–output ratio and the failings of policy on a number of levels.

CHAPTER 7

The Global Financial Crisis

'Bad causes, bad results' — Japanese proverb

CARDIAC ARREST

In the second half of 2007 the global financial system entered a period of acute and escalating crisis that was to reach its apogee towards the end of 2008 with the collapse of the US investment bank Lehman Brothers. The burgeoning solvency issues of the banks and other financial institutions around the world triggered what was then the most dramatic economic downturn of the post-war period: a recession that was not only very deep, but also disturbingly obdurate. It exerted an enduring malign influence.

As a result, Japan, which had seemingly finally put its own domestically generated financial crisis behind it in the early 2000s, was consumed by something altogether more pervasive. Indeed, the GFC appeared, for a time, to be little short of a matter of life or death for the entire capitalist system. It was a truly international calamity from which no country escaped unscathed. Furthermore, to those who had observed Japan's bubble era and subsequent lost decade, including the country's policymakers, there was to be much that was depressingly familiar about this episode. It is therefore worth taking a detour and dwelling on it in some detail.

The essential specifics of the GFC are sobering.

Between 2007 and 2009, the pre-tax profits of the world's largest 1,000 declined from $800 billion to a low of $100 billion. The return on equity for US banks, which had long averaged around 15%, went negative for a period. Bank and investment bank equity prices fell on average by between 60% and 80% before recovering, significantly underperforming overall equity indices, while bank credit default swap (CDS) spreads leapt from around 20 basis points to peak around 450 basis points.[1] Total global bank assets as a percentage of GDP stopped growing and even edged down for a period. In the major economies, NPLs jumped from between 1% and 2% of the outstanding total to between 7% and 8%. Lending standards became eye-wateringly tight and credit growth collapsed, turning negative in many advanced economies. Gross capital flows to emerging markets fell by almost two-thirds from their pre-crisis highs, with cross-border loans turning sharply negative.

In the broader financial markets, the major stock indices typically fell from peak to trough by something in the region of 50%. Measures of market volatility surged to unprecedented levels. The funding markets seized up. Corporate bond spreads blew out. Corporate bond issuance, and in particular ABS issuance, slumped. In the desperate search for safe havens, long-term government bond yields sank to unprecedented lows. Real estate markets plummeted, with the fall in US real house prices approaching a third.

The macroeconomic landscape was similarly devastated. Global real GDP declined marginally in 2009, the first drop since 1945. World trade volumes suffered a 17% retrenchment. The peak-to-trough falls in output in individual economies were unlike anything seen in the post-war era – they exceeded double digits in some cases. Investment spending, and in particular residential construction spending, bore the brunt of the downturn. Gross fixed capital formation fell on average by around 14%. Unemployment surged, exceeding 10% of the workforce in many countries, and within these totals the long-term jobless came to account for a significantly increased proportion.

Inflation cratered (albeit after a lag) as previously elevated commodity prices slumped and, in the process, transmitted the crisis to the developing world; corporate pricing power evaporated; wages stagnated. Annual CPI measures of price pressure turned negative for a period in many countries, and inflation expectations dropped alarmingly.

Policy rates rapidly gravitated towards the zero bound, where they had been in Japan for around a decade. Budget deficits swelled towards the equivalent of around 10% of GDP as cyclical developments caused tax revenues to slump and welfare-related outlays to surge, while there was widespread resort to activist fiscal policies to support financial sectors and economies more generally. This in turn led to sharp increases in public sector debt burdens, with the average advanced economy figure swelling to more than 100% of GDP in gross terms. The recession also marked the onset of a further slowdown in productivity and potential output growth.

The grave crisis that engulfed the world between 2007 and 2009 and cast a shadow over the next decade had its origins, for the most part, in the United States and its financial sector. Fundamentally, however, it was a huge market failure and a story of how two basic human motivators – fear and greed – conspired in an environment of permissive macroeconomic policies and a lax regulatory framework to break both trust and confidence and encourage a catastrophic financial and economic meltdown.[2]

It is not easy to get to grips with the principal mechanisms involved because the crisis was truly universal and systemic. It had multiple overlapping and often-complex causes that mutated and malignly interacted with one another both within and across borders. The crisis was intrinsically non-linear. It is therefore almost certainly pointless to look for a single trigger or tipping point. When a system is teetering on the verge of collapse, almost anything can elicit it. And besides, a tipping point is a place or a moment, not a cause.

MACRO EXCESS

For a decade or more leading up to 2007, the major advanced economies had had – or certainly their policymakers had perceived themselves as having – difficulty in maintaining aggregate demand at an adequate level. Growth rates had generally trended lower, with sluggish business investment an important contributing factor. Central banks were tending to undershoot their mandated inflation targets. Consistent with the writings of Keynes, Kalecki and Marx, globalization played a role in this. As China, India and other relatively low-wage emerging economies became more integrated into the system of world trade, there ensued more intense competition, an excess supply of workers, and a related shift in factor shares in favour of profits and against labour. Inequality remained high, and the general tendency was, if anything, for it to increase.

While the emerging Asian economies were well placed to export their way out of this problem, that option was not really open to the world's largest economic entities; that said, Japan, as we have seen, enjoyed more success than most. Hence, in the United States, partly for these reasons but also on philosophical and domestic political grounds, fiscal policy became unambiguously expansionary in an effort to support domestic spending. The Bush administration cut taxes in 2001 and did so again in 2003, at the same time as electing to fight a major war. This resulted in some 4 percentage points of GDP of fiscal largesse over four years. Other countries, particularly those in the euro area, were more circumspect, as was Japan, as we have seen, but the United Kingdom ploughed a similar expansionary fiscal policy furrow to the United States for at least part of the immediate pre-crisis period.

Policy interest rates first trended progressively lower, and then, if anything, central banks erred on the side of accommodation once they began to be normalized. Taylor rule calculations suggest that, in aggregate, the official interest rates of the OECD economies as a whole were around 180 basis points 'too low' in 2003 and 270 basis points too low in 2004. By this standard, it was only in 2007 that they returned to their appropriate level.

This widespread monetary accommodation was transmitted to other countries via fixed, quasi-fixed or artificially depressed exchange rates, thereby amplifying the whole effect. This was particularly the case in the emerging economies.

All the while, macroeconomic imbalances were accumulating, particularly importantly in the United States. The broadly defined US budget deficit amounted to some 5% of GDP from 2002 to 2008. This compares with an average of just 0.5% in the five previous years, and an average from 2001 of just over 2% of GDP for the euro area.

US house prices almost doubled between 2000 and 2006. This exceeded the rise in the 'Roaring Twenties'. At the peak of the boom, US housing investment accounted for some 6.75% of GDP – far above its long-term trend of between 3% and 5%. The rise in property prices helped to push household net worth from 400% of GDP to 490% of GDP, encouraging personal consumption to surge. Meanwhile, the ratio of household indebtedness to disposable income, which had been rising gently since World War II, took off, surging by 40 percentage points in just seven years.

As a consequence of the relative strength of domestic spending, from 2001 the US economy absorbed considerably more resources than it produced, running a current account deficit that averaged a little over 5% of GDP.

It would not be correct, however, to pretend that the course of the US economy was unwelcome to others: had the US authorities not sustained the growth of domestic demand, economic growth everywhere else in the world would have been weaker. The Europeans and others, including the Japanese, were happy to piggyback on the United States's growing excesses and disequilibria.

At the time these circumstances were undoubtedly sufficiently novel for it to be hard to know for certain how they would ultimately play out. Nevertheless, there were some important pointers.

First, there was what might be termed the *reductio ad absurdum*. No entity – be it an individual, a household, a company, a government or a country – can indefinitely consume more than it produces. There comes a point, even for the world's largest economy, where lenders start to become circumspect about extending further credit.

Second, there are trusted rules of thumb that should have been heeded: the Qvigstad rule, for example, posits that trouble lies ahead for an advanced economy if any of its key macroeconomic indicators – the budget deficit (as a percentage of GDP); the current account deficit (as a percentage of GDP); or the inflation rate – exceeds a value of 4.[3] On that basis, the US data had been flashing red every year since 2002 in respect of its current account deficit; since 2003 in respect of its public sector deficit; and in 2008 in respect of its inflation rate, which peaked above 5%. A number of other major economies, including the United Kingdom, also breached at least one of the Qvigstad rule ceilings.

However one looks at it, the global macroeconomic configuration was unsustainable, and particularly so in the United States. As the American economist Herbert Stein famously observed: 'Things that can't go on for ever, don't.'[4] The only issues were when and how the inevitable correction would come about.

FREE-FOR-ALL

The pervasive light-touch regulation of the pre-crisis period had its roots in two theoretical propositions.

The first was that well-designed monetary policy is all that is needed to encourage financial stability. This meant monetary policy based on the New Classical–New Keynesian synthesis, focused predominantly on low inflation and delivered by an independent central bank.

The second was that, on average, financial markets price risks correctly. This was a conclusion drawn from the efficient market hypothesis (EMH), which, notwithstanding what had happened in Japan in the 1980s, implied quite simply that bubbles and crises could not occur.

These two propositions left the conventional wisdom of policymakers in 2007 broadly as follows. Financial market prices provided an indication of rationally evaluated economic value. Securitization, based on the development of new liquid markets, had enhanced the allocation of resources and the stability of the financial sector. The riskiness of financial assets could be determined by mathematical means, so as to elicit dependable quantitative metrics of trading risk. Market discipline was an effective mechanism to moderate excessive risk taking. Financial innovation is generally constructive, as market competition should ensure that innovations that do not provide value added do not survive.

Hence, it followed that markets will generally prove to be self-correcting, with market discipline a more effective instrument than government regulation and oversight. The primary responsibility for the management of risk should lie with the senior management and boards of individual firms as they are better placed than regulators to assess threats to particular business models and they can be relied upon to make appropriate decisions for their institution about the balance of risk and return. Satisfactory customer protection is likely to result not from product regulation or direct intervention in markets but by ensuring that those markets are as free from interference and as transparent as possible.[5]

In hindsight, these were very misguided assumptions.

It is now appropriate to consider the ways in which the unsustainable underlying macro forces interacted with one another in this remarkably permissive context to bring about the inescapable adjustment.

THE ROAD TO CRISIS

In November 1999 a fundamental change that had long been observable in US financial framework conditions was finally recognized and formalized by the abolition of the Glass–Steagall Act – a change in which Alan Greenspan, then chair of the Federal Reserve, played an important role. This act had both founded the Federal Deposit Insurance Company (FDIC) and separated commercial and investment banking in an effort to eliminate conflicts of interest that arise, as they did in the 1930s, when the granting of credit-lending and the use of credit-investing were undertaken by a single entity. In the wake of Glass–Steagall's abolition, such conflicts multiplied once again.

Equally important, however, were the six principal ways in which behaviour unfolded. These can be summarized as follows.

Savers, seeking yield, were relatively relaxed about moving into assets that historically had been judged risky, in part because inflation was quiescent by the standards of recent decades. Indeed, at the beginning of the new millennium many – including senior policymakers at the Federal Reserve such as Ben Bernanke, strongly influenced by the persistently sub-target level of inflation – considered deflation to be the greater threat.

Banks and investment banks borrowed extensively on the wholesale money markets, lending the proceeds to households through mortgages and other loans, fuelling the property market and prices.

Mortgage misselling became rife, particularly in the United States. Salespeople were frequently paid per sale while bearing no responsibility for the consequences. They therefore lent to people who had little hope of servicing their loans over the longer term, often eschewing any downpayment, offering low initial 'teaser' mortgage rates and providing negative-amortization loans, whereby the difference between a low mortgage rate and the market rate was added to the loan principal.

Investment banks, responding to the search for yield, developed increasingly complex and highly geared investment vehicles, such as ABSs, mortgage-backed securities (MBSs), collateralized debt obligations (CDOs) and CDSs. Many of these securities were fashioned around mortgage loans, a sizeable portion of which were sub-prime, or poor quality, in nature, but which were sliced, geographically diced and combined with lower-risk loans in a such a way as they could be concealed from view.

By 2006 sub-prime mortgages accounted for 23.5% of the overall US mortgage market, up from less than 10% in the late 1990s, and 70% of all new mortgages fell into this category. Of these, more than two-thirds were so-called 2/28 adjustable-rate mortgages (ARMs): 30-year home loans with an initial two-year fixed interest rate, after which the rate floated based on an index rate plus a margin. It could be argued that these were hardly mortgages at all but rather leveraged bets on the direction of house prices.

Banks created off-balance-sheet special purpose vehicles (SPVs) that acted like mini-banks but operated beyond the bounds of bank regulation. They issued short-term debt (mainly in the form of ABCP) to investors and used the cash raised to buy longer-term assets from their parent companies. Many of the assets purchased were drawn from the alphabet soup of new financial vehicles, some of which would be divided up and mixed and matched into ever more complex securities. This was an approach widely adopted by Lehman Brothers.

The overall numbers involved were huge. In August 2007 SPVs linked to the large US financial institutions had assets of more than $300 billion. Legally, these shell companies were independent entities, but in practical terms they were attached to their parents, which provided them with guaranteed credit lines to be drawn down if needed.

This 'shadow banking system' was not confined to SPVs, however. It went much further, extending to hedge funds, private equity firms and other highly leveraged and largely unregulated financial entities. Indeed, the latter provided the core of the demand side of the trade in the investment banks' increasingly exotic financial product development and further contributed to an explosion of leverage. It is estimated that in 2007 the global shadow banks held assets of some $60 trillion – more than 25% of the total financial system.

The net result was to disperse the risks embedded in the new financial products around the world. However, despite the assumptions made by policymakers, there was little understanding of the true extent of these risks in the event of a crisis or, indeed, of where the risks were concentrated. Nor was there much understanding of the practicalities of unwinding highly leveraged portfolios of such products at a time when a large number of investors were seeking to do the same thing.

Meanwhile, although official interest rates remained low by the standards of previous decades, monetary policy had for some years been on a tightening trend. In 2007 this tightening appeared to reach a critical mass such that not only did US real estate prices begin to roll over, but a broad spectrum of riskier asset values turned. Confidence and trust suddenly collapsed, and leverage, which until that moment had seemed like everyone's friend, turned into a savage enemy.

DROPPING THE BALL

There has been much debate as to why this situation was allowed to develop, but it seems clear that much of the explanation lies in the misguided precepts of the regulatory regime. The regulators did a poor job. They relied too heavily on the assumption that companies were 'doing the right thing' while having too few ways to check whether they actually were. They failed to achieve a basic alignment of risk and reward or of financial regulation with financial activity.

Financial crises tend to occur when innovation outpaces the ability of regulators to understand what is going on. A policymaking community brought up on, and wedded to, the basic tenets of the rational expectations hypothesis (REH) and the EMH appears to have been both complacent and ignorant. For example, like much of the economics and financial market cognoscenti, Federal Reserve chairs Alan Greenspan and Ben Bernanke were, in the early to mid 2000s, both in denial about the degree of excess in the US housing market and the potential for an economy-wide housing collapse.

At the same time, because they often work in silos, the regulators can fail to grasp the interconnectedness of different areas of the financial system. This means that when a bubble inflates, it is hard to know the full extent of it until it has burst. This is particularly the case if you believe that bubbles are exceptionally rare, or indeed that they cannot exist.

Many participants in the excesses of the noughties were strongly incentivized to keep the good times going. One-sided incentive structures at financial institutions encouraged traders to make unwarrantedly risky bets. If they paid off, they themselves were paid handsomely, but if they failed, it was someone else's money that was lost and they were allowed to move on. But this cannot be the whole story. Traders did not function in a world without individual risk limits, even if they could be unduly generous – the ultimate responsibility therefore rests with the banks' managements (often ex-traders themselves), who set the guidelines.

Risk analysis, contrary to the authorities' assumptions, was often poor. This had various dimensions. Within the banks and investment banks, many economists – though fewer in the United States – warned repeatedly about the unsustainability of the global, and in particular the US, macroeconomic configuration. Unfortunately, however, while economists in general are proficient at identifying disequilibria, they are much less adept at predicting when or how they will unwind. This meant that their advice was ignored by traders, salespeople and business heads within the financial sector. It was not seen as practical enough.

At the same time, some risk managers were insufficiently concerned that the mathematical risk models they used did not adequately take underlying macroeconomic risks into account. They just blindly 'turned the handle' on their computer programs, without any notion of the broader context.

For their part, many senior risk managers were reluctant to admit that they did not really understand their own bank's risk models. Certainly, most managements did not appreciate that, for contractual or for reputational reasons, sponsors would not be able to avoid responsibility for their supposedly off-balance-sheets products.

Risk management had become increasingly model and statistics based, with value at risk (VaR) analysis at its core, not least because it was consistent with the EMH and the regulators encouraged it. However, this technique is over-reliant on the past to predict the future. In particular, it had two serious limitations. First, while there were many observations around the medians of the various distributions examined, information about the extremities, which is where the catastrophic risk lies, was sparse, particularly after 15 years of exceptionally low macroeconomic volatility. In practice, the probabilities of extreme events were obtained almost wholly by assumption. Second, framework conditions evolve, and accommodating this required a structural approach, which a statistical distribution alone could not provide. In the limit – and therefore, it was hoped, only occasionally – the model simply might not describe reality at all.

Senior corporate management proved unwilling to act. Unduly focused on their company's quarterly reports, many senior executives felt unable to 'leave money on the table'. Chuck Prince, the chair and chief executive of Citigroup, implicitly spoke for the majority in July 2007 when he said: 'When the music stops, in terms of liquidity, things will be complicated. But as long as the music is playing, you have got to get up and dance. We are still dancing.'[6]

Boards of directors proved too weak, or too ill informed, to challenge apparently successful CEOs in financial companies. Managements increasingly seemed to be running companies for themselves, and shareholders proved unwilling, or unable, to rein in senior executives.

'Grade inflation' by the credit rating agencies (CRAs) implied, for example, that a mortgage vehicle rated as 'triple A' (the highest rating that the CRAs could offer) carried the same risk as similarly dubbed major advanced-country government bonds. The principal reason for this remarkable state of affairs was that the agencies were paid by the issuers of the securities (the banks) rather than the investors. Meanwhile, CDOs and other derivatives were so complex that investors became overly reliant on the CRAs.

Financial sector capital ratios proved to be inadequate, given the leverage that had been permitted to accumulate. When asset values collapsed, not only did the shareholders lose all but the investment banks were revealed to have reached systematic importance. The total amount that the financial sector had written off by 2009 – well over $1 trillion – was more than 100 times its collective VaR assessment of 18 months previously.[7]

The procyclical impact of mark-to-market valuation techniques exacerbated the capital inadequacy of banks. When crashing 'fire-sale' values are used by auditors to value a bank's assets, they induce fire sales to spread, thereby making matters worse.

A deficient understanding of corporate self-interest led regulators – from the chair of the Federal Reserve down – to believe that each company's management would always have their company's survival as their primary objective and would therefore avoid actions that might unduly jeopardize that survival. However, this faith underestimated three important forces: management's own personal short-term goals; the unawareness of many CEOs of the scale of the risks of macroeconomic origin to which they were exposed; and the degree to which competitive pressures obliged each to do broadly what all the others were doing.

The multilateral organizations failed to press the point. The BIS was one of the few to sound a loud warning, but it was largely ignored. The IMF, the OECD and the ECB also made cautionary noises about macro and financial developments, but they were not loud enough or clear enough, and in the policy world as a whole, much as in the investment banks, few really wanted to listen. Politics inevitably intervened. There are few if any votes in terminating bull markets in asset prices.

And so it was that the crisis developed, slowly at first, but then increasingly rapidly, before it came to a head at the end of 2008.

CHAPTER 8

Out of the Frying Pan …

'Even monkeys fall from trees' — Japanese proverb

HITTING THE WALL

As stated in the previous chapter, Japan was hit extremely hard by the GFC. Initially, however, buoyant sales to Asia and to oil producers benefiting from the high crude prices of the time sustained Japanese exports in the face of declining US demand, to the extent that for a fleeting period it created an illusion of 'decoupling'. Indeed, even as exports to the US fell in the autumn of 2007, total export volumes continued to expand at double-digit annual rates.

Shipments to Asia and other regions soon faltered, however, such that overall export volume growth had slumped into negative territory by Q2 2008. At the same time, the strength of commodity prices, which went far beyond the oil markets, briefly pushed headline CPI inflation up above 2% for the first time since the consumption tax hike of 1997. This eroded corporate profitability as firms had difficulty in fully passing on higher input costs, and it also squeezed real household income growth. Consequently, domestic demand weakened.

The economy as a whole began to contract in mid 2008, after which time the impetus of the downturn intensified in dramatic fashion. Real GDP fell by a cumulative 9.3% between Q2 2008 and Q1 2009, with the decline in activity especially precipitous around the turn of the year. The output gap, which had previously been positive, became cavernously negative, approaching the equivalent of 8% of potential output on some measures. The irony was, however, that after all the fragility and dysfunction in the Japanese financial sector in the 1990s and early 2000s, it was the manufacturing sector and net exports – long Japan's two major comparative advantages – rather than a reprise of the banking crisis that largely drove the sudden plunge in activity.

FINANCIAL EXCEPTIONALISM

Japanese financial institutions were relatively insulated from financial turmoil. Burned by the traumas of the post-bubble period, the banking sector had latterly focused on more conventional activities. Its exposure to risky assets was thereby relatively limited. Banks directly or indirectly held only a small amount of subprime-related products and were less involved in originate-to-distribute type activities than their US and European counterparts. Indeed, the book value of Japanese banks' subprime-related products was just ¥1 trillion at the end of the 2007/2008 financial year (equivalent to about 0.2% of GDP) and had declined by half by the end of the following financial year, when it accounted for only 1% of their Tier 1 capital, although the loss ratio was high at 72.8%.

Nor did Japan experience the inflation in real estate prices that played out in many other OECD countries in advance of the crisis. Between 2000 and 2008 the ratio of house prices to income in Japan dropped by 22 percentage points, in contrast to gains of 20 points or more elsewhere. The sharp decline reflected the fact that land prices continued to fall for much of this period. It was only in 2006–7, after 15 consecutive years of decline, that average nationwide land prices finally temporarily exhibited some stability, and this largely reflected increases in Tokyo.

This is not to deny that Japanese banks expanded their mortgage lending to households in the early 2000s. However, this was largely a consequence of the decision made in 2001 to gradually reduce new loans provided by the HLC, in preparation for its privatization in 2007. Between the 2001/2002 and 2008/2009 financial years, 20% of outstanding housing loans shifted from the HLC to the banks, and the positive turn in overall loan growth in 2006 was in significant part down to increased lending for real estate related purposes. That said, in line with the FSA's guidelines, notably relating to loan-to-value ratios, lending behaviour remained prudent, and this helped Japan to avoid a debt-driven housing price boom.

The implementation of the Basel II banking supervision accords, announced in 2004, also served to temper Japanese banks' appetite for risk. In contrast to other countries, where it encouraged banks to engage in mortgage loans and securitization, in Japan Basel II raised the minimum required capital of the larger – internationally diverse – banks because of their substantial equity holdings.

The undeveloped domestic securitized product market, together with the limited penetration of the originate-to-distribute business model, further acted to shield Japanese banks from the global crisis. Securitization had received some encouragement from the late 1990s through the creation of a specified legal framework with preferred tax treatment in the context of efforts to address the NPL issue. However, the ensuing expansion was limited and from a very low base. The securitized product market peaked at the equivalent of 1.7% of GDP in the 2007/2008 financial year, before contracting to only 0.8% of GDP in the 2008/2009 financial year.

Finally, while the particular nature of the pay and incentive structures of Japanese banks had been partially culpable for low profitability, limited innovation and the extensive delays in addressing the NPL problems of the 1990s, they subsequently served to stymie the sort of cavalier risk-taking behaviour witnessed across the financial sectors of many other countries. The average salary of management-level employees was significantly lower in Japan than in most of its major competitors, especially after the previous crisis. There was also less emphasis on large bonuses based on individual performance, while the pattern of internal promotions encouraged caution rather than speculation.

Despite these mitigating factors, however, a sharp deterioration in financial conditions still contributed to the Japanese economy's sudden and precipitous reversal. Lending standards became stricter. Interest rate spreads increased. There were difficulties in issuing CP and corporate debt.[1] Equity prices slumped: the Nikkei index began to lose altitude in the spring of 2007 and had declined to new post-bubble lows by early 2009. And the yen's enduring safe haven status – reflecting Japan's structural current account surplus and the country's huge pool of external assets – encouraged a near 30% appreciation in real terms. All these factors combined to depress domestic spending, and especially business investment.

The weakness of the equity market, which, given what was happening in the United States and elsewhere, was initially concentrated on financial stocks, also led to a significant erosion in bank capital, which was still somewhat fragile even before the crisis. Although banks had reduced equity holdings from over 8% of total assets in 1999 to less than 2% at the time of the GFC – a figure well below the legal limit – equity prices remained crucial to the soundness of banks. Unrealized capital gains on bonds and equities, which reached ¥11 trillion in 2007, had turned to losses of around ¥2 trillion both for major banks and for regional financial institutions by Q1 2009. With 45% of unrealized gains counted as capital and with unrealized losses deducted from it, the equity price decline reduced banks' capitalization significantly. Although net business profits remained positive, the ordinary profit of all banks fell into negative territory in the 2008/2009 financial year for the first time in six years, as did their return on equity. One of the few bright spots was that the aggregate NPL ratio stayed broadly constant at around 2.5% of total advances. However, the disposal of NPLs rose from ¥1.1 trillion in the 2007/2008 financial year to ¥3.1 trillion (0.7% of loans outstanding) in the 2008/2009 financial year as borrowers came under increasing duress.

EXPORT SHOCK

Notwithstanding these financial considerations, what really poleaxed the Japanese economy was a slump in the global demand for more advanced industrial products.

As the GFC reached a gut-wrenching crescendo in the latter half of 2008, companies and consumers around the world slashed their investment and durable-goods outlays. The demand for cars, information technology goods and machinery, all of which accounted for a larger share of production in Japan than in the other major economies, collapsed. The manufacturing sector's difficulties were further exacerbated by Japan's heavy trade exposure to Asia, and especially to the more recently industrialized economies, such as Korea and Taiwan. Growth slowed sharply there too, while the yen's dramatic rise around this time was heavily skewed towards the currencies of these countries.

Export volumes had tumbled some 40% by early 2009. The peak-to-trough decline in industrial production amounted to around one-third in a little over 12 months. Nothing like this had been seen before in the modern era. Business confidence crumpled, especially at SMEs. Bankruptcies soared once again. The external surplus declined by more than half between 2008 (3.2% of GDP) and 2009 (1.4% of GDP).

By mid 2009 the unemployment rate had surged to an unprecedented 5.7% of the workforce, wages were falling sharply, the headline CPI was declining at annual rate of around 2% just a year after it had been increasing at a similar pace, and market-determined medium-to-long-term inflation expectations had slumped even further into negative territory. In addition, land prices once again began to fall at an accelerating rate, leading to balance-sheet adjustments that put additional pressure on the corporate and financial sectors.

THE MORE POLITICS CHANGED, THE MORE IT STAYED THE SAME

As was the case in a number of countries, the GFC and its aftermath proved to be a period of considerable political turbulence and uncertainty. The LDP's grip on power, slipping since Prime Minister Koizumi Junichi left office in 2006, was lost entirely in the wake of the crisis, just as had been the case in the immediate aftermath of the bursting of the bubble. After a succession of short-lived prime ministers – chosen on the basis of internal power dynamics within the LDP – had failed to inspire confidence, the electorate lost patience with the vagaries and eccentricities of politics as usual.[2] In a general election in late August 2009 the opposition Democratic Party of Japan (DPJ) won an overall majority. Outwardly centre-left (it professed to model itself on the

United Kingdom's New Labour) and led by Hatayama Yukio, it opted to govern in coalition with the Social Democratic Party and the People's New Party.

However, the inexperienced, ideologically ill-defined and fissiparous DPJ itself subsequently went through a series of flawed leaders and internal conflicts, and it never succeeded in capturing the imagination or the trust of the population.[3] Relations with both the United States and China soured during the DPJ's time in office and it too found that maintaining popularity in challenging economic times was a tough task, especially in the wake of the further chaos and disruption wrought by the 2011 Great East Japan Earthquake (also known as the Tōhoku Earthquake). Its own hold on power lasted only until the end of 2012, when, with a resurrected Abe Shinzo back as leader, the LDP won a landslide victory after the vexed issue of the consumption tax once again proved toxic for an incumbent government.

The final DPJ administration, led by Noda Yoshihiko, had passed legislation (with, it should be stressed, LDP support) authorizing a rise in Japan's most important indirect tax to 8% in April 2014, then to 10% in October 2015, on the assumption that certain macroeconomic conditions were met.

Remarkably, given the abject failure of his first term in office, Abe's second spell as prime minister would see him become Japan's longest-serving leader. He secured further election victories in 2014 and 2017. After a brief and uninspiring interlude, the LDP's political dominance was re-established.

FINANCIAL FIREFIGHTING

Despite the political turmoil of the time, however, and in contrast to the 1990s, the authorities responded quickly and forcefully to the financial crisis. Some important lessons appeared to have been learned, and as in 2001 and 2002 the scale of the emergency with which they were confronted concentrated their minds, as indeed did the fact that some of the primary casualties on this occasion were among the politically powerful manufacturing elite.

In the financial sector, a range of policies were aimed at stabilizing markets and sustaining credit flows.

The FSA announced a range of measures to support equity prices, including greater freedom for firms to purchase their own stock and the curbing of speculation through greater disclosure of market positioning and restrictions on short selling. To help the capital position of the banking sector, the FSA also decided to reactivate the government's BSPC, originally established in January 2002, and resume purchases of equities held by banks. The upper limit of purchases was raised to ¥20 trillion (4% of GDP) as part of an economic package announced in December 2008, although the actual sum bought was a fraction of this figure.

The calculation of bank capital was relaxed so as to prevent excessive fluctuations in CARs from hampering bank intermediation. In particular, the treatment of the valuation of profits and losses on bonds with zero risk weights for internationally operating banks was no longer included in capital estimates. For domestically operating banks, unrealized losses from equities and corporate bonds were similarly excluded from capital estimates.

The legal framework for the injection of public capital into depository institutions was resuscitated in December 2008 with relaxed conditionality. The total budget for such injections was set at ¥12 trillion.

To help sustain lending to SMEs, the FSA altered the conditions under which loans would be classified as non-performing. Certain remaining public financial institutions – the Japan Finance Corporation, the Development Bank of Japan and the Shoko Chukin Bank – also provided emergency loans and guarantees to borrowers.

Bank lending growth actually picked up as the crisis unfolded, although this in the main reflected expanded lending to large companies as their access to direct financing in the capital markets dried up. Loans to SMEs continued to decline, as they had done since mid 2007.

THE BOJ AGAIN REVERTS TO THE UNCONVENTIONAL

For its part, the BOJ had no option but to unwind the gradual policy of monetary normalization that had been in place since early 2006 and revert to various unorthodoxies. After all, based on Taylor rule analysis, the warranted policy rate at this time was somewhere between minus 3% and minus 4%. As the crisis unfolded, the Bank became increasingly active in implementing a suite of measures to re-establish financial market stability, to facilitate corporate financing, to lower and flatten the yield curve, and to moderate exaggerated risk premia.

The measures can be summarized as follows.

First, the BOJ was a participant in the system of inter-central-bank foreign exchange swap lines initiated by the US Federal Reserve and extended to Japan in September 2008 in the context of unprecedented risk aversion and a severe global shortage of dollar funding. Following the collapse of Lehman Brothers, the BOJ accessed more than $100 billion from the Fed to on-lend to domestic commercial banks.

Second, the pace of outright purchases of JGBs by the Bank was increased from the ¥14.4 trillion annual rate prior to December 2008 to a ¥21.6 trillion annual rate (equivalent to ¥1.8 trillion a month, or 4% of GDP) in March 2009, and the range of bonds accepted in these operations was also expanded.

Third, the Bank facilitated lending to the corporate sector through outright purchases of CP and corporate bonds.

Fourth, in December 2009 the BOJ introduced a 'funds-supplying operation' for three months at the policy interest rate. The total amount of loans was initially set at ¥10 trillion yen (2% of GDP), doubled to ¥20 trillion (4% of GDP) in March 2010, and then increased by a further ¥10 trillion in August 2010, taking the total to ¥30 trillion or 6% of GDP. The BOJ also decided in June 2010 to supply up to ¥3 trillion in one-year loans at the policy rate to financial institutions lending to companies in 'growth industries', such as environment-related sectors and health care. While it did not directly involve itself in which companies received such credits, this did in effect amount to a form of industrial policy.

Fifth, following the example set by the government, the BOJ resumed its purchases of investment-grade equities held by financial institutions in February 2009. By the end of July 2009 it had acquired stocks worth ¥38.1 billion.

Finally, the BOJ lowered its policy rate from 0.5% to 0.3% in October 2008, in concert with moves by other major central banks, and then to just 0.1% in December 2008. It was effectively back at the zero-interest-rate bound less than three years after it had been abandoned.

Despite these initiatives, after an initial spike to the equivalent of more than 25% of GDP at the end of 2008, the BOJ's total assets remained fairly constant at around this level until early 2011. Its balance sheet had therefore actually expanded more rapidly under the QE policy of 2001–2006, when it had also peaked at a higher level: around 30% of GDP. This muted expansion of the Bank's balance sheet following the GFC was also in contrast to the sudden sharp increases seen in the United States and the euro area, although these economies suffered greater financial turbulence and dysfunction than did Japan.

Following the onset of recovery in mid 2009, financial conditions returned to something akin to the status quo ante and it was possible to scale the level of support back. The banks also returned to profitability in the 2009/2010 financial year and gradually improved their financial performance thereafter.

By these criteria, the actions of the FSA and the BOJ had been broadly successful.

FISCAL REPRISE

On the fiscal policy front, successive governments eschewed the restraint of the Koizumi years and fell back on large-scale discretionary expansion. The medium-term plan to limit spending with a view to achieving a primary budget surplus in the 2011/2012 financial year was necessarily cast aside, and a series of stimulus packages were launched.

Two supplementary budgets were brought down in the 2008/2009 financial year, and there was additional stimulus both in the regular budget for the 2009/2010 financial year and in a further supplementary budget approved in May 2009. Remarkably, this brought the total number of fiscal packages since the early 1990s to 17.

In aggregate, the budgetary stimulus around the GFC amounted to some 4.7% of 2008 GDP: the second highest among the G7 countries and above the average of 3.9% for OECD countries adopting such programmes.

Increased spending, at 4.2% of GDP, accounted for the bulk of the stimulus in Japan, whereas it was almost evenly divided between higher spending and tax reductions in the OECD as a whole. Transfers to firms and households accounted for about half of the increased spending, the idea being that this would deliver a rapid boost to spending power. For households, the key component was a supplementary fixed-sum income payment of ¥12,000 ($125) for each person between 19 and 64 years of age and ¥20,000 for everyone else. The share allocated to public investment was substantially lower than during earlier episodes of fiscal expansion, when it accounted for almost four-fifths of the total. This change reflected an explicit effort to avoid investing in unnecessary infrastructure. The composition of public investment also changed. To improve the quality and energy efficiency of public buildings, including schools, the allocation to facility expenses was increased from an average of 17% of total public investment in the previous three episodes of fiscal stimulus to 40% over the course of 2008–9.

The expansive thrust of fiscal policy no doubt helped to alleviate the recession somewhat, but in conjunction with the effects on revenues and spending of a still-deep economic contraction, it rapidly unwound the progress made on the budget deficit and public debt during the early 2000s. The consolidated budget shortfall swelled to almost 10.5% of GDP in 2009, while the gross burden of government debt surged beyond 200% of GDP, or more than twice the average of the advanced economies. Thankfully, lower interest rates helped to cap debt service outlays: net interest payments remained around 0.5% of GDP between 2008 and 2010. This was above the near-zero figure of the mid 2000s but still very low by international standards.

Beside the knock-on effects of a near-zero policy rate, the fall in government borrowing costs and their stabilization at a low level reflected three considerations.

First, Japan, unlike many of its major competitors, had abundant domestic savings and, as we have already noted, a structural external surplus and an unprecedented stock of net external assets. Although the household saving rate declined significantly after 2000, it was offset during the first half of the decade by rising corporate surplus saving as firms deleveraged. When corporate surplus saving declined in 2006–7 in the context of strong output growth, this also boosted tax revenues, thereby reducing government net borrowing and helping to maintain domestic saving and low interest rates. Gross national saving averaged close to 27% of GDP around the time of the GFC and its immediate aftermath. This compares to figures of 15.5% for the United States, 13.7% for the United Kingdom and 25.9% for Germany.

Second, some 50% of outstanding government debt was recycled through the operations of the broader public sector by the BOJ, Japan Post and Insurance and the remaining other domestic institutions, which had a limited incentive either to trade their holdings actively or to sell them. The remainder of JGB holdings were heavily concentrated in private financial institutions and particularly in the banks and insurance companies, where BIS regulations, their safety during deflationary periods and various investment rules and asset allocation models and practices all provided powerful incentives to retain them. Households, non-financial firms and foreigners each held less than 10% of the outstanding amount.

Finally, the financial crisis resulted in a flight of capital to safer assets, pushing down the interest rates on government bonds everywhere.

Notwithstanding Japan's high domestic saving rate and the strength of underlying demand for government bonds, the rapid accumulation of deficits and debt over the course of the GFC in the context of continuing population ageing rendered the country's public sector finances more unsustainable than ever. At some stage, to stave off default, the nettle of enduring fiscal consolidation would have to be grasped.

The necessary priorities were all too familiar. Once recovery had fully taken hold and the various measures in the stimulus packages had been phased out, there would have to be discretionary spending cuts, extending to a lower government wage bill, better prioritization of investment outlays and reform of social insurance programmes, including further increases in the pension eligibility age. This was particularly the case because, in December 2008, the government approved a plan to upgrade the social welfare system, moving it closer to the European model. The income and corporation tax bases would also have to be significantly widened, while a substantial increase in the politically sensitive consumption tax was unavoidable, leaving a trap door for future governments.

In an effort to pay lip service to the need for budgetary restraint, new fiscal targets were set out in June 2009, but these necessarily had to be revised a year later as the ramifications of the GFC and the associated policy actions on the public accounts lingered. The Fiscal Management Strategy of 2010 looked to halve the combined central and local government primary deficit by the 2015/2016 financial year and move it back into surplus by the 2020/2021 financial year. However, the plans, such as they were, were as ever dependent on optimistic assumptions about growth and prices, and they lacked detail. The sense was that Japan had yet fully to come to terms with its public sector solvency issues. And, of course, the following years were to see further shocks to the economy and the response to them make the task of fiscal consolidation harder still.

ANOTHER EPHEMERAL RECOVERY

The positive impetus of fiscal policy, together with an improvement in domestic financial conditions and a rebound in exports, especially to China, meant that the economy, and particularly its production sector, began to pick up in Q2 2009, as the inventory cycle turned. The share of Japanese exports going to China (including Hong Kong), which had increased from 12% to 21% between 2000 and 2007, rose further to 25% around this time. Moreover, the healthy state of the corporate sector's balance sheet going into the GFC meant that when demand turned upwards, the business community was not unduly constrained in its response by excess debt, labour or capacity. The threat of an extended period of economic stagnation was thereby mitigated.

While export growth moderated after its initial surge, in part due to slowing demand from Asia and yen appreciation, it was nonetheless sufficient to trigger a rebound in business investment starting in late 2009. Personal consumption also contributed positively to growth in late 2009 and the first half of 2010, as wage growth – particularly bonus payments – rebounded from the precipitous declines seen in 2009.

The DPJ-led government that took office in September 2009 also rapidly implemented a further 1.5 percentage points of GDP of fiscal stimulus, although this was funded in part by scrapping some of the unfinished projects in the previous government's fiscal packages. The new stimulus had a different complexion to many of its post-bubble antecedents. In addition to an expansion of credit guarantees for lending to SMEs, it focused on increased employment subsidies, government job-creation programmes and an extension of subsidies for purchases of energy-efficient vehicles and home appliances, the sales of which subsequently soared.

The overall pace of recovery from the GFC – around a 4.5% annual rate between Q1 2009 and Q3 2010 – was outwardly impressive. Nevertheless, output at the end of this period was still some 2% below its peak prior to the 2008 crisis; there was a substantial output gap; and, despite help from higher global commodity prices, Japan was the only OECD country facing entrenched deflation. Business and consumer confidence then once again began to roll over in the middle of 2010. For all its apparent vibrancy, the cyclical upswing was not self-sustaining. The final quarter of 2010 was to see the onset of a renewed downturn, which, as we shall see, was subsequently greatly exacerbated by another dreadful natural disaster.

The abrupt termination of Japan's post-GFC recovery towards the end of 2010 was initiated by the exhaustion of previous stimulus measures, including the scaling back of some of the government's energy-efficiency consumer subsidy programmes, a renewed slump in export volumes in the face of more yen strength, and the depressing impact of the European sovereign debt crisis, not least on stock prices, which remained close to their all-time lows. Persistent deflation had also meant that, despite the lowering of the policy rate towards zero, real interest rates, both short and long, had risen consistently for the 18 months following the Lehman Brothers bankruptcy. Monetary conditions had tightened.

STILLBORN GROWTH STRATEGY

It was ironic that just ahead of this renewed downturn, the DPJ government launched its New Growth Strategy. Presented in June 2010 at the same time as the revised Fiscal Management Strategy, it differed from the reform policies of previous governments, which, it was argued, were excessively 'market fundamentalist' in nature and had worsened unemployment and exacerbated income inequality. Rather, in addition to revisions of the regulatory and institutional frameworks, it looked to improve the economy's performance through a combination of fiscal incentives, including targeted spending, tax measures, credit guarantees and public lending.

The stated goal was to raise the economy's potential growth rate from the 0.5% average rate of the previous decade to a 2% pace over the course of the next, while also overcoming deflation. As a result, it was suggested, the unemployment rate would fall below 4% and the public finances would become more sustainable.

Seven key areas were highlighted for attention – green innovation; health care and the financial sector; Asian economic integration; local revitalization; the innovation system; and employment and human resources – and the strategy outlined 21 related projects, with an implementation timetable for each through the 2013/2014 financial year and targets to achieve by the 2020/2021 financial year. In order to oversee their implementation, a 'New Growth Strategy Realization Promotion Council' was established in September 2010. It was chaired by the prime minister and included participation from relevant ministers, the governor of the BOJ, business and labour representatives and private experts.

The criticism of previous reform programmes was politically loaded and somewhat harsh, even though, as we have noted in earlier chapters, they were often repetitious, unduly aspirational in tone, excessively incremental in nature and frequently shied away from frontal attacks on the most powerful vested interests and obdurate impediments to growth. Supply-side reform had nevertheless delivered important gains to Japanese consumers. For example, the Cabinet Office estimated that regulatory reform raised consumer surplus by ¥17.6 trillion (3.5% of GDP) between 1995 and 2005. Japanese joblessness and inequality also remained significantly below the levels observed in most of the country's major competitors.

Making the New Growth Strategy work was always going to be challenging given the government's commitment to, and the undoubted necessity of, longer-term public debt consolidation. At the very least it would need to involve a significant improvement in the way that public spending was allocated and applied, together with early and comprehensive tax reform. Some argued that it should not have been limited to specific sectors but rather extended across the entire economy if it was to raise productivity to the extent required. Given that the working-age population was projected to shrink by 10% by 2020, achieving the 2% real growth target implied that productivity growth would have to accelerate significantly from the 1% average annual rate of the previous decade.

Against this difficult background, the strategy seemed to put too little weight on fostering entrepreneurship and a business-friendly environment through initiatives that reduced the cost of creating new firms, strengthened international trade and investment linkages, rolled back agricultural protection, boosted service sector competition and freed up venture capital. It was also important that credit guarantees were not allowed to stymie the process of creative destruction and that the planned privatization of Japan Post was seen through.

TRAUMA TRIAGE

Disappointingly, a May 2012 assessment of the New Growth Strategy found that only 10% of the measures put forward in 2010 had been successfully implemented. Moreover, the DPJ's plans were in any case soon overtaken by events, both economic and political.

With the economy stalling in the latter half of 2010, the immediate priority for the authorities once again became demand stimulus rather than supply-side enhancement. They were compelled to embrace new macroeconomic policy action.

First, in mid September, the MOF initiated a bout of intervention by the BOJ in the foreign exchange markets – the first in some six years – to stem the rise in the yen that was widely seen as an important catalyst for the economy's renewed malaise. However, as is typical with such unilateral operations, its effects were temporary. The yen remained firm.

More pertinently, the government also launched two further fiscal stimulus packages, with the first amounting to 0.2% of GDP and the second to just over 1.0%. These included an expansion of support for the labour market and the extension of some of the remaining incentives to buy energy-efficient consumer durables. These initiatives were financed in part by tax revenue windfalls and lower-than-expected debt service costs.

As far as monetary policy was concerned, in seeking to clarify its understanding of medium-to-long-term price stability first issued in March 2006, the Bank explicitly stated in December 2009 that it would not tolerate zero or negative inflation. This was no doubt welcome. But the low 1% midpoint of its categorization of price stability remained. Furthermore, its actions over the course of the first three quarters of 2010, during which consumer prices continued to fall and real rates rose, hardly suggested that its overall approach to bringing about a sustained positive rate of inflation had changed substantively. Under the guidance of Shirakawa Masaaki, the Japanese central bank was an inherently conservative animal.

By October 2010, however, it was clear that something more had to be done to arrest the economy's latest slide and the enduring tendency of prices to fall. The BOJ's response was to introduce what it grandiosely titled a strategy of 'comprehensive monetary easing'. The policy rate was edged down from 0.1% towards zero, and the old commitment to keep it there until price stability was in sight, conditional on avoiding certain financial imbalance risks, was resurrected.

A decline of just 10 basis points in the policy rate could hardly be described as a dramatic policy adjustment. But more importantly, borrowing from the actions of other central banks during the crisis, not least the Bank of England, the BOJ also established a formal asset purchase programme (APP) to reduce risk premia and sustain asset prices.

The APP embodied the Bank's existing ¥30 trillion funds supplying operation, together with a commitment to buy ¥5 trillion (equivalent to 1% of GDP) of assets over a one-year period. Initially, the latter included ¥3.5 trillion of JGBs in addition to those purchases made under its existing market operations, and ¥1.5 trillion of private assets, extending to corporate bonds, CP, exchange traded funds (ETFs) and Japanese real estate investment trusts (J-REITs).

EARTHQUAKE

Before these new fiscal and monetary policy initiatives had much chance to bear fruit – real GDP fell by around 1% in Q4 2010, and little improvement was expected in Q1 2011 – on 11 March 2011 the north-eastern seaboard of the country was struck by what became known as the Great East Japan Earthquake. Not only did this compound the challenges the economy faced, it also served to highlight some of Japan's unaddressed underlying structural weaknesses, not least its overprotected, sclerotic and costly agricultural sector and the need to reform electricity supply and accelerate the development of renewable energy.

Registering 9.1 on the Richter scale, the Great East Japan Earthquake was the fifth strongest in recorded history and resulted in a powerful tsunami with waves as high as 38 metres. The two destructive natural phenomena together left more than 19,000 people dead or missing. In addition to the devastating human toll, property damage was estimated by the government at ¥16.9 trillion (about 3.5% of GDP).

The shock to economic activity was immediate. Financial conditions tightened sharply as uncertainty mounted and risk appetite drained away. Industrial production fell by more than half in the month of March in Miyagi prefecture and by more than 30% in neighbouring Iwate and Fukushima. This led to a nationwide plunge of almost 16.0% at a time when output was still some 12.0% below its early 2008 peak. Real GDP fell just under 2% in the first half of 2011.

The immediate impact of the Great East Japan Earthquake in both human and economic terms was much greater than that of the 1995 Great Hanshin Earthquake (although both rank far behind the 1923 Great Kanto Earthquake touched on in chapter 1). Moreover, the government's estimates of the damage caused quoted above do not extend to the effects of the meltdown at the Fukushima nuclear plant that was triggered by the earthquake and tsunami. This forced the evacuation of hundreds of thousands of citizens and led to the subsequent suspension of operations at all of Japan's 50 nuclear power plants, which had hitherto supplied nearly a third of the nation's electricity – Japan was one of the world's most nuclear-dependent economies. Widespread energy saving followed, both mandated and voluntary, weighing on the subsequent recovery process.

The disruption of energy resources and production supply chains over the first half of 2011 was not confined solely to Japan. By disturbing international trade linkages and just-in-time inventory management, the world economy was affected as well. At this juncture, Japan accounted for some 8.5% of global GDP but a fifth of all semiconductor output and two-fifths of global flash memory chips. More than 10% of the total supply inputs of some US electronics products was imported from Japan, while overseas Japanese corporate affiliates overwhelmingly relied on procurement from the home country. This was especially the case for electric machinery and precision instruments. Many manufacturers in the United States, the European Union and Asia had to pause or reduce production because of a shortage of Japanese components. The number of cars manufactured worldwide dropped by almost 30% in the wake of the earthquake. Growth across the OECD economies was significantly slower in 2011 than in 2010. The same was true in the developing world.

DAMAGE LIMITATION AND RENEWAL

Following the disaster, Japanese policymakers once again had to respond to a huge and novel shock, the immediate consequences of which were extremely difficult to come to terms with.

The government rapidly launched a ten-year reconstruction programme focusing on the three prefectures mentioned above that had been the most impacted. The 'Basic Guidelines for Reconstruction' included ¥19 trillion (4% of GDP) of remedial spending for the period spanning the financial years 2011/2012 to 2015/2016, some ¥17 trillion (3.6% of GDP) of which was embodied in three supplementary budgets and the budget for the 2012/2013 financial year. The first two supplementary budgets, which passed in May and July 2011, naturally focused on relief of devastated areas. The much bigger third supplementary budget in November 2011 was more focused on reconstruction per se. The incoming Abe government then subsequently expanded the five-year spending target to ¥25 trillion, with some of the extra spending factored into its initial January 2013 fiscal package and the budget for the 2013/2014 financial year.

The additional outlays were financed by so-called reconstruction bonds. These would be redeemed primarily via subsequent tax increases, notably surcharges on corporate income tax over the financial years 2012/2013 to 2014/2015 and on personal income tax for 25 years. However, spending cuts and the sale of some state-owned assets would also play a role.

Needless to say, the costs of reconstruction weighed heavily on Japan's already unsustainable public finances and further complicated the requirement for long-term fiscal consolidation. Indeed, the first half of 2011 saw a slew of downgrades of Japan's credit status by various rating agencies. A revised medium-term Fiscal Management Strategy, issued in August 2011, still paid lip service to the halving of the combined central and local primary government deficits by the 2015/2016 financial year, and the achievement of a primary surplus in the 2020/2021 financial year, but the challenge was now much greater. The overall consolidated budget deficit once again swelled to just short of 10% of GDP in 2011 and remained around 9% of GDP over the next two years. The burden of gross government debt meanwhile rocketed upwards towards 250% of GDP – more than a third higher than that of Greece, the country at the epicentre of the European sovereign debt crisis. Even in net terms – that is to say, adjusted for the government's stock of financial assets – the debt burden increased to just short of 130% of GDP, or approaching twice the advanced economy average of around 70%.

Nevertheless, bond yields continued to trend down, dropping below 1% towards the end of 2011. Japan's continued proneness to deflation undoubtedly played an important role in this, but more than ever Japanese policymakers were thankful for the nation's abundant domestic savings and the particular distribution of JGB holdings.

The ability of Japan to finance its reconstruction programme at super low interest costs was also eased by the further actions of the BOJ. Over the course of the 21 months following the earthquake, it steadily ratcheted up its asset purchase programme, and particularly its JGB buying, to over ¥100 trillion, or some 21% of GDP, while dramatically expanding its fund supplying operations. Indeed, by October 2012 the latter had no upper limit.

The Bank's expansive actions were important in sustaining the payments system and preventing excessive financial turbulence too. The sharply increased demand for liquidity in the wake of the earthquake was accommodated and domestic markets and institutions remained resilient. An initial bout of panic selling in the domestic equity market (it was at one stage down some 18%, wiping out nearly ¥57 trillion in market capitalization) subsided after a few days, although key indices continued to languish at levels that were a fraction of their December 1989 highs. Meanwhile, a series of interventions coordinated with other G7 central banks helped to moderate currency volatility, cap the still elevated yen and reduce the contagion risks to other asset classes and economies.

The BOJ was helped in its efforts to maintain financial stability by the fact that the banks had little exposure to the regions most impacted by the earthquake. At the end of 2010 the three hardest-hit prefectures accounted for just 2.4% of total outstanding loans. This is not to suggest that local banks did not suffer, but they did not pose a major nationwide systemic problem. As for the insurance companies, the major firms' solvency margins were more than adequate to absorb the costs, while the government provided assistance for the sector where residential claims were concerned. The corporate sector was also well positioned to weather the crisis. While its overall debt to equity ratio was high at around 175%, it held a lot of liquid assets, profitability had recently improved, corporate defaults were moderate and the credit ratings of most companies were high.

GROUNDHOG DAY

Despite continued currency strength and severe electricity shortages, underpinned by robust public sector demand, Japan's economy initially rebounded strongly from the effects of the earthquake and tsunami. Real GDP expanded by some 3.7% between Q2 2011 and Q1 2012. Private consumption, business confidence, industrial production and exports all traced a similar positive path, and the unemployment rate edged down towards 4% of the workforce. Even the rate of deflation moderated somewhat for a period, although stock and land prices continued to languish. On the other hand, the combination of sluggish world trade, yen strength and the need for Japan to import alternative sources of energy (principally oil and liquified natural gas) in the wake of the Fukushima disaster meant that the external surplus fell to just 1% of GDP in 2012 – its lowest level since the early 1980s. Indeed, for a period towards the end of the year, the current account went into deficit, briefly sparking fears that in future Japan might have to depend on the generosity of foreign investors to finance its budget deficit.

The cyclical bounce once again proved all too brief, however, stalling in Q2 2012, with output barely above the previous peak established in Q3 2010 and still some 1.2% below its Q1 2008 pre-GFC level. Japan subsequently fell into recession for the third time in five years, while the easing of deflationary pressures proved all too modest and fleeting. More than two decades after the collapse of the 1980s bubble, the economy was contracting once again and consumer and asset prices had yet to stabilize, despite almost 15 years of near-zero policy interest rates and the central bank's repeated resort to unconventional action.

The decline in output in the latter three quarters of 2012 reflected in part the fading of post-earthquake government spending but was also down to weak external conditions. The global recovery from the GFC had lost momentum as the widespread resort to fiscal policy support around the depths of the crisis was simultaneously unwound, the European sovereign debt crisis rumbled on, and China, the primary source of the initial global rebound in activity, slowed down.

Just as they had done in the two previous downturns, export volumes fell sharply as a consequence of Japanese industry's concentration in capital and intermediate goods and in discretionary consumer products. The yen was also at this stage some 45% above its 2007 level in nominal effective terms and 24% higher in real terms. Against the Korean won – an increasingly important cross rate for Japan – it had appreciated more than 80% over this period.

Against this background, business confidence waned and industrial production fell back to a level around one-fifth below its 2008 peak, feeding back negatively into business investment. The one bright spot was private consumption, which was sustained by resilient employment trends and the continuation of some government subsidies for the purchase of environment-friendly vehicles.

REGIME CHANGE

Exports stabilized towards the end of 2012, leading to a rebound in output growth in the first quarter of 2013. More importantly, this period also saw the 'second incarnation' of Abe Shinzo as prime minister. Six years on from his first short and less-than-sweet term of office, Abe was this time presented to the electorate as a courageous reformer akin to his mentor Koizumi Junichiro, who was determined to achieve economic revival.

Re-elected as LDP president in September 2012, Abe's advisors convinced him that Japan had fallen into a trap in the mid 1990s and had remained there ever since. In short, slow growth and deflation had dramatically undermined the public finances, but the exhaustion of conventional monetary policy and intermittent efforts to achieve fiscal consolidation had prevented successful reflation. The economy was stuck in a quasi-equilibrium of deficient nominal GDP growth and policy ineffectiveness. The trap could only be sprung if deflation were defeated once and for all – and this meant thinking more outside the box. Abe was therefore, from the outset of his general election campaign, strongly committed to a bolder and more unconventional economic policy. What is more, as it became increasingly likely that the LDP would return to office under his leadership, the markets began to discount this change of approach. The yen finally began to adjust lower, and the stock market rallied strongly.

The policy regime change of early 2013 that became known as Abenomics was presented as an economic revival plan that marked a clear break from the incrementalism of previous policies. It encompassed three elements – or, in the terminology of the new prime minister, 'three arrows'.[4]

The first arrow of Abe's strategy was more aggressive unconventional monetary stimulus. The second was 'fiscal flexibility'. This amounted to more short-term government largesse centred on the old default option of public investment, which would dovetail with the monetary expansion. However, it would be followed by a shift to long-term consolidation once the economy was growing sustainably and prices were rising. The third arrow was a revitalized programme of structural reform to boost productivity and the supply side of the economy over the medium to long term; this, it was suggested, would also be easier to see through if deflation were overcome and the economy back on its feet.

One of Abe's first practical initiatives was to reconstitute the CEFP that had played an important role in the formulation of economic policy under the Koizumi governments but that had been cast aside by the DPJ administrations. At the first CEFP meeting in January 2013, the prime minister argued that the BOJ should set aside its existing conservative inflation objective and instead aim rapidly to achieve an annual rate of increase in the CPI of 2% – a rate similar to that of most other major central banks.

Echoing Hayami Masaru, his predecessor but one, Governor Shirakawa had long been sceptical about specific targets and was unconvinced that monetary expansion could deliver sustained positive inflation in a rapidly ageing, low potential growth economy, where there was limited scope to bring growth forward from the future. However, he was clearly being put under enormous political pressure to fall in behind Abe.[5] In the end, after much agonizing, Shirakawa concluded that he had little choice but to toe the new government's line. The alternative would be to risk the Bank being formally stripped of its independence and to see his own removal from office.

Hence, after the subsequent BOJ Policy Board meeting at the end of January, a joint statement with the government was released to the effect that the Bank would in future pursue an explicit 2% inflation target and aim to achieve that target at the earliest possible time. Furthermore, it would adopt an open-ended approach to asset purchases (there was as such no specified termination date) and boost the APP by a further ¥10 trillion, taking it up to ¥111 trillion (23% of GDP).

Subsequently, however, Shirakawa announced that he, along with his two deputies, would leave office three weeks before their five-year term expired. This opened the way for Abe to appoint Kuroda Haruhiko – a veteran reflationist, a former senior MOF official and the president of the Asian Development Bank – as his replacement. There were also other important personnel changes at the Bank, including the selection of the academic Iwata Kikuo, another longstanding critic of the BOJ, as one of Kuroda's two deputies.

In exploring the criticisms of the Bank prior to Kuroda's elevation, it is noteworthy that – notwithstanding the various initiatives taken in the wake of the earthquake and the success it enjoyed in maintaining financial stability – the expansion of the Japanese central bank's balance sheet had continued to fall short of that seen in the United States, the euro area and the United Kingdom, both in nominal terms and as a percentage of GDP. At the same time, the effectiveness of its increasingly expansive government bond-buying operations had been constrained by its overwhelming focus on shorter-maturity debt: assets that were very close substitutes for the central bank reserves that the BOJ in effect offered in return.

Treasury Bills and JGBs with a maturity of between one and three years accounted for some 90% of the Bank's APP; private assets a mere 10%. The portfolio balance effect of QE – the associated reduction in term and risk premia in fixed-income and other markets – was therefore limited. It would have been more substantive had the Bank prioritized longer-term bonds and private assets. The feeling among Abe's advisors and beyond was that the Shirakawa BOJ had soft-pedalled on QE and that it was less than fully committed to it. This was set to change.

Following the first meeting of the Bank's Policy Board after he had taken office in April, Kuroda announced a yet more aggressive programme of monetary expansion given the moniker 'quantitative and qualitative easing' (or QQE). The intention was to double the monetary base (currency in circulation plus commercial bank reserves held at the BOJ) from ¥138 trillion (28% of GDP) at the end of 2012 to ¥270 trillion at the end of 2014 in an effort to achieve the new 2% inflation target within an initial horizon of two years.

As part of the process, the BOJ's JGB holdings would rise at an annual pace of around ¥50 trillion, extending to all maturities, such that the average remaining maturity of its holdings would increase to about seven years, equivalent to the average maturity of the entire outstanding stock of JGBs. At the same time, the Bank's ETF and J-REIT purchases would rise to ¥1 trillion and ¥30 billion, respectively.

Finally, the Bank's forward policy guidance was again strengthened: it would sustain this unreconstructed expansionary approach until the inflation target was met 'in a stable manner'.

The desire was to address the criticisms of the previous policy regime, send an unambiguous message regarding the Bank's intentions with regard to inflation, make clear there would be no premature tightening similar to that seen in 2001 and 2006, and thereby significantly change the expectations of both the markets and economic agents in general in regard to the future outlook trend in prices. Even if it was not directly underwriting the government's issuance of bonds as had been done in the early 1930s, the BOJ policy was converging on the strategy adopted by Takahashi Korekiyo at that time.

Turning to the second arrow of Abenomics, in keeping with the notion of growth first and budgetary consolidation later, the incoming Abe government announced a ¥10.3 trillion (2.2% of GDP) fiscal stimulus package in January 2013. This was composed of public works spending, aid for small businesses and investment incentives.

Where the third arrow was concerned, the government offered little initial detail, although in mid March Abe announced that, building on a DPJ initiative, Japan would enter negotiations to join the Trans-Pacific Partnership (TPP), a sophisticated trade grouping the United States was seeking to assemble with much of Asia. The hope was that this could be a mechanism to enhance competition across the economy and through which the government would be able to enact future reforms to liberalize certain long-sheltered sectors of the Japanese economy, most notably agriculture. It was, in short, a deliberate resort to *Gaiatsu* to foster domestic change.

Overall, the initial months of Abenomics saw the new government deliver its easier elements – essentially, monetary and fiscal reflation. The more challenging aspects of the policy – specifically, an extended period of fiscal consolidation amounting to as much as 10 percentage points of GDP and including a significantly higher consumption tax, plus new supply-side reforms – would have to be faced later.

In the meantime, however, medium-to-long-term market-determined inflation expectations broke higher, moving up towards 2% for the first time since the bubble burst. The yen's nominal trade-weighted value fell by 20%, and the long-depressed Nikkei 225 stock index rose by 30%. The latest cyclical upswing, which had begun at the very end of 2012, rapidly gathered momentum. Helped by the yen's adjustment lower and the rally in the equity market, the economy expanded strongly over the course of the year, registering growth of some 2% relative to 2012. Headline CPI inflation also turned positive. Abenomics seemed to be working.

BETTER THAN IT MIGHT HAVE BEEN?

Thanks to the belated banking and corporate sector restructuring of the early 2000s, Japan avoided many of the worst aspects of the financial meltdown that consumed numerous other economies during the GFC and its aftermath. However, its experiences proved no less demanding for its policymaking community and served further to extend the nation's post-bubble era of output volatility, diminished underlying performance and expectations, and persistent deflation. Nominal GDP at the time of Abe Shinzo's return as prime minister remained almost 9% lower than its Q4 1997 peak. Moreover, the fact that it was the travails of its export-dependent manufacturing sector – long its comparative advantage and often the envy of the world – that provided the initial catalyst for many of the problems it faced during this period was a particularly unexpected development with which to come to terms. In this context, the yen's safe-haven status and persistent strength regularly seemed more trouble than they were worth.

Japan suffered three sharp recessions in a mere five-year period following the GFC, and while that which followed the Great East Japan Earthquake and tsunami of March 2013 was in effect an unavoidable act of God, the underlying message was that, for all the policy interventions and painful adjustments in the early years of the new century, the economy remained fragile and vulnerable to shocks. It was only in the third quarter of 2013 that it regained the level of real GDP achieved in Q1 2008. Prices continued to fall for the most part. Unsurprisingly this led to a period of political turmoil and change, although it was notable that, at the end of 2012, in extremis the Japanese electorate returned to the bosom of the LDP, the political entity that, for all its foibles and shortcomings, it was most familiar with and that had delivered the economic miracle of the 1950s and 1960s.

The economy's triple dip meant that there could be no sustained normalization of macroeconomic policy. Fiscal policy stimuli of differing shapes and sizes was once again resorted to as a default option, and the nation's public finance metrics deteriorated at an alarming and increasingly unsustainable rate. But at least the same factors that underpinned the yen's persistent strength – high domestic savings, the structural external surplus, the huge pool of external assets and the peculiar nature of Japan's home investment bias – meant that there was no loss of bond market confidence. The nation's huge deficits and massive burden of government debt were comfortably financed. The need for fiscal adjustment could be put off – although not forever. At some stage there would be a reckoning. The only question was when.

Anchored by the BOJ's near-zero policy rate, the term structure remained historically low in absolute and relative terms. The Bank's imagination for supplementary unconventional initiatives also continued to prove fertile, especially post the Lehman Brothers debacle and following the earthquake and tsunami. However, there was a sense under Governor Shirakawa's tenure at the Bank that it was a reluctant innovator, and that it often did not really believe in some of the things it found itself doing, especially where fighting deflation was concerned. In important respects it was going through the motions. It was content to be seen to be doing something.

This was self-defeating. As suggested in chapter 5 when discussing the attitude of Shirakawa's predecessor, Hayami Masaru, monetary stimulus works in significant part through the management of expectations and by the central bank fostering the belief across the economy that it will work. If the governor and some of his senior colleagues suggested they were unconvinced of their policies' success, others would be encouraged to think along the same lines. In this sense, the political pressure for a change in the Bank's modus operandi, and for it to embrace a more unreconstructed approach to monetary reflation after 2013, was unsurprising. Notwithstanding its apparent initial success, however, whether the Bank would subsequently deliver a sustained change in the dynamics of the price level was moot.

Indeed, the same judgement could be applied to the chances of success of Abenomics as a whole. For all the rhetorical flourishes about a new unconstrained approach and the firing of three new policy 'arrows', there are in essence only ever three conduits of economic policy: monetary, fiscal and structural (where the first and the third also embody elements of financial policy). Japan had already been applying them all in some combination or other, often in a pioneering fashion, with the objective of improving the economy's performance since the bubble burst, albeit with the two macro elements doing most of the heavy lifting and structural policy often flattering to deceive.

Perhaps a clearer, more coordinated and coherent approach would produce better results than had so far been achieved, but that clarity, coordination and coherence had to be achieved first, and it would not be easy. Japan faced enormous headwinds, not just from its challenging demographics and the unprecedented state of the public finances, but also because the longer its malaise continued, the more embedded it became into the expectations of firms and individuals.

In its widest sense, successfully implementing the three arrows of Abenomics would take Japanese policymakers into more uncharted waters; it would involve complex sequencing and many difficult trade-offs, and it would have to overcome powerful vested interests. It could easily become unbalanced, descend into outright contradiction and confusion, or go entirely astray, leading to runaway inflation – the opposite of the problem that Japan had struggled with for almost two decades. The proof of the pudding would come in the eating, and at the beginning of 2013, the new prime minister had yet to outline the more testing elements of his approach.

CHAPTER 9

Abenomics and After

'One who chases after two [or three] hares will not even catch one' — Japanese proverb

IMPRESSIVE DURABILITY

Abe Shinzo's second premiership extended from late 2012 until his resignation, again on the grounds of ill health, in August 2020. This was during the middle of the Covid-19 pandemic and a year or so after Emperor Naruhito had ascended to the thrown following the abdication of his father Akihito, also on the grounds of ill health.[1]

Abe's second term of office was the longest in Japan's history and thereby provided a stark contrast to his first brief and unsuccessful spell as Japan's political figurehead. It also coincided with the longest cyclical upswing of the post-war era: an expansion that lasted until late 2019.

HESITANT PROGRESS

This expansion was quite different to the raucous booms of the High Growth Era of the 1950s and 1960s or, for that matter, the bubble economy of the late 1980s. The average annual real GDP growth rate for the years 2013–2019 was a little under 1%: a figure akin to that of the 'lost decade' of the 1990s, lower than that seen during the run-up to the GFC and some way below that enjoyed by Japan's major competitors. There were, in addition, several setbacks along the way, which, while they never evolved into what was considered a full-blown recession, slowed the economy's progress and sometimes halted it altogether, leading to contraction. These hiatuses, like those that had preceded them over the previous 25 years, reflected fiscal policy adjustments – in particular two further increases in the consumption tax – and deteriorations in the external growth and exchange rate environments.

During this period the country's challenging demographics, and in particular its declining and rapidly greying population, came increasingly to the fore. As suggested previously, having peaked in the late 2000s the population was now in decline. By 2060 it was expected to drop by some 25% to a level last seen in the late 1950s, sparking significant depopulation in many rural areas. The labour force was likely to fall by even more, and with Japanese life expectancy the longest in the world, the old-age dependency ratio – the ratio of those aged 65 and above to those of working age (15–64) – would exceed 75%.

All this acted further to undercut the economy's already diminished growth potential to between 0.5% and 1% a year. It also further depressed the 'natural', or 'equilibrium', real rate of interest, which, together with low inflation, diminished the ability of monetary policy to reflate the economy.[2] And it necessitated the diversion of mounting resources into pensions and health and social care while amplifying uncertainty about the future. Quite how Japan would adjust to these circumstances was unclear. There was no historical template for it to follow.

Labour productivity continued to disappoint in absolute and relative terms, and there was a marked increase in the performance gap between larger manufacturing firms at the technological frontier and others, especially SMEs in the service sector. Productivity declined in more years than it increased, and the average annual productivity growth rate for the years 2013–2019 was around zero. Consequently, the absolute level of productivity remained some 30% below the average for the top-performing OECD economies and substantially further adrift from the United States, which increasingly outpaced its rivals based on this crucial metric.

This is not to deny that there were some important reforms made over the course of these years in areas such as corporate governance, female participation, the structure of the tax system and Japan's trading relationships. Environmental policy also became increasingly important, and significant initiatives were launched to move the country towards carbon neutrality. But, in aggregate, structural policy again fell short at a time when the size and nature of the trials facing the country demanded more ambition and more conspicuous progress.

Personal consumption spending was persistently weak after 2013 but especially so in the years 2014 and 2019, when the consumption tax was further increased. Business investment offered a more consistently positive contribution to growth – and was better balanced between firm size, manufacturing and services, and equipment and structures – than during the previous upswing, but it faded somewhat after 2015, despite a consistently historically high share of profits in GDP and a huge and growing pool of corporate savings.

Growth in the capital stock more or less ground to a halt in the face of faster rates of depreciation and scrapping where tech investments were concerned. The average age of the economy's plant and equipment increased noticeably as a result.

Notwithstanding the customary intermittent episodes of largesse when growth undershot expectations and/or political expediency intervened, the impulse of fiscal policy was for the most part contractionary. The headline and primary consolidated budget deficits therefore trended down, but progress failed to match the government's targets. The aggregate burden of public debt, already far higher than in Japan's major competitors, escalated further, reaching levels unseen in Japan since the end of World War II. Only rock-bottom interest costs; the concentration of debt ownership in the hands of domestic investors, including, increasingly, the BOJ; and a structural external surplus afforded Japan any fiscal policy space.

The contribution of net exports to growth was initially negative following the disruptions caused by the Great East Japan Earthquake and tsunami, but it became consistently positive in the mid 2010s before reversing course again towards the end of the decade. Import penetration trended gently higher, while Japan's share of world exports was stable at between 3.5% and 4.0%, as it continued to move up the value-added chain, its specialization in technologically complex goods deepening. Once the effects of the extraordinary events of early 2013 had faded, the foreign balance stabilized at between 3% and 4% of GDP. The gross saving rate remained extraordinarily high, but it was no longer the merchandise trade balance that dominated the economy's external performance. Rather, it was rapidly growing tourist arrivals, which increased sixfold between the end of the GFC and mid 2019, and in particular it was the substantial income that Japan earned on a high, rising and well-diversified pool of external assets. By the early 2020s these amounted to more than 70% of GDP. Despite the government's huge indebtedness, because of the private sector's thrift Japan remained by some margin the world's largest creditor nation.

Where prices were concerned, the deflation that had dogged Japan since the late 1990s was to some extent tamed, but however defined, inflation remained exceptionally low and consistently undershot both the BOJ's 2% CPI-based target and the rates seen in most of Japan's competitors. Much of the variation in inflation from period to period was driven by international commodity and exchange-rate trends. But inflation expectations, whether market-derived or survey-based, were reluctant to move upwards.

Low inflation and inflation expectations – together with labour market dualism and, most conspicuously, a rising share of relatively poorly paid part-time workers – weighed heavily on the process of wage determination. Although Japan enjoyed persistently full employment – the unemployment rate dropped to a 25-year low over this period – and the output gap became increasingly positive, wage inflation was beset by inertia. The average annual rate of growth in compensation per employee was about 0.6%. Japan's Phillips curve – the graphical relationship between labour market slack and wage growth – was, like its LM curve, close to horizontal.

Persistently low inflation meant that nominal interest rates plumbed new depths, with a considerable proportion of the term structure dropping into negative territory for much of the period. Borrowing costs were anchored by the acutely depressed level of the main policy rate, which itself was pushed into negative territory from February 2016, and further constrained by other increasingly unconventional monetary policy initiatives pursued by the BOJ. However, the entire world was locked into a low-growth, low-inflation, low-interest-rate equilibrium in the wake of the GFC, as the level of desired investment consistently fell short of the level of desired savings. Japan was not alone in experiencing negative policy interest rates, or bond yields, and the ability of any central bank to escape this subdued equilibrium was limited.

As for real assets, the stock market traced a similar path to the real economy, in that it gradually trended upwards, albeit with a number of corrections and retreats. But it remained far removed from its late-1989 peak. Property prices also resumed the tentative recovery that had begun in the previous decade, although, apart from where condominiums were concerned, the pace of improvement was glacial. Even at the end of the decade, overall land prices remained only about two-thirds of the peak established in mid 1991.

On a brighter note, although profitability remained low, especially where regional entities were concerned, the banking sector was liquid, well capitalized and stable throughout. There was no reprise of the NPL problem. Even more encouragingly, Japan's annual growth in real GDP per head accelerated after 2012 to a rate of around 1.3%, which was close to the OECD average. And more impressively still, real GDP growth per head of the working-age population averaged some 2.3% a year between 2012 and 2019 – half a percentage point higher than the OECD average. For those in work, living standards improved quite rapidly.

In examining this extended period of shallow and hesitant expansion in more detail, it is perhaps best to view it through the lens of the three arrows of Prime Minister Abe's overarching economic policy framework, including how they interacted with one another. Let us begin with monetary policy.

THE OUTER LIMITS OF MONETARY POLICY

The 2010s saw the BOJ continue to set much of the global agenda for unconventional monetary policy. Finally fixated on overcoming deflation and returning the country to enduring price stability, the Japanese central bank embraced additional initiatives that for most of the post-war era would have been unthinkable. Unsurprisingly, as the monetary arrow of Abenomics evolved through numerous policy iterations and internal BOJ reviews, it was beset by controversy and the results were mixed. As time went on, it also became increasingly unclear how the Bank could disengage from its burgeoning unorthodoxies, assuming that it ultimately achieved its mandated goal of sustained 2% inflation.

As suggested at the end of the previous chapter, the more expansive approach announced in April 2013 initially appeared to be working. BOJ policy had been closely coordinated with the burst of fiscal stimulus embodied in the February supplementary budget. Indeed, the Bank began to purchase more JGBs than were being issued, effectively more than fully financing the government and thereby following in the footsteps of the Takahashi strategy of underwriting the bond market in the early to mid 1930s. Financial conditions eased as term premia and longer-term interest rates declined, stock prices spiked higher and the yen depreciated. Bank lending growth accelerated and investment portfolios were gradually rebalanced.[3] Real GDP growth moved well above potential, inflation expectations firmed up, and the deflation that had been so pervasive since the GFC was overcome. Consumer price and wage inflation returned to positive territory, with the annual rate of headline CPI inflation rising to around 1.5% in late 2013; the underlying rate peaked just below 1.0%.

This success was short lived, however. Following an increase in the consumption tax to 8% at the beginning of April 2014, real GDP slumped by almost 2% in the second quarter and recovered only gradually over the next six months. At the same time, the oil market slumped, the price of Brent crude halving during the second half of the year, while other international commodity markets also weakened. In this environment, CPI inflation – excluding the one-off impact of higher indirect taxation – fell back towards zero, as indeed did inflation expectations and the rate of increase in wages.

The BOJ had no choice but to recognize that it would not reach its 2% inflation target anytime soon, and in October 2014 it increased its annual target for net JGB purchases from ¥60 trillion to ¥80 trillion, extended the average maturity of these purchases to 7–10 years to compress longer-term yields, and tripled the rate of its acquisitions of ETFs and J-REITs (the most 'qualitative' of its easing measures) to ¥3 trillion a year. By early 2015 the Bank's balance sheet had swollen to the equivalent of some 65% of GDP – more than double what it was when QQE was initiated. However, these policy changes only came about via a close 5–4 vote by the Policy Board. There were many within the Bank, and beyond, that had reservations about the effectiveness of the stance being taken and fears about the associated side-effects.

The yen subsequently renewed its decline into year end, while stock prices rose to levels last seen in the run-up to the GFC. The economy enjoyed a better start to 2015, with the level of real GDP bouncing back above its previous Q1 2014 peak. Progress thereafter was sluggish, however. Fiscal policy remained contractionary, even though Abe took the decision to postpone a further hike in the consumption tax from October 2015 to April 2017. The yen reversed course and began to strengthen. Bank lending growth flattened off. CPI inflation failed to pick up, running around zero throughout 2015. Nor was there any obvious improvement in inflation expectations or wage growth, and by late 2015 the stock market was falling once again.

The BOJ's somewhat surprising response to these disappointing outcomes – there had been little active discussion of such a move in advance, and once again it was only agreed to after a close 5-4 Policy Board vote – was to follow the example of the Swiss National Bank, the Swedish Riksbank and the ECB and introduce a negative interest rate policy (NIRP). A rate of –0.1% was imposed on financial sector excess reserves, to complement QQE. To ease the impact on profitability when these reserve balances at the Bank were the equivalent of more than 50% of GDP, and more than 25% of total bank assets, a three-tier reserve deposit system was introduced, with only the top (marginal) tier – a modest proportion of the total – subject to the new negative rate.

However, concerns about banking profitability meant that the BOJ's scope to push its policy rate further into negative territory was limited.[4] For similar reasons, it could also be argued that it might have made more sense to use a negative policy rate before embracing QE and forcing commercial banks to hold large quantities of excess reserves that the Bank effectively subjected to a tax.

Notwithstanding these limitations and shortcomings, the policy helped both to lower market rates further, with the 10-year JGB yield dropping below zero, and to accelerate portfolio balancing. However, there was at first little discernible effect on the yen, on inflation expectations, on stock prices or on risk seeking at the banks, and confidence in the ability of the BOJ to hit its inflation target remained lacking. There were also concerns about market functioning, as liquidity in the JGB market subsequently declined. Negative rates had costs as well as benefits and were far from a game changer. The economy remained sluggish in 2016, while CPI inflation dropped back below zero in the middle of the year[5] and wages remained largely stagnant.

Faced with these troubling circumstances, the government took the decision in mid 2016 further to postpone the proposed increase in the consumption tax to 10%, pushing it out to October 2019, while the BOJ once again expanded its ETF purchases to ¥6 trillion a year. By this stage, however, concerns were mounting about the sustainability of QQE and the NIRP. In addition to the worries about market liquidity and banking-sector profitability, speculation mounted that the collateral needs of the banks, the balance sheet constraints of insurers and the asset allocation targets of pension funds could together conspire to force the BOJ to taper its bond purchases. The fear was that there would quite simply not be enough JGBs available for it to buy.

As a consequence, in September 2016, following a comprehensive review of monetary policy, the Bank took the decision by a 7–2 majority on the Policy Board to de-emphasize its annual ¥80 trillion JGB purchase target and instead commit to holding the 10-year JGB yield around zero in addition to maintaining its negative policy rate. At the same time, it sought to strengthen its forward policy guidance and its influence on inflation expectations by committing to expand the monetary base until inflation exceeded 2% and 'stayed above it in a stable manner'. Through the lens of real interest rates, the monetary stance would therefore become more expansionary as inflation converged on the newly refined target.

Confusingly, the Bank added that it expected initially to continue to buy JGBs more or less in line with the then-existing pace of ¥80 trillion a year (equivalent to some 16% of GDP), although the amount of JGB purchases was now in effect endogenous. It is impossible to control the quantity and price of an asset at the same time.

Beyond the contradictory rhetoric, the BOJ's hope was that its commitment to a zero 10-year rate would be sufficiently credible for it to disengage somewhat from the bond market while also allowing it to shape the yield curve in such a way as to sustain bank profitability and insurance and pension fund returns. In this it was successful. The Bank's JGB purchases declined to ¥58 trillion in 2017, ¥37.6 trillion in 2018 and less than ¥20 trillion in 2019, although its holdings of government bonds and the total size of its balance sheet continued to escalate towards the equivalent of 100% of GDP, far larger than those of the other major central banks with the exception of the Swiss National Bank. Meanwhile, the yield curve developed a marked 'hinge' or 'kink' around the 10-year maturity. There was a significant steepening out to 40 years.

The decision to effectively fix the cost of government borrowing represented a further blurring of the lines between monetary and fiscal policy and an embrace of Takahashi-style monetary finance, with its attendant moral hazard risks. When challenged on this, the Bank claimed that its independence hinged on the continued maintenance of its inflation-targeting framework and that it could and would tighten policy in whatever way necessary if the target were met. But, as Takahashi found out to his peril in the mid 1930s, the politics of policy normalization could be problematic. This would especially be the case in the event that excessive inflation resulted from the government pursuing an irresponsible fiscal policy or, for that matter, if the Bank's desire for higher interest rates increased debt service costs to the extent that the government's discretionary spending plans were crimped. Only time would tell if politicians would prove amenable to the BOJ continuing to plough an independent furrow.

The aftermath of the introduction of so-called quantitative and qualitative easing with yield curve control, or QQE with YCC, saw real rates fall, stocks rally, the yen's rise curtailed and a modest acceleration of bank lending growth. With the fiscal stance also moderately expansionary for a period, the economy picked up again. Real GDP growth in 2017 was, at 1.7%, the strongest outcome since 2013, although there was little follow through into the following year. CPI inflation also moved back into positive territory in 2017 and 2018, although this again in part reflected swings in oil and other commodity prices.

After 20 years of near-zero inflation, inflation expectations remained stubbornly muted, and the BOJ continued to find itself repeatedly having to downgrade its inflation forecasts, to the extent that in April of 2018 it announced that monetary policy would no longer be tied to a specific time frame for meeting its inflation target. Notwithstanding some acceleration encouraged by tripartite dialogue between government, employers and employees; tax incentives; and regular generous increases in the minimum wage, wage inflation continued to run at such a depressed level that hitting the 2% inflation target was impossible.

Although the monetary arrow of Abenomics had yet to hit the bull's eye, Kuroda Haruhiko was reappointed for a second term as BOJ governor by Prime Minister Abe in April 2018. By this stage, however, there were renewed concerns about the sustainability and distortions associated with the BOJ's increasingly unorthodoxy approach. Bond market liquidity remained low, and fears were again building about excessive risk taking in the economy. The Bank's deep involvement in the equity market via its extensive ETF purchases also raised hackles. It had come to own more than 75% of the ETF market, which indirectly put it in the top ten shareholders of 40% of all listed companies.

Responding to these issues, in July the BOJ widened the acceptable range for the 10-year JGB yield to zero plus or minus 20 basis points and announced that its ETF and J-REIT purchases would in future be dictated by market conditions. To address speculation that these moves were precursors to a formal tightening of policy, it further finessed its forward guidance, explicitly committing to keeping short- and long-term rates low for an extended period.

The economy stalled once again in the second half of 2018 in the face of a weakening of global growth, heightened uncertainty over international trade policy and another bout of exchange rate strength. There was a brief rebound as spending accelerated in advance of the long-delayed consumption tax hike to 10% in October 2019, but thereafter activity once again fell sharply. Real GDP contracted almost 3% in the final quarter of the year, barely stabilized in the first quarter of 2020, and then slumped dramatically as the Covid-19 pandemic hit. In this environment there could be no dramatic improvement in the inflation situation. Underlying wage and price pressures remained negligible. The BOJ's 2% target was still out of reach.

There was pressure for the Bank to do more to sustain growth in 2019, but by this stage it had few options left beyond resorting to ever more heterodox variations on the theme of monetary finance. These were rejected and it settled instead for further tweaking its forward guidance to clarify its reaction function and convince the markets and the public that monetary policy remained contingent on the path of inflation.

After more than five years of Abenomics, the low natural rate of interest and the obduracy of depressed inflation expectations continued to undermine monetary policy. Shirakawa Masaaki's pessimism about how much a central bank could achieve in the circumstances confronted by Japan – and in particular bearing in mind its demography and its low future growth potential – retained considerable veracity. For all Kuroda Haruhiko's efforts, the BOJ and the economy still seemed to be stuck on the flat portion of the LM curve, as they had been since the 1990s. Quite what sort of endogenous shock would change this was unclear.

FISCAL FLAMMERY

As already noted, the second (fiscal policy) arrow of Abenomics was initiated with yet another sizeable public-investment-heavy stimulus package, amounting to some 2.2% of GDP. With its positive impact on the economy still playing out and growth firm, however, in the autumn of 2013 Abe decided to ignore those of his colleagues who argued in favour of 'growth first and retrenchment later' and to proceed with the first stage of the proposed increase in the consumption tax, from 5% to 8%, in April 2014.

The rationale was that serious fiscal consolidation was long overdue, the economy seemed to be robust enough to shrug off the tax hike, and the higher rate of indirect taxation would provide a more sustainable basis for the future burden of social spending. While it was accepted that the tax hike would temporarily weaken economic growth, in also announcing a further ¥5 trillion stimulus package, Abe hoped to mitigate these effects and underpin a subsequent rebound in activity.

Unfortunately, once again the impact of a tightening of fiscal policy exceeded expectations, especially where private consumption spending was concerned. Notwithstanding Abe's countermeasures, the overall budgetary stance was tightened by around 1.5% of GDP in 2014 and the cyclical upswing suffered a significant setback, with output only returning to its Q1 2014 level a year later.

Chastened, Abe decided to delay the second stage of the tax rise scheduled for October 2015 until April 2017 and called a snap election on the issue of his economic strategy. The LDP and its *Komeito* party coalition partners comfortably won, retaining a two-thirds majority in the Lower House of the Diet.

However, notwithstanding the fact that the economy had temporarily stalled, the budget situation did seem to be improving. With the share of government revenues in GDP boosted by a higher indirect tax take to a level closer to that seen in other advanced economies, the consolidated deficit dropped to 3.7% of GDP in 2015, well under half what it had been in the wake of the GFC. Indeed, progress was sufficient for the government to recommit to its 2010 goal of achieving a primary surplus in the combined central and local budgets by the 2020/2021 financial year, although it promised to review this pledge in 2018 should the shortfall have fallen to 1% of GDP by that time.

This recommitment all too rapidly looked over optimistic. The disappointing tone of growth and the threat of renewed deflation in mid 2016 saw the prime minister announce a further delay in the scheduled rise in the consumption tax to 10% until October 2019. Furthermore, the government initiated another substantial fiscal stimulus package – amounting to some 1.5% of GDP and extending to public investment, disaster alleviation and help for SMEs – that would dovetail with the BOJ's NIRP and YCC policies. The middle years of the decade also saw a much-needed reform of corporate taxes that included a series of reductions in the headline rate to below 30% by the 2018/2019 financial year. The impulse of fiscal policy therefore turned positive again in 2016 and 2017. Growth rebounded to just under 2%, but the headline consolidated budget deficit swelled once more, rising to 5.0% of GDP.

When the promised review of the government's fiscal strategy was conducted in 2018, it concluded that the achievement of balance in the central and local government budgets in the 2020/2021 financial year was out of reach. The target date was pushed out until the 2025/2026 financial year. A number of further expansionary initiatives, amounting to around 1% of GDP, were also subsequently announced with the aim of reducing the volatility of output around the next consumption tax hike. These included the retention of an 8% rate on food and non-alcoholic drinks – a significant distortion of the tax system – higher public investment in the 2019/2020 financial year, support for car and house purchases, vouchers for low-income households and those with fewer than three children, and points rewards for cashless payments at small retailers.

Nevertheless, fiscal policy was contractionary over the course of 2018 and 2019 by just under a percentage point of GDP in cumulative terms, and the economy could not sustain the more positive momentum of 2017. The front-loading of expenditure ahead of the consumption tax hike was, as the government hoped, less dramatic than in 2014, but it was still followed by an unexpectedly large and sharp drop in economic activity in the fourth quarter of 2019, especially where durables outlays were concerned. The weakness of the economy towards the end of the year was further exacerbated by Typhoon Hagibis, the most intense for decades.

With the exchange rate once again on a rising trend, with global growth and exports soft, and with wage growth still languishing, real GDP contracted by 0.4% in 2019. The long and shallow upswing had ground to a halt. December 2019 saw the announcement of a further ¥26 trillion fiscal package, of which some ¥9.4 trillion (1.7% of GDP) was central and local government spending. This was designed to pull the economy out of its latest funk and sustain spending beyond the Tokyo Olympics, then scheduled for mid 2020. But all of this was to be overtaken by events.

In reviewing the second arrow of Abenomics, the raw facts show that, despite two increases in the politically vexed consumption tax and the halving of the government's net interest burden over a seven-year period, Japan's consolidated budget deficit was still around 3% of GDP in 2019, with the primary shortfall about 2.5% of GDP and the gross debt ratio some 224% of GDP and rising. With demographic pressures on the public finances only set to grow, the fiscal situation remained perilous. The 'fiscal flexibility' of the second arrow of Abenomics had not addressed Japan's budgetary problems.

That said, the persistent inability of the monetary arrow to drive inflation up to the BOJ's target played a central role in this failure. Nominal GDP, which is the denominator in calculations of the deficit and the debt burden, increased at an average rate of just 1.5% a year between the end of 2012 and the end of 2019. At the same time, Japan's fiscal strategy over this period remained flawed on a number of levels. It lacked sufficient upfront identification of specific revenue and expenditure measures and rules. The government's baseline projections were built on optimistic assumptions. There was the risk, perhaps even the certainty, that whatever its plans at the start of any fiscal year they would be altered through the improvisations of supplementary budgets as shocks hit the economy and/or political necessity intervened.

Fiscal policy therefore lacked consistency, persistence and credibility. Instead, it was a source of uncertainty and unpredictability. One is forced to conclude that it would have benefited from a new independent institution to provide unbiased forecasts, to inject greater transparency and oversight into the budgetary process, and to make more explicit the priorities and trade-offs inherent in the government's longer-term budgetary challenges. The existing external bodies advising the MOF (the Fiscal System Council) and the prime minister (the Council on Economic and Fiscal Policy) did not possess the autonomy, the clout or the resources to do the job.

As the new decade dawned, therefore, the task facing Japan's fiscal policy-makers remained daunting, and it was about to become harder still because of Covid-19. Stabilizing the debt burden and then bringing it down in a sustained manner would require not just the realization of the BOJ's inflation target, but a primary budget surplus of many percentage points (5 or more) of GDP. To achieve this, the consumption tax rate would have to converge with VAT rates in other countries, which averaged around 20%. There would need to be higher environmental taxes, other reforms to broaden the overall tax base, and tighter control over spending, not least where health and social care and local government outlays were concerned. All this would take time and be politically fraught. The risk was that politicians – who, to that point, had not taken too many egregious liberties with the latitude afforded them by the central bank financing the government – took an easier way out by repudiating some of the debt, and in particular that on the BOJ's balance sheet. At the end of 2019 the central bank held almost 50% of the outstanding total of JGBs.

THE THIRD ARROW FALLS SHORT

Given Japan's significant productivity shortfall and the need to address the impact of demographics both on the labour force and on the economy more broadly, it could be argued that the third arrow of Abenomics was the most important of all. Of course, the more success the monetary and fiscal arrows enjoyed, the easier it would be to make progress on structural reform. In this sense the three arrows were potentially mutually reinforcing, but the fact remained that the success or failure of structural policy would be the dominant determinant both of whether Japan overcame the enormous challenges it was confronted by and of the country's long-term economic performance.

Hence, the most pertinent question for Abe Shinzo and his government was whether they could avoid falling into the same traps as previous administrations where this complex area of policy was concerned. As we have already seen, initiatives aimed at improving Japan's supply-side performance had for decades tended to be atomized, subject to repetition, disjointed, slow-moving, too aspirational in tone and unduly cautious where they encroached on the most politically sensitive ground and where they might involve significant short-term output costs. Progress had been patchy and disappointing up to 2013. The time for a more aggressive approach was long overdue.

Unfortunately, a review of the following six years of supply-side policy reveals many all-too-familiar traits and characteristics: a plethora of often-confused and recurrent announcements that lacked coherence and underlying substance; the creation of new quangos; caution in the face of opposition from vested interests and long-held biases in public attitudes and opinion; gradualism in implementation relative to the manner in which fiscal and monetary policy were employed; and a sense at the end of the period that opportunities had been missed and there was still a great deal to be done. That said, there were some notable achievements, and looking back we get a sense that, in some important respects, necessity had become the mother of invention.

At the outset of Abenomics in early 2013, there was a lengthy list of well-known, often-overlapping, supply-side shortcomings that needed to be addressed. The outstanding policy agenda can be summarized as

- raising female and elderly participation;
- increasing access for foreign labour, which accounted for just 1.1% of the workforce;[6]
- the encouragement of FDI, the annual inflow of which had been negligible in 2012 and the stock of which, at around 3.5% of GDP, was one of the lowest in the OECD;
- better corporate governance, to release the large outstanding stock of retained corporate earnings (between 2010 and 2019 and before the Covid-19 and Ukraine War shocks, corporate savings averaged some 23% of GDP and dominated Japan's high overall savings rate);
- the enhancement of business dynamism and the freeing up of moribund capital in 'zombie companies';
- the weaning of the inefficient SME sector off public sector credit guarantees and collateral-based borrowing;
- the encouragement of more risk capital, both from the banks and from venture capitalists;
- the further deregulation of agriculture, energy, health and professional services;
- tax reform, not just to facilitate fiscal sustainability and intergenerational equality, but also to improve the incentive structure, not least through a reduction in the share of direct taxes; and, finally,
- the fostering of competition, and thereby the diffusion of innovation and higher prospective returns on new investment through greater trade openness.

Over the following six years, structural reform at least touched on all these areas.

The third arrow of Abenomics was initially launched as the Japan Revitalization Strategy in June 2013, and it embodied a medium-to-long-term target for real output growth of 2.0% a year, which, given the prospective decline in the labour force, implied productivity growth of some 2.5% a year. However, beyond the government's commitment to TPP, and the intention to develop low-regulation Special Economic Zones further, there was little of great substance that was new.

By late 2013, however, notwithstanding the innate conservatism on social issues of Abe and his party, he had acknowledged the importance of raising the profile and contribution to the economy of the female labour force, and he promised to accelerate the provision of more affordable, high-quality childcare facilities to encourage it. At the same time, in order more sustainably to address the effects on energy supply of the Fukushima disaster and to reduce production costs, Abe had also announced a long-overdue comprehensive liberalization of the electricity industry that would abolish price controls, reduce regional monopoly power and separate power transmission from generation. Japan's nuclear programme was also cautiously restarted.

Early 2014 saw Abe supplement his commitment to the TPP by negotiating a new trade deal with the EU, and in March it was announced that the low-regulation Special Economic Zones would include Tokyo and Osaka, which together accounted for more than 40% of GDP. Over time, the total number of these special areas would swell to ten, although their reliance on local governance proved to be an enduring impediment to their development.

A little more flesh was put on the bones of reform in June 2014, although the package of measures announced fell into the familiar trap of amounting to a large number of minor – often seemingly random – rule changes and ambitions. It did, however, include initiatives to encourage the corporate sector to adopt more efficient and outward-looking business practices. Despite business opposition, in addition to a new Stewardship Code brought in in February to encourage greater institutional investor activism in the search for enhanced corporate value, a Corporate Governance Code was introduced that required firms to appoint outside directors on a 'comply or explain' basis. A new stock index, the JPX-Nikkei Index 400, was also set up to promote firms with good governance and disclosure records.

What is more, as noted earlier in the chapter, to encourage higher investment and wages, a further progressive reduction in the combined national and local rate of corporation tax – which was, at 37% in the 2013/2014 financial year, still one of the highest in the OECD – to around 30% was announced, together with a broadening of the associated tax base.

After the initial configuration of Abenomics lost traction, Abe attempted to reanimate his economic strategy by launching 'Abenomics 2' in September

2015. This encompassed three new 'arrows' – a strong economy, more support for families with children, better social security – and three associated targets: the boosting of nominal GDP to ¥600 trillion in 2020 (an increase of more than 10%); an increase in the birth rate to 1.8; and, by the mid 2020s, a society in which no one needed to leave their job to care for their elderly parents. These were laudable, if challenging, objectives, but notwithstanding a law passed in April 2016 to force large companies to set numerical targets for the employment and promotion of women, follow-up was slow and patchy. Structural reform continued to fall short of requirements, with gaps in important areas, long implementation horizons, questionable prioritization and an inadequate system of assessment and follow-up.

The labour market remained a crucial area in need of transformation, in that its institutional structure stunted labour supply and productivity and made the BOJ's inflation target harder to achieve. Importantly, while female participation had long been on a rising trend, the rate still lagged behind that in many of Japan's competitors. At the same time, as the population had begun to shrink, there had been a substantial increase in the share of non-regular, or part-time, workers, most of whom were female, as women sought to balance the demands of childcare, housework and elderly care. By 2015 this share stood at some 37% of the total employed, up from 20.3% in 2004. These workers were typically paid lower wage rates and offered fewer non-wage benefits than regular employees. They enjoyed less job security and bargaining power. And they were granted limited access to on-the-job training.

Consequently, not only was the pass-through from high profits and an increasingly tight labour market to wage inflation weakened, but so too was the quality of human capital and the motivation of a considerable proportion of the workforce. There was therefore a need both to eliminate the sizeable disincentives to female full-time work in the tax and social security systems and also to promote intermediate employment contracts that better balanced job security and wage and benefit levels, to improve training for non-regular employees and to introduce more formal job descriptions and a stronger reporting framework. This meant a direct assault on the long-standing and still-commonplace systems of lifetime employment,[7] seniority-based pay and mandatory retirement that made it almost impossible to fire regular workers, restricted horizontal job mobility and pushed workers out at 60, forcing them into much-lower-paid jobs if they wished to continue to work.

A 'Work Style Reform' agenda was unveiled in March 2017, with associated legislation passing the following June. This encouraged 'Equal Pay for Equal Work' and sought to moderate labour market duality. However, notwithstanding the introduction of a cap on overtime hours, an increased minimum wage, guidelines to avoid gender discrimination and continued emphasis on the expansion of childcare facilities, the new directives were easy to circumvent and fell short of the comprehensive programme outlined above. The government also subsequently restricted any increase in foreign labour to the Special Economic Zones and the highly skilled, when it was medium- and low-skilled workers that were in shortest supply.

Turning to trade policy, a 12-nation TPP deal was struck in October 2016 that committed Japan to sharply lower tariff and non-tariff barriers, not least on agricultural goods. However, the Trump administration withdrew the United States from the arrangement in March 2017, significantly reducing its potential benefits to signatories. Japan reacted by seeking an agreement with residual participants and by pushing ahead with the proposed deal with the European Union to foster trade and competition while also offering a counterbalance to China's growing hegemony across Asia. With Japan taking the lead in negotiations, a Comprehensive and Progressive Agreement for Trans-Pacific Partnership (CPTPP) was signed in March 2018 and came into force in December of that year. The EU Economic Partnership Agreement was eventually signed in July 2018 and entered into force in February 2019. As a result, the share of Japanese trade covered by free-trade agreements increased, importantly, from about a quarter to some 70%.

Elsewhere, the process of deregulation meandered on in a piecemeal and inconsistent manner, not least in the designated Special Economic Zones. Electricity, gas and agriculture saw the most significant changes, with the latter inter alia subject to significant reform of an overbearing cooperative system that had hitherto limited entrepreneurship and new market entrants. However, the restructuring of telecoms and professional services lagged, and – notwithstanding the assault on cooperatives – agriculture still enjoyed huge subsidization. Support to agricultural producers averaged some 47% of gross farm receipts in the years 2016–2018. This was down from some 63% in the late 1980s but was still 2.5 times higher than the OECD average. Consumer spending on agricultural products was 1.8 times what it would have been in the absence of government policies. As for SMEs, a modest reform of the credit guarantee system was enacted in June 2017. However, in that year such support remained equivalent to more than 4.0% of GDP.

As the business expansion matured towards the end of the 2010s, there were some further reforms, although there was a sense of dwindling enthusiasm and a loss of focus on the part of the government. The Abe administration looked increasingly tired, and the prime minister was more and more consumed by the controversial issue of the constitutional reform he was so keen to achieve and by a series of favouritism scandals. That said, the Corporate Governance Code was further revised in June 2018 to incentivize more reductions in cross-shareholdings and to encourage greater transparency in the appointment and dismissal of CEOs, although there remained a reluctance directly to target retained earnings through the tax system. Restrictions on banks investing in other banks were also reduced, and the GPIF introduced incentives for its external asset managers to take a more activist approach in their equity portfolios. And in October 2019 Japan and the United States signed agreements regarding market access for agricultural and industrial goods as well as on digital trade that would take effect in January 2020. On a more negative note, in November 2019 the government introduced legislation that made it harder for foreign investors to take stakes in national-security-related industries such as aerospace, telecoms and computer software.

The government also began to focus more squarely on the environment and greener growth. At this time, while Japan's production-based CO_2 intensity was around the OECD average and the energy intensity of production was falling and below that of other OECD countries, exposure to air pollution was about a third above the OECD average, the recycling of waste was substandard, the renewable energy share was relatively low and the gap with other countries widening, and environmental taxes were inadequate, especially on coal. Fossil fuels still accounted for 88% of Japan's energy supply in 2019.

The government's overriding target was to cut greenhouse gas emissions by 25% below their 2013 levels by 2030, but the decarbonization of electricity supply was a major challenge, especially in the wake of the 2011 nuclear accident. In that year, nuclear power had provided around a third of total electricity but this fell to just 3% in 2015. The intention was to raise the percentage back up to 20%–22%, but to do so the industry had to overcome some of the most stringent nuclear standards in the world. The process would therefore be slow.

In aggregate, however, Japan's greenhouse gas strategy was deficient, not least because there remained an unwillingness significantly to raise the price of carbon through the tax system. The carbon tax introduced on selected energy products in 2012 was set at too low a level. Indeed, environmentally friendly taxes as a whole remained the fourth lowest in the OECD.

In conclusion, it would be churlish to deny that the period of Abenomics ushered in at least the foundations of some notable supply-side reforms and achieved some successes.

The corporate sector was changing. By 2018 the share of firms in the first section of the TSE that had at least two outside directors had risen more than fourfold, to more than 91%, and this acted to draw in more external capital. However, this success had to be set against the fact that the BOJ's dominance of the ETF market was acting to blunt corporate governance reform.

The overall labour force participation rate jumped from 73.9% in 2012 to 79.5% in 2019. That of females increased from 63.4% to 72.6%, and for those over 65 it rose from 19.9% to 25.3%. The increase in female participation was particularly marked for women in their thirties, where the activation rate had historically been aberrantly low relative to other advanced economies. There was a sharp increase in the number of female graduates with children, while approaching 50% of the female workforce was in a job following marriage or the birth of their first child. There was, moreover, greater flexibility in the way that workers were employed.

Competition, meanwhile, was enhanced through greater openness to trade, and the economy's incentive structure was improved via the drop in the corporate tax rate towards the OECD average of around 28% and various deregulatory initiatives.

On the other hand, these achievements were small beer when stacked against a demographic tsunami that the IMF suggested could slash GDP by some 25% by 2050. In the meantime, female participation was still held back by disincentives that were hard-wired into the tax and social security systems, which meant that, despite being diluted somewhat in 2017, women remained heavily underrepresented in leadership roles. Labour market dualism endured, as did a sizeable gender pay gap. While the importation of foreign employees had no doubt increased, they remained heavily excluded, accounting for just 2% of the labour force. The governance of the corporate sector might have begun to change for the better and become more focused on returns on assets, but neither this, nor a lower corporate rate, had encouraged a significant rundown of its longstanding huge cash cushion. That would require much bolder and more politically fraught action, such as formal limits on cross-shareholdings, efforts to ease M&A activity or even a big cut in depreciation allowances or a punitive tax on retained earnings. Inward FDI might have increased but it remained chronically low, at around 0.8% of GDP a year, in flow terms; the OECD average was some 2.5% of GDP. Risk capital was still in short supply. The SME sector was still over-protected. Business dynamism remained lacking, not least because of shortcomings in the insolvency regime. The ownership of farmland by non-agricultural groups was still restricted. The Special Economic Zones had disappointed.

Other structural issues had also come to the fore while Abenomics was in place. While Japan remained a global leader in the use of robotics, there was, for example, growing evidence of a shortfall in the use of digital technology. Now that government investment was less to the fore in countercyclical policy, the public sector capital stock, like that of the private sector, was rapidly ageing, and it also increasingly appeared to be unduly distributed across areas of depopulation. And with climate change accelerating, environmental policy needed to become much bolder.

When all is said and done, at the end of 2019 the economy's huge productivity shortfall, especially relative to the United States, remained, and potential growth continued to languish at between 0.5% and 1.0% a year. The economy also retained a heavy reliance on exports. In 2020 the International Institute of Management Development placed Japan 34th in its competitiveness rankings, seven places lower than when Abe Shinzo came to power, while the World Bank's ease of doing business rankings had Japan in 29th, nine places down on 2012.

In this context, it is difficult but to conclude that the third arrow of Abenomics failed to hit the target.

COVID – SHOCK AND HORROR

With the economy already in trouble – and the long, shallow, hesitant and uneven Abenomics expansion seemingly drawing to a close – Japan, like the rest of the world, was banjaxed by a huge and novel shock: the Covid-19 pandemic. Nothing like it had been seen since the Spanish Flu pandemic of 1918–1920, and it was to have profound effects on both demand and supply.

The first case of Covid infection in Japan came in mid January 2020, and the pandemic hit hard from the spring. Although Japan's post-war constitution prevented the government from instituting curfews, it reacted by declaring a number of formal states of emergency that ushered in a range of increasingly geographically targeted confinement measures that discouraged mobility and services consumption. Together with the Japanese public's customary attention to hygiene (as demonstrated, for example, by the widespread wearing of face masks and regular hand washing during the cold and flu season), significant voluntary behavioural changes, and the implementation of test, track and trace programmes, this acted to moderate the rate of infection.

Nevertheless, it proved difficult to bring the spread of Covid entirely under control. As elsewhere, there were waves of infection that intermittently put intense pressure on the health service and that saw restrictions on activity – both voluntary and imposed – ebb and flow. Japan's vaccination programme began slowly, but by mid 2021 it had accelerated, with more than 75% of the population having been vaccinated by April 2022. Overall, despite a greater reliance on voluntary confinement than elsewhere, Japan emerged from the pandemic with lower rates of infection and death than most advanced economies.

Real GDP fell 7.7% in the second quarter of 2020 as various restrictions on activity constrained consumption and investment spending. The peak-to-trough decline in output between Q3 2019 and Q2 2020 was 9.8%, exceeding the 8.8% drop between Q1 2008 and Q1 2009 during the GFC. Unsurprisingly, employment contracted in this environment, having already weakened at the end of 2019; wage growth turned sharply negative; price deflation beckoned once again; and the stock market suffered a severe, if short-lived, slump. This period also saw the onset of a four-year-long 30% slide in the yen's trade-weighted value, during which the dollar/yen rate dropped to levels last seen in mid 1990.

The economy bounced back strongly in the second half of 2020 thanks to government support and as it was gradually reopened, such that the average rate of decline for the year was 4.1%. However, difficulties in containing infections subsequently led to a series of setbacks, albeit less dramatic than those seen in 2020. The recovery in trade was also uneven, with supply bottlenecks in some places hindering growth, and inbound tourism – hitherto a rapidly growing aspect of the economy – collapsed and took an extended period to recover. This in part reflected the postponement of the Olympic and Paralympic games. Originally planned for 2020, they were ultimately held in July and August 2021, albeit within the context of a city-wide state of emergency and without spectators because of the residual effects of the pandemic. Japan's economy still benefited from some ¥9 trillion of outlays associated with the preparation of the games over the years 2014–2020 (a boost to real GDP growth of some 0.2–0.3 percentage points a year), but in being denied a large inflow of foreign visitors and currency, the country lost an estimated ¥1.4 trillion (1% of GDP) of additional expenditure that would have provided a significant short-term boost to output in 2021.[8] It was not until Q1 2023 that real GDP surpassed its previous peak. The atmosphere around the 2020/2021 games was the antithesis of that in 1964.

Depressed by policy interventions such as a reduction in mobile phone charges as well as the extended weakness of aggregate demand, CPI inflation remained negative until the final quarter of 2021. At that stage, the headline CPI index, which had of course been boosted over time by a succession of consumption tax hikes, was a mere one percentage point higher than in Q4 1998. It was no surprise, therefore, that inflation expectations showed no sign of reviving and converging on the BOJ's target.

The external surplus, which had been very strong at the end of the 2010s, averaging some 3.8% of GDP, fell back to under 2% of GDP in 2022, as the fall in public saving during the pandemic more than offset the rise in private saving. However, it rebounded to its previous level and beyond in 2024, as tourism arrivals exceeded their previous peak and with the income surplus continuing to play a dominant role.

The huge and sudden setback to the economy meant that previous policy priorities, in particular around the budget and fiscal consolidation, had to be cast aside. The government was thrown headlong into crisis mode.

A series of huge stimulus packages, financed by three supplementary budgets during the 2020/2021 financial year, were announced that in total amounted to ¥103 trillion, or some 18.5% of GDP. The measures included wide-ranging health-related spending and sought to provide financial relief to households, maintain employment and offer credit lines to the corporate sector. The latter extended to cash transfers to individuals and firms, the deferment of tax and social security obligations, an easing of macroprudential and other financial regulations, and more concessional loans and loan guarantees. The outstanding amount of loan guarantees to SMEs nearly doubled during the pandemic, to the equivalent of some 7% of GDP, in the process reversing the slow and steady decline over the previous decade.

These interventions prevented a spike in bankruptcies, capped the rise in the unemployment rate at just 3.1% in October 2020, and precluded any significant deterioration in the health of the financial sector. NPLs remained low, and the major banks' capital adequacy stayed in line with the other major advanced economies. However, policy had only a limited effect on consumption and investment as the transfers were largely saved in the environment of heavily constrained movement. The household saving rate peaked at 22% of disposable income, more than four times its pre-pandemic level.

Public spending surged, accounting for a record 45.6% share of GDP in 2020. The overall fiscal impulse into the economy in that year amounted to some 3.5% of GDP, and it was unwound only slowly thereafter. Unsurprisingly, the consolidated budget deficit exploded higher, blowing out to 9.0% of GDP in 2020 – the same level as during the GFC – and remaining at 6.2% of GDP in 2021. It only returned to its 2019 level of 3.0% of GDP in 2024. The primary deficit traced a similar path, peaking at 8.6% in 2020. Any hopes of returning to balance by 2025 were lost. Perhaps most concerning of all, the gross debt burden increased from 224% of GDP in 2019 to 241% in 2021, thus reaching a level last seen in World War II.

For its part, the BOJ retained its existing QQE and YCC framework but rapidly increased its provision of liquidity to financial markets in both yen and US dollars; it also provided more support for commercial bank lending via a number of conduits, including a fourfold increase in its purchases of commercial paper and corporate debt. By expanding its asset purchases it eased risk premia and financial conditions and sustained financial stability. The money supply, however defined, surged, as it did in most economies, while the Bank's balance sheet increased by some 22% in 2020 to exceed the equivalent of 120% of GDP; its rise continued thereafter. Private sector credit growth accelerated sharply, reaching some 6.3% year-on-year by the end of 2020.

In March 2021 the BOJ released the results of another internal policy review that confirmed the value of its 2% inflation target, QQE and YCC, a negative policy rate and its overshooting commitment. However, the review did result in some tweaks to the Bank's strategy, including a plus or minus 25 basis point fluctuation range for the 10-year JGB yield target and a relaxation of its heavy commitment to ETF purchases during the pandemic. Over the rest of the year, other emergency measures were also unwound, and the central bank's balance sheet began to stabilize around 130% of GDP.

AFTER ABE

By the time that the so-called Reiwa imperial era[9] superseded the Heisei imperial era in May 2019, Abe Shinzo was – like so many of his predecessors – consumed by scandals and his popularity was very much on the wane. With the onset of the Covid-19 pandemic and the disruptions and disquiet it wrought on Japanese society, his resignation became increasingly inevitable. When it finally came, in September 2020, he was replaced by long-serving Cabinet Secretary Suga Yoshihide.[10]

Suga had been a close ally of Abe and he committed to sustaining the Abenomics approach to policy, but he lacked his predecessor's charisma. He resigned after just a year because of his low approval ratings. Neither the pandemic, the slow vaccine rollout, nor the delayed, spectator-free, Olympics had done him any favours. Suga was replaced in early October 2021 by the more youthful Kishida Fumio, a former defence and foreign affairs minister, who had most recently chaired the LDP Policy Research Council and who also broadly hewed to Abe's vision. He immediately led the LDP to victory in a general election, albeit with a slightly reduced majority. However, he too was to see his popularity plummet in the face of a series of financing and right-wing influence-peddling scandals.

Despite the sharp deterioration in Japan's major fiscal metrics during the pandemic, Kishida followed his electoral success with a record ¥78.9 trillion (14.6% of GDP) package of policy measures. Designed to underpin recovery, foster greater income equality and enhance the economy's future resilience, it extended to generous cash handouts for households, and in particular those with children, students and low earners; it expanded corporate tax breaks to boost wages, subsidies to small firms, a ¥10 trillion university endowment fund, money for vocational training, and subsidies to build microchip plants; and it provided discounts for domestic travel. Furthermore, in March 2022 fuel subsidies were significantly increased as oil prices rose.

Even more so than with the myriad previous stimulus packages announced since the bursting of the bubble economy, however, the headline figure of Kishida's post-election package exaggerated the underlying impact on the economy. This was in part because it included a limited allocation to public works, but most importantly of all because it had to be put into the context of the natural winding down of the exceptional level of policy support provided during the pandemic. Even allowing for the onset of a major effort to increase

Japan's defence capability,[11] the overall fiscal policy impulse over the years 2021–2024 was actually contractionary to the tune of some four percentage points of GDP, the share of public spending in GDP fell back towards 40%, the consolidated headline and primary budget deficits declined towards 3% of GDP, and the gross burden of debt stabilized around 240% of GDP.

Nevertheless, despite the onset of war in eastern Europe and all the dislocations that caused for the global economy, Japan enjoyed a period of reasonable expansion from late 2022 until mid 2023, supported by the release of pent-up domestic demand, a rebound in tourism arrivals and various supply-chain improvements. The labour market tightened once again, and the unemployment rate trended back down towards 2% of the workforce. However, the upswing subsequently lost momentum and real activity turned down into early 2024. At the time of writing, in early 2025, real GDP had only just returned to its previous Q2 2023 high.

What changed in a more sustained way was the inflation environment. The annual rate of CPI inflation moved sharply higher after the onset of the Russia–Ukraine conflict, eventually peaking above 4% in early 2023 before trending down somewhat. Headline consumer price pressures had not approached this level since early 1991. While global commodity price trends played an important role in the rise in inflation, as indeed did the yen's sustained decline, it is noteworthy that various measures of underlying inflation also picked up to levels not seen for even longer – since the early 1980s.

In this environment, inflation expectations and wage growth moved into higher ranges than had been seen for decades, while in early 2024 stock prices finally exceeded the peak established at the end of the bubble period. There was therefore a growing hope that inflation would finally settle around the 2% inflation target.

The BOJ widened its target band for the 10-year JGB yield again in December 2022 to zero, plus or minus 50 basis points, before de-emphasising the importance of longer-term rates in policy during the course of 2023. Then, with renowned academic Ueda Kazuo installed by Prime Minister Kishida as a replacement for long-serving Governor Kuroda Haruhiko in March 2024, the Bank ended its negative interest rate and YCC policies.[12] This was the first formal tightening of monetary policy since February 2007.

The pandemic and its aftermath added to the urgency of structural reform in Japan. The need to enhance productivity, further increase labour participation, combat climate change and address the economy's other longstanding supply-side shortcomings became even more acute, and new challenges also emerged. For example, the pandemic underscored Japan's position as a conspicuous laggard in the adoption of digital technology by businesses, especially within the public sector. The latter hindered the response to Covid by delaying the 2020 cash handout programme. At just 20% of the total in the early 2020s, the role of cashless payments was far below that in Japan's competitors. In Korea, for example, the figure was above 90%.

Despite the pressures on policymakers during this extraordinary period, some structural policy initiatives did emerge.

A digital transformation strategy was implemented to boost digitalization across central and local government, while offering tax credits to businesses to encourage investment in this area.

The government's environmental policy objectives became more ambitious. In line with the United States and the European Union, Japan committed to a target of net zero greenhouse emissions by 2050 and an intermediate target of a 46% reduction from the 2013 level by 2030, although meeting these targets would be challenging given the low starting point on renewables, the still-limited integration of regional power grids and the inadequate use of market-based instruments. The gradual restarting of the nuclear programme would help, however.

In July 2021 the BOJ also released a climate strategy aimed at managing the associated financial risks and supporting 'green' financial markets. At the end of that year it began to offer financial institutions zero-rate loans and exemptions from the negative rate imposed on some reserves if they increased climate-related advances.

In November 2021 the government signed the Regional Comprehensive Economic Partnership (RCEP) agreement, the first free trade agreement among the largest economies in Asia. It was expected to eliminate about 90% of the tariffs on imports between its signatories within 20 years of coming into force while also establishing common rules for e-commerce, trade and intellectual property.

Finally, in 2021 the Corporate Governance Code was further modified to enhance board independence; to promote diversity through hiring targets for women and foreigners; and to encourage the greater consideration of sustainability, environmental and social issues.

HITS AND MISSES

Abenomics went through numerous iterations and shifts in emphasis as it fell short of expectations and responded to events, in the process extending the period of innovation and experimentation in Japanese policymaking. Nevertheless, it also had more in common with earlier regimes than is sometimes recognized. As noted at the end of the previous chapter, there are only ever really three conduits of economic policy, and while the government wanted to present an appearance of greater coherence and coordination in its approach, the detailed policy mix was often flawed, lacking in balance, if not downright wrong-headed.

While Abenomics may have failed to live up to the hype that surrounded it, it had its successes. BOJ Governor Kuroda's efforts to break with the central bank's hitherto somewhat defeatist approach to monetary policy delivered some constructive results. Under his tutelage, the Bank managed to further ease monetary conditions, lower real interest rates and encourage portfolio rebalancing. This provided the backdrop to an extended – if modestly paced and stuttering – recovery, during which corporate profitability improved and employment was increasingly full. Deflation was tamed to an important degree, and a floor was thereby established under price expectations. Importantly, the threat of a downward spiral of prices, wages and profits was repelled. The price paid was that monetary policy became increasingly exhausted and blurred with fiscal policy, with associated moral hazard risks and uncertainties about how it might be unwound.

More pertinently, consumer price inflation, although typically positive rather than negative after 2013, consistently failed to reach the BOJ's 2% goal. The inability of the Bank to hit its prescribed target was by this stage no longer unique to Japan, but the parlous condition of the nation's public finances was, and sub-target inflation greatly added to the difficulties of putting them on to a more sustainable footing. Under Abenomics fiscal policy also lacked sufficient institutional oversight and consistency. Planned budgetary restraint lacked a convincing programme of specifics and was in any case regularly moderated or reversed to ameliorate negative demand shocks. Targets were based on optimistic assumptions and continued to be overshot.

The public sector debt burden mounted to ever more extraordinary levels. This also acted to deplete the nation's once sizeable public sector net worth, such that by 2017 it had dropped to zero. A semblance of control and the confidence of the markets continued to be maintained only because of historically low global interest rates; the mass recycling of debt within the public sector; and, in particular, via the balance sheet of the BOJ, the home bias of the local investment community, and the still large current account surplus and absence of reliance on foreign investor inflows.

Some important supply-side reforms were forthcoming, especially where the labour market, trading relations, corporate governance and (to a lesser extent) agriculture, the environment and the tax system were concerned. However, the demographic shock with which Japan was confronted continued to metastasize and weigh heavily on the performance of the economy. Growth potential continued to decline. Beset by a virulent form of secular stagnation, Japan remained a poor imitation of its former all-conquering and confident self.

Corporate sector savings and cross-shareholdings were still excessive, capping profitability and constraining aggregate demand. A large productivity shortfall remained, with SMEs an enduring drag on efficiency, and many of the most egregiously underperforming sectors at the beginning of the period were still at the bottom of the pile towards the end. Structural shortcomings – such as bureaucratic overreach; a shortage of FDI; agricultural protection; regulatory excesses in the service sector; and, no doubt encouraged by public opinion being tilted against more immigration, a shortage of foreign labour – continued to fester, while new weaknesses, such as inadequate digitalization, reared their heads.

There remained an underlying mistrust of market forces and an interventionist mindset. There was a tendency to pick the low-hanging policy fruit. Perhaps it would have been more productive to pursue a narrower focus in this area of policy – a third arrow strategy of less breadth and more depth.

The long, ponderous upswing of the 2010s was seemingly in its death throes when the Covid pandemic struck in the spring of 2020, triggering a contraction on a par with that of the GFC. Japan dealt with this episode better than most, not least because of deeply embedded elements of its social and cultural make-up. The boundaries of the BOJ's unconventional monetary policy were also further stretched and, as elsewhere, fiscal policy was employed on a grand scale, albeit at the cost of a further significant deterioration in the condition of the public finances and deepening uncertainty about the future tax burden and scale of government. Supply-side reform was set back, but perhaps less so than might have been imagined. For its part, after the relative stability of the Abe era, Japanese politics again reverted to unfortunate type from 2020 onwards in the guise of a series of scandals, financial malfeasance and prime ministerial musical chairs.

Notwithstanding the return of politics as usual, the years following the pandemic did see two unexpected positive developments.

First, moderate inflation at last returned after three decades in which it had been uncomfortably low. This owed less to the actions of policymakers – and particularly the BOJ, although they did nothing of substance to prevent it – and more to external forces, and in particular international commodity price trends and the impact of Covid and the war in Ukraine on supply chains.

Second, by 2024 there was talk among commentators and the investment community of a Japanese corporate renaissance following a decade or more of governance reform and an apparent change in corporate mindset. With profitability on the rise, firms bringing in more external expertise to their board rooms, paying more in dividends, selling off unprofitable units and increasingly willing to buy back their own shares, interest in the stock market both at home and abroad had been rekindled. The major market indices finally exceeded their late-1989 highs. Shareholder activism and private equity dealmaking soared.

It remains to be seen, however, whether these trends can be sustained in the face of Japan's deepening demographic crisis and in an increasingly inward-looking and politically volatile world.

CHAPTER 10

Conclusions and Prognoses

'Fall down seven times, stand up eight' — Japanese proverb

EBBS AND FLOWS

Japan's post-war economic history is an extraordinary narrative of highs and lows, triumphs and disasters, policy hits and misses, and both serendipitous and inopportune external interventions. The country has progressed through devastation and humiliation; reconstruction and renaissance; hubris and excess; anguish and denial; and, finally, painful adjustment and gradual reconstitution – even if the latter phase remains incomplete and beset by uncertainty and enormous demographic and other challenges. If the immediate aftermath of World War II saw Japan a reviled, pariah state, 80 years later, although past its point of peak influence and no longer the source of envy and disruption it had been, it is, as the world's fourth largest economy, a vital and highly developed cog in the global wheel, admired for its continued high-tech manufacturing excellence, its grit and its social stability. Just as few predicted the nation's remarkable rise in the late nineteenth century, there was also little expectation in 1945 that it could trace such an exceptional path and be rehabilitated in this way. And now, in the middle of the third decade of the twenty-first century, how it copes with its latest trials will have important implications for much of the rest of the world.

The country's resurrection was initially shaped by US oversight and support in the context of a humbling military occupation and then galvanized by the economic and geopolitical requirements of the Cold War, and in particular by three years of conflict on the Korean peninsula. Thereafter, protected by the US security umbrella, sustained by a young, well-educated, highly skilled and motivated workforce, guided by a powerful bureaucracy with a strong sense of national purpose, and able to draw on important lessons from its initial emergence from backwardness, it made the most of a sympathetic and dynamic international background.

This process of developmental catch-up was further underpinned by industrial practices and structures that proved well-suited to its circumstances; by political stability under the leadership of a single, dominant, business-friendly party of government – what might in effect be termed something close to a benign dictatorship; and by an extended willingness to sacrifice current consumption for longer-term investment. In the meantime, its record of macroeconomic policy management was generally sound. Major errors were avoided. The underlying processes of expansion were largely allowed to play out unencumbered, and often actively encouraged. The net result was two decades of unprecedentedly rapid, export-driven progress within the context of a distinctive – some would argue unique – form of capitalism.

By the 1970s, however, the constructive influence of many of these considerations had begun to wane, and Japan's convergence with the more advanced economies was to a significant extent complete. It was also increasingly viewed as a competitive threat, not least by the United States, rather than as a strategic ally that could be indulged or simply an admirable illustration of developmental success. This was especially the case as it emerged from both two major energy price shocks and what was to prove a much more challenging decade for the global economy in better shape than most other countries.

The 1980s saw Japan at the zenith of its economic power and influence. Growth might have slowed from the heady pace seen in the 1950s and 1960s, but the country's economy was still expanding significantly faster and more consistently than those of its major rivals while also avoiding the extended inflationary excesses, high levels of unemployment and associated political and social strife witnessed elsewhere. A continued focus on capital accumulation and overseas sales, most conspicuously across its highly efficient manufacturing sector, enabled it to accumulate huge external surpluses and increasingly expand its industrial footprint overseas in other economies that had lower cost structures and/or large internal markets. Many of its business practices were seen as an example for others to follow, even if resentment and suspicion of its accomplishments and global reach mounted.

This outperformance and industrial hegemony became increasingly unsustainable, however. The country's demography had become less supportive and was progressively developing into a more binding constraint on growth. The longstanding emphasis put on capital accumulation was subject to increasingly diminishing returns. Japan's manufacturing- and export-dependent economic model faced new challenges, and it was increasingly unfit for domestic purpose or acceptable to the rest of the world. There was therefore a growing requirement that the economy evolve. The country's long-sheltered service sector needed to be opened up to greater competition, the pervasive but now increasingly suffocating influence of the bureaucracy had to be reduced, innovation and individual entrepreneurship needed to be fostered, and greater consumer sovereignty encouraged.

But for all the detailed and perspicacious published diagnoses of the new direction in which Japan should travel, fundamental reform – as has so often been the case across numerous epochs and societies – proved socially and politically contentious and was, in important respects, beset by inertia.

One area in which this was less the case, however, was in the financial sector – from the 1980s onwards, at least. There, laxer regulation enhanced competition, expanded the financing options available, spawned new investment products and opportunities, and encouraged entities to take on additional, often questionable, risk. Together with lingering biases in the tax and regulatory structures, inadequate oversight of the banks and an inappropriate macro policy mix designed in significant part to satisfy Japan's external critics in the United States and beyond, this encouraged growth to become increasingly driven by asset price inflation and a rapid build-up of corporate debt. Stock and land prices surged to reach extraordinary, and increasingly divisive, levels. And with this came unacceptable levels of dishonesty, corruption and fraud across business, the bureaucracy and the political class. For all its outward success and the international envy it inspired, the Japanese economic miracle had become grotesquely distorted and unsound by the late 1980s.

The dramatic and inevitable adjustment to this period of egregious excess began at the end of 1989, after the MOF and the BOJ had reached the conclusion that the asset price boom had to be curtailed. However, engineering a soft landing in such circumstances proved an impossible task. There was no repeat of the remarkably successful adjustment to higher energy costs in the 1970s. Instead, what transpired was a rout.

The collapse of the so-called bubble economy in the early 1990s represented a massive shock in terms of wealth destruction and negative financial and corporate sector fallout, which took an extended period to assimilate and address. After such a protracted interlude of success, it was difficult to take on board the new and more straitened circumstances confronting the nation, especially as the asset price reversal came to interact malignly with the nation's increasingly challenging demographic profile. Nor was the process of adjustment helped by certain cultural values and customs, and in particular the motivational importance in Japanese society of shame and 'face'. All this said, the Japanese were not alone in failing fully to recognize and adjust to their more chastened circumstances: most of the rest of the world also took some time to understand that the era of Japanese economic superiority was over and that the country's developmental model had its shortcomings and a finite lifespan.

The initial policy response to the deflation of the bubble fell some way short of requirements. The BOJ went on fighting asset price inflation for too long, it was too slow to change course, and it was too timid when it eventually did so. Lacking transparent forward-looking independent oversight, the subsequent easing of fiscal policy was publicly overstated, too episodic, inefficient and frequently distorted by the idiosyncrasies of Japan's political system. Supply-side policy adjusted only slowly, such that many longstanding, and politically challenging, issues remained inadequately dealt with, and productivity and structural dynamism and adjustment were stymied.

The biggest failure of policy at this time, however, was the choice – and it was a choice – not to confront the financial sector's difficulties head on and instead to hope that they could be brazened out over time through forbearance. This was, in essence, a strategy of wishful thinking encouraged by previous triumphs and rooted in the psychological make-up of Japanese society alluded to above. It also ignored both the country's own painful experience with asset price deflation and banking sector dysfunction in the 1920s and the experience of other economies confronted by financial crises in the modern era. The approach emasculated monetary policy, put an undue onus on fiscal policy to sustain economic activity, stymied supply-side reform, increased the economy's vulnerability to new shocks, and rendered the inevitable adjustment process longer and more painful.

It took two more iterations of the financial crisis – at the end of the 1990s and early in the new millennium – and the subsequent arrival of a somewhat different kind of political leader in the form of Koizumi Junichiro before the necessary response was finally delivered – a response that, crucially, included the injection of large-scale public funds and the significant consolidation of the banking sector. By this time, however, an entire decade had been lost, and in a remarkable turnaround in international public perception, 'Japanification' had already become a derogatory term for economic policy failure, stagnation and relative decline.

Once the financial sector fallout from the bursting of the bubble had been definitively addressed, it became clear that the Japanese economy was operating in a new and very different environment. The self-confidence and hubris of the 1980s had been superseded by caution and uncertainty. The country's ageing demographic profile was increasingly to the fore, reducing growth potential by more than half and necessitating that it confront culturally challenging issues such as immigration, low female participation and the dismantling of the lifetime employment system that had been such a signature element of its initial post-war miracle.

By the early 2000s other advanced economies, including the United States, were also finding it increasingly hard to sustain domestic demand growth at accustomed and acceptable rates. At the same time, competition from China and the rest of Asia had become more acute. This put Japan's manufacturing export prowess under duress and generally made life more difficult, not least via associated movements in its terms of trade. The latter deteriorated (at their greatest extent) by 51.2% between Q3 1986 and Q1 2022, in large part as a result of China pushing up the prices of the commodities that it and Japan imported while pushing down the prices of the manufactured goods that it and Japan exported (or increasingly, in Japan's case, used to export). This in turn resulted in a huge shortfall in real gross domestic income (which rose by 45% over this interval) relative to real gross domestic product (which rose by 60.5%).

Not least because of the macro policy failures of the 1990s, low inflation, and sometimes deflation, had become increasingly embedded into the economy's superstructure. The public finances had been decimated by the burgeoning necessities brought about by an ageing population, slow growth and the wastefully executed intermittent fiscal expansion of the 1990s; they were in urgent need of protracted and painful repair. But a shift towards budgetary consolidation again distorted the policy mix, putting excessive onus on the BOJ to manage the business cycle. The BOJ's policy rate became stuck around zero, and it found itself increasingly having to resort to unfamiliar and unorthodox techniques to sustain output and prices, even as important members of its leadership failed to believe in them fully and thereby diluted their effectiveness. In the background, despite occasional sound and fury – and the odd major initiative – supply-side policy plodded on in an aspirational, piecemeal and often-reticent manner. Japan continued to save too much, with the corporate sector particularly culpable in this regard, while much of non-manufacturing remained excessively protected from the chill winds of competition.

Towards the end of the first decade of the new millennium, in seeking to sustain economic growth at acceptable levels, the United States and other countries fell into a similar trap to the one Japan suffered from in the 1980s. Across the developed world, these years were marked by unduly loose monetary policy, lax financial supervision, rapid debt accumulation and asset price excess, and these mistakes were followed by an inevitable sharp adjustment in output, financial sector dysfunction, uncomfortably low inflation and historically low interest rates.

With some irony, although the recently cleaned up and slimmed down Japanese financial sector avoided most of the pitfalls to which others succumbed, the economy as a whole suffered an especially deep downturn in late 2009 because its super-efficient manufacturing sector was hit by a slump in world trade and there was limited room for a monetary policy response. This episode also further exacerbated the country's public finance issues; left deflation more deeply embedded than ever; and, for a brief period; seemed to suggest that the LDP might lose the grip on power it had held more or less continuously since the mid 1950s. The subsequent recovery was then set back by the devastating Great East Japan Earthquake and tsunami and the subsequent meltdown at the Fukushima nuclear plant.

Political failings around these disasters brought about the rapid return of the LDP and Abe Shinzo to power. Abe's first brief spell as prime minister had been an abject failure, but he now came committed to what was portrayed as a new, more coherent and forceful economic policy agenda in the form of the 'three arrows' of 'Abenomics', although in truth it had rather more in common with previous regimes than was generally admitted.

Abenomics also proved anything but constant in form. It went through numerous iterations and changes in emphasis. Its record was mixed, with the economy continuing to struggle under the weight of demographic change and confronted by an altogether more testing international environment than had prevailed before the GFC. Japan experienced a long and shallow expansion through the 2010s during which employment was increasingly full and deflationary pressures eased somewhat. But growth potential continued to fall, dropping below 1% a year, and sporadic episodes of contraction, albeit brief ones, inevitably became more commonplace.

At the same time, despite increasingly unconventional monetary policy and the BOJ taking the entire issuance of government debt onto its already swollen balance sheet in an echo of the Takahashi strategy of the early 1930s, CPI inflation still failed to match its now formally mandated 2% a year target.

Fiscal policy, meanwhile, was conflicted: it was torn between the intermittent need to support growth when the economy stalled and/or political imperatives intervened and the increasingly urgent need to bring the public finances under sustainable control. Despite some progress on the budget deficit, the overall position was grim, with the government debt burden lurching ever higher and public sector net worth declining towards negative territory. The situation was only kept under control by low global interest rates, high domestic savings and the particular configuration of the demand for Japanese safe assets, including the huge role played by a burgeoning BOJ balance sheet. But at least there was no repetition of the descent into outright fiscal dominance and loss of budgetary control that was seen in the later 1930s. In this sense, twenty-first-century Japanese politicians proved to be cut from a different cloth to their pre-war predecessors.

Finally, supply-side policy – notwithstanding some accomplishments in areas such as trade, female participation, corporate governance and the environment – was hardly transformed. Indeed, it often gave the impression of having become an endless palimpsest of relaunches and announcements replete with redundant aspirational minutiae. Industrial and labour market dualism endured. Business dynamism was constrained. Japan's productivity gap with its major competitors remained – indeed, relative to the United States, it widened. That said, one must question whether any other country could have conducted supply-side policy significantly better than Japan did in the difficult circumstances it faced – and this applies to the entire period from the 1980s onwards. The record elsewhere hardly puts Japan to shame. Indeed, in some instances it is far worse.

The extended post-Fukushima recovery had largely run its course when the Covid pandemic delivered another large and novel shock – not just to Japan, but to the world as a whole. The economy swooned dramatically again, although this time, curiously, the 'sudden stop' in output growth was the result of deliberate acts of policy designed to protect the population and the health care system.

Just as they had hindered the post-bubble adjustment, Japan's social and cultural mores on this occasion helped it to deal with the new crisis better than most, but such success came at a price. Uncertainty and uneasiness about the future burgeoned further. The public finances were dealt yet another sharp blow, pushing the debt burden to new record highs; this was in effect unavoidable, though, with the government having no choice but to step in to keep businesses afloat and sustain incomes during the duration of the pandemic. And in making its contribution to addressing the crisis, the BOJ was driven even further into unconventional territory, its initiatives increasingly akin to a form of fiscal policy.

The period under review ended with the world trying to re-establish the supply chains that had been disrupted by the pandemic and the onset of the war between Russia and Ukraine. The latter had little direct impact on Japanese trade, but it sent global commodity prices soaring, raising input costs, squeezing household real incomes and further complicating the process of recovery. However, the Russia–Ukraine war had one obvious positive effect: CPI inflation in Japan was driven up to such an extent and for such a period that there was hope that the longstanding deflationary mindset could be overcome and that inflation might finally settle around the BOJ's target. The return of inflation, together with the reform of corporate governance and global trends, also acted to encourage something of a resurgence in the stock market, driven by interest both at home and abroad. In what was an important psychological milestone, the index peaks set as long ago as December 1989 were finally exceeded, while in the meantime shareholder activism and private equity dealmaking blossomed – although whether this can be sustained remains moot.

BROADER LESSONS

All this leads us to the question of what the post-war Japanese experience means for the rest of us in 2025? What lessons can we draw from it?

First and foremost, perhaps, Japan's recent history provides confirmation that capitalist economies – even those that retain considerable governmental influence, even socialistic elements – are remarkably resilient and dynamic entities. Over the long term, their default setting has been to grow. They can overcome the most egregious and traumatic of setbacks and retain an extraordinary ability to expand and evolve. That said, the potency of these processes of resilience and evolution depend on the external environment and the manner in which the international rules within which an economy operates are framed and policed. They are also beholden to the strength and agility of a country's institutions; the stability and practical mindedness of its political system; the culture, quality and motivation of its workforce, management and public bureaucracy; and the flexibility and appropriateness of the entire gamut of domestic policy. The Japanese experience confirms that while good policy might not always deliver an optimal outcome, it goes a long way towards it – and bad policy almost inevitably results in a bad outcome.

Second, asset price bubbles, such as that experienced in Japan in the late 1980s, are extremely damaging phenomena. Their extent is hard to grasp in real time, but they are often born out of extended periods of apparent financial stability, and they thrive on poorly framed or inadequate regulation and oversight; a skewed and unduly lax macro policy mix; and arrogance and self-congratulation on the part of policymakers, business managers and the population at large. They are associated with excessive appetite for risk and rapid debt accumulation. They drive unsustainable booms. They are socially and politically divisive. They breed financial malfeasance and political sleaze. And they are inevitably followed by asset price busts; recessions; and extended periods of balance sheet adjustment and slow growth, worryingly low inflation (or even deflation) and stubbornly low interest rates that constrain the effectiveness of monetary policy and leave central bankers operating in unfamiliar and demanding territory.

To prevent asset booms running out of control, policymakers need to do three things. First, they need to be mindful of complacency and of the lessons of history. Second, they need to keep a close eye on financial imbalances and changes in investor behaviour. And third, if they detect the development of immoderation, if at all possible – and it is never a simple political task deliberately to stand in the way of people making money – they need to act early to nip it in the bud. This does not, of course, mean that economic policy should be aimed in its entirety at managing the financial cycle. This would lead to impossible conflicts of interest and be a certain recipe for broader macro instability. What it does mean, however, is that the financial – or so-called macroprudential – tools honed since the GFC should form an important and transparent part of the policymaker's armoury across the business cycle, and that in some exceptional circumstances, monetary and fiscal policy should also to some extent lean against the wind of asset market excess.

Supposing that such interventions are not forthcoming, or that they are too slow or too timid to engineer a soft landing – and unfortunately, it is not just the Japanese example but the entire historical record of bouts of asset inflation that suggests that they are rarely robust enough do so – then the need to act quickly equally applies to dealing with the after-effects of an asset bust. Beyond rapidly and sustainably adjusting macroeconomic policy to the subsequent inevitable change in cyclical dynamics and being willing if necessary to champion unconventional tools in the process, it is important that losses are transparently recognized, that compromised assets are removed from balance sheets, that the financial system is rapidly recapitalized, that those guilty of criminality are held to account, and that lasting reforms are put in place to reduce the chances of repetition. Forbearance is rarely, if ever, a viable alternative strategy.

Third, Japan's demographic challenges hold important lessons for everyone. All the major economies are now confronted by falling birth rates, slowing population and workforce growth and ageing societies, even if few will experience these phenomena to the degree that Japan has and is. The message here is clear. In such circumstances, financial incentives should be used to increase the birthrate. The participation of the workforce should be maximized through adequate childcare provision; the prioritization of education, training, retraining and life-long learning; and the appropriate tailoring of the regulatory and tax environments. And finally, controversial as it is in today's world, the encouragement of inward migration, albeit in such a manner that new arrivals possess the skills that are in shortest supply and can be satisfactorily integrated into society.

At the same time, with productivity growth rather than labour input increasingly the dominant source of potential growth, structural policy in general should take centre stage and be kept under constant review. In addition to the labour-market-related priorities outlined above, this means a focus on strong but not inflexible institutions (legislative, operational and informational), the provision of good infrastructure, the maintenance of open and competitive markets, and reasonable and fair overall tax burdens.

That said, as the Japanese example amply demonstrates, there should be no illusions about the political and social difficulties of managing extended structural change when most of the benefits come only after a long lag but the associated costs are more immediate and typically fall most heavily on powerful vested interests. Structural policymaking therefore needs to be evidence based. It needs to be concrete and feasible. Where appropriate, it should borrow from best practice elsewhere. It should provide protection for the most vulnerable in society, and it requires at least the tacit acceptance of the majority of the population that it is necessary. In this, it helps if there is a significant amount of cross-party support, if it is driven by strong leadership and if the electorate can see that the process is being overseen by people who are qualified to do the job. Having agents of change or supportive 'points of light' across society can also help.

It may also make sense, at least at the outset, to concentrate on driving through a relatively small number of important initiatives rather than taking a scattergun approach and trying simultaneously to make progress across a broad spectrum, although it is important that positive momentum is sustained and that any narrow prioritization does not descend into a strategy of merely picking low-hanging fruit. The establishment of early 'wins' in the reform process can build momentum for additional initiatives, although this in turn means that there must be an ability to assess and credibly demonstrate progress both quantitatively and qualitatively. It must also be recognized that structural policies interrelate both with one another (in this sense, their positive effects can over time feed off each other) and, as they can have short-term output costs, with macroeconomic policy. They should not be considered in isolation.

This brings us to a fourth lesson: that of the importance of the policy mix. Too often, and especially from the mid 1980s onwards, Japan's policy mix was lopsided and out of kilter. Generally, too much emphasis was put on macro policy to achieve the desired goals, while structural policy – including, importantly, financial policy – frequently lagged, was poorly framed or just misguided. Macroeconomic policy also has only a finite influence. Sagely delivered within the context of transparent and sensible rules, and provided it is not used hyperactively to 'fine-tune' demand, it can contribute significantly to evening out the business cycle. But doing this successfully also requires the fiscal and monetary elements to be appropriately calibrated. An undue burden should not be placed on one, as was frequently the case with Japanese monetary policy, even though, following the bursting of the bubble, the circumstances in which it was employed were for much of the time less than conducive to its success. At the same time, macroeconomic policy, however it is constructed, cannot do much to influence the underlying performance of an economy over the longer term. This is the job of structural policy.

To be fully successful, economic policy needs to be balanced and formulated in such a way that its different elements complement rather than clash with one another.

A TENTATIVE LOOK AHEAD

All of which brings us to the final question that needs to be addressed: where does Japan go from here?

The recent increase in interest in the corporate sector's earnings potential is, without doubt, a source of optimism, but, as noted across much of the previous narrative, Japan's prospective demographics are extremely daunting. The birth rate has collapsed to around 1.2 children per female, and it has been below the level necessary to sustain the population since the mid 1970s. The overall population peaked in the late 2000s at just under 128 million and is projected to drop to around 100 million in 2050 and then to some 64 million by 2100 – half the peak. Supported by the nation's extraordinary longevity, the proportion of elderly citizens will rise to just under 35% of the population by the middle of the century, and it will still amount to more than a third of the population at its end. The working-age population will fall by something in the region of 40% from its highs by 2050.

These statistics are unparalleled for a peacetime economy and their implications are hard to grasp. They imply a huge drop in population density and outright depopulation across many rural areas; intergenerational income and wealth inequalities are likely to become increasingly burning political issues; unanticipated social issues are expected to flare up. It seems unavoidable that potential growth will continue the decline seen since the 1960s, and at some stage will surely turn negative. In a dramatic break with the past, the overall size of the economy will therefore shrink significantly, pushing it rapidly down the global country rankings. It is just a matter of how much and when. As we noted in the previous chapter, at the end of the 2010s the IMF estimated that, in the absence of significant reform, the long-term contraction in output in Japan could amount to some 25%.

Of course, what matters from the perspective of living standards and, thereby, social and political stability is not the absolute size of an economy but, rather, the progress of real GDP per capita, and by this measure Japan has largely held its own over recent periods, which is comforting. Nevertheless, persistently falling overall real GDP is an unfamiliar phenomenon that could have unfortunate psychological effects on the population that encourage a negative feedback loop, accelerating the process of decline.

There are also numerous other uncertainties confronting Japan. For example, in the area of macroeconomic policy, how can the crisis in the public finances be addressed before the exceptional considerations that have acted to maintain market confidence in the nation's solvency ebb away? Is it possible for Japan to grow to any significant extent and at the same time bring the huge burden of public debt under control? Can the BOJ realistically provide any major offset to an extended period of fiscal restraint? How will the BOJ operate in an environment of negative growth potential and a persistently negative neutral interest rate? Will this require a digital currency to engineer deeply negative interest rates? What should happen to its inflation target? Should it be reduced? Should it be abandoned? After all, the older the population becomes, and the more pensioners there are, the less likely it is that there will be any appetite for rising prices. Will there be any other options but to embrace wholesale financial repression or to repudiate a sizeable portion of the public sector's outstanding debt? What would that mean for the BOJ's balance sheet, solvency and credibility – and more broadly?

Then there is climate change to consider. Addressing it will be disruptive and expensive. How will environmental considerations interact with the demographic shock and the parlous condition of the public finances? Will it add to the prospective downdraft affecting potential growth or ameliorate it? Could its consequences be the catalyst to push the budgetary situation over the edge? Could action to tackle climate change conceivably result in another renaissance for the economy?

Turning to politics, Japanese society, for all its longstanding idiosyncrasies, has proved remarkably stable through the economic vicissitudes of the past 40 years. Indeed, it is hard to imagine how any other modern-day state would have dealt so well with the challenges Japan has faced. Moreover, so far at least, the country has largely escaped the recent global rise of populism and nationalism, although arguably the latter has never entirely gone away.

But how much does Japan's outward social stability reflect its enduring ethnic homogeneity and the fact that it is so geographically difficult for unauthorized migrants to reach? What will happen if the door to legal immigration continues to swing open? After all, Japan has considerable historical form where prejudice and autocracy are concerned. Quite how a resurgence of such tendencies would play out is difficult to foresee with any precision but it is unlikely to result in a smooth ride for an economy and society already facing so many other challenges.

Nor is the international economic environment comforting. Potential growth is substantially lower everywhere than it was, and aspirations and expectations are not being met. The globalization of the late-twentieth/early-twenty-first century, meanwhile, is now in headlong retreat. Protectionism and bilateralism are on the rise; the rules-based international institutions established at the end of World War II, from which Japan benefited so much, are under growing strain, if not in their death throes; while the economic and geopolitical threat from China shows little sign of easing. Such circumstances do not augur well for a shrinking, export-dependent economy with few natural resources, and with whom many of its neighbours retain an axe to grind from the middle of the twentieth century. At the very least, these considerations are likely to require subtle diplomacy on Japan's part. Are its politicians and bureaucrats up to the job? Recent successes in developing the country's trading relations across Asia and with Europe are encouraging, but how will Japan cope if the United States, long its protector, continues to turn inwards, become more transactional in its approach to international relations and increasingly takes on the role of disruptor?

Dwelling too much on these issues and uncertainties can undoubtedly be depressing, and it is easy to think oneself into a state of despair about the future. However, the fact is that Japan has little control over many of them.

One is therefore left with the conclusion that the best strategy for Japan to follow is to seek to minimize the prospective decline in growth potential and the absolute level of GDP and to try to protect itself against future shocks. This means making the most of its existing comparative advantages and accelerating the process of structural reform that has been ongoing over recent decades but that has so far fallen short of requirements. At the risk of merely reciting a menu of policy perfection, this implies casting aside the residual tendencies towards physiocracy, gerontocracy, misogyny and xenophobia; giving technology – and in particular AI – every chance to substitute for an increasingly acute labour shortage; and returning to a very familiar list of supply-side priorities.

Inter alia, Japan must seek to ensure that sufficient resources are available to sustain the country's excellent infrastructure. It must maintain the emphasis put on open trading relationships and education. It must provide better active labour market policies. It must look to further boost the birthrate and extend affordable childcare. It must deliver more tax reform, including, importantly, higher indirect taxes, more onerous taxation of carbon and the reduction of the disincentives for women to work. It must continue the deregulation of services and agriculture, and the encouragement of FDI. It must seek out greater efficiency in healthcare provision and gradually ease restrictions on migration, especially for the semi-skilled and low skilled. It must further the encouragement of shareholder value, and in particular the reduction of cross-shareholdings, and therefore facilitate the release of the huge reservoir of dormant corporate savings.

This is a truly daunting to do list in such unforgiving circumstances. Over the past 150 years or so, for all its social and cultural quirks and occasional unfortunate misadventures, Japan has for much of the time exhibited remarkable fortitude, resilience and adaptability. It would appear that it will have to continue to do so. Perhaps more than ever.

Selected Charts

The following twelve charts were created by the author with help from Silja Sepping to provide a graphic depiction of some of the more important longer-term macroeconomic trends described in the text. They are all drawn from publicly available data provided by the OECD, the IMF or official Japanese government statistical sources

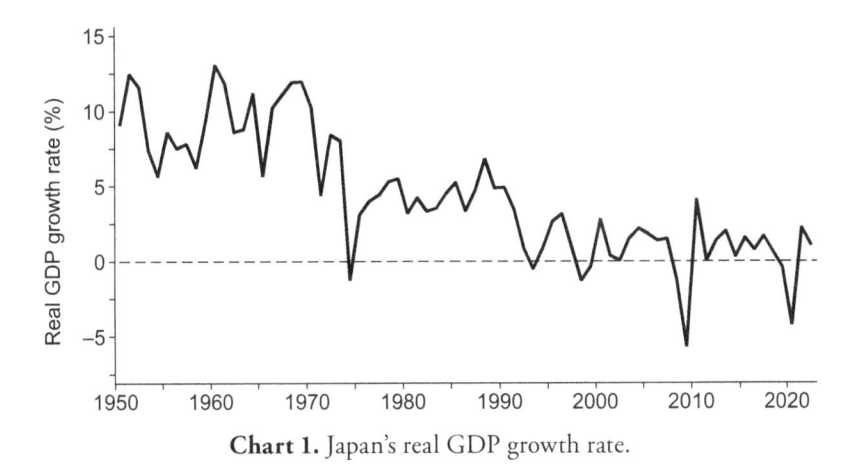

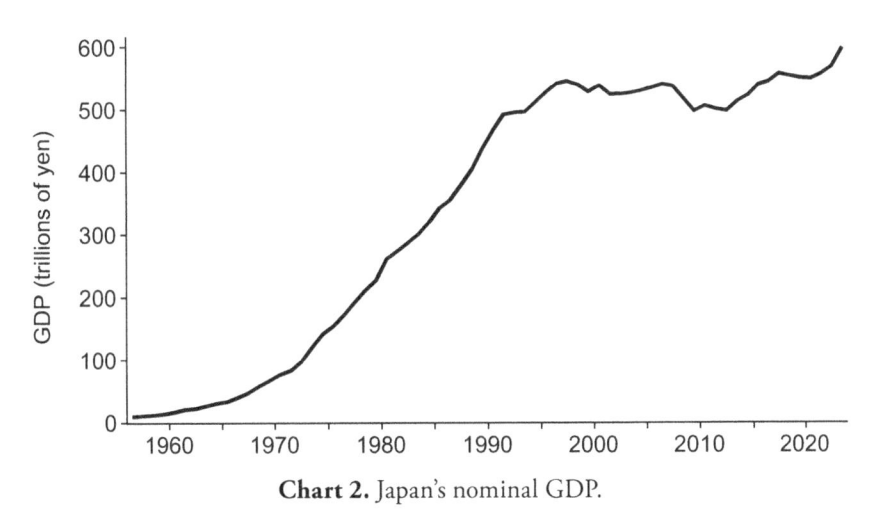

Chart 1. Japan's real GDP growth rate.

Chart 2. Japan's nominal GDP.

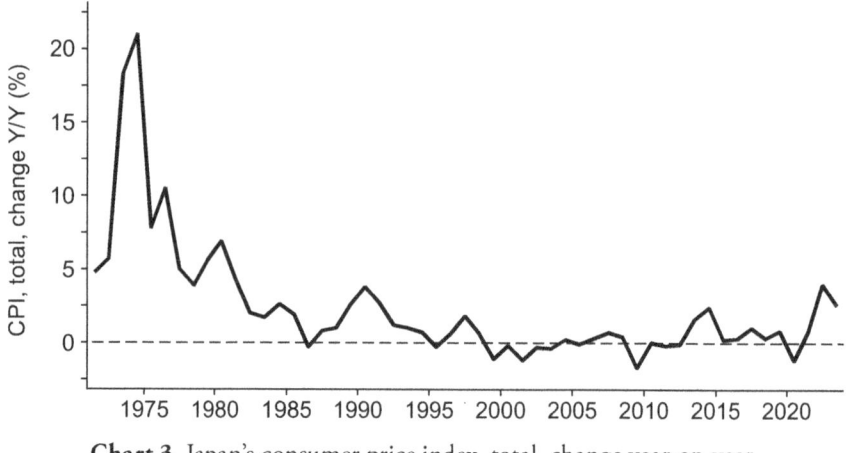

Chart 3. Japan's consumer price index, total, change year-on-year.

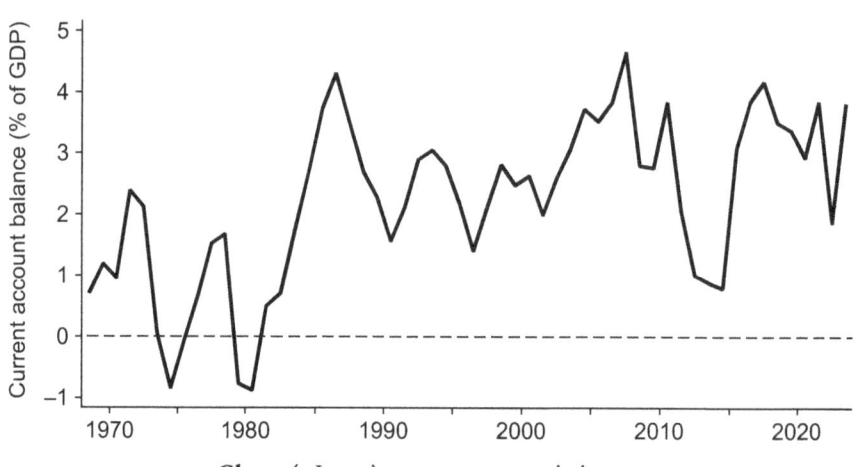

Chart 4. Japan's current account balance.

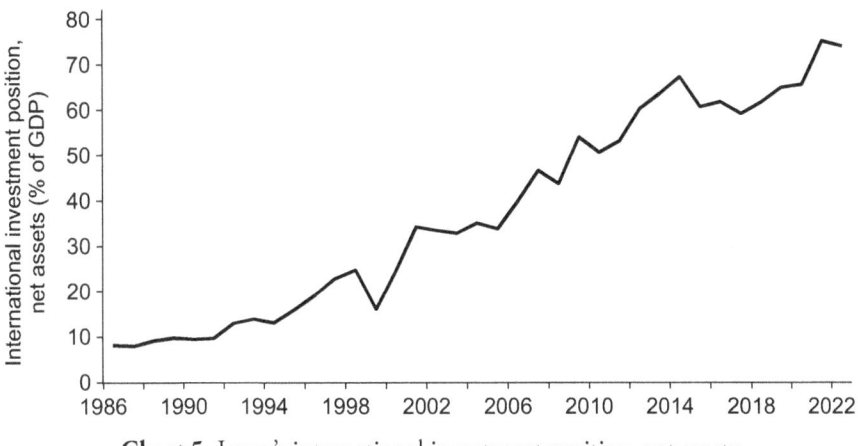

Chart 5. Japan's international investment position, net assets (as a percentage of GDP).

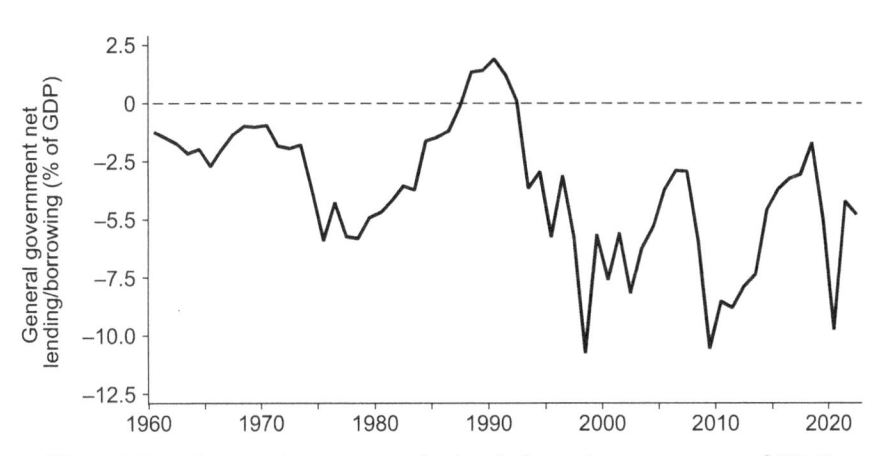

Chart 6. Japan's general government budget balance (as a percentage of GDP).

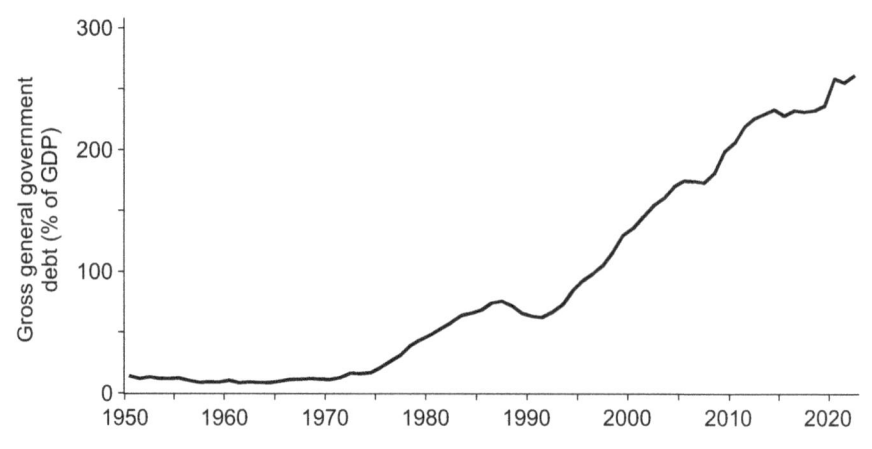

Chart 7. Japan's gross general government debt (as a percentage of GDP).

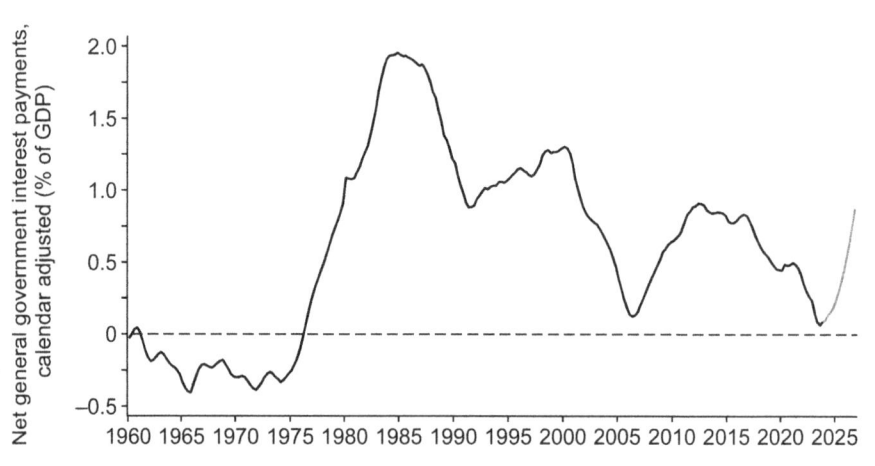

Chart 8. The Japanese government's net interest payments (as a percentage of GDP).

Chart 9. Nikkei 225 and Japanese land prices.

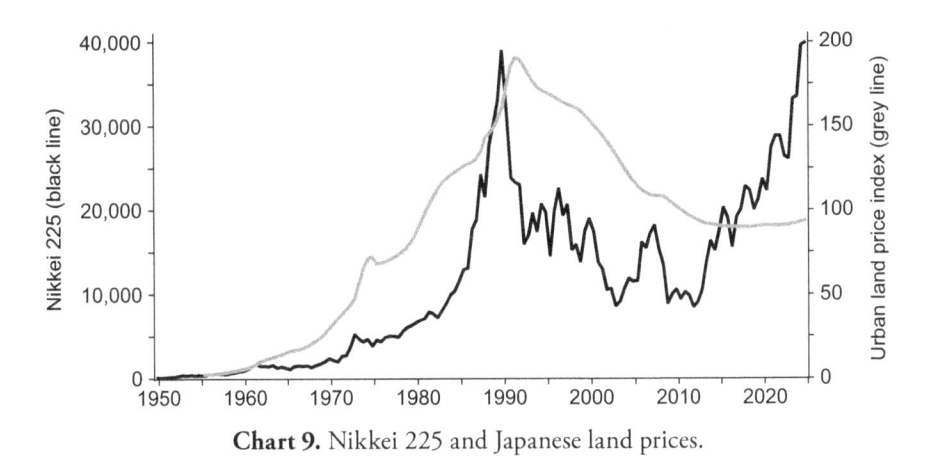

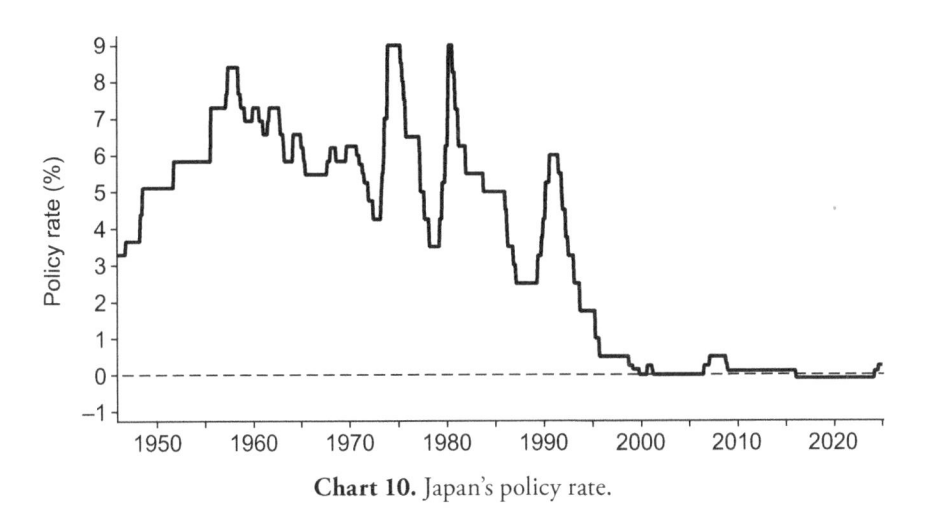

Chart 10. Japan's policy rate.

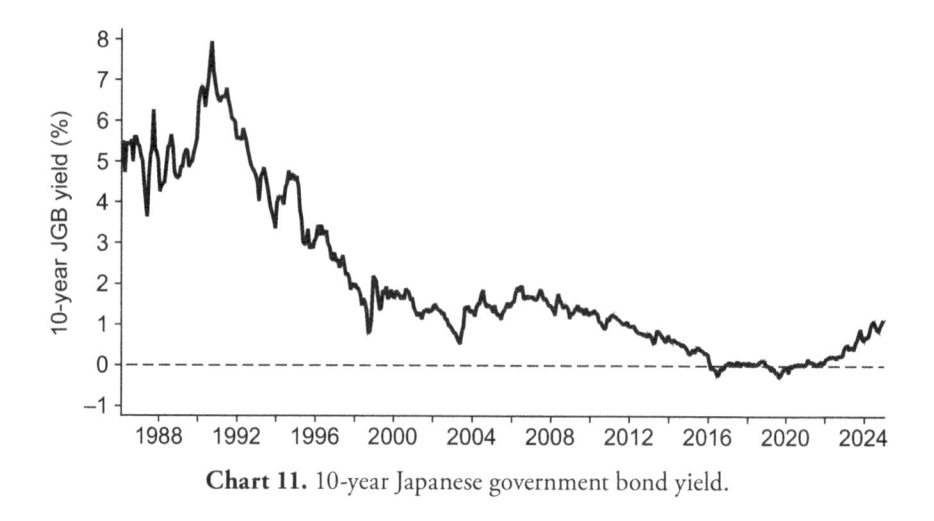

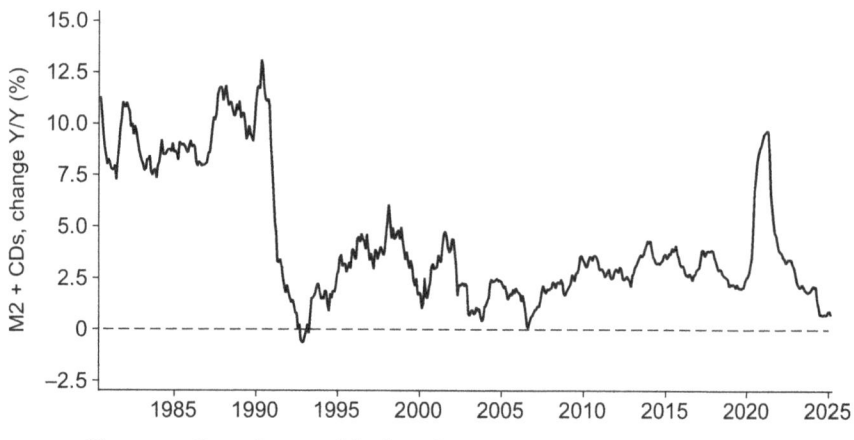

Chart 11. 10-year Japanese government bond yield.

Chart 12. Growth rate of the broad monetary aggregate, M2 + CDs.

Bibliography and Sources

The primary statistical sources used throughout the book are the websites of the Bank of Japan, the Japanese Ministry of Finance, the Japanese Cabinet Office, the BIS, the OECD and the IMF. Two other key resources were Angus Maddison's *The World Economy in the 20th Century* (1989, OECD, Paris) and the Maddison Project at the University of Groningen (https://www.rug.nl/ggdc/historicaldevelopment/maddison/). For the sake of consistency, and to avoid confusion, I gravitated towards the most recently revised data. However, it is worth noting that, in some instances, the revisions were substantial. Contemporary perceptions could therefore be somewhat at variance with my narrative.

For the pre-World War II era I relied on various Bank of Japan sources – particularly *Hundred-Year Statistics of the Japanese Economy*, published in July 1966 – together with a range of secondary sources. There is therefore a lack of consistency and the figures used for that period should consequently be taken as illustrative.

CHAPTER I. SETTING THE SCENE

Allen, G. C. 1958. *Japan's Economic Recovery*. Oxford University Press.
Bank of Japan. 1996. Annual review. Fiscal policies under the new deal in the United States and the Takahashi fiscal policy in Japan. Bank of Japan, Tokyo.
Bernanke, B., and H. James. 1991. The gold standard, deflation, and the great depression: an international comparison. In *Financial Markets and Financial Crises*, edited by G. Hubbard, pp. 33–68. University of Chicago Press.
Bass, G. 2023. *Judgement at Tokyo*. Picador, London.
Bollard, A. 2020. *Economists at War*. Oxford University Press.
Cargill, T. 2000. Monetary policy, deflation, and economic history. IMES Discussion Paper 2000-E-30, September, Bank of Japan, Tokyo (https://www.imes.boj.or.jp/research/papers/english/00-E-30.pdf).
Cha, M. 2003. Did Takahashi Korekiyo rescue Japan from the Great Depression? *Journal of Economic History*, volume 63(1), March.
Dower, J. 1993. *Japan in War and Peace*. Fontana, London.

Dower, J. 1999. *Embracing Defeat: Japan in the Wake of World War II*. Norton, New York.
Eichengreen, B. 1995. *Golden Fetters*. Oxford University Press.
Harding, C. 2018. *Japan Story: In Search of a Nation – 1850 to the Present*. Allen Lane, London.
Harding, C. 2020. *The Japanese: A History in Twenty Lives*. Allen Lane, London.
Itō, T. 1992. *The Japanese Economy*. MIT Press, Cambridge, MA.
Kindleberger, C. 1973. *The World in Depression 1929–39*. University of California Press, Los Angeles, CA.
Kuronoma, Y. 2009. Showa depression: a prescription for 'once in a century crisis'. Japan Centre for Economic Research, Tokyo (https://www.jcer.or.jp/eng/pdf/kuronuma0904.pdf).
Large, S. 1992. *Emperor Hirohito and Showa Japan*. Routledge, London.
Maddison, A. 1989. *The World Economy in the 20th Century*. OECD, Paris.
Mizuki, S. 2013. *Showa 1926–1939: A History of Japan*. Drawn and Quarterly, London.
Mizuki, S. 2014. *Showa 1939–1944: A History of Japan*. Drawn and Quarterly, London.
Murphy, R. T. 2014. *Japan and the Shackles of the Past*. Oxford University Press.
Nakamura, T. 1983. *Economic Growth in Pre-War Japan*. Yale University Press, New Haven, CT.
Nakamura, T. 1998. *A History of Showa Japan 1926–89*. Tokyo University Press.
Ohno, K. 2018. *The History of Japanese Economic Development*. Routledge, London.
Overy. R. 2025. *Rain of Ruin: Tokyo, Hiroshima and the Surrender of Japan*. Allen Lane, London.
Patrick, H. 1971. The economic muddle of the 1920s. In *Dilemmas of Growth in Pre-war Japan*, edited by J. Moody. Princeton University Press.
Pilling, D. 2014. *Bending Adversity: Japan and the Art of Survival*. Penguin, London.
Romer, C. 2013. It takes a regime shift. Recent developments in Japanese monetary policy through the lens of the Great Depression. *NBER Macroeconomics Annual*, volume 28(https://www.journals.uchicago.edu/doi/full/10.1086/674609).
Shibamoto, M. and M. Shizume. 2011. How did Takahashi Korekiyo rescue Japan from the Great Depression? IMES, August, Bank of Japan, Tokyo (https://docslib.org/doc/8896134/how-did-takahashi-korekiyo-rescue-japan-from-the-great-depression).

Shizume, M. 2002. Economic developments and monetary policy responses in interwar Japan: evaluation based on Taylor rule. Discussion Paper 2002-E-7, BOJ/IMES (https://www.imes.boj.or.jp/research/papers/english/me20-3-3.pdf).

Shizume, M. 2007. Sustainability of public debt. Evidence from pre-World War II Japan. Kobe University Discussion Paper 201, March (https://www.rieb.kobe-u.ac.jp/academic/ra/dp/English/dp201.pdf).

Shizumi, M. 2009. The Japanese economy during the inter-war period: instability in the financial system and the impact of the World Depression. Bank of Japan/IMES, Tokyo (https://www.boj.or.jp/en/research/wps_rev/rev_2009/rev09e02.htm).

Shizume, M. 2019. A history of the Bank of Japan 1882–2016. Working Paper E1719, Waseda Institute of Political Economy, Tokyo (https://www.waseda.jp/fpse/winpec/assets/uploads/2014/05/No.E1719.pdf).

Smethurst, R., and M. Matsuura. 2000. Politics and the economy in pre-war Japan. Discussion Paper JS/00/381, Suntory Centre, LSE, London (https://papers.ssrn.com/sol3/PIP_Journal.cfm?pip_jrnl=1005204).

Storry, R. 1960. *A History of Modern Japan*. Penguin, London.

Tasker, P. 1987. *Inside Japan*. Penguin, London.

Thomas, E. 2023. *Road to Surrender: Three Men and the Countdown to the End of World War II*. Elliot and Thompson, London.

Van Wolferen, K. 1989. *The Enigma of Japanese Power*. MacMillan, London.

CHAPTER 2. RECONSTRUCTION AND RENAISSANCE

Allen, G. C. 1958. *Japan's Economic Recovery*. Oxford University Press.

Bank of Japan. 2015. Bank of Japan's monetary policy in the 1980s: a view perceived from archived and other materials. Monetary and Economic Studies, November, Bank of Japan, Tokyo (https://www.imes.boj.or.jp/research/papers/english/me33-5.pdf).

Bass, G. 2023. *Judgement at Tokyo*. Picador, London.

Dower, J. 1993. *Japan in War and Peace*. Fontana, London.

Dower, J. 1999. *Embracing Defeat: Japan in the Wake of World War II*. Norton, New York.

Harding, C. 2018. *Japan Story: In Search of a Nation – 1850 to the Present*. Allen Lane, London.

Harding, C. 2020. *The Japanese: A History in Twenty Lives*. Allen Lane, London.

IMF. Various years. World economic outlook. IMF, Washington, DC.

Itō, T. 1992. *The Japanese Economy*. MIT Press, Cambridge, MA.

Johnson, C. 1983. *MITI and the Japanese Economic Miracle: The Growth of Industrial Policy, 1925–75.* Stanford University Press.
Jones, R. 1997. *Bank of Japan Law: Evolution, not Revolution.* Lehman Brothers, Tokyo.
Jones, R. 2014. *The Itinerant Economist: Memoirs of a Dismal Scientist.* London Publishing Partnership, London.
Large, S. 1992. *Emperor Hirohito and Showa Japan.* Routledge, London.
Maddison, A. 1989. *The World Economy in the 20th Century.* OECD, Paris.
Mauro, P., R. Romeu et al. 2013. *A Modern History of Fiscal Prudence and Profligacy.* IMF, Washington, DC.
Mizuki, S. 2014. *Showa 1944–1953: A History of Japan.* Drawn and Quarterly, London.
Mizuki, S. 2015. *Showa 1953–1989: A History of Japan.* Drawn and Quarterly, London.
Murphy, R. T. 2014. *Japan and the Shackles of the Past.* Oxford University Press.
Nakamura, T. 1981. *The Post-War Japanese Economy: Its Development and Structure.* Tokyo University Press.
Nakamura, T. 1998. *A History of Showa Japan 1926–89.* Tokyo University Press.
OECD. Various years. Economic outlook. OECD, Paris.
OECD. Various years. Economic survey of Japan. OECD, Paris.
Ohno, K. 2018. *The History of Japanese Economic Development.* Routledge, London.
Patrick, H. 1980. The post-war economic history of Japan. Discussion Paper 349, April, Economic Growth Centre, Yale University.
Pilling, D. 2014. *Bending Adversity: Japan and the Art of Survival.* Penguin, London.
Shizume, M. 2019. A history of the Bank of Japan 1882–2016. Working Paper E1719, Waseda Institute of Political Economy, Tokyo (https://www.waseda.jp/fpse/winpec/assets/uploads/2014/05/No.E1719.pdf).
Storry, R. 1960. *A History of Modern Japan.* Penguin, London.
Tasker, P. 1987. *Inside Japan.* Penguin, London.
Thomas, E. 2023. *Road to Surrender: Three Men and the Countdown to the End of World War II.* Elliot and Thompson, London.
Van Wolferen, K. 1989. *The Enigma of Japanese Power.* MacMillan, London.

CHAPTER 3. THE BUBBLE ECONOMY

Bank of Japan. 1990. A study of potential pressure on prices. Special Paper 186, February, Bank of Japan, Tokyo.

Bank of Japan. 1991. Recent balance of payments developments in Japan. Special Paper 208, Bank of Japan, Tokyo.

Bank of Japan. 2015. Bank of Japan's monetary policy in the 1980s: a view perceived from archived and other materials. Monetary and Economic Studies, November, Bank of Japan, Tokyo (https://www.imes.boj.or.jp/research/papers/english/me33-5.pdf).

Baumgartner, U., and G. Meredith. 1995. Saving behaviour and the asset 'bubble' in Japan. Occasional Paper 124, IMF, Washington, DC.

Bayoumi, T., and C. Collyns (eds). 2000. *Post Bubble Blues: How Japan Responded to Asset Price Collapse*. IMF, Washington, DC.

Cecchetti, S., H. Genberg, J. Lipsky and S. Wadhwani. 2000. Asset prices and central bank policy. CEPR, London.

Harding, C. 2018. *Japan Story: In Search of a Nation – 1850 to the Present*. Allen Lane, London.

IMF. Various years. Article IV assessment of Japan. IMF, Washington, DC.

IMF. Various years. World economic outlook. IMF, Washington, DC.

Ito, T. 1992. *The Japanese Economy*. MIT Press, Cambridge, MA.

Koo, R. 2008. *The Holy Grail of Macroeconomics: Lessons from Japan's Great Recession*. Wiley Asia, Singapore.

Jones, R. 2014. *The Itinerant Economist: Memoirs of a Dismal Scientist*. London Publishing Partnership, London.

Mizuki, S. 2015. *Showa 1953–1989: A History of Japan*. Drawn and Quarterly, London.

Miller, G. 1996. The role of a central bank in a bubble economy. *Cardozo Law Review*, volume 18.

Murphy, R. T. 2014. *Japan and the Shackles of the Past*. Oxford University Press.

OECD. Various years. Economic outlook. OECD, Paris.

OECD. Various years. Economic survey of Japan. OECD, Paris.

Ohno, K. 2018. *The History of Japanese Economic Development*. Routledge, London.

Pilling, D. 2014. *Bending Adversity: Japan and the Art of Survival*. Penguin, London.

Nakamura, T. 1998. *A History of Showa Japan 1926–89*. Tokyo University Press.

Shiratsuka, S. 2003. The asset price bubble in Japan in the 1980s: lessons for financial and macroeconomic stability. BIS Papers 21, BIS, Basel (https://www.bis.org/publ/bppdf/bispap21e.pdf).

Van Wolferen, K. 1989. *The Enigma of Japanese Power*. MacMillan, London.

Wood, C. 1992. *The Bubble Economy*. Atlantic Monthly Press, New York.

CHAPTER 4. THE BUBBLE BURSTS

Aghevli, B., T. Bayoumi and G. Meredith. 1998. *Structural Change in Japan: Macroeconomic Impact and Policy Challenges*. IMF, Washington, DC.

Bank of Japan. Various years. Annual review. Bank of Japan, Tokyo.

Bayoumi, T., and C. Collyns (eds). 2000. *Post Bubble Blues: How Japan Responded to Asset Price Collapse*. IMF, Washington, DC.

Bordo, M., T. Ito and T. Iwaisako. 1997. *Banking Crises and Monetary Policy: Japan in the 1990s and the US in the 1930s*. Unpublished, University of Tsukuba.

Cecchetti, S., H. Genberg, J. Lipsky and S. Wadhwani. 2000. Asset prices and central bank policy. CEPR, London.

Economic Planning Agency. Various years. Economic survey of Japan. EPA, Tokyo.

Harding, C. 2018. *Japan Story: In Search of a Nation – 1850 to the Present*. Allen Lane, London.

IMF. Various years. Article IV assessments of Japan. IMF, Washington, DC.

IMF. 2002. When bubbles burst. IMF world economic outlook, chapter 2. IMF, Washington, DC.

IMF. Various years. World economic outlook. IMF, Washington, DC.

Koo, R. 2008. *The Holy Grail of Macroeconomics: Lessons from Japan's Great Recession*. Wiley Asia, Singapore.

Jones, R. 1990. Yasushi Mieno: an appraisal of his first year as BOJ governor. Economic Report 32, December, UBS Phillips and Drew, Tokyo.

Jones, R. 1991a. BOJ monetary policy: overkill or prudence? Economic Report 36, March, UBS Phillips and Drew, Tokyo.

Jones, R. 1991b. How far for the ODR? Economic Report 38, July, UBS Phillips and Drew, Tokyo.

Jones, R. 1991c. Fiscal policy: taking up the slack. Economic Report 39, August, UBS Phillips and Drew, Tokyo.

Jones, R. 1992. Japan after the fifth ODR cut. Economic Report 44, July, UBS Phillips and Drew, Tokyo.

Jones, R. 1995a. Bank of Japan watching: a guide. July, Lehman Brothers, Tokyo.

Jones, R. 1995b. Fiscal fairytale or Keynesian kinetic – an analysis of Japan's latest economic stimulus package. Lehman Brothers Asian Economic Focus, September, Tokyo.

Jones, R. 2014. *The Itinerant Economist: Memoirs of a Dismal Scientist*. London Publishing Partnership.

Matsui, K., and H. Suzuki. 1997. Deregulation: breaking the 10,000 commandments. Goldman Sachs Portfolio Strategy, February, Tokyo.

Murphy, R. T. 2014. *Japan and the Shackles of the Past*. Oxford University Press.

Nakaso, H. 2001. The financial crisis in Japan during the 1990s: how the Bank of Japan responded and the lessons learnt. BIS Paper 6, BIS, Basel (https://www.bis.org/publ/bppdf/bispap06.pdf).

OECD. Various years. Economic outlook. OECD, Paris.

OECD. Various years. Economic survey of Japan. OECD, Paris.

OECD. 1999. Regulatory reform in Japan. OECD, Paris.

Ohno, K. 2018. *The History of Japanese Economic Development*. Routledge, London.

Pilling, D. 2014. *Bending Adversity: Japan and the Art of Survival*. Penguin, London.

Obstfeld, M. 2009. *Time of Troubles: The Yen and Japan's Economy, 1985–2008*. University of California, Berkeley, CA.

Turner, G. 2003. Solutions to a liquidity trap. Japan's bear market and what it means for the West. GFC Economics, London.

CHAPTER 5. THE CRISIS DEEPENS

Aghevli, B., T. Bayoumi and G. Meredith. 1998. *Structural Change in Japan: Macroeconomic Impact and Policy Challenges*. IMF, Washington, DC.

Bank of Japan. Various years. Annual review. Bank of Japan, Tokyo.

Bank of Japan. Various years. Minutes of monetary policy meetings. Bank of Japan, Tokyo.

Bayoumi, T., and C. Collyns (eds). 2000. *Post Bubble Blues: How Japan Responded to Asset Price Collapse*. IMF, Washington, DC.

Bank for International Settlements. Various years. Annual report. BIS, Basel.

Bordo, M., T. Ito and T. Iwaisako. 1997. *Banking Crises and Monetary Policy: Japan in the 1990s and the US in the 1930s*. Unpublished, University of Tsukuba.

Cargill, T. 2000. Monetary policy, deflation, and economic history. IMES Discussion Paper 2000-E-30, September, Bank of Japan, Tokyo (https://www.imes.boj.or.jp/research/papers/english/00-E-30.pdf).

Cecchetti, S., H. Genberg, J. Lipsky and S. Wadhwani. 2000. Asset prices and central bank policy. CEPR, London.

Economic Planning Agency. Various years. Economic survey of Japan. EPA, Tokyo.

Harding, C. 2018. *Japan Story: In Search of a Nation – 1850 to the Present*. Allen Lane, London.

IMF. Various years. Article IV assessments of Japan. IMF, Washington, DC.

IMF. Various years. World economic outlook. IMF, Washington, DC.

Jones, R. 1995b. Fiscal fairytale or Keynesian kinetic – an analysis of Japan's latest economic stimulus package. Lehman Brothers Asian Economic Focus, September, Tokyo.

Jones, R. 1996. Bank of Japan Law: time for a change? Lehman Brothers Asian Economic Focus, April, Tokyo.

Jones, R. 1997. Bank of Japan Law: evolution, not revolution. Lehman Brothers, Tokyo.

Jones, R., and J. Llewellyn. 1999. Japan: a radical proposal. Lehman Brothers, Tokyo.

Jones, R. 2014. *The Itinerant Economist: Memoirs of a Dismal Scientist*. London Publishing Partnership.

Krugman, P. 1998. It's baaaack! Japan's slump and the return of the liquidity trap. September, Brookings Institute, Washington, DC (https://www.brookings.edu/articles/its-baaack-japans-slump-and-the-return-of-the-liquidity-trap/).

Koo, R. 2008. *The Holy Grail of Macroeconomics: Lessons from Japan's Great Recession*. Wiley Asia, Singapore.

Lincoln, E. 1998. Japan's financial problems. Brookings Papers on Economic Activity 2, Brookings Institution, Washington, DC.

Murphy, R. T. 2014. *Japan and the Shackles of the Past*. Oxford University Press.

Nakaso, H. 2001. The financial crisis in Japan during the 1990s: how the Bank of Japan responded and the lessons learnt. BIS Paper 6, BIS, Basel (https://www.bis.org/publ/bppdf/bispap06.pdf).

OECD. Various years. Economic outlook. OECD, Paris.

OECD. Various years. Economic survey of Japan. OECD, Paris.

OECD. 1999. Regulatory reform in Japan. OECD, Paris.

Ohno, K. 2018. *The History of Japanese Economic Development*. Routledge, London.

Pilling, D. 2014. *Bending Adversity: Japan and the Art of Survival*. Penguin, London.

Obstfeld, M. 2009. *Time of Troubles: The Yen and Japan's Economy, 1985-2008*. University of California, Berkeley, CA.

Shigehara, K. 1996. *Results of Regulatory Reform for Consumers, Innovation and Economic Performance*. OECD, Paris.

Shirakawa, M. 2014. Is inflation (or deflation) always and everywhere a monetary phenomenon? BIS Paper 77, BIS, Basel (https://www.bis.org/publ/bppdf/bispap77e.pdf).

Syed, M., K. Kang and K. Tokuoka. 2009. 'Lost decade' in translation. What Japan's crisis could portend about recovery from the Great Recession. Working Paper WP/09/281, IMF, Washington, DC (https://www.imf.org/external/pubs/ft/wp/2009/wp09282.pdf).

Tett, G. 2003. *Saving the Sun*. Harper Collins, New York.

Turner, G. 2003. Solutions to a liquidity trap. Japan's bear market and what it means for the West. GFC Economics, London.

CHAPTER 6. LEAVING THE LOST DECADE BEHIND

Baba, N., S. Nishioka, N. Oda, M. Shirakawa, K. Ueda and H. Ugai. 2009. Japan's deflation, problems in the financial system and monetary policy. BIS Working Paper 188, BIS, Basel (https://www.bis.org/publ/work188.pdf).

Ball, L. 2008. Helicopter drops and Japan's liquidity trap. Discussion Paper 2008-E-4, March, IMES/Bank of Japan, Tokyo (https://www.imes.boj.or.jp/research/papers/english/me26-7.pdf).

Bank for International Settlements. Various years. Annual report. BIS, Basel.

Bank of Japan. Various years. Minutes of monetary policy meetings. Bank of Japan, Tokyo.

Bernanke, B. 2003. Some thoughts on monetary policy in Japan. May, Federal Reserve Board, Washington, DC (https://www.federalreserve.gov/boarddocs/speeches/2003/20030531/default.htm).

Cargill, T. 2000. Monetary policy, deflation, and economic history. Discussion Paper 2000-E-30, September, IMES/Bank of Japan, Tokyo (https://www.imes.boj.or.jp/research/papers/english/00-E-30.pdf).

Fuji, M., and M. Kawai. 2010. Lessons from Japan's banking crisis, 1991–2005. Working Paper 222, July, ADBI, Tokyo (https://www.adb.org/node/156077/printable/print).

Harding, C. 2018. *Japan Story: In Search of a Nation – 1850 to the Present*. Allen Lane, London.

IMF. Various years. Article IV assessments of Japan. IMF, Washington, DC.

IMF. Various years. World economic outlook. IMF, Washington, DC.

Jones, R. 2005. Japan: escape from the dark valley. December, Abu Dhabi Investment Authority.

Jones, R. 2014. *The Itinerant Economist: Memoirs of a Dismal Scientist*. London Publishing Partnership.

Koo, R. 2008. *The Holy Grail of Macroeconomics: Lessons from Japan's Great Recession*. Wiley Asia, Singapore.

Matsubayashi, Y. 2015. The effort to stabilise the financial system in Japan: an outline and the characteristics of the programme for financial revival. Working Paper 2015/02, March, Bruegel, Brussels (https://www.bruegel.org/working-paper/effort-stabilise-financial-system-japan-outline-and-characteristics-programme).

Matsuoka, M. 2004. End of Japan's lost decade. October, Deutsche Bank, Tokyo.

Matsuoka, M. 2005. Normalisation of business cycle to continue. November, Deutsche Bank, Tokyo.

Matsuoka, M. 2006. Post-quantitative monetary easing regime. March, Deutsche Bank, Tokyo.

McCulley, P., and T. Masanao. 2010. Where exit should be an oxymoron: the Bank of Japan. PIMCO, Newport Beach, CA.

Morgan, P. 2005. Progress of structural adjustment. September, HSBC, Tokyo.

Morgan, P. 2006. Japan monetary policy regime change. March, HSBC, Tokyo.

Murphy, R. T. 2014. *Japan and the Shackles of the Past*. Oxford University Press.

OECD. Various years. Economic survey of Japan. OECD, Paris.

OECD. Various years. Economic outlook. OECD, Paris.

Ohno, K. 2018. *The History of Japanese Economic Development*. Routledge, London.

Pilling, D. 2014. *Bending Adversity: Japan and the Art of Survival*. Penguin, London.

Obstfeld, M. 2009. *Time of Troubles: The Yen and Japan's Economy, 1985–2008*. University of California, Berkeley, CA.

Shirakawa, M. 2014. Is inflation (or deflation) always and everywhere a monetary phenomenon? BIS Paper 77, BIS, Basel (https://www.bis.org/publ/bppdf/bispap77e.pdf).

Sheard, P. 2005. Japan: edging towards reflation. November, Lehman Brothers, Tokyo.

Syed, M., K. Kang and K. Tokuoka. 2009. 'Lost decade' in translation. What Japan's crisis could portend about recovery from the Great Recession. Working Paper WP/09/281, IMF, Washington, DC (https://www.imf.org/external/pubs/ft/wp/2009/wp09282.pdf).

Tett, G. 2003. *Saving the Sun*. Harper Collins, New York.

Turner, G. 2003. Solutions to a liquidity trap. Japan's bear market and what it means for the West. GFC Economics, London.

Ueda, K. 2003. Japan's deflation and policy response. April, Bank of Japan, Tokyo.

CHAPTER 7. THE GLOBAL FINANCIAL CRISIS

Bank for International Settlements. Various years. Annual report. BIS, Basel.

Bernanke, B. 2015. *The Courage to Act: A Memoir of Crisis and Its Aftermath*. Norton. London.

Bernanke, B., T. Geithner and H. Paulson. 2019. *Firefighting: The Financial Crisis and Its Lessons*. Penguin, London.

Blinder, A. 2013. *After the Music Stopped: The Financial Crisis, The Response, and the Work Ahead*. Penguin, New York.

Eichengreen, B. 2015. *Hall of Mirrors*. Oxford University Press.

Geithner, T. 2014. *Stress Test: Reflections on Financial Crises*. Random House, London.

IMF. Various years. Article IV assessments of Japan. IMF, Washington, DC.

IMF. Various years. World economic outlook. IMF, Washington, DC.

IMF. Various years. Global financial stability report. IMF, Washington, DC.

Jones, R. 2014. *The Itinerant Economist: Memoirs of a Dismal Scientist*. London Publishing Partnership.

Jones, R. 2023. *The Tyranny of Nostalgia: Half a Century of British Economic Decline*. London Publishing Partnership.

Jones, R., and J. Llewellyn. 2019. The Global Financial Crisis. Presentation at Birkbeck College, University of London, for the Society of Professional Economists, February.

OECD. Various years. Economic outlook. OECD, Paris.

OECD. Various years. Economic survey of Japan. OECD, Paris.

Ohno, K. 2018. *The History of Japanese Economic Development*. Routledge, London.

Tooze, A. 2018. *Crashed: How a Decade of Financial Crises Changed the World*. Allen Lane, London.

CHAPTER 8. OUT OF THE FRYING PAN ...

Baba., N., S. Nishioka, N. Oda, M. Shirakawa, K. Ueda and H. Ugai. 2009. Japan's deflation, problems in the financial system and monetary policy. BIS Working Paper 188, BIS, Basel (https://www.bis.org/publ/work188.pdf).

Bank for International Settlements. Various years. Annual report. BIS, Basel.

Bank of Japan. Various years. Minutes of monetary policy meetings. Bank of Japan, Tokyo.

Bank of Japan. Various years. Outlook for economic activity and prices. Bank of Japan, Tokyo.

Bank of Japan. 2016. Developments in the natural rate of interest in Japan. *BOJ Review*, 2016-E-12, October, Bank of Japan, Tokyo (https://www.boj.or.jp/en/research/wps_rev/rev_2016/data/rev16e12.pdf).

Fukao, M. 2014. Fiscal consolidation in Japan. Discussion Paper Series 14-E-015, April, Research Institute of Economy, Trade, and Industry, Keio University (https://www.rieti.go.jp/jp/publications/dp/14e015.pdf).

Harding, C. 2018. *Japan Story: In Search of a Nation – 1850 to the Present*. Allen Lane, London.

IMF. Various years. Article IV assessments of Japan. IMF, Washington, DC.
IMF. Various years. World economic outlook. IMF, Washington, DC.
IMF. Various years. Global financial stability report. IMF, Washington, DC.
Jones, R. 2013. Mr. Abe takes the plunge. Comment, September, Llewellyn Consulting.
Jones, R. 2014. *The Itinerant Economist: Memoirs of a Dismal Scientist*. London Publishing Partnership.
Kuroda, H. 2013. Quantitative and qualitative monetary easing and Japan's economy. Speech at a Meeting Held by the Yomiuri International Economic Society in Tokyo, May (https://www.boj.or.jp/en/about/press/koen_2013/data/ko130412a1.pdf).
Matsubayashi, Y. 2015. The effort to stabilise the financial system in Japan: an outline and the characteristics of the programme for financial revival. Working Paper 2015/02, March, Bruegel, Brussels (https://www.bruegel.org/working-paper/effort-stabilise-financial-system-japan-outline-and-characteristics-programme).
OECD. Various years. Economic survey of Japan. OECD, Paris.
OECD. Various years. Economic outlook. OECD, Paris.
OECD. Various years. Going for growth. OECD, Paris.
Ohno, K. 2018. *The History of Japanese Economic Development*. Routledge, London.
Murphy, R. T. 2014. *Japan and the Shackles of the Past*. Oxford University Press.
Pilling, D. 2014. *Bending Adversity: Japan and the Art of Survival*. Penguin, London.
Romer, C. 2013. It takes a regime shift. Recent developments in Japanese monetary policy through the lens of the Great Depression. April, NBER, Washington, DC (https://www.journals.uchicago.edu/doi/epdf/10.1086/674609)
Sheard, P. 2015. Japan's policy trap: deflation is the enemy of fiscal health, fiscal consolidation the enemy of reflation. August, Standard & Poor's Rating Services.
Shirakawa, M. 2014. Is inflation (or deflation) 'always and everywhere' a monetary phenomenon? BIS Paper 77, BIS, Basel (https://www.bis.org/publ/bppdf/bispap77e.pdf).
Syed, M., K. Kang and K. Tokuoka. 2009. 'Lost decade' in translation. What Japan's crisis could portend about recovery from the Great Recession. Working Paper WP/09/281, IMF, Washington, DC (https://www.imf.org/external/pubs/ft/wp/2009/wp09282.pdf).

CHAPTER 9. ABENOMICS AND AFTER

Arbarti, E., D. Botman, *et al.* 2016. Reflating Japan. Time to get unconventional. Working Paper WP/16/157, August, IMF, Washington, DC (https://www.imf.org/external/pubs/ft/wp/2016/wp16157.pdf).

Arslanalp, S., and D. Botman. 2015. Portfolio rebalancing in Japan: constraints and implications for quantitative easing. Working Paper WP/15/186, August, IMF, Washington, DC (https://www.imf.org/en/Publications/WP/Issues/2016/12/31/Portfolio-Rebalancing-in-Japan-Constraints-and-Implications-for-Quantitative-Easing-43161)

Bank of Japan. Various years. Minutes of monetary policy meetings. Bank of Japan, Tokyo.

Bank of Japan. Various years. Monetary policy decisions. Bank of Japan, Tokyo.

Bank of Japan. Various years. Outlook for economic activity and prices. Bank of Japan, Tokyo.

Bank of Japan. Various years. Summary of opinions at the monetary policy meeting. Bank of Japan, Tokyo.

Bank of Japan. 2016a. Developments in the natural rate of interest in Japan. BOJ Review 2016-E-12, October, Bank of Japan, Tokyo (https://www.boj.or.jp/en/research/wps_rev/rev_2016/data/rev16e12.pdf).

Bank of Japan. 2016b. Comprehensive assessment: developments in economic activity and prices as well as policy effects since the introduction of quantitative and qualitative easing. The Background. Bank of Japan, Tokyo (https://www.boj.or.jp/en/mopo/mpmdeci/mpr_2016/k160921b.pdf).

Bank for International Settlements. Various years. Annual report. BIS, Basel.

Bernanke, B. 2017. Some reflections on Japanese monetary policy. Brookings Institute, Washington, DC (https://www.brookings.edu/articles/some-reflections-on-japanese-monetary-policy/).

Fukao, M. 2014. Fiscal consolidation in Japan. Discussion Paper Series 14-E-015, April, Research Institute of Economy, Trade, and Industry, Keio University (https://www.rieti.go.jp/jp/publications/dp/14e015.pdf).

Harding, C. 2018. *Japan Story: In Search of a Nation – 1850 to the Present*. Allen Lane, London.

Hausman, J., and J. Wieland. 2014. Abenomics: preliminary analysis and outlook. Brookings Economic Studies, March, Brookings Institute, Washington, DC (https://www.brookings.edu/wp-content/uploads/2016/07/2014a_Hausman.pdf).

IMF. Various years. Article IV assessments of Japan. IMF, Washington, DC.

IMF. Various years. World economic outlook. IMF, Washington, DC.
IMF. Various years. Global financial stability report. IMF, Washington, DC.
Jones, R. 2014a. Takahashi's ghost. Comment, March, Llewellyn Consulting.
Jones, R. 2014b. Through the looking glass. Comment, November, Llewelyn Consulting.
Jones, R. 2015a. Abenomics – all aquiver. Comment, June, Llewelyn Consulting.
Jones, R. 2015b. Mr. Kuroda's cognitive dissonance. Comment, October, Llewelyn Consulting.
Jones, R. 2017a. Cul-de-sac. Comment, January, Llewellyn Consulting.
Jones, R. 2017b. Hope springs eternal. Comment, October, Llewellyn Consulting.
Jones, R. 2018a. Mr. Kuroda's ever more complex conundra. Comment, February, Llewellyn Consulting.
Jones, R., and J. Llewellyn. 2019a. The global financial crisis. Presentation at Birkbeck College, University of London, for the Society of Professional Economists, February.
Jones, R., and J. Llewellyn. 2019b. Japan: consolidation or repudiation. Comment, August, Llewellyn Consulting.
Koshima, Y. 2019. Japan's public sector balance sheet. Working Paper WP/19/212, IMF, Washington, DC (https://www.imf.org/en/Publications/WP/Issues/2019/10/04/Japan-s-Public-Sector-Balance-Sheet-48687).
Kuroda, H. 2013. Quantitative and qualitative monetary easing and Japan's economy. Speech at a Meeting Held by the Yomiuri International Economic Society in Tokyo, May (https://www.boj.or.jp/en/about/press/koen_2013/data/ko130412a1.pdf).
Kuroda, H. 2017. Quantitative and qualitative monetary easing and economic theory. November, Bank of Japan, Tokyo (https://www.boj.or.jp/en/about/press/koen_2017/data/ko171114a1.pdf).
OECD. Various years. Economic survey of Japan. OECD, Paris.
OECD. Various years. Economic outlook. OECD, Paris.
OECD. Various years. Going for growth. OECD, Paris.
Ohno, K. 2018. *The History of Japanese Economic Development*. Routledge, London.
Sheard, P. 2015. Japan's policy trap: deflation is the enemy of fiscal health, fiscal consolidation the enemy of reflation. August, Standard & Poor's Rating Services.
Shirakawa, M. 2014. Is inflation (or deflation) 'always and everywhere' a monetary phenomenon? BIS Paper 77, BIS, Basel (https://www.bis.org/publ/bppdf/bispap77e.pdf).
Takata, H. 2017. Abenomics. Past, present, and future. September, Mizuho Research Institute, Tokyo.

CHAPTER 10. CONCLUSIONS AND PROGNOSES

Bank for International Settlements. Various years. Annual report. BIS, Basel.
IMF. Various years. Article IV assessments of Japan. IMF, Washington, DC.
IMF. Various years. World economic outlook. IMF, Washington, DC.
IMF. Various years. Global financial stability report. IMF, Washington, DC.
OECD. Various years. Economic survey of Japan. OECD, Paris.
OECD. Various years. Economic outlook. OECD, Paris.

Notes

CHAPTER 1

1. *Japan as Number One: Lessons for America* (Harvard University Press, Cambridge, MA) is a book by Ezra Vogel published in 1979. It argued that Americans should understand the Japanese experience and be willing to learn from it.
2. The Tokugawa (or Edō) period extended from 1603 to 1867, during which Japan was ruled by the Tokugawa Shogunate (military dictatorship) and the country's 300 regional *daimyō* (feudal lords).
3. Samurai were the hereditary military nobility and officer caste of medieval and early modern Japan from the late twelfth century until their abolition in the 1870s during the Meiji era. They were the well-paid retainers of the *daimyō*.
4. The Meiji Restoration restored practical imperial rule to Japan in 1868, consolidating the political system of the country under Emperor Meiji.
5. Prior to the late-nineteenth century, no Japanese emperor had enjoyed uncontested rule for over a millennium.
6. A *Zaibatsu*'s structure typically included a family-owned holding company at the top and a bank that financed the other (mostly industrial) subsidiaries within them.
7. For the sake of consistency with the modern-day custom in economic analysis, I refer to GDP as the standard measure of aggregate output throughout most of the text. In fact, the Japanese authorities, like many others, typically used GNP as their favoured metric until the early 1990s, and it is referred to here where alternative GDP data were unavailable.
8. A military coalition of France, the United Kingdom and Russia, plus Italy from 1915 and the United States from 1917.
9. Shirakawa, M. 2011. Great East Japan Earthquake: resilience of society and determination to rebuild. Remarks at Council on Foreign Relations in New York, April, Bank of Japan, Tokyo (https://www.boj.or.jp/en/about/press/koen_2011/data/ko110415a.pdf).
10. The Washington Naval Treaty was signed by the governments of the British Empire, the United States, France, Italy and Japan. It limited the construction of battleships, battlecruisers and aircraft carriers. It was despised by many in the Japanese navy. Nevertheless, it was not until the mid 1930s that navies began to build battleships once again, and the power and the size of new battleships began to increase.

11 Of the two parties, the political philosophy of Kenseikai (Minseitō) was more free market and small government in tone, while Seiyūkai favoured greater fiscal activism and a larger state.
12 It is widely said that the Mitsubishi *Zaibatsu* controlled the Kenseikai, and the Mitsui *Zaibatsu* the Seiyūkai.
13 By way of example, although Japan had been an ally in World War I, and Japan was one of the major players at the Paris Peace Conference, US President Woodrow Wilson had insisted that clauses in the initial drafts of the Versailles Peace Treaty calling for an end of racial discrimination were deleted. Similarly, in 1924 the US Congress passed the blatantly racist Immigration Act, severely limiting immigration from Japan.
14 This was the so-called Mukden incident. The Japanese troops bombed their own railway but blamed locals.
15 The most serious consideration of returning to gold seems to have come in 1919, 1923 and 1927.
16 Inoue Junnosuke served as BOJ governor from 1919 to 1923 and from 1927 to 1928. He also served as finance minister in 1923 as well as from 1929 to 1931.
17 Takahashi Korekiyo is a remarkable figure in Japanese history. He joined the Bank of Japan in 1892 and served as its governor from 1911 to 1913. In total, he served as finance minister on seven occasions and as prime minister once, between 1921 and 1922. Self-educated, a fluent English speaker, progressive and open-minded, he had a central role as a fundraiser in the Western countries during the Russo-Japanese war and played a key part in addressing the financial crisis of 1927.
18 Keynes's magnum opus *The General Theory of Employment, Interest and Money* was published in 1936. By the early 1930s, however, the great British economist had already sketched out many of his central views on macroeconomic stabilization, and it is known that Takahashi had read some of his work. This included *A Tract of Monetary Reform*, published in 1923, which put the case for a managed currency.
19 Previously, under the gold standard, bank notes could only be issued up to the amount of gold reserves held.
20 The quantitative easing employed by Japan from the early 2000s, and more broadly in the wake of the GFC, overwhelmingly consisted of central bank purchases of government and private sector debt in secondary markets rather than directly from the government itself.
21 The buoyancy of exports in part reflected increased sales to the yen-bloc economies of Korea, Taiwan and Manchukuo.
22 Miwa, T. 2016. Fiscal policy unease and financial repression. June, Nomura Global Markets Research, Tokyo.
23 The total amount of cash that a company has received in exchange for its common or preferred stock issues.
24 It has been suggested that Harry Dexter White – then director of monetary research at the US Treasury but also a Soviet spy – was encouraged by his Moscow handlers to draft for the Roosevelt administration completely unrealistic

demands on Japan to end the US oil embargo, which it was clear would be rejected. This set the scene for Japan's attack on Pearl Harbour. US entry into the war meant, of course, that Stalin no longer had to worry about a Japanese invasion of the Soviet Far East. See Steil, B. 2013. *The Battle of Bretton Woods*, pp. 52–58. Princeton University Press.

25 Zuljan, R. 2003. Allied and axis GDP, Article, ONWAR.com (https://onwar.com/articles/0302wwiigdp.html).

26 Prior to World War II, Korea, Taiwan and Manchuria had enjoyed rapid growth, driven by efforts to improve technology in basic agriculture, substantial investment in infrastructure and modern industrial techniques, better technical education, and the migration of mid-level skills and management from Japan.

CHAPTER 2

1 The author's father, a young rating on the Royal Navy battleship King George V, witnessed both the formal surrender of the Japanese forces and the abject condition of Tokyo and Yokohama and their populations in August 1945. The experiences remained with him for the rest of his life.

2 The occupation was ended by the Treaty of San Francisco, signed in September 1951 and effective on 28 April 1952, after which full sovereignty was returned to the bulk of the Japanese archipelago. However, under the US–Japan Security Treaty, more than 250,000 US troops remained. Even today, there are more than 30,000 US troops in Japan.

3 The constitution formally came into effect on 3 May 1947. It has recently come to light that parts of it were not after all the work of US officials but rather drawn from a document written by liberal Japanese lawyers and journalists during the Taishō era of 1912–1926.

4 Thirty-nine women won seats in the Lower House in the general election of April 1946.

5 RFB financial assistance fell under the unfortunately named category of so-called *Fukkin* loans.

6 Mauro, P., R. Romeu, A. Binder and A. Zaman. 2013. A modern history of fiscal prudence and profligacy. IMF, Washington, DC (https://www.imf.org/external/pubs/ft/wp/2013/wp1305.pdf).

7 The currency reform was named after Joseph Dodge, chairman of the Bank of Detroit and a hardline free-marketeer brought in to advise MacArthur at the end of 1948.

8 A formal Policy Board was also established at this time as the central bank's supreme decision-making body. It was comprised of the governor, four other Bank officials who enjoyed voting rights, and two government 'observers', one from the MOF and, in due course, another from the Economic Planning Agency (EPA). The BOJ's legal foundations were little changed, however, and it therefore ultimately remained beholden to the MOF and the government.

9 It has been suggested to the author that the reason the yen was fixed at 360 to the dollar was that when Japanese bureaucrats asked MacArthur to make a

decision as to what the exchange rate should be, pursuant to his role as Supreme Commander, he replied along the lines of 'I don't know – pick a round number', so they did, 360 being the number of degrees in a circle.
10   There is evidence that the establishment of the LDP was explicitly bankrolled by the CIA to ensure that the Right dominated Japanese politics.
11   Japan had originally been selected to host the 1940 games, but in 1938 the decision was rescinded in favour of Helsinki because of the war with China. World War II meant that the Helsinki games were postponed until 1952.
12   The plan was originally set out in Tanaka, K. 1972. *Remodelling the Japanese Archipelago*. Nikkan Kogyo Shinbusha, Tokyo.
13   The Lockheed Scandal broke in December 1975. It related to the payment of bribes of more than ¥3 billion in connection with sales of aircraft to Japan. Tanaka was arrested in July 1976 for his part in the scandal. As prime minister, he had taken a bribe from Lockheed to persuade All Nippon Airways to purchase Lockheed aircraft for its fleet rather than those manufactured by McDonnell Douglas. He was the first person in Japan to be charged with criminal abuse of the prime ministerial office. His trial lasted almost seven years, at the end of which he was found guilty, fined and sentenced to four years in prison, from where he continued to direct the activities of his LDP faction and remained a powerful kingmaker.
14   Japan's social security account surpluses and the assets built up in it at that time reflected the fact that the pension system was less mature than in the rest of the OECD economies. As such, the ratio of pension recipients to contributors was low. However, that ratio was set to rise inexorably as the population structure aged.
15   The estimates of the impulse of fiscal policy on the economy included here and throughout the book relate to structural, or non-cyclical, changes in the so-called general government definition of the budget balance, which extends to the activities of central government, local government and the social security account. Such estimates are by their very nature imprecise, as they depend in large part on evaluations of an economy's underlying growth potential, which change over time and are often subject to significant revisions. They should therefore be looked at as illustrative rather than definitive.

It should also be noted that in Japan's case (and, for that matter, in the case of other economies), the general government balance is an incomplete indicator of fiscal health and policy momentum as it fails to extend to the broader public sector. Where Japan is concerned, it excludes the Fiscal Investment and Loan Programme (FILP), which for much of the period under discussion in this book – until the 2010s at least – effectively amounted to a second budget. The FILP employed the assets of the social security account mentioned above – essentially pension contributions – together with postal savings and postal insurance funds and with money raised from government guaranteed bonds, all of which were deposited into the MOF's Trust Fund Bureau (TFB). With these funds, the FILP financed a complex network of transfers within the public sector and government and lending operations, including those of the Housing Loan

Corporation. Indeed, for a significant period it accounted for around a quarter of government investment on a national accounts basis. What is more, changes in FILP spending did not necessarily mirror those of other areas of government activity. In the 1980s FILP spending acted to offset some of the fiscal policy tightening driven by the rest of the budget.

When all these considerations are taken into account, the public sector was larger, the fiscal balance less favourable and the burden of net debt higher than suggested by looking just at the general government statistics. As for the overall thrust of fiscal policy, it remained significantly contractionary throughout the 1980s, but to a somewhat lesser degree than is suggested in the main text. Needless to say, the work of economists, and for that matter officials, would be greatly eased by the transparent consolidation of all government operations.

As an aside, the author was once told by a senior MOF official that the reason for the complexity of Japan's public sector accounts harks back to World War II and a desire on the part of officials to hide at least some public funds from the military. The system was then never fully reformed.

16 This happens when inflation or income growth moves householders into higher tax brackets.
17 Privatization was only complete where JAL and a number of smaller corporations were concerned. In the cases of NTT, JT and JNR, the change in business structure was more a process of corporatization than of privatization. The entire business was not transferred to the private sector. Rather, the government divested itself of financial and operational control but retained a sizeable equity stake in the 'privatized' company.
18 Unfortunately, in the face of falling land and stock prices after 1990, the profit on these assets sales was insufficient to meet the JNRSC's interest costs, and the government was forced to provide huge annual transfers to cover the shortfall. In the 1995/1996 financial year, for example, the total sum applied was equivalent to some 1.5% of GDP.
19 The United States rarely acknowledges that it maintained very high tariffs from its foundation in the late-eighteenth century right up to the end of World War II, and that it heavily protected and subsidized its agricultural industries for a long time after it began reducing tariffs on manufactured goods. Indeed, it still does so today. The United States is also reluctant to see its use of subsidies and protectionist Department of Defense procurement policies as an American version of what it accused Japan of doing then and accuses China of doing now. And it never acknowledges that for an extended period America routinely stole intellectual property from Europe.
20 The Plaza Accord was a joint agreement – signed on 22 September 1985 at the Plaza Hotel in New York City – between France, West Germany, Japan, the United Kingdom and the United States. Its aim was to depreciate the US dollar in relation to the French franc, the German deutschemark, the Japanese yen and the British pound by intervening in currency markets and putting in place monetary and fiscal policies sympathetic to that end.

21 The middle-income trap refers to a situation where a country has reached a middling level of GDP per capita but struggles to develop further and fails to attain high-income-country status. Casualties of this phenomenon are particularly numerous in Latin America.
22 Keynes, J. M. 1971. *The Economic Consequences of the Peace.* The Collected Writings of John Maynard Keynes, Volume II. MacMillan, London.
23 This is not to deny that Japan had ever previously exerted a significant influence on 'Western' culture. For example, late-nineteenth-century impressionism owed a great deal to Japanese art. See 'How did Japanese art influence impressionism?' at https://www.thecollector.com/how-japanese-art-influenced-impressionism/ or see 'Japonisme' at https://www.metmuseum.org/toah/hd/jpon/hd_jpon.htm.

CHAPTER 3

1 The 'Heisei boom' was named after the onset of the reign of Emperor Akihito, who assumed the throne on 8 January 1989 and whose era was designated as 'Heisei'. A rough translation of Heisei would be 'peace everywhere'.
2 Mayekawa, H., *et al.* 1986. The report of the advisory group on economic structural adjustment for international harmony. Japan Information Service, 7 April.
3 Mercantilism was a nationalist economic policy designed to maximize the exports and minimize the imports of an economy. It became the dominant school of economic thought in Europe throughout the late Renaissance and the early-modern period (from the fifteenth to the eighteenth centuries).
4 The figures described here refer to movements in the M2 + CDs aggregate on which the Bank of Japan tended to focus much of its attention, even producing quarterly projections for it.
5 The output gap is a broad measure of economy-wide resource utilization, defined as the level of actual output relative to potential, expressed as a percentage of potential.
6 Taylor, J. 1993. Discretion versus policy rules in practice. Carnegie-Rochester Conference Series on Public Policy, 39, pp. 195–214 (https://web.stanford.edu/~johntayl/Onlinepaperscombinedbyyear/1993/Discretion_versus_Policy_Rules_in_Practice.pdf).
7 West Germany's current account surpluses actually exceeded those of Japan in the mid-to-late 1980s, averaging some 4.5% of GDP between 1986 and 1989.
8 The Louvre Accord was an agreement, signed by Canada, France, West Germany, Japan, the United Kingdom and the United States on 22 February 1987, in Paris, that aimed to stabilize international currency markets and halt the decline of the US dollar following the Plaza Accord.
9 This conclusion was first formerly articulated by Dennis Robertson, a Cambridge economist and contemporary of Keynes, in a paper published in 1928. See Robertson, D. H. 1928. Theories of banking policy. Lecture at the London School of Economics, 13 February. (Reprinted in 1966 in *Essays in Money and Interest.* Collins, London.)

10 These capital adequacy requirements are now referred to as BIS I, in that there have subsequently been three more series of such guidelines for banks. The idea was to establish minimum capital standards that international banks should adhere to in order to protect against certain risks. The more significant risk that a bank was exposed to, the greater should be the amount of capital held to safeguard its solvency and overall economic stability. The primary focus of BIS I was credit risk, and to a lesser degree market risk. Operational risk was not addressed at all. The guidelines introduced in 1988/1989 became law in 1992.

11 Mynsky, H. 1986. *Stabilizing an Unstable Economy*. McGraw Hill, New York.

CHAPTER 4

1 Resentment over the introduction of the consumption tax, together with a sex scandal involving previous prime minister Uno Sōsuke, meant that the LDP lost 25 seats in the February 1990 Lower House election. However, led by the relatively undistinguished (even by Japanese political standards) Kaifu Toshiki, the party still retained an overall majority of 19 in the 512-seat chamber.

2 The invasion signalled the beginning of the first Gulf War, which was to continue until the end of February 1991.

3 Home ownership in Japan's major cities averaged around 50%, a much lower share than in the United Kingdom or the United States, for example. As a result, the effects on private consumption of large cyclical variations in property prices were more muted. The impact of asymmetries in the tax regime on the liquidity of the housing market also served to moderate housing wealth effects.

4 Alternatively, it can also be seen as the real rate of interest that balances desired real savings and investment under conditions of full employment. When the real rate of interest exceeds the natural rate of interest, output and prices will slow, and vice versa.

5 *Keizai* means 'economy' in Japanese.

6 The tax elasticity with respect to GDP had averaged around 1.25 in the late 1970s and early 1980s before jumping to about 1.75 during the asset bubble. However, it fell well below 1 between 1991 and 1994.

7 According to the IMF, Japan's automatic stabilizers were at this time only between a half and two-thirds as powerful over a two-year period as was the case in the vast majority of the G7 economies. Only in the United States and Italy were the automatic stabilizers similarly limited.

8 The number of proportional representation seats was subsequently reduced to 180 for the 2000 general election, such that the total number of seats in the House of Representatives was cut to 480.

9 Over subsequent years, the rate of decline in the GDP deflator would consistently outstrip that of the CPI, in significant part because the investment deflator was particularly depressed by technological improvements.

10 Shirakawa, M. 2011. Great East Japan Earthquake: resilience of society and determination to rebuild. Remarks at the Council on Foreign Relations, New York, April. The plunge in stock prices that followed also proved to be the

proximate cause of the collapse of Barings Bank: see https://www.boj.or.jp/en/about/press/koen_2011/data/ko110415a.pdf.

11   The RCC grew out of Tokyo Kyodo Bank, an entity created by the BOJ in 1995 to assume the assets of two failed credit unions – Tokyo Kyowa Credit Union and Anzen Credit Union – that went to the wall in December 1994.

12   Hitherto, only small lot deposits (those up to ¥10 million per depositor; these comprised around half of all bank deposits) had been automatically guaranteed. As we shall see, in December 1999 the government extended the guarantee on large lot deposits until the end of March 2003, and in October 2002 it extended again: until the end of March 2005.

13   The financial crises of the early 1990s in Finland, Sweden and Norway were resolved by rapidly recognizing the extent of loan losses, injecting capital into the financial system in one form or another, and by removing high-risk loans from the banks' balance sheets – and in turn creating a 'bad bank'.

14   It is interesting to note that the Japanese asset bubble of the 1980s and the US asset bubble of the 1920s are similar in terms of the pace of economic growth and interest rate dynamics. However, between 1930 and 1933 the Untied States experienced a collapse in real output of some 8.5%, while between 1991 and 1994 Japan's GDP increased by about 1.5%. Japan actively resorted to fiscal expansion and allowed its budget deficit to widen sharply around the bottom of the business cycle while the United States did not.

15   Rates of return on public investment tended to be much higher in areas of higher per capita income than in areas of low per capita income, yet the poorer the area, the higher the level of public investment spending per capita typically was. Economic activity in poorer areas tended to be very dependent on public sector construction activity. Public investment spending was in effect a large regional aid programme.

CHAPTER 5

1   Despite further intermittent resort to public works spending to boost growth, the share of public investment in GDP subsequently trended downwards until the aftermath of the GFC.

2   The difference between the fixed rates offered by the major banks for housing loans and those offered by the HLC averaged a little below two percentage points for most of the 1990s, but it increased to more than two and a half percentage points for a period in late 1998 before subsiding once again.

3   It should be noted, however, that there is a well-known positive bias in all CPIs, as inter alia they fail to capture the fact that less is bought of goods and services that experience the largest price rises. It was estimated in 1999 that the positive bias in Japan's CPI was about one percentage point. See Shiratsuka, S. 1999. Measurement error in the Japanese consumer price index. *Monetary and Economic Studies*, volume 17(3). Institute for Monetary and Economic Studies, Bank of Japan.

4 It should be added that, given the reluctance among Japanese employers to make people redundant, the headline unemployment rate understated the degree of excess capacity in the labour market.
5 Given the limited equity-related wealth effect in Japan mentioned in chapter 3, it was the huge extent of the fall in the value of household assets, rather than any great sensitivity to asset values, that held back private consumption in the 1990s.
6 As far as a corporate sector wealth effect is concerned, it was estimated by the IMF that each 1,000-point fall in the Nikkei stock index reduced business investment by 0.5%–1.0% over a two-year period.
7 The Japanese state pension system was first introduced in 1890. The system in place in 1996 was initiated in 1961 and took its then current form in 1985. It comprised two tiers. The National Pension Plan offered basic flat rate benefits for all. The second tier was earnings related. Employers' Pension Insurance was available for private sector employees. The Voluntary National Pension Fund was available for the self-employed.
8 The evidence is that the scheme was used most by heavily indebted companies with a higher risk of default. The suggestion is therefore that it may have delayed the process of corporate restructuring.
9 The vouchers appear to have had a very limited impact on spending, largely because of substitution effects. According to the Cabinet Office, the multiplier associated with them was a mere 0.3.
10 In the end, the BOJ suffered some losses as a result of its actions, but the sort of financial and economic collapse suffered in the United States and beyond in the wake of Lehman's failure was avoided.
11 A 'carry trade' refers to an investment strategy in which highly leveraged investors borrow yen at very low rates and invest the proceeds in higher-yielding US dollars.
12 The statement is based on a monetary conditions index (MCI) developed by the OECD and based on movements in real short-term interest rates and the real exchange rate. See OECD. 1999. Economic survey of Japan. OECD, Paris.
13 See chapter 3, and especially note 5 therein.
14 The BOJ expanded the range of eligible collateral to include corporate bonds, loans on deeds, asset-backed commercial paper and other asset-backed securities. It also provided liquidity at longer terms by extending the maturity of its bill purchases and JGB repurchase operations from six months to a year, and it increased the number of counterparties it was willing to deal with.
15 This was the approach recommended by the Nobel Laureate Paul Krugman. See Krugman, P. 1988. It's Baaack. Japan's slump and the return of the liquidity trap' Brookings Papers on Economic Activity 2 (https://www.brookings.edu/articles/its-baaack-japans-slump-and-the-return-of-the-liquidity-trap/).
16 As the twentieth century drew to a close, concerns were raised that the Y2K problem could severely disrupt the world economy. This was a legacy of a computer programming shortcut widely used in the 1960s and 1970s to save computer memory, which was at the time very expensive relative to later decades.

Computer programmers used two digits instead of four – for example, 99 instead of 1999 – to identify the year in the date field in a computer code. As a result, many computer programmes and systems, as well as communication networks and some equipment or machinery with embedded microprocessors, were at risk of failure or serious error in the event that they misinterpreted '00' as '1900' rather than '2000'. Governments and businesses spent considerable resources to address the problem, but there remained considerable uncertainty until the year 2000 came and went. Central banks prepared for the possible increase in the demand for currency by building up inventories during 1999. This extended to US dollars, as it was the world's primary reserve currency. As it turned out, the ultimate effects of the Y2K issue were very limited.

17 See chapter 1, page 18.
18 There is evidence, for example, that some on the Policy Board at this time appeared to interpret this part of the Bank's mandate as targeting zero measured CPI inflation, which would suggest a much less expansive policy than had the target been formally set at 2%. This is particularly the case when some unavoidable positive measurement bias in the CPI is considered.
19 Hayami was a devout Christian – a rarity in Japan. In addition, he had a reputation for plain speaking, which was hardly commonplace, and for eschewing political intrigue. Neither of these traits was very helpful during his time as governor.
20 There was, for example, no comprehensive examination or clean-up of bank balance sheets at this stage.
21 Under US standards, NPLs comprised loans to those in legal bankruptcy, loans in arrears of three months and loans restructured to any degree. Previously, the definition of an NPL in Japan had been less onerous, applying to those in bankruptcy, those six months in arrears and those where the interest rate paid was below the ODR. NPLs were provided by banks on the basis of both the old and new standards at the end of the 1997/1998 financial year.
22 By way of a rule of thumb, the NPL total tended to increase when the economy grew by less than 1% a year and decrease when it grew by more than 1% a year.
23 The Cabinet Office estimated that the average multiplier on public works projects fell from 1.3 in 1991 to 1.1 in 2004.

CHAPTER 6

1 To provide greater clarity about its reaction function, the Bank published a report entitled 'On price stability' in mid 2000 and took the decision to complement its 'Monthly reports' by releasing semi-annual 'Outlook and risk assessments of the economy and prices', while also making Policy Board members' own forecasts public. There remained, however, no formal inflation target as an anchor for expectations.
2 Under normal circumstances, when conducting open market operations, a central bank, as the sole provider of reserves, determines the amount of

reserves to be supplied to the banking system so that the actual overnight rate in the money market (the price of reserves) is akin to the target interest rate, based on its estimate of banks' demand for reserves on that day. In systems where central banks do not remunerate reserves, reserve balances rarely exceed required reserves, as banks have no incentive to hold them. In a crisis, the banks' cautionary demand for reserves tends to rise because of increased concerns over liquidity. The BOJ's policy was designed to ensure that there would be no shortage of reserves, no matter the level of cautionary demand.

3   As noted in the previous chapter, Fukui had resigned from his position as deputy governor of the Bank in 1998 in connection with a bribery scandal involving leaks of financially sensitive information. However, having expressed deep remorse for his actions, he was permitted to return to his old position in 2002, and he was elevated to governor the following year. He remained in place until 2008.

4   The stock purchases also represented a tiny proportion of the BOJ's overall balance sheet (around 1.3%). They were dwarfed by the Bank's JGB holdings.

5   The TIBOR (Tokyo Interbank Offered Rate) was a reference rate compiled by the Japanese Bankers' Association. Most of the reference banks for TIBOR are Japanese banks, while the reference banks for LIBOR (London Interbank Offered Rate) are dominated by non-Japanese banks. The spread between the two indicates the relative degree of stress experienced by these institutions.

6   Negative interest rates emerged in some areas. The currency swap market in particular experienced almost constantly negative rates when foreign banks sought to raise yen to exchange for US dollars. A currency swap was a contract in which, for example, Japanese banks would borrow US dollars from and lend yen to a foreign bank at the same time. The interest rate at which Japanese banks lent yen was near zero. As the credit standing of Japanese banks was lower than that of foreign banks, the yen funding costs for foreign banks became negative. Foreign banks would then deposit the proceeds at the BOJ to register a risk-free profit.

7   Fukuda, who was generally considered to be a 'clean' politician, served as prime minister between 1976 and 1978.

8   Takenaka had been educated in both Japan and the United States, studying for a while at Harvard and at the University of Pennsylvania. He gained his PhD from Osaka University, having previously worked for a period at both the Development Bank of Japan and the MOF.

9   It became the Financial Services Agency rather than Financial Supervisory Agency, subsequent to the latter taking over the functions of its original parent body, the FRC, and becoming an external agency of the Cabinet Office.

10 By way of example, in September 2001 Mycal – Japan's fourth largest retailer – had filed for bankruptcy, yet none of its major creditors had placed it in a high-risk category. When it failed, the company owed the Mizuho Group ¥316 billion, of which ¥150 billion was not covered by collateral or loan loss reserves.

11　The Basel Committee on Banking Supervision is a committee of banking supervisory authorities that was established by the central bank governors of the Group of Ten (G10) countries in 1974.
12　This was akin to the US Chapter 11 process.
13　Between 1992 and 2002 Japan had dropped from fifth place to nineteenth place.
14　In actual fact, it was neither direct write-offs nor increased provisioning that solved the NPL problem. It was the recovery.
15　Dating back to the work of David Ricardo in 1820, this is a controversial theory that depends on a number of unlikely assumptions, including perfect capital markets and fully rational expectations. There is little evidence of it being operative in the real world apart from in the most extreme circumstances of fiscal excess.
16　For example, nominal GDP expanded sevenfold between 1970 and 2007, while over the same period national land prices rose only threefold, with the divergence progressively increasing as the 1980s asset bubble deflated.
17　The Policy Board's practical definition of price stability would be reviewed every year and could therefore be adjusted as the personnel on it changed. Members served a five-year term, and there was at least one newcomer to the group every year.
18　The upward biases in CPIs typically reflect three considerations: the tendency of consumers to buy less of those goods and services the prices of which rise most; failure to adjust fully for quality improvements; and failure fully to reflect the addition of new goods and services. Efforts had been made to improve the Japanese CPI since the mid 1990s, and the BOJ stated in March 2006 that any upward bias in the Japanese CPI at that time was insignificant. However, the conclusions reached by research conducted outside the Bank were less sanguine, with one study suggesting that the bias was close to 2%! It is also worth noting that when, in August 2006, the base year of the index was shifted from 2000 to 2005, the inflation rate declined by half a percentage point, taking it back down to zero.
19　The changes were aimed at improving the process of building inspections after a scandal in 2005.
20　Shirakawa took over from Fukui in April 2008.
21　Shirakawa's term as governor of the BOJ was controversial from the outset. The government's favoured candidate to replace Governor Fukui was originally the deputy governor, Muto Toshihiro. But Muto's nomination was rejected by the Upper House of the Diet because of his extended career at the MOF before he became deputy governor. Shirakawa, a conservative Chicago University trained economist and longstanding BOJ official, was something of a compromise candidate for the top job.
22　This was a phrase coined by Ben Bernanke, the former chair of Federal Reserve. For four years through the summer of 2007, global real GDP expanded at an average rate of about 5% a year – its highest sustained rate since the early 1970s.

CHAPTER 7

1. CDSs are akin to insurance policies. The buyer pays a regular fee to the seller, who will pay out in the event of a default on a loan. They allowed risky assets to be removed from bank balance sheets, thereby freeing up capital for alternative uses. The buyer of a CDS does not necessarily have a corresponding loan on its books. CDSs can therefore be a vehicle for pure speculation on a default.
2. The rest of this chapter is drawn from a February 2019 presentation at Birkbeck College, University of London, by the author and Dr John Llewellyn for the Society of Professional Economists.
3. Qvigstad, J, J. Llewellyn, N. Husom Vonen and B. Dharmasena. 2012. The 'rule of four'. *Business Economist*, volume 3(1), pp. 31–44 (https://www.researchgate.net/publication/283086000_The_Rule_of_Four).
4. Quoted by Paul Krugman in the *International Herald Tribune*, 5 November 2003. Others remember Stein slightly differently, but the point remains the same. See, for example, Greenspan on Stein at www.nabe.com/am2000/grnspnvid.htm.
5. Turner, A. 2009. *The Turner Review: A Regulatory Response to the Global Banking Crisis*. FSA, London.
6. *Financial Times*, 10 July 2007. Cited by John Gapper. See Jones, R. 2023. *The Tyranny of Nostalgia: Half a Century of of British Economic Decline*, chapter 9.
7. Nugée, J. 2009. Failure and reconstruction: the financial sector in 2008 and 2009. A personal view of the financial crisis for EFFAS-EBC. See https://slideplayer.com/slide/6846436/.

CHAPTER 8

1. The malfunctioning of the capital markets forced firms to increase borrowing from banks, resulting in a surge in loan demand by large firms in the fourth quarter of 2008. Consequently, loan growth in the fourth quarter of 2008 doubled to 4%, while loans to small enterprises fell, reflecting increased credit risk.
2. Following Abe Shinzo's departure in September 2007, LDP veteran Fukuda Yasuo took over. He resigned just a year later to be replaced by Aso Taro, who was in office for an even shorter period.
3. Hatoyama resigned in June 2010 and was replaced by Kan Naoto, who was then replaced by Noda Yoshihiko at the end of August 2011. Noda lasted 15 months before he lost the general election of December 2012 and was replaced by the returning Abe Shinzo.
4. The employment of this term was a reference to Mori Motonari, a sixteenth-century lord who had supposedly told his three sons that they would be stronger if they worked as a team. It was easy to break the shaft of one arrow but much harder to break three bound together.

5 Shirokawa, M. 2014. Is inflation (or deflation) always and everywhere a monetary phenomenon? BIS Paper 77, BIS, Basel (https://www.bis.org/publ/bppdf/bispap77e.pdf).

CHAPTER 9

1 Symbolically, Naruhito and his wife had just a single child.
2 For example, if the natural real rate of interest is 0.5% and the expected inflation rate is zero, then the nominal policy rate must be set at less than 0.5% to provide any stimulus – and probably at less than zero to provide a significant boost to an economy.
3 This was also encouraged by the decision of the government's Public Pension Investment Fund, which had more than $1 trillion in assets under management to increase its weighting towards foreign assets from 17% to 23%.
4 The BOJ also introduced a disincentive for banks to convert reserves into cash by charging 10 basis points on any significant rebalancing of bank liabilities.
5 This in part reflected the deregulation of communication services.
6 The typical figure in Japan's competitors varied from 3% to 13%. In some countries, such as the United Kingdom, Canada and Switzerland, it was far higher.
7 Just under 40% of employees were 'lifetime employees' in 2016.
8 Osada, M., *et al.* 2016. Economic impact of the Tokyo 2020 Olympic Games. January, Bank of Japan, Tokyo (https://www.boj.or.jp/en/research/brp/ron_2016/data/ron160121b.pdf). See also Nagahama, T. 2022. The economic impact of the Tokyo 2020 Games. February, Dai-Ichi Life Research Institute, Tokyo (https://www.tokyoupdates.metro.tokyo.lg.jp/en/post-603/).
9 The closest English translation of Reiwa is 'beautiful harmony'.
10 Abe was subsequently assassinated at a 2022 election campaign event. His assassin had a vendetta against the Unification Church, which he believed Abe was a supporter of.
11 In so doing, Kishida fulfilled one of Shinzo Abe's priorities. Japan had long kept its military spending to less than 1% of GDP. Kishida's plan was to raise it to 2% of GDP by 2027.
12 Ueda had previously served on the BOJ Policy Board between 1998 and 2005, but he was a surprise choice as he was neither a current BOJ nor MOF official.

Index

1940 system, 48

Abenomics, xi, 178–181, 183 et seq,
    196 et seq, 214
    'Abenomics 2', 196 et seq
Abe, Shinzo, xi, 142, 163, 173, 176 et seq,
    186 et seq, 194, 196, 198, 201, 204,
    208, 214–215, 257**n**, 258**n**
accounting methods, 67, 69, 77, 93, 113,
    121, 129, 132–133, 139
    mark-to-market, 97, 132, 158
Accounting Standards Board of Japan, 132
adjustable rate mortgages, 155
administrative guidance/procedures, 28, 33,
    69, 88, 140
    Administrative Procedures Law, 90
    Administrative Reform Committee, 90
advanced industrial products, 162
aerospace, 199
agriculture, 3, 6, 32, 45, 51, 247**n**
    deregulation of, 57, 58, 118, 120, 179,
        195, 198, 207, 221
    productivity of, 58
    protection of, 90, 170, 198, 208
aircraft, 10, 245**n**, 248**n**
airport capacity, 140
air tickets, 140
air travel, 57
aluminium, 19
Amano, Tameyuki, 13
Amaterasu (Sun Goddess), 11
anti-monopoly law, 24, 57–58, 139
armed forces, 14 et seq, 19, 23–24, 74
Asahi Bank, 133
Asano corporation, 29
Asia, vii, viii, 5, 7, 9, 16–18, 24, 30, 43–44,
    46, 92, 96, 98, 105, 134, 151, 159,
    162, 168–169, 173, 179, 198, 206,
    213, 221
    crisis, 102 et seq, 108, 113, 115, 119–120
    economic integration of, 169
    newly industrializing economies (NIEs),
        56
Asian Co-Prosperity Sphere, 18

Asian Development Bank, 177
Aso, Taro, 257**n**
assassination, 11, 15, 258**n**
asset-backed securities (ABSs), 127, 150,
    253**n**
asset prices, ix, 35, 158, 171
    inflation, 9, 59–61, 63, 69, 79, 91, 133
    deflation, ix, 69, 71, 78, 100, 134, 147,
        175
Aum Shinrikyo cult, 83
austerity, 7
autarky, 4
autocracy, 5, 11, 220
automobiles (cars), 30, 37, 57, 134, 45–46,
    96, 162, 173
aviation, 19
Axis pact, 17

'bad bank', 252**n**
balance of payments constraint, 8
    pre-World War I, 8
Bank of France, 83
Bank for International Settlements (BIS), 12,
    158, 243, 251**n**, 258**n**
    capital adequacy requirements and, 65,
        68, 98, 114, 167, 229, 243
Bank of Japan (see also monetary policy),
    13 et seq, 32, 46, 50, 69, 72 et seq,
    80 et seq, 113, 117, 132 et seq,
    177 et seq, 186 et seq, 192 et seq,
    197, 199, 202, 204 et seq, 211,
    219–220, 252**n**, 255**n**
    Act, 17
    asset purchase programme (APP), 135,
        171, 174, 177, 203
    balance sheet of, 16, 20, 107,
        108 et seq, 128, 144, 165, 177,
        187, 189, 194, 203–204, 207,
        214, 255**n**
    climate strategy of, 206
    credibility of, 39, 63, 110, 111, 220
    establishment of, 7
    fund supplying operations, 174
    independence of, 63, 112, 126, 177, 189

joint statement on inflation target (with government), 177
Law, 18, 109 et seq
lending facility, 108, 144
negative interest rate policy (NIRP), 188, 192
Policy Board, 110, 127, 143, 177–178, 187–188, 189, 247**n**, 254**n**, 256**n**, 258**n**
official interest rates/policy rate, 14, 25, 33, 35–36, 40, 43, 52–53, 61 et seq, 74 et seq, 87, 92, 95, 108, 119, 126, 143–144, 150–151, 155, 164 et seq, 169, 171, 180, 186, 188–189, 203, 213, 227, 254**n**, 258**n**
reaction function of, 254**n**
reserve ratio requirements, 33
solvency of, 220
stand-by facility, 127
stock holdings of, 144
Tankan survey, 136
three-tier reserve deposit system of, 188
zero interest rate policy (ZIRP), 76, 92, 109, 119, 125 et seq, 142 et seq, 150, 165–166, 169, 171, 175, 180, 213
banks, commercial, ix, x, 10, 14 et seq, 25, 28 et seq, 42–43, 61 et seq, 85 et seq, 91 et seq, 103–104, 107–108, 123 et seq, 141 et seq, 154 et seq, 160, 163 et seq, 174, 178, 186 et seq, 199, 211–212, 251**n**
assets of, 149, 188
audits of, 113–114, 133, 158
balance sheets of, 61, 79, 112, 114, 115, 124, 128, 132, 135, 252**n**, 253**n**, 254**n**, 257**n**
Bank Shareholdings Purchase Corporation, 133, 163
capital of, 68, 69, 80, 84, 89, 98, 112 et seq, 133, 135, 145, 158, 161, 164, 203
capital gains of, 68, 77, 84, 100, 161
collateral of, 43, 52, 61, 72, 79, 86, 91, 98, 100, 114, 125, 130, 147, 189, 195, 255**n**
core capital of, 84
cost structures of, 130
credit default swaps (CDSs) of, 149
cross share holdings of, 78, 124
deregulation of, 50, 52, 54, 60, 68 et seq, 86, 97 et seq, 155, 156, 203, 211, 216

directors/executives of, 77, 115, 157
equity holdings of, 127, 161
excessive risk taking of, 101, 153, 191
failures of, 104, 114
Financial Revitalization Committee (FRC), 113–114, 255**n**
Financial Revitalization Law and, 113
foreign, 21, 70, 104, 255**n**
global assets of, 149
inspections of, 132
lending, 39, 48, 52, 62–63, 66, 68, 70, 74 et seq, 92, 95, 100, 103, 112, 116, 135, 139, 144–145, 164–165, 187–188, 190, 203
mergers of, 115, 129
'main banks', 28, 68, 83, 117
management of, 115, 129, 130
mega, 130
overbanking and, 7
overseas activities of, 62, 70, 77, 87, 98
preferred equity injections and, 114, 246**n**
profitability of, 68–69, 77, 85, 96, 100, 103, 115, 119, 130, 141, 146, 149, 161, 165, 188, 189
public fund application (recapitalization), and, 112 et seq, 124, 129, 130, 132
reserves of, 108, 126, 142, 144, 177, 178, 188, 206, 254**n**, 255**n**, 258**n**
regional, 6, 17, 91
regulation of, 42, 52 et seq, 68, 71, 153, 155–156, 203, 216
subordinated debt issuance and, 77, 80, 112, 114
supervision of, 69, 103, 117, 119, 121, 145, 160, 213
stocks of, 115, 135, 144, 149
takeovers of foreign banks, 70
'Total Plan' for, 113 et seq
US, 149, 163
window dressing of accounts and, 114
Zaibatsu and, 6, 17, 245**n**
bank notes, 14, 246**n**
Bank of Tokyo Mitsubishi, 115
bankruptcy, 10, 75, 79, 82, 98, 100, 107, 114, 124, 129, 132, 162, 169, 203, 254**n**, 255**n**
Basel Committee, 256**n**
Basel II, 160
board auditing committee, 133
'bear the unbearable', 21
Bernanke, Ben, 156, 256**n**
'Big Bang' in financial sector, ix, 97 et seq, 100

black market, 21
Black Monday (1987 stock market crash), 59, 62
board directors, 115, 157, 196, 199
   outside, 196, 199
book value, 160
'bridge bank', 10, 113
Bretton Woods, 25, 34
Britain: *see* United Kingdom (UK)
brokerage commissions, 104
brokerage houses, 59, 97
bubble economy, the, xi, 49 et seq, 77, 79, 83, 98, 116, 120, 143, 183, 204, 211
budget balance (see fiscal policy), 5, 10, 28, 30, 40–41, 48, 101–106, 119, 141–142, 164–167, 178, 207, 225, 249**n**, 252**n**
   defence, 41
   deficit, 13, 15, 25, 35, 39, 41, 82, 93, 101–102, 126, 142, 150, 152, 167, 173, 175, 185, 193, 205, 214
   local government balance, 105, 115, 126, 138, 158, 192 et seq, 248**n**
   primary balance, 33, 138, 165, 167, 173, 185, 192–193, 194, 203, 205
   supplementary, 84, 105, 106, 113, 137, 166, 173, 187, 193, 202
   surplus, 33, 41, 53, 65, 74, 102, 165, 194
   US, 44, 152
Bundesbank, 61
bureaucracy, 11, 22–23, 25, 28, 45, 47–48, 50, 209, 211, 216
Bush administration, 151
business confidence, ix, 14–15, 30, 53, 59, 71, 74 et seq, 84, 95, 99, 104, 109, 113, 115, 118–119, 124, 127–128, 133–134, 151, 155, 162, 168, 175, 180
business dynamism, 7, 195, 200, 215

cabinet, 5, 11, 253**n**, 254**n**, 255**n**
   Cabinet Planning Board, 16
   Cabinet Office, 23, 106, 131, 170
   Cabinet Office Council for Regulatory Reform, 139
call money rate, 53, 74, 76, 80, 92, 108, 119, 144, 150, 164 et seq, 169, 171, 180, 186, 188–189, 203, 213, 227, 258**n**
Canada, 110
capital account, 30–31
capital accumulation, 6, 120, 210
capital adequacy, 65, 68–69, 80, 103, 112, 203, 251**n**
   requirements, 114, 164

capital controls, 13
capital flight, 13
capital flows, vii, 16, 103, 150
capital gains, 54, 60, 89, 100
   unrealized, 66 et seq, 77, 84, 161
capital goods, 56, 91, 96
capital losses, total, 99
capital stock, 20, 31, 185
   public sector, 200
   retirement, 136
   wartime destruction, 22, 28
cartelization, 15, 17, 28, 117
cash dispensers, 97
cashless payments, 192, 206
certification, 45, 57, 89, 140
chemical attack, 83
chemicals, 10, 20, 30, 36
children, 101, 106, 192, 200, 204, 219
   childcare, 141, 197–198, 217, 221
Chile, 110
China, viii, 12–17, 24, 45, 116, 134, 151, 163, 168, 175, 213, 220, 248**n**, 249**n**
   hegemony, 7, 198
   Sino-Japanese war, and, 7
city farms, 67
Civil Rehabilitation Law, 133
civil service, 5, 41
climate change, 200, 205, 220
Clinton administration, 113
coal, 19, 22, 28, 199
coalition government, 80–81, 105, 141, 163, 192
Cold War, 24, 26, 32, 209
collateralized debt obligations (CDOs), 154
colonialism, 5, 7 et seq, 12, 14, 16, 17 et seq
combat deaths, 19
competitiveness, 7, 13, 27, 33, 38, 42, 44, 87, 96, 120, 139–140, 145, 158, 201, 210
commercial paper, 127, 253**n**
commodity prices, 53–54, 150, 159, 168, 190, 215
company housing, 29
Comprehensive and Progressive Agreement for Trans-Pacific Partnership (CPTPP), 198
concentration of capital, 17
Confucianism, 4
conscription, 16
consensus building, 51, 104, 121
constitution, 11, 14, 201, 247**n**
   Bismarkian, 5
   post-war, 23, 34, 198
   reform, 198

construction, 28, 30, 38, 51–52, 66–67, 79–80, 96, 105, 117, 120, 145, 150
consumer, the, 6, 9, 14, 16, 25, 31 et seq, 38–39, 45, 55 et seq, 89, 96, 119–120, 134, 143, 162, 168 et seq, 175, 187, 205, 207, 224, 252**n**, 256**n**
   banks, 32
   choice, 140
   confidence, 84, 119, 125, 168
   culture of, 4, 31
   finance companies and, 68
   prices: *see* consumer price index (CPI) and inflation
   sovereignty, 120, 211
   surplus, 170
consumer price index (CPI), 25, 35 et seq, 44, 55, 63, 74, 76, 78, 83, 92, 96, 99, 127–128, 143–144, 150, 159, 162, 177, 179, 186 et seq, 202, 205, 214–215, 224, 251**n**, 252**n**
   bias in, 254**n**, 256**n**
'convoy system', 85–86, 91
Cooperative Credit Purchasing Company (CCPC), 79, 85, 97
corporate balance sheets, 78, 100, 128, 147
corporate bond issuance, 150
corporate bond spreads, 150
corporate financing, 62, 164
corporate governance, 69, 117, 184, 195–199, 206–207, 214–215
   code, 196, 198, 206
corporate management, 103, 157
corporate pricing power, 150
corporate restructuring, 14, 120, 128–129, 135 et seq, 253**n**
corruption, 11, 22, 27, 80, 98, 131, 141, 211
cost of capital, 119
Covid-19 pandemic, 183, 191, 194–195, 204–205, 208, 215
   behavioural changes and, 201
   confinement and, 201
   death rates and, 201
   hygiene and, 201
   infection rates and, 201–202
   mobility and, 201
   pent-up domestic demand and, 205
   service consumption and, 201
   state of emergency and, 202
   vaccination and, 201, 204
credit controls, 25
credit demand, 99

credit guarantees, 106, 168 et seq, 195, 198
credit rating agencies (CRAs), 106, 157
credit supply, 99
creditor nation, 9, 44, 47, 185
creditors, 69, 109, 132–33, 255**n**
crime, 11, 21, 27
criminals, 60
cross shareholdings, 28, 57, 67, 69, 77, 124, 139, 198, 200, 207, 221
crowding out, 14, 33, 127
cultural factors, impact of, 5, 8, 32, 88, 120, 146, 208, 211, 215, 221
currency swaps, 255**n**
current account balance (balance of payments), 9–10, 36–37, 40 et seq, 56–57, 175, 217, 224
   German, 61, 250**n**
   surplus, 10, 37, 42, 45, 49, 50, 54, 56, 61, 70, 74, 79, 87, 89, 92, 96, 99, 120, 134–135, 161–162, 166, 180, 185, 202, 210
   US, 44, 152
Czech Republic, 110

Daichi Kangyo Bank (DKB), 115
Daiwa Bank, 133
death penalty, 11
debt, 12 et seq, 18–19, 47, 66–67, 80 et seq, 88–89, 92 et seq, 117–118, 120, 123 et seq, 130, 132–133, 136–137, 154–155, 160, 177, 205, 207, 211, 213 et seq
   bad, 10, 79, 81, 98
   corporate, viii, 77, 95, 132, 133, 136, 148, 161, 203, 211, 253**n**
   European sovereign crisis, 169, 174, 175
   forgiveness, 88
   gold standard and, 12
   government, 9–10, 12, 14–15, 19, 25, 33, 39, 41–42, 49, 53, 80, 82, 93–94, 101, 106, 118, 123, 126, 137, 143, 150, 167, 170, 174, 180, 185, 193–194, 203 et seq, 214–215, 219–220, 226, 249**n**
      debt service costs, 33, 39, 41–42, 49, 82, 101, 137, 166, 167, 171, 190
      effective rate of interest on, 137
      treasury bills, 14, 178
   household, 152
   Japan National Railways (JNR), 42
   Minsky and, 71 et seq
   monetization, 109, 214

INDEX

private sector, viii, 14, 25, 64, 67, 117, 124, 130, 145, 168, 213, 216, 246**n**
  real value, 12, 25, 92
  repudiation, 220
  subordinated, 77, 80, 114
  war, 8, 12
decoupling, 159
defence capability, 26, 34, 41, 204–205
deflation, viii, ix, 9, 12, 52, 58, 79, 82 et seq, 92 et seq, 103, 109, 111, 118–119, 123, 127–128, 134, 137–138, 143, 146, 154, 167 et seq, 174–175, 176, 179–180, 185 et seq, 192, 201, 207, 212–213, 215–216, 258**n**
demobilization, 22
Democratic Party, 27
Democratic Party of Japan, 162
denialism, historical, 142
dependency theory, 32
deposit guarantee, 108
Deposit Insurance Corporation (DIC), 86, 91, 97, 112, 113, 114
depreciation, 26, 36, 185, 200
deregulation, 25, 31, 40, 53, 69, 81, 87, 90, 99, 105, 121, 131, 195, 198, 221, 258**n**
  financial, 50, 52, 54, 57, 68
derivatives, 43, 171
destocking, 96
devaluation, 13, 34
Diet, the, 11, 27, 38, 54, 60, 80, 82, 85, 110, 257**n**
  elections, 73, 81, 141, 251**n**
  House of Peers (original upper house), 5
  House of Representatives (lower house), 5, 73, 81, 141, 192, 247**n**, 251**n**
  House of Councillors (modern-day upper house), 165
digitalization, 200, 206, 208
diplomacy, 221
disclosure, 100, 113, 163, 196
  lack of, 7, 69, 91, 100
discounted cash flow accounting methodology, 132
discounting, 89
discrimination, 8, 197, 246**n**
disposable income, 55, 96, 152, 203
  real, 96
distribution system, 4, 16, 45, 51, 57, 88–89, 117, 157
dividends, 208
Dodge, Joseph, 247**n**

'Dodge Line', 25
domestic demand, 6, 39–40, 50, 54 et seq, 75–76, 92, 98, 116, 120, 134, 152, 159, 205, 212
durable goods, 96, 162, 171, 193
Dutch East Indies, 18
dynamic capital buffers, 65
dynamic liquidity buffers, 65

e-commerce, 206
economic miracle, viii, ix, xi, 3, 27, 31 et seq, 70, 73, 92, 180, 211–212
Economic Planning Agency, 88, 247**n**
economies of scale, 32, 58
education, 4, 6, 16, 23, 33, 47, 140, 217, 221, 247**n**
efficient market hypothesis (EMH), 153
eigyo tokkin accounts, 59
elderly care, 197
electoral reform, 81
electorate, 11, 27, 64, 131, 142, 162, 176, 180, 218
electrical machinery, 10, 20, 30, 36, 134, 173
electricity, 9, 20, 117, 119, 140, 172, 175, 196, 198, 199
emperor, 5, 10 et seq, 16, 21 et seq, 55, 80, 183, 245**n**, 250**n**
  Akihito (Heisei), 183, 250**n**
  Hirohito (Showa), 10 et seq, 16, 21 et seq, 55, 80
  Matsuhito, (Meiji), 5, 10 et seq, 245**n**
  Naruhito (Reiwa), 183, 204, 258**n**
  Yoshihito (Taishō), 10
employment, 10, 29, 37, 123 et seq, 147, 169, 176, 181, 210, 203, 246**n**
  conditions, 23, 51
  excess, 136
  full, 15, 40, 74, 123, 185, 207, 214, 251
  growth, 55, 76, 96
  part-time, 26, 125, 136, 140, 185, 197
  protection, 140
  public, 138
  rationalization, 90
  temporary, 125, 136
energy, 16–17, 34 et seq, 175, 196
  costs, 36, 40, 211
  deregulation, 139, 195
  efficiency, 34, 40, 166, 168–169, 171–172
  intensity, 199
  prices, 76, 210
  renewable, 172, 199

saving, 36
taxation, 199
engineers, 7
Entente Powers, 8
entrepreneurship, 6, 12, 29, 51, 131, 170, 198, 211
entry restrictions (barriers to entry), 45–46, 68, 91, 117, 140
environmental policy, 34 et seq, 165, 176, 200, 206–207, 214, 220
   carbon neutrality, 184, 199
   greenhouse gas strategy, 199
   taxes, 107, 194, 199
equality, intergenerational, ix, 195, 219
equilibrium real interest rate, 61, 78, 92, 184, 186
equity market, 59, 68, 73, 155, 179, 191
   debt/equity swaps, 133, 174
   issuance, 77
   portfolios, 75, 119, 127, 160–161, 199
   prices, 100, 124, 149, 161, 163
ethnic homogeneity, 4
Europe, 5, 8, 17, 22, 26, 33, 37–38, 41, 45, 49, 52, 56, 59, 108, 140, 152, 160, 167, 205, 221, 249**n**, 250**n**
   European Central Bank (ECB), 158, 188
   European Economic Community (EEC), 37, 46, 64
   European Enlightenment, 16
   European Union (EU), viii, 173, 198, 206
   EU Economic Partnership Agreement, 198
   euro area, 151
   Euroyen market, 43
   sovereign debt crisis, 169, 174–175
exchange controls, 43
exchange rate, 13–14, 16, 21, 25, 51, 58, 65, 79, 125, 129, 152, 183, 190, 193, 248**n**, 253**n**
   endaka fukyo (high yen slump), 46, 70
   fixed, 7, 32, 34
   floating, 34
   implicit guarantees of, 103
   intervention in, 87, 128, 171, 174
   quasi fixed, 103
   real, 10, 12, 13
   undervalued, 32
exchange traded funds (ETFs), 171, 187
exports, 9, 12, 14, 26, 32, 55, 75, 115, 124–125, 134–135, 168, 175–176, 193, 201, 246**n**, 250**n**
   market share, 50, 56, 79, 92
   net, 38, 44, 46, 54, 96, 99, 137, 159, 185

extension of voting rights, 11
external assets, 3, 47, 49, 56, 70, 161, 166, 180, 185

face, importance of, 9, 211
factor shares, 151
Fair Trade Commission (FTC), 24, 25, 139, 140
farmers, 7, 14, 45
Federal Deposit Insurance Company (FDIC), 154
finance companies, 52, 95
financial deregulation, 50, 52, 54, 60, 68 et seq, 86, 97 et seq, 155–156, 203, 211, 216
financial faultlines in the 1920s, 9
financial oversight, 10, 28
financial panic, in the 1920s, 9
financial repression, 18, 48
Financial Supervisory Agency (FSA), 97, 113, 132–133, 160, 163 et seq, 255**n**, 256**n**
   credibility of, 115
financial system, 9–10, 33, 50, 52, 54, 60, 68 et seq, 70–71, 84, 86, 97, 110, 119, 149 et seq, 155–156, 216–217, 252**n**
Finland, 60
fire sale of assets, 106, 157
fiscal policy (*see also* budget), 12 et seq, 40 et seq, 51, 65, 92, 112, 119, 166 et seq, 176 et seq, 183, 189 et seq, 207, 212 et seq, 220, 246**n**
   'automatic stabilizers', 78, 94, 251**n**
   cash transfers, 203–204
   Council on Economic and Fiscal Policy and, 131, 194
   defence spending, 24, 26, 41, 205
   drag, 42
   expansion/stimulus, 13–14, 38, 44, 78, 80 et seq, 87, 102, 104 et seq, 126, 136 et seq, 151, 166, 168, 171, 178, 180, 187, 192, 203, 212, 213, 252**n**
   fine-tuning, 40
   Fiscal Investment and Loan Programme (FILP) 107, 141, 248**n**
   Fiscal Management Strategy, 167, 169, 173
   Fiscal Structural Reform Act (FSRA), 102
   Fiscal System Council, 194
   flexibility (Abenomics), 176, 193
   'golden rule', 33

independent fiscal institution need for, 193
multipliers, 93, 120, 253**n**, 254**n**
packages, 78, 81, 88, 96, 106, 108, 120, 124, 125, 166, 168, 171, 173, 178, 192, 193
public investment, 7, 13, 27, 33, 35 et seq, 45, 54, 58, 78, 80 et seq, 87, 93, 96, 102, 105–106, 115, 124, 126, 136, 138, 166, 176, 178, 192, 204, 252**n**, 254**n**, 255**n**
public spending share in GDP, 102
restraint/consolidation, 8, 12, 14–15, 36, 38, 41, 43–44, 53 et seq, 98, 101–102, 105, 124, 126, 138, 167, 168, 173, 176, 179, 188, 191 et seq, 202, 205, 220, 249**n**
space, 185
sustainability, 108, 195
Fisher, Irving, 13
flash memory chips, 172
food, 19, 21, 22, 45, 47, 192
forbearance, 86–87, 91, 100, 217
foreign currency, 17
reserves, 22, 33
swap lines, 164
foreign direct investment (FDI), 79
inward, 6, 28, 58, 89, 140, 195, 200, 208, 221
outward, 57, 97
foreign experts, 6
fossil fuels (*see also* coal), 199
France, 17, 31, 83, 245**n**, 249**n**, 250**n**
Bank of, 83
free markets, 6, 121
distrust of, 121
free trade agreements, 206
freedom of speech, 16
French Indochina, 17, 18
fuel subsidies, 204
Fuji Bank, 115
Fukai, Eigo, 13
Fukuda, Takeo, 131, 255
Fukuda, Tokuzō, 13
Fukuda, Yasuo, 257**n**
Fukui, Toshihiko, 111, 126, 142, 255**n**, 256**n**
Fukushima disaster, xi, 172, 175, 196, 214–215
funding markets, 150
Furukawa, 29

Gaiatsu, 34, 42, 57, 113, 179
gangsters/organized crime, 60, 71

general elections, 5, 80–81, 162, 176, 247**n**, 251**n**, 257**n**
Genro, 11
gerontocracy, 121
gerrymandering, 121
Germany, 17, 20, 31, 39, 62, 167, 249**n**, 250**n**
Gilbert islands, 20
Gini coefficient, 31
Glass–Steagall Act, 154
global economy, 9, 134, 145, 205, 210
Global Financial Crisis (GFC), ix, 65, 104, 123, 126, 129, 145, 149 et seq, 159–169, 175, 179, 183 et seq, 201 et seq, 208, 214, 217, 246**n**, 252**n**
global IT boom, 124
globalization, 116, 151, 221
gold, 7, 8, 9, 12 et seq, 34, 246**n**
reparations, 8
gold standard, 7, 8, 9, 12 et seq,
government bonds/JGBs (*see also* fiscal policy and government debt), 74, 164, 171, 189, 194,
construction, 33
functioning of market for, 188
reconstruction, 173
underwriting of, 14–15, 178, 187
yields, 63, 75, 108, 127, 129, 144, 150, 165, 174, 186 et seq, 203, 205, 228
government consumption, 53
government debt, 8, 9, 15, 25, 41–43, 49, 53, 93, 106, 167, 174, 180, 214, 226
service costs, 39, 82, 101, 137, 166, 171, 190
governments of national unity, 16
grade inflation, 157
Great Depression, ix, 10 et seq, 104, 118, 146
Great East Japan (Tohoku) Earthquake, 163, 172 et seq
'Basic Guidelines for Reconstruction', 173
tsunami, 172 et seq, 185, 214
Great Hanshin Earthquake, 83, 95, 172
Great Kanto Earthquake, 9
Greece, 174
green growth, 199
green innovation, 169
Greenspan, Alan, 154
gross domestic product (GDP), real, 8, 104, 108, 187–188
growth rate, 9, 31, 35–36, 40, 54, 75, 96, 99, 115, 125, 135, 175, 183, 187, 190, 223

per capita growth rate, 187, 219
per capita level, 19, 36, 93, 99, 135, 159, 172, 180, 186 et seq, 191, 193, 201–202, 205, 219, 250**n**
gross fixed capital formation, 32, 150

Hagibis typhoon, 193
Hamaguchi administration, 12
Hata, Tsutomu, 80
Hatayama, Yukio, 163
Hashimoto, Ryūtarō, 81, 105, 130
Hayami, Masaru, 111, 125–126, 177, 180, 254**n**
Heisei boom, 49
High Growth Era, 21 et seq, 120, 183
Hirohito, 10, 23–24
    divinity of, 23
    as symbol of the state, 23
    as war criminal, 24
Hitler, Adolf, 17
Hokkaidō, 104
Hokkaidō Takushoku Bank, 98, 104
holding companies, 24, 117, 141, 245**n**
homeownership, 75
Honda corporation, 37
household assets, 55, 253**n**
household savings, 24, 32
    rate, 36, 56, 124, 166, 203
household wealth effect, 55
housework, 197
housing, 20, 29, 51, 54–55, 58, 60, 66–67, 68, 77, 80, 85, 89, 100–101, 103, 153, 156, 160, 248**n**, 251**n**, 252**n**
Housing Loan Corporation (HLC), 68, 78, 81, 96, 160, 252**n**
Hosokawa, Morihiro, 80–81
human capital, 20, 45, 140, 197

Ikeda, Hayato, 30
    Income Doubling Plan, 30
imbalances, viii, 9, 91, 116, 152, 216
imperialism, 5
imports, 10, 17, 22, 26, 30 et seq, 46–47, 57, 213, 250**n**
    penetration, 49, 53, 55, 89, 140, 185
    prices, 35, 39–40, 56, 58
    raw material, 32, 56, 175
    substitution, 32
    tariffs and restrictions, 6, 13–14, 28, 31, 56, 58, 90, 206, 249**n**
    volumes, 46, 56, 79, 96, 99
income per capita, 31, 135, 145, 252**n**

income tax, 5, 13, 62, 54, 65, 67
    cuts, 82, 88, 93, 102, 105, 106, 138, 145, 173
India, 20, 151
Industrial Bank of Japan (IBJ), 115
industrial policy, 14–15, 43, 165
Industrial Revitalization Corporation of Japan (IRCJ), 133–134
industrial revolution, 8
industrialization, 6–7, 27, 30, 32, 34, 56, 162
industry (see also manufacturing), 9, 19–20, 22 et seq, 29–30, 32, 45–46, 48–49, 62–63, 66, 77, 175, 196, 199
    dualism of, 29
    heavy, 6, 19
inequality, 31, 141, 151, 169, 170
infant mortality, 4
inflation, ix, 9–10, 19, 25 et seq, 32, 61 et seq, 72 et seq, 93, 127 et seq, 143 et seq, 150 et seq, 171, 184 et seq, 249**n**, 256**n**, 258**n**
    asset price, viii, ix, 49 et seq, 63–65, 67, 69, 72, 103, 109, 211–212, 217
    consumer price, 16, 35 et seq, 44, 49, 53, 55, 63, 72 et seq, 92, 125 et seq, 143, 158, 177, 179, 187–188, 190, 202, 207, 214–215, 254**n**
    Dodge Line and, 25 et seq
    expectations, 107–108, 125, 150, 163, 179, 185, 187–188, 189–190, 191, 202
    grade, 158
    land price, 58, 67, 160
    late 1930s, 15 et seq
    low, 83, 92, 96, 110, 145, 184 et seq, 213, 216
    OPEC I and, 35 et seq
    OPEC II and, 39 et seq
    post-war, 21 et seq
    target, 108, 129, 143–144, 151, 153, 177–178, 187, 189–190, 194, 197, 203, 205, 207, 220, 254**n**
    war, 9, 16 et seq
    world, 7
influence peddling, 11
infrastructure, 8, 13, 30, 43, 84, 125, 166, 217, 221, 247**n**
Inoue, Jonnosuke, 12
interbank market, 62, 86, 104, 107, 108, 129, 255**n**
intermediate goods, 175
international policy coordination, 46, 61, 64
international trade linkages, 19, 172

international capital markets, 7
international competition, 9, 116, 140, 146
International Monetary Fund (IMF), 34, 158, 200, 219, 247**n**, 251**n**, 253**n**
  rescue packages, 103
institutional architecture, 27, 41, 47–48, 50, 70, 109–110, 169, 197
insurance sector, 37, 77, 141, 167, 174, 189, 248**n**
  life insurance sector, 32, 84, 98, 130
  policyholder yields, 98
Inukai, Tsuyoshi, 13
invasion, 20, 247**n**, 251**n**
inventory adjustment, 31, 74, 92, 134, 168
investment, viii, 28, 32 et seq, 49, 52 et seq, 70, 74 et seq, 82–83, 87 et seq, 100 et seq, 119–120, 145, 147, 150, 162, 171, 178, 180, 184 et seq, 191–192, 195, 200 et seq, 210–211, 247**n**, 251**n**
  'accelerator', 124
  business, 36, 38, 40, 44, 55, 59, 74, 76, 79, 91–92, 96, 102, 124, 134, 136, 151, 161, 168, 176, 184, 206, 253**n**
  efficiency, 75, 100
  home bias of, 180, 207
  housing/residential, 52–53, 75, 79, 82, 145, 150
  portfolio, 100, 180, 187
  public, 6, 33, 35 et seq, 53, 78–79, 83, 87, 93, 96, 102, 105–106, 115–116, 120, 124, 126, 137, 166–167, 176, 191–192, 200, 249**n**, 252**n**
  tech, 115, 185
investment banks, ix, x, 130, 149, 154 et seq
IS-LM analysis, 92–93, 186, 191
Iwata, Kazumasa, 144
Iwata, Kikuo, 177
Iwate, 172

'Japan as number one', 3
Japan Finance Corporation, 164
Japan New Party, 80 et seq
Japan premium, 86, 104, 113, 115
Japan Railways (JR), 42 et seq, 79, 246**n**, 249**n**
Japanification, viii
job-creation programmes, 168
judiciary, 5, 117
junta, wartime, 142
Jusen, 85, 114
'just in time' inventory management, 37, 172

Kalecki, Michal, 151
Kenseikei, 11
Keynes, John Maynard, 13 et seq, 31, 47, 105, 151, 246**n**, 250**n**
Keynesianism, 13 et seq, 31, 40, 78, 92, 151, 153
Kishi, Nobusuke, 142
Kishida, Fumio, 204–205, 258**n**
Kobe, 83
Koizumi, Junichiro, 130 et seq, 162, 165, 176–177, 212
Kokutai, 5, 11, 16, 22
Komeito party, 192
Korea, 7, 8, 13, 17, 19, 20, 36, 162, 206, 209, 246**n**, 247**n**
  war, 26 et seq
  won, 175
Krugman, Paul, 253**n**, 257**n**
Kuroda, Haruhiko, 177–178, 190–191, 205, 207
Kwantung army, 11

labour market, 19, 39, 76, 116–117, 124, 171, 185–186, 205
  active labour market policies (ALMPs), 140, 221
  disputes in 1920s, 10
  dualism, 140, 185, 197, 215
  'Equal Pay for Equal Work', 197 et seq
  female graduates in, 200
  female leadership roles in, 200
  flexibility of, 117, 124
  job security in, 29, 197
  job-placement firms, 117
  labour force, 101, 184, 194, 196, 199–200
  labour force, female, 196
  labour shortage post-World War II, 10
  low female participation in, 102, 138, 140, 184, 195 et seq, 212, 214
  low-skilled workers in, 221
  on-the-job training in, 29, 197
  overtime, 37, 76, 92, 124, 136, 197
  reform, 140, 207
  share, 136
  slack, 186, 253**n**
  temporary workers in, 117
  tightness of, 76, 197, 205
  vocational training in, 204
  'Work Style Reform', 197 et seq
  World War II and, 19
  weakness of, 116
land, vii, xi, 5, 93, 118
  collateral, 53, 91, 100
  leasing laws, 66

prices, 9, 42, 50, 53, 55 et seq, 61, 65 et seq, 71, 74–75, 79, 85–86, 89, 91, 98 et seq, 113, 120, 125, 143–144, 160, 162, 175, 186, 211, 227, 256**n**
  reform, 23
  regulation of, 65 et seq,
  tax treatment of, 65 et seq
  unutilized, 67
League of Nations, 12
Lebensraum, 12
Lehman Brothers, 107, 149, 155, 164, 169, 180, 253**n**
lending (credit) conditions, 35, 52, 91, 105
liberal parliamentary democracy, 11
Liberal Democratic Party (LDP), 27, 35, 38, 43, 54, 73, 80–81, 105, 118, 130–131, 141–142, 162–163, 176, 180, 192, 204, 214, 248**n**, 251**n**, 257**n**
Liberal Party, 27
LIBOR–TIBOR spread, 129, 255**n**
licensing, 45, 57
liquidity, 7, 14, 76, 92, 157
  countercyclical buffers and, 64
  corporate, 52
  interbank, 107 et seq, 125 et seq, 142, 174, 203
  JGB market, 188 et seq
  liquidity trap (Keynesian), 78, 253**n**
  real estate market, 130
  stock market, 127
liquified natural gas, 175
living standards, 36, 116, 135, 219
loan classification, 129, 132
loan loss provisions, 84, 91, 130, 252**n**
loan-to-income ratios, 64
loan-to-value ratios, 64
loan write-offs, 112
London, 8, 43, 60, 97, 255**n**
Long Term Credit Bank (LTCB), 98, 114
looting, 21
Los Angeles, 60
lost decade, 72, 118 et seq, 123 et seq, 149, 183, 237 et seq
  1920s, 9
Louvre Accord, 62, 250**n**

MacArthur, Douglas, 21–24, 247**n**
machine tools, 30
machinery, 10, 36, 46, 55, 92, 162, 173, 254**n**
macroeconomic imbalances, 152

macroeconomic policy (*see also* fiscal policy and monetary policy), 14, 70, 87, 92, 121, 150, 153, 156, 180, 210, 217 et seq
macroeconomic risks, 157–158
macroeconomic (in)stability, 7, 64, 157, 246
macroeconomic theory, 92
macroprudential policy, 64–65, 203, 217
Malaya (Malaysia), 18
malnutrition, 21
Manchuria (Manchukuo), 12 et seq
manufacturing, 4, 9, 20, 31, 46, 79, 92, 96, 120, 135, 139, 184, 209
  capacity utilization of, 74
  exporters, 88, 115, 124, 159, 179, 210, 213
  GFC and, 162 et seq
  heavy, 16, 26
  import penetration, 53, 57
  SMEs, 116
  trade surplus, 44, 57
mark-to-market accounting, 97, 132, 158
market discipline, 153
market distortions, 50, 119, 138, 141, 190
market failure, 150
market fundamentalism, 169
market segregation (in finance), 97
market volatility, 104, 150
Marshall Plan, 22
Marx, Karl, 151
Marxist theory, 31, 151
mathematical risk models, 156
Matsushita, 37
Matsushita, Yasuo, 83, 110
Matsukata, Mayayoshi, 7
Mayekawa, Haruo, 50,
Mayekawa Report, 50, 250**n**
Meiji restoration, 4 et seq, 36, 247**n**
Meiji era, 22, 29, 47, 120, 245**n**
mercantilism, 44, 50, 250**n**
merchants, 7
mergers and acquisitions (M&A), 57, 117, 140, 200
Micawberism, 121, 145
microconomic policy (*see also* structural policy/reform), 15, 28, 51, 94
microchip plants, 204
mid-level officers, 11
middle class, 31
Mieno, Yasushi, 63, 74, 83
migration, 65, 90, 102, 208, 212, 217, 221, 246**n**, 247**n**
militarists, 13, 15

military, vii, 5, 7, 10
Ministry of Agriculture, 45
Ministry of Finance (MOF), 14–15, 18, 33, 41, 61, 63, 69, 74, 77 et seq, 97, 110–111, 126, 128, 131, 137, 171, 177, 194, 211, 247**n**, 255**n**, 256**n**, 258**n**
    Budget Bureau, 28
    Trust Fund Bureau, 43, 248**n**, 249**n**
Ministry of International Trade and Industry (MITI), 28, 34, 45
Ministry of Munitions, 28
Minseitō, 11, 12
Minsky, Hyman, 70 et seq
misogyny, 221
Mitsubishi Corporation, 7
Misuho Financial Group, 115
Mitsui and Company, 7
Miyagi, 172
Miyazawa, Kiichi, 60
mobile phone charges, 202
modern monetary theory (MMT), 14
monetary conditions, 67, 80, 96, 108, 125, 128, 169, 207, 253**n**
monetary policy (*see also* Bank of Japan), 14, 51, 60, 93, 108 et seq, 153, 155, 164 et seq, 171 et seq, 176, 186 et seq, 195, 212 et seq
    comprehensive monetary easing, 171
    comprehensive review of, 189
    coordination with fiscal policy, 13 et seq, 93, 119
    forward guidance and, 109, 127, 129, 190, 191
    laxity of, 53, 60, 63–64, 65, 108, 119, 171
    normalization of, 62, 144, 151, 164, 180, 189
    portfolio balance effect of, 178
    tightness/restraint, 8, 12, 15, 18, 40, 59, 63, 74 et seq, 78, 82, 119, 155, 205
    transmission mechanism (effectiveness) of, 61, 92, 111, 126, 144, 184, 207, 212, 216
    quantitative easing (QE), 14, 110, 126 et seq, 137, 142–144, 165, 178, 187–188, 190, 203–204, 246**n**
    quantitative and qualitative easing (QQE), 178, 187–188, 190
    quantitative and qualitative easing and yield curve control (QQE+YC), 190, 203–204
    unconventional (*see also* QE, QQE and QQE+YC), 109, 111, 119, 125 et seq, 164 et seq, 186 et seq, 214
monetary base, 108, 128, 178, 189
monetary growth, 14, 40, 52, 61, 63, 74, 75, 76, 92, 95, 125, 128, 217
    broad, 35, 52, 74, 75, 76, 95, 125, 128
monetary system, 7
money politics, 35, 81
moral hazard, 120, 128, 133, 207
Moret, Clement, 83
Mori, Motonari, 257**n**
Mori, Yoshirō, 130–131
mortgage arrears, 100, 254**n**
mortgage-backed securities, 152 et seq
mortgage mis-selling, 154
multilateral organizations, 158
Mussolini, Benito, 17
Muto, Toshihiro, 256**n**

Nagoya, 32
Nakajima Corporation, 29
Nakasone, Yasuhiro, 41, 50, 54, 131
Nanking, 16
National Bank of Belgium, 7
national income, 3, 9, 15, 20, 31, 34, 102, 136
national savings, 6, 167
    National Savings Promotion Bureau, 18
National Tax Agency, 66
national wealth, 20
nationalism, 3, 5, 11, 26, 41, 131, 220, 250**n**
natural disasters, vii, 9, 83, 169
Nazi Germany, 12, 18
negative-amortization loans, 154
negative equity, 100
net investment income (current account), 56, 57
net worth, 99 et seq
    household, 100, 152
    non-financial corporate sector, 100
    private sector, 118
    public sector, 207, 214
New Classical–New Keynesian synthesis, 153
New Deal (US), 13, 22
New Growth Strategy, 169–170
    Realization Promotion Council, 169
New York, 43, 70
New Zealand, 110
Nippon Credit Bank (NBC), 98, 114
Nissho Iwai, 111
non-banks, 63, 68, 77, 85, 91

non-performing loans (NPLs), 77–78,
    84, 86, 97–98, 103, 112 et seq,
    124–125, 129 et seq, 145, 150, 161,
    186, 203, 254**n**
  write-offs, 84, 91, 112, 115, 130, 132,
    256**n**
Noda, Yoshihiko, 163, 257**n**
non-financial corporate sector balance, 53,
    78
non-linearity, 151
non-manufacturing, 76, 116, 133, 135, 139,
    146
non-tariff barriers to trade, 31, 45, 198
Nordic financial crisis, 91
nuclear power, 37, 172, 196, 200, 206, 214

Obuchi, Keizō, 105, 130
occupation, 21 et seq, 39, 41, 48, 54, 209,
    247**n**
off-balance-sheet products, 157
oil, 17, 30, 43, 56, 74, 79, 94, 159–160,
    175, 187, 190, 204
  OPEC I, 35 et seq
  OPEC II, 39 et seq
  producers, 159
Okura Corporation, 29
Olympic Games:
  1964, 30
  2020 (2021), 193, 202, 204, 258**n**
on-the-job training, 29, 197
one-party state, 27, 121
Organisation for Economic Co-operation
    and Development (OECD):
  Concerted Action Programme of, 39
  membership of, 30–31
Osaka, 6–7, 32, 59, 196
out-of-court-settlements, 132–133, 139

Papua New Guinea, 20
Paris Peace Conference, 9
parliamentary debate in the 1920s, 11
patronage, 27, 48, 121, 141
Pearl Harbour, 17
Peking (Beijing), 16
pension system, 37, 102, 107, 137, 184,
    253**n**, 258**n**
  benefits, 101
  contributions, 33, 248**n**
  eligibility age, 168
  funds, 97, 189
  obligations, 101
  spending cap on, 138
  social security account and, 248**n**
People's New Party, 163

personal consumption, 48, 50, 53, 74–75,
    82, 96, 124, 134, 137, 144, 175,
    184, 191, 201, 220, 251**n**, 253**n**
  share in GDP, 55
Philippines, the, 18
Phillips curve, 186
physical assets, 20
Plaza Accord, 46, 51, 56 et seq, 249**n**
police, 11
policy error, 61, 119, 144
political class, 47, 85, 211
political scandal, 27, 34, 60, 81, 111, 198,
    204, 208, 251**n**, 255**n**, 256**n**
  Lockheed, 38, 248**n**
political uncertainty/instability, ix, 103
pollution, 34, 199
population (demography), 3, 18–19,
    32 et seq, 65, 87 et seq, 106, 111,
    116 et seq, 137 et seq, 146–147,
    163, 181, 191, 193–194, 207 et seq,
    247**n**, 248**n**
  ageing, 41, 51, 54, 82, 92, 101, 116, 120,
    137, 140, 146, 167, 184, 213, 219,
    220, 248**n**
  birth rate, 33, 101, 107, 197, 217, 219
  decline, viii, 19, 78, 82, 88, 170, 184,
    197, 219
  density, 4
  growth, 10, 33, 41, 47, 217
  life expectancy, 4, 101, 138, 184
  ratio of elderly to working age, 101, 184
  rural, 184, 200, 219
  urban, 10, 131
  working age, 58, 70, 184, 186, 219
  young, 33, 45, 131
potential (trend) growth rate, 39, 88, 101,
    169, 177, 201, 218, 219, 220
pound sterling, 13
Post Office System, 179
  assets, 141
  Japan Post, 141 et seq, 167, 170, 248**n**
  Ministry of Post and Telecommunications,
    43, 45
  postal insurance, 141, 167, 248**n**
  postal savings, 6, 32, 43, 131,
    141 et seq
  reform, 141 et seq
prejudice, 8, 220
Presley, Elvis, 130
price controls, 45, 196
price stability, 40, 73, 110, 143, 171, 187,
    254**n**, 256**n**
Prince, Chuck, 157
private equity, 155, 208, 215

privatization, 131, 138, 161
  Housing Loan Corporation (HLC), 160
  Japan Airlines (JAL), 42, 249**n**
  Japan National Railways (JNR), 42, 45, 79, 249**n**
  Japan Post, 141 et seq, 167, 170
  Japan Tobacco (JT), 42, 79, 249**n**
  Nippon Telegraph and Telephone Corporation (NTT), 42, 79, 90, 106, 118, 249**n**
productivity, ix, 31–32, 37, 50, 56 et seq
  agricultural, 58
  growth, 31, 50, 88, 101, 138 et seq, 150, 170, 184, 196, 217
  level, ix, 31–32, 37, 57, 116, 135, 238 et seq, 147, 170, 176, 184, 194 et seq, 205, 207, 215
  shortfall, 194 et seq
  total factor productivity (TFP), 147
professional associations, 140
professional services, 195
promotion of women, 197
prompt corrective action (PCA), 97, 112
proportional representation, 81
protectionism, 9, 27, 50, 208, 220, 249**n**
prudential rules, 103
public funds, application to financial sector, 10, 79, 85, 91, 112 et seq, 132 et seq, 212, 249**n**
public sector demand, 175

quangos, 195
Qvigstadt rule, 152–153, 257**n**

racism, 8, 246
railways, 8, 9, 20
  privatization of, 42, 43, 45, 79, 246**n**, 249**n**
rational expectations, 156, 256**n**
Reagan, Ronald, 40, 41–42, 44, 64
  Reaganomics, 40
real estate (*see also* land), 35, 52–53, 75 et seq, 84 et seq, 91 et seq, 115–116, 130, 150, 155
  capital gains on, 60
  developers, 52, 85
  hoarding, 89
  holdings, 99, 124
  investment, 52, 79
  investment trusts (J-REITs), 171, 178, 187, 190
  lending, 63–64, 91
  prices, 60, 66–67, 79, 85, 89, 93, 99, 115, 118, 160

recession, 16, 31, 64, 91, 105, 108, 118, 183
  1948–1949, 25
  1975, 36 et seq
  1991, 73 et seq
  1998, 113 et seq
  2000, 124–125, 134, 145
  2010s, 179 et seq
  GFC, 150 et seq
Reconstruction Finance Bank (RFB), 25 et seq
Recruit Cosmos Corporation, 60
Reichsbank, 18
Regional Comprehensive Economic Partnership (RCEP) agreement, 206
regulated industries, 42, 50, 57, 88
  highly regulated industries, 50, 57, 88
Reiwa imperial era, 204, 258**n**
relief programmes, 13
reparations, 22
repatriation, 22
research and development (R&D), 32, 147
Resolution and Collection Bank, 85
Resolution and Collection Coporation (RCC), 113–114, 132 et seq, 252**n**
Resona Bank, 133
resource misallocation, 50, 120, 137, 144
retailing, 51, 55
retail sales, 102
retirement, mandatory, 197
Reverse Course, 24 et seq
Ricardian equivalence, 137
Ricoh Corporation, 37
Riksbank (Swedish), 188
risk control, 86, 103
  managers, 156–157
  models, 156–157
robotics, 200
Roosevelt, Franklin Delano, 13
Rubin, Robert, 87
rural areas, 6, 9 et seq, 15, 27, 45, 81, 131, 142, 184, 219
Russia:
  Russia–Ukraine war, 205
  Russo–Japanese war and, 8
  Russo–Japanese war debt, 8, 12
  sovereign default, 108

Saudi Arabia, 35
Samurai class, 4
San Francisco, 60
Sanwa Bank, 115
Sanyo Securities, 104
savings, viii, 25, 48, 86, 100, 109
  corporate, 184, 195, 207, 221

desired, 186, 251**n**
domestic, 32, 166, 174, 180, 214
excess, 53, 118
national, 6, 18
postal (*see also* postal system), 32, 43, 131, 141 et seq, 248**n**
private, 118
public, 202
schools, 4, 33, 166
Seiyūkai, 11, 13
Self-Defence Force, 34
service sector, 4, 37, 58, 82, 88, 116, 118, 124, 138 et seq, 146, 170, 184, 195, 198, 201, 208, 211, 221, 258**n**
shadow banks, 155
shame, as motivating force, 121, 211, 215
Shanghai, 16
shareholders, 48, 69, 132, 157, 190, 208, 215, 221
Sharp Corporation, 37
Shinkansen (bullet train), 30, 40
Shintō (State Shintō), 5, 23
shipbuilding, 19
Shirakawa, Masaaki, 145, 171, 177, 180, 191, 256**n**
Shoko Chukin Bank, 164
shopping vouchers, 106, 192
Showa financial crisis, 10
silk, 12
single member parliamentary seats, 81
sinking funds, 13
small and medium-sized enterprises (SMEs), 78, 81, 91, 106, 130, 145, 162, 164, 168, 184, 195, 198, 200, 203, 207
small shops, 89
socialization of risk, 120
social Darwinism, 5
Social Democratic Party of Japan, 163
social security system, 33, 41, 45, 94, 117, 140, 197–198, 200, 248**n**
contributions, 102, 107, 137, 203
social stability, 24, 51, 209, 220
social unrest, ix, x, 11–12, 30, 104, 210
social welfare, 78, 139
European model of, 167
Socialist Party (JSP), 27, 81
Sony Corporation, 36
Soviet Union, 24
Spanish flu, 201
Special Economic Zones, 196, 198, 200
special purpose vehicles (SPVs), 155
speculation, 72, 91, 120, 161, 163, 189, 257**n**

stagnation, viii, 98, 123–124, 168, 212
in the 1920s, 9 et seq
secular, 207
standards, 29, 57
accounting, 132
building, 145
capital, 251**n**
lending, 150, 161
living, 20, 36, 116, 135, 219
NPL, 113–114, 254**n**
nuclear safety, 199
state-owned factories, 6
steel, 19, 20, 31, 36
Stein, Herbert, 153
stewardship code, 196
stock exchange, 6, 59
stock market, 12, 64, 77, 128–130, 176, 186, 188, 202, 215
1987 crash, 54, 70
exposure of households to, 75
JPX-Nikkei index 400, 196
Nikkei-225 index, 59, 67, 73 et seq, 83, 115, 124–125, 143, 161, 179, 227
Nikkei-225 index, PE ratio, 67
Tokyo Stock Exchange (TSE) first section, 199
strategic bombing campaign (US), 19
Structural Impediments Initiative (SII), 58
structural reform, viii, 51, 37 et seq, 84, 102–103, 116 et seq, 139, 194 et seq, 205, 221
Abenomics, 'third arrow' and, 176 et seq, 196 et seq,
Japan revitalization strategy, 196 et seq
Special Economic Zones and, 196, 198, 200
subsidies, 14, 41–42, 176
agricultural, 45, 57, 90, 170, 198, 249**n**
employment, 168
energy, 168, 204
housing, 68
industrial, 6, 25, 33
sub-prime assets, 160
Suga, Yoshihide, 204
Sumita, Satoshi, 61, 63
Sumitomo corporation, 7, 29, 94
supply chains, 172, 208, 215
supply side, the, 176
shortcomings of, 195
Swiss National Bank, 188
Switzerland, 44, 188, 258**n**
synthetic fibres, 30

INDEX

Taiwan, 7, 13
Takahashi, Korekiyo, 13 et seq, 105, 109, 119, 127, 128, 187, 189, 214, 246**n**
take-off, 4
Takenaka, Heizō, 132, 255**n**
Takeshita, Noboru, 54, 60
Tanaka, Kakuei, 35–36, 38, 41, 130, 131, 248**n**
Taylor rule, 61, 108, 144, 151, 164, 250**n**
tax, 6, 28, 42 et seq, 51, 53 et seq, 80, 85, 90, 117, 120, 126, 150, 166 et seq, 190 et seq, 203, 206–207, 211, 249**n**
  base, 5, 54, 194, 196
  burden, 33, 107, 208, 217
  capital gains, 65 et seq, 89
  corporation, 106, 138, 167, 192, 200, 204
  deferred tax assets, 133
  direct/income, 5, 13, 40, 42, 65, 67, 82, 102, 105–106, 138, 145, 173, 195
  distortions, 57, 88, 192
  elasticity, 78, 251**n**
  environmental, 107, 194, 199, 221
  indirect/consumption, 5, 13, 40, 42, 54–55, 60, 63, 65, 67, 82, 98, 102, 105 et seq, 137–138, 143, 160, 163, 167, 179, 183–184, 187–188, 191–193, 202, 251**n**
  inheritance, 65 et seq, 89
  land, 58, 65 et seq, 89, 118
  multiplier, 94
  reform, 25, 54, 65, 82, 170, 176, 195, 221
  revenue, 53, 74, 78, 93, 101, 167, 171
'teaser' mortgage rates, 154
technological development, 3–4, 6–7, 28, 32, 34, 55, 184, 251**n**
terms of trade, 35, 39, 55, 56, 99, 213
textiles, 12, 46
Thatcher, Margeret, 40–41
  Thatcherism, 40, 97, 131
thrift, 32, 47, 185
time deposits, 133
tourism, 47, 49, 57, 185, 202, 205
trade openness, 195
trade unions, 23, 25, 36–37
transparency, 90–91, 110, 194
  lack of, 69, 91, 103, 113, 120, 140, 146
Tōjō, Hideki, 17, 24
Tokugawa Shogunate, 4
Tokyo, ix, 6, 10, 30, 32, 43, 49, 70, 83, 247**n**, 255**n**, 258**n**
  fire bombing of, 19
  land prices, 59 et seq, 160
  Special Economic Zone, 196
  Tokyo War Crimes Trial, 24
Toyota Corporation, 37
Truman administration, 24
Trump, Donald, 198
tuberculosis, 21
two-party political system, 81
  pre-war, 11

Ueda, Kazuo, 205, 258**n**
Ukraine, 195, 205, 208, 215
uncertainty, 91, 93, 103–104, 108, 110, 130, 147, 172, 184, 190, 193, 208–209, 212, 215, 254**n**
unemployment, 12, 22, 25. 36, 40, 64, 75–76, 78, 96, 99, 124–125, 136, 145, 147, 150, 162, 169, 175, 185, 203, 210, 253**n**
unequal commercial treaties, 6
unit labour costs, 96
United Financial of Japan (UFJ), 115
United Kingdom (UK), x, 5, 8–9, 13, 97
United States (US), vii, viii, xi, 3 et seq, 16 et seq, 35, 37, 40, 53, 59 et seq, 67–68, 70, 77, 86, 88, 92, 100, 127, 139, 142, 149, 150 et seq, 160–161, 165, 167, 172–173, 178, 184, 198 et seq, 215, 221, 246**n**, 251**n**, 252**n**
  aid, 22, 24, 26
  current account, 44
  dollar, 4, 12, 13, 21, 25, 32, 34, 39, 44, 46, 51, 52, 56, 62, 74, 79, 82, 83, 87, 96, 164, 202, 203, 247**n**, 249**n**, 250**n**, 253**n**, 254**n**, 255**n**
  dollar funding shortage, 164
  dollar/yen exchange rate, 21, 52, 82, 83, 96, 202
  external liabilities, 3
  Federal Reserve, 61, 154, 156, 158, 164, 256**n**
  house prices, 152
  housing investment, 152
  loan standards, 113
  military, 4, 21, 22, 247**n**
  navy, 4
  oversight of Japan, 22, 209
  recession of 1937–38, 16
  Republican Party, 24, 44
  US-Japan security umbrella, 22, 26, 30, 34, 131, 209, 247**n**

Treasury bonds, 109
unemployment, 99
universal suffrage, 11
university endowment fund, 204
Uno, Sosuke, 251**n**
urbanization, 4, 10

value-at-risk (VAR) analysis, 157–158
vested interests, 195
Volcker, Paul, 63, 83
voluntary export restraints (VERs), 45, 56

wages, 16, 99, 116, 125, 137, 150, 162, 196, 204, 207
   basic, 37, 92
   bonus payments, 26, 37, 92 124, 136, 161, 168
   inflation, 37, 38, 44, 76, 96, 186, 187, 197
   minimum, 190, 197
   overtime, 37, 76, 92, 124, 136, 197
   performance-based, 136
   real wage resistance, 37
   seniority-based, 29, 33, 117, 121, 136, 197
   structure, 136
   wage-price spiral, 74
Wall Street Crash (1929), 12
war materiel, 18, 26
warehousing fees, 89
Washington Naval Treaty, 10
waste recycling, 199
welfare state, 37, 40
White, Harry Dexter, 246**n**
white supremacy, 17
wholesale prices, 84, 99
window guidance, 33, 36, 39, 43, 62, 64, 76, 106, 114
working age population, 3
World War I, 8 et seq,
   post-war boom, 9
World War II, 3, 10, 15 et seq,

xenophobia, 221

Y2K problem, 109
Yamaichi Securities, 104, 107
Yamato race, 11
Yasuda Corporation, 7
yen, vii, 22, 39, 42 et seq, 51 et seq, 79, 96, 147, 161–162, 179–180, 201, 204, 249**n**
   abandonment of gold standard and, 13
   Abenomics and, 176 et seq, 187 et seq, 190
   Covid-19 and, 210 et seq
   carry trade, 108, 253**n**
   effective, 103, 108, 175
   endaka fukyo (high yen slump), 46, 70
   Fukushima earthquake and, 175–176
   GFC and, 162, 168–169
   intervention and, 128, 171, 174
   link to silver, 7
   link to gold, 7
   post-war value, 25
   real effective, 56, 125, 134
   revaluation in early 1970s, 34–35
   safe haven status, 161, 179
   stabilization in 1949, 25
   strength following Asian crisis, 103, 108
   strength in late 1980s, 46 et seq, 53, 55–56, 58
   strength in the mid 1990s, 82–83, 87, 92
   Takahashi policy and, 14 et seq
   trading bloc, 13–14
   undervaluation in 1950s and 1960s, 34, 42
   weakness in early 1980s, 44
   weakness post-bubble, 73–75
yield curve, 129, 164, 189–190, 203–204
   inversion, 63
Yokohama, 10, 32, 247**n**
Yom Kippur War, 35
Yoshida, Shigeru, 23, 26.

Zaibatsu, 6, 9, 11, 17, 18, 24, 25, 29, 94, 245**n**, 246**n**
Zaitech, 59
zombie firms, 195